"THIS WAS NO ΦΥΧΝΗ PICNIC!"

"THIS WAS NO ΦΥΧΝΗ PICNIC!"

2.4 Years of Wild and Woolly Mayhem
in Dawson Creek

BY JOHN SCHMIDT

GORMAN & GORMAN LTD.
Publishers of Fine Canadian Books
Box 460, Hanna, Alberta T0J 1P0
Telephone (403) 854-3366 – (403) 627-3252

Typesetting and book design by
The Hanna Herald.
Printed and Bound in Canada.

John Schmidt, 1923 —
"THIS WAS NO
ΦYXNH PICNIC"
Includes Index —
ISBN 0-921835-12-4

DEDICATION

This book is dedicated to my son, John P. Schmidt, news editor of the Ayr News in Ontario. His counsel and assistance were appreciated.

The Artwork

The cover and 15 drawings are from the pen of Dr. Josephine Parrott, P.S.C., of Salmon Arm, B.C.

CONTENTS

John Schmidt

John T. Schmidt was born at Ayr, Ont., in 1923. By age 13 he was a journeyman cow milker and Linotype operator. At age 15 he'd had enough of illiterate French teachers at Ayr Continuation School and received the rest of his education at the Ayr News, owned by his father, and on the road. In 1947 he went to the Kitchener-Waterloo Record as a Linotype operator and later a farm writer. In 1958 he was hired by The Calgary Herald as a farm writer. In 1986 he was fired by the Calgary Herald as a madman. While there, he used his expense account creatively to do the research for this book and another, Growing Up In The Oil Patch, published in 1989. It won critical acclaim in Canada, the United States and Iran, but was a grammatical disaster. He now lives at Chancellor, Alberta, because nobody knows where it is. There are no sacred cows in that country as Schmidt has punctured them all. He writes a farm column for 15 southern Alberta weekly newspapers. He passes for a grey-haired mysterious oil sheikh as there are 100 million barrels of oil under his property. Other occupants of the household are his wife, Margaret, a retired school teacher and world traveller, and dog, Moses, formerly an American Express credit card holder. Schmidt and Moses take turns being Exchequer of Chancellor.

INTRODUCTION

This short, irreverent and hilarious docu-drama of a war on Canadian soil may be read from front to back, back to front or both ways from the middle. In this respect it was put together like the Alaska Highway.

Had any lucid person in the bar of the Dewdrop Inn in Dawson Creek, B.C., on Dec. 6, 1941, predicted it would be possible to go by road the 1,520 miles from there to Fairbanks, Alaska, next year, he'd have been laughed out of town. The next day he'd have been a prophet.

The Japanese attack on Pearl Harbor Dec. 7 touched off the spark that saw that road built. With only minimal continental defences, the attack scared the pants off the Americans so badly they brushed all critics aside and built the road as a secondary defence against the imperial might of Japan. It was built through a territory of bush, muskeg, rivers, lakes, mountains and permafrost; most of it not even surveyed. Some of the mountains had never been traversed and new passes had to be located.

It was the genius of a U.S. Army Corps of Engineers general (who looked like the cartoon figure, Mr. Magoo) who found a way to do it. Gen. W.M. Hoge was his name and his answer was to deploy seven regiments of engineering troops from both ends and at various points in the middle to work towards each other. On Dec. 6, 1942, it was possible to travel from Mile Zero at Dawson Creek to Fairbanks.

No matter from which end the book is started, the reader may wonder why there are some contradictions and repetitions. This is because each person interviewed had a different perception of this immense project, which took off in all directions at once and which created 2.4 years of wild and woolly mayhem in Dawson Creek.

Although each person in Dawson Creek had a front-row-centre seat to observe the Herculean manoeuvres, no single person knew what was happening at any one time on this military chessboard. This also applied to some of the high-ranking American officers on the scene. They were unaware of all forces controlling the movements of men and machinery.

It was strictly incidental that behind the tightest cloak of secrecy in any American military zone, the road was woven into three other activities:

1. The 624-mile Canol road and pipeline were built to oil supplies at Norman Wells, N.W.T., to feed an oil refinery the U.S. Army built at Whitehorse, Y.T.

2. The mining and removal of uranium oxide from mines at Port Radium, N.W.T., on Great Bear Lake to the University of Chicago stadium. Here the Manhattan Project brought together scientists and materials to manufacture the first atomic bomb. The A-bomb was used to blast two Japanese cities to smithereens. The bomb not only frightened all of Japan but the rest of the world ever since.

3. Use of the Alaska Highway as a staging route along which 10,000 American lend-lease war planes were flown to the Eastern front in the Alsib project. This project marked the beginning of the end for Adolf Hitler's wehrmacht, which had almost succeeded in bringing the Soviet Red Army to its knees. Many of these planes ended up in the decisive Battle of Stalingrad.

The Americans were in Dawson Creek in force for 2.4 years. The army would have been there a great deal longer staggering around in the primitive trackless bush going in circles or up cul de sacs had it not been their generals were assisted at the south end by some Ontario Department of Highways survey crews who had developed several new techniques for locating routes. The techniques were developed in the Northern Ontario bush in preliminary site location for the Trans-Canada Highway. The crews were pulled off their work and sent north to introduce these techniques to U.S. army engineers.

In the more mountainous sections, the work of Les Cook, a Pincher Creek, Alberta, bush pilot, in finding a new pass that cut construction time was noteworthy.

Even after the army had driven all the centre line stakes and established levels, the business of building a road in a hurry was no sinecure. Every construction stiff and bulldozer had to be transported hundreds of miles to the job site from the United States. Some two dozen contractors from Ontario were also asked to participate. This movement of machinery and supplies choked every rail siding between Minneapolis, Minn., and Dawson Creek.

The job in "the middle of nowhere" was a place for neither the timid nor the unwilling. This prompted several of the big contractors to erect this famous hiring hall sign:

THIS IS NO PICNIC

> Working and living conditions on this job are as difficult as those encountered on any job ever done in the United States or foreign territory. Men hired for this job will be required to live and work under the most extreme conditions imaginable. Temperatures will range from 90 above to 70 below.
>
> Men will have to fight swamps, rivers, ice and cold. Mosquitoes, flies and gnats will not only be annoying but will cause bodily harm. If you are not prepared to work under these conditions, **do not apply**.

It is from this adjuration the book derives its name; but in the past tense and with today's vernacular added.

The stories were recorded in the early 1960s while those interviewed still had vivid recollections.

Between that time and the emergence of the dope-crazed society of the 1990s, a number of social revolutions have taken place in Canada: the feminist, the activist church, the racist, the multiculturism, the native rights, the human rights, history revisionism, the environmental and the affirmative action. Because of the transitory nature of such fads, they have been ignored in the writing to present a true picture of the day and age in which the wartime events took place.

It was no f---ing picnic when, in a desperate effort to build a 2,000-mile telephone line in the middle of winter by using dynamite, an American contractor managed to blow up and burn the downtown core of Dawson Creek.

The death toll of this catastrophe made this village of 700 at the northern terminus of the Northern Alberta Railway realize it was in a shooting war. Previously its citizens had been somewhat sheltered from war by distance.

To atone for this catastrophe, the benevolent Americans brought in city planners and helped create one of Canada's model, best-laid-out cities. Like the rest of the world following that war, Dawson Creek was never the same again; nor has it looked back.

1

American Contractors Blow Up Dawson Creek

At 6:37 p.m. Feb. 13, 1943, a disaster in Dawson Creek brought home to its residents the fact Canada was in a real shooting war. They were hit by an explosion of 60 cases of dynamite and 20 cases of electric percussion caps.

The force of the roaring, tearing blast stopped the exterior clock on the Canadian Bank of Commerce at 6:37. The hands remained in that position for several years as a mute reminder that the blast presumably killed 21 persons and injured 150. They were killed or maimed with the same stuff that was killing or maiming millions in war theatres in Asia and Europe.

The fire which triggered the dynamite blast spread over half the downtown section of the town, built mostly of wood.

The official death toll was five, but 15 other people among the heavy transient population were never accounted for in the cloak of secrecy imposed on the town's greatest disaster by the U.S. Army. The U.S. military contended as late as 1982 the casualty list was not 21. Dwight D. Oland, historian, U.S. Army Centre for Medical History at Washington, D.C., said then: "A search of the records shows nothing to indicate more than five were killed and they were civilians."

That night martial law was declared. Many townspeople alleged the secrecy was used to cover up the actual number of casualties. The U.S.

Army never published a list. The only admission on its part was that five were killed.

However, despite the boom-town fever which raised the population to 4,200 from 700 in the space of a year, Dawson Creek still retained its character as a large country town with few secrets. The Roman Catholic priest let it out the next morning 28 had been killed. This figure was scaled down to 21. Some of the injured died.

* * *

Harold Havig, a Stettler trucker, recalled:

I met a top army officer a few days later and asked him how many of his men had been killed. He said eight. They were shipping bodies back to the U.S. on the train for several days afterwards. We never knew the truth concerning the casualties. I am sure those 10 GIs chain-handling dynamite were all killed.

There were reports of men who had left home and who headed up there and were never heard of again. Some bodies could not be identified.

Of course, any admission of civilian deaths by the army left it open for lawsuits by survivors.

I saw them recover some bodies from the wreckage. One man was a horrible mess. He had all his eyes burned and he was still breathing.

A dead man was discovered in the haymow of a nearby stable a couple of days after the fire. It was never established whether he had died in the explosion or not.

A U.S. Army uniform hung on a telephone wire for several days before anyone thought to haul it down. It was not determined whether the owner was dead or alive.

Two truckers looking around the rubble several days afterward noticed a shoe under a piece of plywood. Upon closer investigation, it turned out to be a leg and the leg belonged to a dead girl. They pulled out the body and reported it.

* * *

Making the situation difficult was the constant movement of workers. Among them were employees of two U.S. construction companies which were being pressed by the U.S. Army to complete the 2,000-mile Cantel telephone line to Fairbanks from Edmonton. In the rush to complete the line, a blueprint for calamity had been drawn up beforehand. The prime contractor for the phone line, Miller Construction of Indianapolis, Ind., had applied to the federal government in Ottawa — and received — a number to locate a temporary powder magazine in downtown Dawson Creek and buy dynamite. The rationale for the short-cut was that there was a wartime emergency.

The location of the magazine was a small frame warehouse fronting the Alaska Highway. Owned by W. E. Stein, it was actually a stable, the second storey of which was still filled with hay. It was rented from him by Miller Construction and the Oman-Smith Company of Nashville, Tenn., a sub-contractor on the north end of the line.

The dynamite and caps were stored here as, at that time, there were no regulations in the criminal code or the Explosives Act on handling dynamite once a licencee bought it. Therefore, contrary to all laws and regulations and dictates of common sense, the dynamite and caps were stored in the small building in the heart of town — even though there was a powder magazine at the W. H. Harvey and Son construction camp eight miles north of town. It was regularly used by the companies.

By Dec. 1, 1942, the phone line had been completed to Dawson Creek under difficult circumstances. To expedite the work, both companies were using the dynamite to blast post holes.

Handling dynamite is a calculated risk. Although new dynamite in the hands of experienced men is relatively safe to handle, it is only safe providing it does not receive a sharp impact. It can even be burned without necessarily exploding. In its proper use, a percussion cap provides the impact to set it off.

Hundreds of truckloads had been forwarded up the highway without incident. The dynamite itself might not have been so bad, but storing the 20 cases of percussion caps beside it set the stage for catastrophe. Even in isolated powder magazines caps are stored some distance from the boxes of dynamite sticks for safety.

For convenience, the Oman-Smith Company had requisitioned the explosives through Miller Construction Company which, in turn, had ordered them from Canadian Industries Ltd. in Edmonton. The caps had arrived Feb. 10 and were picked up by an Oman-Smith truck driver, Eddie Ray Jones. The dynamite arrived Feb. 12 and, as Jones was busy at another job, Robert S. Nelson, purchasing agent for Miller, told an employee named Barnhardt to pick it up. Both shipments were taken to the Stein warehouse to await forwarding.

How that warehouse caught fire is still a matter of conjecture.

Although the commonly-held supposition was that an employee with a welding torch repairing a "down" truck set off the blaze at 6:20 p.m., Floyd Wilson, grocer and at that time a deputy chief of the volunteer fire brigade, said in his opinion the fire was set. The possibility of sabotage was never ruled out.

* * *

The dangerous material was being handled and transported with nonchalance and indifference to its dangerous qualities by Jones and Co., as a transcript from a preliminary hearing indicates. The British Columbia attorney-general laid a charge of criminal negligence against Miller. Jones was examined by his counsel, Gordon S. Wismer, later the attorney-general of B.C., before Magistrate M. S. Morrell:

Q. Were those caps in the warehouse the day the accident occurred?
A. Part of them was.
Q. What happened to the others?
A. We loaned some to Miller Construction.
Q. How did Barnhardt happen to get the dynamite instead of you?
A. Well, I had too much work and Nelson sent Barnhardt down to give me a hand.
Q. Did you ask Barnhardt to get the dynamite for you?
A. That was his job.
Q. Did you ask Barnhardt to get it?
A. I don't know that he got it. I told him to take care of it.
Q. Do you know of your own knowledge what happened to that dynamite?
A. I did not see him put it there.
Q. Did you ever see that dynamite in the Oman-Smith part of the building (the rear portion)?
A. I don't remember. I had just picked up the caps the day before.
Q. Did Nelson get those caps which were later borrowed by Miller?
A. I think he picked them up.
Q. Where were you the day the accident occurred?
A. I was down at the 843rd Signal Corps warehouse all day.
Q. Were you in the Oman-Smith warehouse at all that day?
A. I carried the boys up from the bunk shack after breakfast and brought them home for supper. (Jones was stationed at Whitehorse but had come to Dawson Creek to truck dynamite up the highway. While there he stayed at Miller's headquarters, which was a shed which could

house six people located two miles west of town. The Oman-Smith crew lived there, too.)

Q. What time did you leave the warehouse for supper?

A. About six o'clock. We were last to leave.

Q. Did you lock up the place? Did you leave anybody there?

A. There was nobody left.

Q. Did you have any signs or anything on that building stating there were explosives in it?

A. Not to my knowledge.

Q. Was the building fixed up in any way as a magazine for storing powder?

A. No.

Q. Where did you store the caps in the building Feb. 10?

A. In the back part.

Q. Were they near the partition?

A. Yes.

Q. While you were at supper at Miller's did anything happen?

A. Yes, Nelson came in and said the warehouse downtown was on fire. We all jumped up from supper and drove down as fast as we could.

Q. Just tell us what took place, Mr. Jones.

A. We got down there and we all scattered out running around every way hollering to people to get back. We told them there were explosives. We kept pleading and begging them to get back but they didn't pay much attention. The crowd kept getting thicker and thicker. Then the blast went off. I was kind of dazed. We was all kind of stunned. We all finally got back out to the bunk shack. The ones that could.

Q. Did anything happen to the building after you got there?

A. It blowed up.

Q. Was it on fire when you got there?

A. The front part of the building was on fire.

Q. Did you see the fire burning before the explosion took place?

A. Yes, sir.

Q. Was the whole building demolished by the force of the explosion?

A. Well, I couldn't say. I was rolled around pretty bad. I couldn't say what happened afterwards.

Q. Was it blown up?

A. Yes, I seen it blow up.

Q. Who was in charge of the Oman-Smith warehouse in Dawson Creek?

A. Barnhardt and I was, I guess. If anyone was in charge I guess we was in charge.

Q. Did you receive any instructions from anybody in Miller Construction or from your company as to how you were to receive any explosives that came in by train?

A. No, sir.

Cross examination by Alex D. B. Young, appearing for the Crown:

Q. The explosives arrived Feb. 10 and 12. Did you notify the authorities or the police you were storing explosives in the building?

A. No, we didn't. We didn't intend to have them there any time at all. We were supposed to have some trucks ready to take them north but we didn't.

Q. Your instructions were to expedite the shipment of goods to northern points by truck from Dawson Creek?

A. Yes, sir.

Q. As soon as you picked up the dynamite from the boxcar you put it in your trucks and sent it north?

A. Yes, sir.

Q. I suppose with the bad weather you had difficulty keeping the trucks rolling?

A. It seems the trucks which came down always had to have repairs — and we had to do the best we could.

Although Jones was present at the preliminary hearing, he had left the country and could not be found for the trial Oct. 2 and 3, 1943. The preliminary hearing transcript became a trial exhibit.

* * *

Back in Dawson Creek the fateful night in 1943, it was well below zero and a raw wind was blowing when the alarm was turned in. This, coupled with the time of day, prevented higher casualties. Many persons who normally would have rushed to the fire were kept indoors by the cold and the fact they were at the evening meal. Even so, 500 quickly showed up even before the town usually began to fill with soldiers from the nearby army camp. Dawson Creek was not big enough to maintain a full-time fire brigade. Deputy Chief Wilson recalled:

We depended upon untrained volunteers and a "chemical truck" with a tankful of water. Lack of equipment and water hampered us. Nevertheless, we set about the task with courage and about 10 GIs started chain-handling those boxes of dynamite and other burning material out of the building. They weren't particularly afraid of the dynamite — but they didn't know about the presence of those caps. We sent to the army for assistance and the army sent men and a couple of water-carrying tankers.

Most of the spectators were not aware of the dynamite. When, at last, Oman-Smith and Miller employees spread the word people didn't seem to be concerned either. Strangely, few started to run. They left reluctantly and then only when military police and B.C. Provincial Police under Michael Leo Bagallies started shooing them away.

When I saw the dynamite catch fire (burning with a bluish-yellow flame) I pulled my men back behind some lumber piles in Burrows Lumber Company yard to wait for the inevitable moment when the caps caught fire.

The fire at that point appeared to be just about under control then. The GI firemen were reluctant to withdraw as quickly as us. Some were still on the roof when the blast let go.

With the need for dynamite for coping with the mountainous terrain, Dawson Creek was literally overrun with the stuff. Had people generally known about it after the explosion, there would no doubt have been an exodus. For instance, most of the spectators that hectic night were unaware of the fact that two trucks of dynamite had been sitting on the street two blocks from the scene.

The drivers from Oman-Smith were afraid to go near them to move them. They weren't moved until the next day.

After the big one, minor explosions continued to dog the firemen as percussion caps continued to go off.

* * *

A thing that scared hell out of the military and civilian officials during an inspection tour the next day was that many unexploded caps were lying around the crater waiting to go off and injure the unwary, it is recalled by Dick Panter, a general superintendent of the R. Melville Smith Company:

While tending the wounded, St. Joseph's Hospital staff ran into an emergency. They ran out of beds and bedding as the wounded came in faster than they could be accommodated. Officials sent over to us for help. Fortunately, we had a warehouse full of the stuff they needed. As I was in the middle of taking care of this emergency another came up. Some excited workers from the camp got hold of me and began jabbering:

"A fellow over at the new camp has gone crazy and he's got a lot of dynamite. Come and get him."

Nobody would go near him so I commandeered a pick-up truck and drove out to him and said:

"What's the matter?"

He was almost incoherent.

We had been digging a sewer trench from the new camp down to the creek and he was working on it. We had left half a case of dynamite in the hole for the night. This was perfectly legal, as we had taken steps to protect it in case kids came around. In the excitement he had become a little hysterical and had gone down and picked up the dynamite and was running around with it in his arms trying to find a safe place in case there was another explosion. So I said:

"Put it in my truck."

He put it in. Everything was dandy — and the emergency was over. The thing that struck me as funny was that there was this whole gang of fellows standing 100 feet away — and nobody would go near him.

The day after the explosion the RCMP and officials from the fire marshall's office visited our camp. The pompous and officious sergeant had learned about my encounter with the fellow at the sewer trench. He asked:

"Where is the dynamite now?"

"It's in my truck," I said. "And naturally it should be there, don't you think?"

The sergeant also heard we had about eight cars of dynamite stored in town and more was coming. He said:

"I understand you have these cars of dynamite in town."

"Yes," I said.

"Well, you gotta get it out."

"Where do you want me to put it?"

"Send it to Pouce Coupe or somewhere."

"They don't want it in Pouce any more than we want it here," I protested, "Besides, it's here legally."

"How much more have you got in town at the magazine?"

"Oh, I think there's about eight cars."

"Well, how much? Don't you know?" he huffed.

"I don't know."

"Who's in charge?"

"I am."

"Well, why don't you know?"

"Because I haven't been around the magazine for a couple of hours."

Unmollified, the sergeant asked: "Well, what are you going to do about it?"

"We're going to get it out of town as fast as we can get trucks."

"How long will it take?"

"I don't know."

"Well, who the hell's in charge?"

"I am."

I had him, this stuffy pompous character. I didn't give him the satisfaction of knowing that I had a warehouse superintendent who probably knew exactly how much was there. He didn't realize that in assessing danger one case is as dangerous as 400. He should have realized we were going to move it as fast as we could get trucks, which weren't too plentiful.

I also had an encounter with Major-General Steele, who came from Ottawa. He was a lovely old gentleman, the head of the government department which controlled the use of explosives — but not those used against the enemy. He laid down the law to us. I'll frankly admit we were breaking it as far as the loading of trucks went.

We had big four-wheel-drive trucks and the law said we could pile boxes only one tier deep. This wasn't practical as we were sending trucks on 1,000-mile round trips.

To follow the letter of the law, a driver could not stop and leave his truck within a mile of a settled area or camp. The people who made these regulations never visualized such a situation as ours. Obeying the letter of the law meant our drivers wouldn't be able to stop at a camp to eat, sleep or do anything else and could only carry a quarter of a load.

I remember coming out the door with General Steele to go to dinner. A big FWD truck pulled up beside the cookshack all decked out in "explosives" signs. The driver jumped down and went in to eat. The general said:

"Well, there you are now: a truckload of dynamite parked right in camp."

I said: "General, maybe it's empty."

And I went over and looked in. There was a layer of dynamite boxes on the floor. I turned to him:

"You win," I laughed.

What he didn't know was that we were driving the trucks a mile outside town and doubling them up because we couldn't afford to follow regulations. As far as this was concerned, this was a foolish regulation. We took some leeway because we faced an emergency situation. The general knew he had to shut his eyes to some of these things. He didn't make any objection to having dinner while the truck loaded with explosives sat outside the door.

* * *

The casualness with which dynamite was handled is related by Herb Mowat, a foreman with Don Construction Ltd. of Toronto:

When I arrived in March, 1943, I was met in Dawson Creek by six men in a truck. They were all dressed up.

"What have you been doing?"

"Oh," one replied, "we've been pallbearers at a funeral."

"Who died?"

"One of our buddies was working on the tower of the Kiskatinaw River bridge about 100 feet above the river. He stepped off a horizontal beam onto what he thought was another beam. There wasn't anything there and he fell onto the rocks and was killed."

They had two cases of dynamite in this truck and we were travelling over a pretty rough road. The cases were bouncing around. I wasn't very comfortable. I said:

"If you don't drive more carefully we're going to need pallbearers for this crew."

They thought this was a big joke. I was glad when they stopped at a shanty a few miles down the road and left the dynamite there.

* * *

They called those devil-may-care workers "powder monkeys." They were too reckless with explosives to suit the tastes of John Fisher, who was with a nine-man pile-driving crew of the E. W. Elliott Company of Seattle. He recalled:

Building a bridge across a small creek, I had a four-wheel-drive truck with a winch on the front end. I was having difficulty trying to hold a pile straight with the winch cable, despite the fact I had all the brakes on. I noticed some planks under the truck and asked the boys to remove them so I could get a better footing. A powder monkey came running up:

"Don't move those planks," he yelled.

"Why not? What's the matter?"

"Under those planks I have 100 sticks of dynamite ready for use."

"You stupid fool," I exploded. "Here, how'd you like to get in here and drive this truck?"

He did so nonchalantly — as if there was no danger at all. Just plain reckless he was.

Great quantities of explosives were used for excavating cuts. We'd see convoys of 15 or 20 trucks with capacity loads and red warning streamers. Everything on the road would give way to them.

A small incident on the road near Fort St. John put a stop to vehicle thefts for a while. An Indian stole a command jeep from the 843rd Signals and took off for the Condill Hotel there to quench his thirst. He was enjoying a quiet bottle of beer when the police finally spotted the jeep.

If an Indian can turn pale, this one did. A burly military policeman took him outside and showed him a dozen sticks of dynamite and a handful of caps under the seat. A good jolt could have sent him to the Happy Hunting Grounds.

* * *

Back at the scene of the tragic explosion, the force of the blast scattered every animate and inanimate object without discrimination, it was recalled by Dick Panter:

My glasses were blown away. My coat was split up the back. To add to the difficulties, the fire brigades were temporarily knocked out. This prevented them from dousing small fires that started after the blast — fires that normally could have been tapped out. The main fire burned up all the battered buildings over six blocks, eventually causing $500,000 damage.

In the seconds, minutes and hours after the explosion, the townspeople witnessed dozens of unbelievable incidents and acts. For instance, they could not comprehend what forces had been let loose to blow all the tires off a parked car. One landed on a roof. The shock waves would skip one or two and the next one would be flattened.

* * *

After the blast, everyone was immobilized for a minute. Then some, who were knocked down, got up and ran for blocks. Don Leach, then running Union Tire shop, was an eyewitness:

I was standing 150 feet away by the railroad tracks when I saw the dynamite start to sputter. I turned around and started to run but had gone only a few steps over the icy ground when the big boom hit. I can still feel the way it picked me up off the ground bodily. Being in motion, I didn't fall; but in the seconds between the high-pressure shock wave and the big boom I could hear dozens of bodies plopping to the frozen ground.

I was one of hundreds who lost their hats. I recovered mine later but the next day 100 hats were still lying around the streets. People's possessions and clothes were found scattered all over town.

* * *

One man who found his hat was W. H. Brown, a Greyhound bus driver. He recalled:

The drivers had a corner room on the second floor of the Dewdrop Inn. When the fire alarm rang I grabbed my sheepskin coat and fur hat to see what was happening. The rest weren't interested as they were getting ready to take off for a dance at Fort St. John.

When word started to spread about the dynamite I started to retreat through an alleyway in which three trucks were parked. They were between me and the blast. They broke its force but, even so, when I woke up I was lying in the middle of the street wondering if I was hurt and would get run over.

I finally realized I was all right. In my shock for some unaccountable reason I ran back up the alleyway, picked up my hat and headed for the hotel.

When I passed the hardware store I saw the whole side had been blown away and everything in the bins was lying on the sidewalk two feet deep.

The air was filled with burning debris. However, it went over the heads of most of those who were in close. But this was not the case of a red-hot tire from the fire in the Oman-Smith warehouse. It was blown at eye-level across the street where it hit a wooden building with such force it left the manufacturer's imprint on the building.

People reported sore stomaches for several days because of the pressure. Tommie Gregg, a Northern Alberta Railways engineer, said the terrific concussion took his breath away for 20 minutes. Nothing happened to the log blacksmith shop except one log was blown out of the side. The heels blew off a new pair of boots worn by one man.

In one home, both the front and back doors were blown inside. They passed each other in the tiny room, circled a glass china cabinet and never so much as scratched it.

* * *

Another of the Greyhound drivers who worked out of the former chicken coop which served as an office across the alley from the burning warehouse was Bud Armstrong. He recalled:

We won ourselves an immortal place in the history of Dawson Creek by forming the Great Greyhound Evacuation Squad. Once organized, we went into high gear to save a row of houses east of the fire. One of the boys pinched a tractor unit and hooked it into a spare trailer and we took off to save the Weiss family home. By the time we arrived the power had gone off but it was as bright as day. However, it was pitch black inside the house.

Weiss wanted us to save his wife's precious china. We grabbed the china cabinet, tilted it back to keep the dishes from falling out and went to the back door. We fell on the icy steps but, curiously, not a dish broke. We loaded it onto the trailer. Back in the house there was a lot of fumbling and grunting as the guys banged into each other carrying out pieces of furniture.

Somebody figured the red-hot kitchen stove should be saved. They managed to handle it with leather gloves, clumping it to the door a foot at a time. Reaching the door they found it wouldn't go through. Somebody grabbed an axe and smashed the door frame.

We managed to manhandle it onto the trailer. We took it inside and we dropped it — right on top of the china cabinet.

Of course, every piece of china we had worked so hard to save broke.

This established our reputation. The Great Greyhound Evacuation Squad didn't win any medals for their heroic efforts. After the fire cooled off people began to see the funny side of our serious efforts and could laugh about it.

To cap it all off: After all the havoc we caused at the Weiss house, it didn't even catch on fire!

We lost all our office furniture and equipment. However, my efforts to save this stuff is the only reason I am alive. I was slithering across the road on glare ice with the top drawer of a filing cabinet when the dynamite let go. The protection offered my chest by the drawer and the fact my feet went out from under me were what saved me. I was flung into the ditch head-first. When I recovered my senses I leaped up and discovered I was blind. I reeled over to the railway station where some guys were standing.

"I'm blind," I moaned.

"Wipe the mud off your glasses and you'll be able to see a lot more," guffawed one of the bystanders.

We never recovered any of our office furniture, typewriter and stationery. The U.S. Army placed the area under tight security when some looting started. A GI with a rifle stopped me the next day when I went to pick up the pile.

He forced me to go to the army post to obtain a permit. When I was away the stuff was picked up and they could never locate it.

Just after the explosion, the Dewdrop Inn caught fire. We decided we had better evacuate it. We ran into our room and emptied dresser drawers onto blankets and hollered at other guests to do the same and bring them down to a bus which Brown had driven around. They threw a lot of stuff from a second-storey balcony onto the roof racks. Driving away, burning embers set the stuff afire — but we managed to douse the fire and drive to safety.

Jack Tait carried out two kids belonging to a family, one under each arm, screaming with fright. He had been frightened, too, when the blast blew him out into an alley.

After the fire there was nowhere for us drivers to go so we drove to an empty lot and lived in it for two nights. We then moved into the Dawson Hotel and later into the army barracks. The bus office was moved into the old French-safe-distribution station, then into the army headquarters building.

The only Greyhound employee hurt was Bert Wilson, a spare driver from Airdrie, Alta., who arrived on a crowded train a few minutes before the explosion. He had joined people in the railway yards, who were blown under boxcars and off the top of cars and injured. A canthook was flung at him and knocked off his kneecap. He was never able to drive a bus again and received a $2,000 injury award.

He was one of 18 evacuated by plane to Edmonton hospitals that night to relieve the burden on St. Joseph's. Some of the victims were still in the hospital in 1945 and others carried permanent scars and disabilities.

* * *

As J.H. Vollans, NAR yardmaster, recalled:

Wilson was put out of commission the same way as Harry Newton, the station agent, who received a broken wrist when a distributor cap from a truck being repaired in the Oman-Smith building flew through a station window.

A young stenographer went into hysterics when her hair caught fire.

Comical but close was something which blew out of a building and cut the seat out of a new pair of pants being worn by George Elliott, a trucker.

Never explained was an incident in a restaurant. A man and a woman, strangers to each other, were sitting 15 feet apart. After the explosion the baby the woman was holding was found on the man's knee. Both swore they hadn't moved.

Another railroader and I had our supper and were heading for Milo Grubb's barber shop, a small wooden one-storey building. We were blown 30 feet. We thought sure as hell the Japanese had arrived and some of the U.S. Army people did, too.

We hurried back to the station and watched the scene in horror. I began to realize if I had reached the barber shop I might not have gotten off as easily as a big fat man who was blown out of the chair onto the street and suffered severe cuts. Next morning there was nothing left of the building but the floor with two burned-up chairs standing forlornly in the middle.

Men were also knocked off roofs of homes and businesses onto which they had climbed to douse sparks. Many received broken bones from flying tools, timbers, broken glass, tire chains and red-hot tires. The tires rained down everywhere and that's how deputy fire chief Wilson lost his grocery store.

The most serious loss, however, was the destruction of 6,000 ration books.

The army acted quickly to contain the fire. It commandeered tank trucks from gasoline-hauling contractors and construction companies and put them to work hauling water from Pouce Coupe. They pumped water into one big tank truck they had available for fighting fires.

When it was all over the NAR received plaudits for the best effort in supplying water to fight the fire. We had four locomotives, each with tenders of 8,000 to 10,000 gallons capacity, laying over in Dawson Creek that night. We shuttled them back and forth between our water tank and the team track which ran into the area where most of the fire was. The army filled its tank truck from the engine tenders. That water kept the whole town from being razed completely. Had the NAR not been able to supply the water the fire would have jumped the main street because of the strong wind.

* * *

To add to the eerie scene, hundreds of spools of copper telephone wire were blown out of the warehouse. Stu McAlpine, a government agricultural worker, then driving a truck, recalled:

Some of the unravelled spools went as far as 500 feet. Many who became entangled in them were badly frightened. It was hard to tell if they were live electric wires. Some of the fire trucks and other traffic drove unwittingly into the thousands of feet of tangled wire and bogged down. Most were forced to stay there until morning.

The soldiers later claimed the wire was as much a menace as any weapon the enemy could have contrived.

* * *

There were some lucky escapes from the holocaust. One was by Harold Havig, who remembered:

In the late afternoon I was helping Joe Kossick, a friend, install new brake linings on his truck. When we finished about 10 to 6 I had to take off on a rush delivery to Fort St. John.

Joe and Ed Breault, a lawyer, were assisting two soldiers to hoist a hose to the roof of a blacksmith shop near the fire. When the blast came Joe was knocked out and Breault was never heard of again.

When Joe came to, two soldiers were in the throes of death, kicking him in the stomach. One had a large sliver of wood driven through his throat. Joe was deaf for six months and never did fully recover his hearing. He received a large amount in disability compensation.

Had I been there I would have been helping at the fire. As it was I was unloading my freight at the Hudson's Bay Company store when the phone rang.

"Dawson Creek is on fire. Just look," said the store manager when he returned. We could see red in the sky 50 miles away.

"The whole town is on fire," he said. "That was the telephone operator who called me to say she had to evacuate the central switchboard. All the lines had burned out and the building was then on fire."

When I returned the next morning the fire area was cordoned off and armed GIs patrolled the streets to prevent looting. Nobody was allowed to take pictures.

As the army had helped to bring order out of chaos, any civilian resentment which had built up against the U.S. military previously quickly evaporated that night because the town officials had asked them to step in to declare martial law. In the panic after the explosion all stores were evacuated. Thousands of dollars worth of goods were dumped onto the streets by owners before the army took over. Much of it was needlessly dumped, leaving it prey to looters and the weather — until the army stepped in to provide security.

The most urgent need was caring for the injured. The army had summoned ambulances and soon there were sirens screaming all over the place. The injured were despatched to hospitals in them as well as trucks, light deliveries and cars. The most seriously injured were brought to St. Joseph's RC Hospital and it was soon overtaxed as was a Red Cross emergency unit. Others were treated at the railhead dispensary of the 341st Engineering Regiment.

* * *

Mrs. Floyd Wilson, a practical nurse and part-time worker at the hospital, told what it was like that night:

It began for me as I was getting ready to go down and open our only movie theatre, a 250-seat house owned by Joe Garfin, who also ran the American Lunch restaurant. I worked nights as cashier. When the explosion came it blew away all the prize house plants I had arranged on the window sills. This was only a small part of the damage to the house but for me it was a tragedy as the plants meant a lot to me in our winter.

My first thought was for Floyd, who was fighting the fire. When I was assured he was safe I headed for the hospital to help. However, a big military policeman wouldn't let me in. I didn't have my uniform on and he didn't believe me. I became a bit hysterical and proceeded to hit him but he remained adamant. Later I came across the priest and he got me past the guard.

All the lights had been put out and it was 15 minutes before they were able to get the emergency system working.

There were terrible scenes in the overcrowded hospital: wounded lined up in the halls and more arriving every few minutes. It looked like a slaughter house. Dr. Leo Giroux and Dr. Stoker were working on the most serious cases. Later Dr. Lau, a Chinese from Spirit River, drove 100 miles to help. They were terribly short of nurses. Mrs. K. O. Aspol had come in but they needed more. They ran out of plaster of paris and antibiotics.

The army radioed Fort St. John and they sent Doris Davidson and Mrs. William Koeniger of Winnipeg by car. The road was very slippery and the car went out of control and ran into the ditch several times but by super-human strength they managed to push it out and keep going. They worked all night in the operating room under difficult circumstances.

A special plane was despatched from Fort St. John with urgently needed supplies. It almost didn't make it. The runway was only partially completed at the time and not lighted for night flights. To light the runway, they made flares out of piles of wood soaked in gasoline.

Airport officials feared the pilot might hit the power pole at the end of the runway so they asked the power be shut off again. However, they had placed flares too near the end of the runway and the pilot did hit the pole but he managed to recover and land.

* * *

Sister Superior Theresa was so busy it was impossible to record the names of some of the patients as they were admitted. Dick Panter recalled one case of an injury that didn't get into the records:

We had a Chinese bull cook named Mah Sett Ying, a small man under five feet who weighed only about 85 pounds. He was standing at the window of a Chinese restaurant downtown when the blast blew in the window and he had a great many small cuts on his face. He came back to camp bleeding and excited. I took a look at him before we patched him up and said:

"You're not going to die, Mah Sett. You have a lot more blood left."

Poor Mah Sett had a bigger problem later on that spring when R. Melville Smith moved its camp north of Fort Nelson. He refused to go — and nobody could understand why. We all felt bad because he was useful to us — even if he did sell 25-cent and 50-cent lottery tickets on which nobody ever won. Then one day Bruce Ballah of the Unemployment Insurance Commission asked him the reason.

"I tell you," he said, "if I go up there the Amelicans think me a Jap and they shoot."

Ballah was able to assure him this would not happen but he was scared silly. However, after a holiday in Edmonton he came up the road and everything was dandy.

* * *

Another trucker heading back to Dawson Creek that night was Paul Loiselle, whose house was five blocks from the blast:

"I reached town at 4 a.m. Because of all the fire hose and tangled wire and debris I couldn't get through town with my truck. I walked into our house and found it empty and all the windows blown out. There was no furniture. I found my wife was staying with a friend. She and this friend had been standing by the Dawson Co-op Store when they were warned an explosion was coming.

"Grabbing our daughter in her arms, they headed for home. Just as they were going into the house the blast let go and blew her and the child into the ditch. Where they had been standing by the co-op eight tons of red-hot tire chains landed. There was a pile of chains half-way up the wall. But the store was the only building in the block not destroyed."

* * *

Dick Panter had one more crisis to contend with before the night was over. He recalled:

I had to have 20 "stolen" trucks parked outside the R. Melville Smith garage in the path of the fire removed to safety. The story of how we "stole" the trucks was almost as hectic as the rescue operation.

We put in a requisition for them originally through the U.S. Army. We figured they'd be shipped direct to us. A shipment of 20 Studebaker trucks to the Public Roads Administration arrived. PRA said:

"These are your trucks."

I received them and put them in service. A while later a sergeant from one of the army camps came in and said:

"I wish you would come and take delivery of your 20 trucks."

"What trucks?" I asked.

"There are 20 Studebaker 6x6s down here addressed to the R. Melville Smith Company."

Somebody had goofed. This was a clear duplication of a requisition. But we wasted no time looking a gift horse in the mouth and I sent all the boys I could lay hands on from behind desks at the office to go over and steal those trucks before anybody started asking questions as we needed them badly. Trucks were at a premium at that time and we would have been penalized had we failed to move the dynamite, food and supplies up the road before the spring break-up. So I took them without turning a hair — and now they were sitting outside the garage ready to get burned up.

It was a close call but we saved them.

To prevent the recurrence of fires — a series of disastrous blazes had already plagued the town — an order issued by President Franklin D. Roosevelt of the U.S. made it mandatory for every camp in Dawson Creek and on the Alaska Highway to organize and maintain a trained fire brigade.

A trained man from Texas was sent in to instruct firemen. Eventually there were 20 firefighting units with water tanks located at the army base, in the town, the PRA camp, the R. Melville Smith camp and several smaller camps.

Immediately after the fire, and despite the fact it was in the cold of mid-winter, the town administration took steps to install a $250,000 water and sewer system. Water was piped 12 miles from the Kiskatinaw River and a reservoir with a 1.5-million-gallon storage capacity was dug for fire protection.

The town fathers took on the problems of rebuilding with a stroke of genius. In a day when town planners were regarded in the same light as witch doctors, they called in a town planner to redesign the central core. They felt Dawson Creek would some day become a city and wanted it laid out aesthetically and for utility. Their optimism and courage were justified for, despite some opposition, they followed the planners all the way.

Today the city is one of the most attractively laid-out on the continent.

During the Oct. 2 and 3 trial of Miller Construction for criminal negligence, Judge Woodburn rendered a guilty verdict and fine of $10,000.

However, in a very interesting decision, the B.C. Appeal Court reversed Woodburn's decision Nov. 24, 1943, on the grounds Miller did not have the dynamite "under its charge and control" and therefore no conviction should have been registered. Oman-Smith was the actual culprit and it wasn't charged. The appeal court also rejected Woodburn's finding the two companies were prime contractor and subcontractor — even though witnesses said this was so — and thus Miller was in no way responsible for acts and defaults of Oman-Smith.

Gordon C. Miller of Linton, Ind., company president, denied Oman-Smith was a sub-contractor but his company received no extra remuneration for building 500 miles of line Oman-Smith was unable to finish under its contract.

In the trial, Judge Woodburn pointed out he could have fined Miller $25,000 "but I felt, while not excusing the criminal negligence of which I find it guilty, the wartime emergency and rush under which the work was done to some extent mitigated the circumstances. I accordingly impose a lower fine."

The Crown did not re-lay the charges against Oman-Smith a second time. Whether it was possible the cause of justice was best served or whether Oman-Smith was no longer on the scene is not known. However, the cause of justice was served when the American government agreed to assume financial responsibility amounting to $1 million in damages, death and injuries — a large sum for that country in those days.

Teams of arbitrators were sent in, hearings were held and the injured compensated as well as the families of the dead. Most of the cost of rehabilitation of buildings was paid. It all took time but it came out a better town than it went into the war.

After raising hell over mosquito net shortages, Washington sent Gen. Hoge a boxcarful.
US ARMY
MOSQUITO
NETS

2

Project Almost Beyond Imagination

When the Americans came into the Canadian Northwest Feb. 16, 1942, and announced they intended to construct a 1,500-mile highway to Alaska, they did more to assist northern development in the next 2 1/2 years than the Japanese had been able to hold back in the previous 40.

In these days when the federal government is handing out wartime reparations to citizens of Japanese descent, many recipients do not have any idea of how their honorable ancestors held this country back — or they have forgotten. It is an almost unbelievable fact of history the blame for holding back northern development may be laid squarely at the door of Japan. It's all the more astounding and ironical in the light of later events in which Japan is given credit for creating the impetus which was responsible for the real opening of the Canadian North by forcing the construction of the Alaska Highway to protect this continent.

Japan effectively held back northern development from the turn of the century, despite the efforts of Russian, Canadian and American politicians to shove back the frontiers.

Alaska had agitated for a railroad up the Rocky Mountain Trench to give it a link with the mainland U.S. and/or the Soviet Union. But any moves in this direction had been scuttled by the Japanese as one of the terms of armistice when they licked the Russians in the Russo-Japanese war. The Japanese general staff feared such a railroad would encircle Japan. They wanted none of it.

Heeding continued Alaskan agitation in the 1930s for a link, President Franklin D. Roosevelt appointed the International Highway Commission in 1938 with Senator Warren D. Magnusson of Washington State as chairman. The commission selected three routes for a road through Canada and recommended construction on the road start in 1939.

When the Japanese heard of this recommendation they were able to exert enough pressure to halt actual construction. Hirochiro Nemichi, the Japanese consul in Vancouver, was instructed to fly to Whitehorse in 1939 to make a direct report to his government on the proposed route. At the same time the Japanese entered a strong protest to the Chamberlain government in London, stating it would consider construction of such a highway through Canada against their interests. Canada was still under the diplomatic umbrella of Great Britain then, with a ruling Privy Council in England.

Because of further protests to Ottawa and Washington the highway was not started. However, work on an aerial route survey quietly continued.

Air service to the Yukon had been initiated in the early 1930s by bush pilots using skis in winter and floats in summer. As traffic increased and scheduled service from Vancouver and Edmonton was established, pressure had been put on the Canada Department of Transport to build all-weather airports and navigational aids in 1936. However, Ottawa was slow to move on the project and it was not until 1939 — when the onset of the Second World War loosened the funds available for such purposes — that an airway survey was finally launched.

Ground surveys were undertaken at Fort St. John, Grande Prairie, Fort Nelson, Watson Lake and Whitehorse for landing strips of 3,000-foot minimum, suitable for extension, each to be served with radio range stations for instrument flying. Emergency landing strips were to be located 100 miles apart.

When Canada entered the war in September, 1939, the survey parties were still in the field. There was talk of withdrawing the surveyors to help set up airports for the Commonwealth Air Training Scheme but it was decided to allow them to complete their work. This they did in January, 1940. The reports they sent to Ottawa came to the notice of the Canada-U.S. Permanent Joint Board on Defence in September.

One of the joint board recommendations was the construction of an airport at Fort Nelson. The order to proceed was given Nov. 13, 1940.

Coincidental with the DOT effort in Canada, the Civil Aeronautics Board of the U.S. had been building civilian airports in Alaska like mad in a program it undertook in 1939. Reluctant to do anything that might irritate the Japanese, the U.S. Congress consistently refused to vote money for Alaska defence. However, the CAB seemed to have unlimited funds for building airports of such size and at such places they could be immediately taken over by the military.

The Japanese knew all about this immense program — some of the companies (Morrison-Knudsen and Lytle-Green) which later had contracts on the Alaska Highway were given contracts for airport construction. The Japanese protested. But the CAB continued its purportedly civilian program.

Whether this program plus the DOT program were factors which ultimately led to the Japanese decision to go to war with the U.S. is debatable. Suffice it to say that it probably saved Alaska from a complete Japanese take-over in the spring of 1942. The CAB program, too, probably resulted in Alaska being the most air-conscious state in the U.S.

* * *

Jim Millar's Western Construction and Lumber Company of Edmonton was given the contract for the Fort Nelson Airport. Alex Johnston was the superintendent and he recalled:

We had done a fair amount of work in rough country and were familiar with building of winter roads. That's why we got the job without public tender. Another thing about the contract I considered unusual was the DOT's right hand didn't know what its left hand was doing.

This became apparent when it took me more than a month to get government funds released so I could place orders for equipment and supplies — including bulldozers, trucks, sawmill, well-drilling outfit, planing mill and earth-moving equipment.

Canada has been at war two years then and equipment was scarce. It was impossible to buy a Cat in Edmonton. We did manage to scrounge one on the strength of the fact we were engaged in war work. We dug up another in Calgary and a third in Vancouver.

There were two ways of getting our outfit to Fort Nelson.

One was via the Mackenzie River system to Fort Simpson, then via the Liard and Fort Nelson rivers. But this plan was scratched as the DOT said the shipment wouldn't arrive on site until July 1. There was a great urgency to get it on the ground by the beginning of the construction season in late April.

The other plan was to use Dawson Creek as a staging area, hire a 28-man crew and take our shipment in by Cat train over a 325-mile winter trail. We were all ready to go Jan. 1 even though we didn't get the go-ahead until Dec. 18. We thought we could move the stuff over that trail before spring break-up but weren't sure.

For some reason which was never explained some boneheaded bureaucrat in Ottawa held up the start of the project six weeks — a delay which nearly spelled doom for the whole thing.

Because of this pinhead we didn't get away from Dawson Creek until Feb. 8 with our Cat train which consist of five cabooses on runners weighing 50 tons each. We made it through by Mar. 31.

We discovered the trail was good enough to run trucks over it 225 miles to the Sickanni Chief River. A trucking contract was given E. J. Spinney of Dawson Creek to move 400 tons to that river. The last 100 miles was a pack trail which had to be improved with bulldozers and this gave us the most trouble. We were supposed to go back and pick up that tonnage but an early spring break-up caught us and this couldn't be done.

The DOT hired a couple of old Northern hands, Knox F. McCusker, a pioneer land surveyor, trail blazer, big game guide and rancher, and Lloyd Gething, who operated a coal mine west of Fort St. John and was a barge operator, to move the gear by river. This proved to be a losing proposition as the water was too low for navigation that year. They used 32-horsepower kickers on home-made 48-foot scows.

When the fall freeze-up came we were finally able to send out a Cat train and move the stuff in. We were engaged in this job Dec. 7, 1941, when we heard the Japanese had attacked Pearl Harbor.

On our trek into Fort Nelson with the Cat train the last 100 miles was hard going. To move over it we had to use the bulldozers to knock down trees eight to 14 inches in diameter.

When we reached the Muskwa flats at Fort Nelson, two unusual things occurred. The crew was greeted by Chief Bellyfull of the local Indian band dressed in a Royal Navy uniform with gold braid and brass buttons. The chief had been given the uniform by the Hudson's Bay Company.

I wish some of our critics around Dawson Creek who said we'd never make it had been on hand to see that sight. The Indians didn't really know what to make of the snorting bulldozers pulling trains which were handled by hard-up homesteaders we had hired around Fort St. John.

The other unusual incident was that four days after we reached Fort Nelson, two men came down with the measles. It was hard to understand how they got them as they hadn't had contact with anyone for 1 1/2 months.

The RCMP came up from the Indian village and ordered us to place them in quarantine, get in a doctor to prevent the disease from spreading to the Indians.

The only thing I could muster for an isolation ward was a caboose. It was full of potatoes but I dumped them on the ground and insulated them with moss. (A caboose was a bunkshack on runners.) I put in a couple of bunks and ordered them to stay there a couple of days.

The RCMP, stationed in the filth and squalor of that Indian village, seemed to have a chip on their shoulder. They reported us to Ottawa for unsanitary conditions, of all things.

There was no water available — and that's the reason we brought in that drilling outfit. The experts laughed at us and said we'd never find water with it, either; we'd have to pump it up 300 feet from the Fort Nelson River.

However, I had a Cat digging a hole for a basement. He was down about five feet when the skinner came over to the office:

"Alex, I'm in trouble. I've struck water."

"Good God, man, there's not supposed to be water on this whole hill."

"Well, there's lots of it now."

Sure enough, he was in water. I said to one of the guys:

"Dig a hole."

He went down 10 feet below where the Cat was and there was all kinds of water. We made a crib and put around the hole and installed a pump and had ourselves a nice shallow well.

About a month later this RCMP type came along and saw our well. He said our installation was unsanitary. He sent a report to the DOT in Ottawa.

Well, by God, they sent a health inspector right from Ottawa with top travel priority. When the man showed up he was much impressed with the set-up we had created out of the bush.

"You fellows have done a wonderful job."

The cop had also reported us for using a few old lumberjack methods in the heating set-up.

"But, look," he said, "I have to justify a trip out here. I've got to order you to make a couple of small inconsequential changes — like covering the well with a couple of galvanized iron sheets."

That's what we did — and no more was heard of it.

Next year we had to have more water as the airport was expanded and decided to put the well-drilling outfit to work. We didn't get water but we discovered the Fort Nelson gas field.

The DOT engineering supervisors on the project were Homer Keith and Wilhelm W. Kelland. They were living in tents on the job site. Our job was to enlarge the small field which the Yukon Southern Air Transport (predecessor of the Canadian Pacific Air Lines) had hacked out of the bush the previous two winters. YSAT had brought in some equipment via the Mackenzie River route and we took that over. Their gasoline arrived from Norman Wells by barge and so did the asphalt for paving the runway.

We experienced a great many difficulties. They should have made available a chartered plane for the job — as was the case at Watson Lake. It would have saved money. Keith couldn't see it, though, and said we could use the scheduled YSAT. Here's an instance of what I mean.

It cost $68 to fly a man in from Fort St. John. The pilot would cram one more man onto the plane and as much high-priced freight as possible — and take off and leave the man's tool kit and baggage sitting on the tarmac because it was non-revenue. The air line didn't want to hire extra men to handle non-revenue poundage. Another instance:

We broke a part on a Cat and tied it up one day. The part was lying in the airport at Fort St. John and no aircraft were coming through. Homer Keith came bustling in and wanted to know why we were tied up.

"It's too far to walk to Fort St. John," I said.

"Oh, why didn't you say so? I'll go and get it," he said. And with that he wound up the DOT plane and took off for Fort St. John. We had the Cat moving the same day. Had not he come around the Cat might have been tied up a week. Another incident:

An American pilot came in and headed for the cook shack for breakfast of bacon and eggs.

"Well," replied the cook, "you'll have to wait till they fly in from Fort St. John. The eggs are still sitting at the airport there."

The next day the same pilot landed in Fort Nelson again. He walked into the cook shack with a 30-dozen crate of eggs on his shoulder.

I had wanted them to haul in some cement on the Cat train. They didn't do it. They finally wound up flying in several batches from Edmonton at $30 a hundredweight. Nails were also flown in at the same rate.

There were difficulties with Kelland as he had never been on a construction project involving heavy equipment before. He didn't understand how machinery worked. For example:

When I was engaged in clearing the 58-acre radio range station, about three miles away, a small clutch part broke and this made it impossible to put a bulldozer in gear. I went for another Cat to pull it back to the repair shop. Kelland came hustling up:

"Why not put the other Cat on the scraper?"

"The other Cat can't be used on this scraper."

"Why can't it?" he demanded.

"Because," I said, "there's a winch on the other Cat and there's a power control on this one. It would take longer to change over than to tow in this Cat and weld the part."

The construction of the Fort Nelson airport was an epic in Canadian construction but the real big action didn't start until Feb. 21, 1942, when William M. Hoge of Booneville, Mo., showed up here with Homer Keith who drove him over the winter road.

* * *

Hoge was a colonel and head of the U.S. Army's Engineer Replacement Center at Fort Belvoir, Va. He had headed a group of military and civilian engineers into Canada to determine the feasibility of a military road to link all the new airports being built in Alberta, British Columbia, the Yukon and Alaska for continental defence.

The fact that he was able to penetrate 325 miles into the wilderness by private car was a key factor in his decision to recommend the U.S. Army proceed with the project.

For the U.S. military, the construction of the Alaska Highway was a complete about-face. While it was earlier stated the Japanese had effectively stymied construction for years by representations to London, Ottawa and Washington, the powerful U.S. military authorities — who could have influenced the U.S. government to build the road — had consistently refused for years to recommend its construction on the grounds they considered its value as a defence measure was negligible. The military stoutly maintained this attitude right up to Oct. 6, 1941, despite the deterioration in the international situation.

At that time it was prodded into its endorsation as a "long-range defence measure" by Mayor F. H. LaGuardia of New York City, chairman of the American section of the U.S.-Canada Permanent Joint Board on Defence. He got President Franklin Roosevelt's ear and the president ordered selection of a route.

The attack on Pearl Harbor galvanized the government and military into joint action. At that time it was decided construction should proceed and the road should link up the airports on the Northwest Staging Route, as it was then named. Approval came Feb. 11, 1942.

* * *

The military wasted no time in despatching Hoge to Edmonton, he recalled to the author in an interview in an exclusive big old businessmen's club in downtown Cleveland in 1968:

The first I had ever heard of the Alaska Highway was Feb. 12, 1942, when I was called to Washington to meet Major-General C. L. Sturdevant, assistant chief of engineers. He had been a division engineer in the Philippines when I went there to command the 14th Engineering Regiment in 1935. He told me I had been selected to carry out a reconnaissance by going up there to figure out the logistics of building a road through unfamiliar wilderness.

They had nothing in Washington but a rough map used by bush pilots. Nobody knew anything much about the country between the airports. At that time I did not realize the magnitude of the test that faced us: to hack a pioneer road for a distance equal to the distance from Toronto to Saskatoon.

We decided to tackle the project by breaking it into pieces and getting engineering units working separately from both ends toward the centre and from the centre towards the ends. At that, we weren't sure where we could get men into the centre. The most difficult point was Watson Lake as it then could only be reached by Wrangell, Alaska, up the Stikine River, portaging to Dease Lake and then along the Dease River.

Although we had not made any formal arrangements with Canada for construction of the highway, I arrived in Edmonton Feb. 19 to determine whether construction was feasible. Accompanying me were Col. R. D. Ingalls, commanding officer of the 35th Engineering Regiment from Fort Ord, Calif.; Lieut.-Col. A. E. Mueller from the Quartermaster Corps, United States Navy, and C. F. Capes, a senior highway engineer from the Public Roads Administration, Denver, Col.

Our job was to pick the brains of every Canadian who knew anything about the North to assess the feasibility of construction. After we talked to everyone we could in Edmonton, we took off for Dawson Creek over the Northern Alberta Railways. At that time there were rumors afloat I had made an offer to lease or purchase the NAR. However, neither I nor any of my staff ever made such an offer. This may have been done by Sturdevant or by the U.S. War Department.

Arriving in Dawson Creek, we were met by Homer Keith. He offered to drive us over the road in his car to Fort Nelson.

I left Mueller behind there to study the feasibility of making contracts with various people to furnish trucks to haul enough oil, gas and rations to Fort Nelson to support a regiment for six months. He found this entirely feasible because we offered to pay them $65 a barrel to haul gas in there. In fact, many farmers and others later went out and bought trucks for no other purpose when they heard the rate we were offering.

I also ran into Knox McCusker who was stationed at Horse Track, the stopping point on the road near the Sickanni Chief River. He was keeping an eye on the last of the supplies cached there awaiting transportation to the Fort Nelson Airport and bringing some of his maps up to date. I took him back to Fort St. John. We spent most of one night going over his maps and talking about the country and the obstacles we might face. One of the things we hadn't realized was the winter road would become useless in the summer time as it traversed frozen muskeg. He suggested taking it further west along the foothills.

The result of this trip was that I ordered an engineering regiment moved into Fort Nelson over the winter road before the spring break-up and have it work towards Watson Lake rather than try to move it into Watson Lake from Wrangell and work south. In the first place, I didn't know when the Japs might close the sea lanes. In the second place, it would be too much effort struggling with equipment and supplies for what we'd get out of it. Mueller assured me he had lined up enough local truckers to move in supplies before the thaw. After that the troops would be sealed in and have to work their way out.

Although McCusker's knowledge of the country north of Fort Nelson was sketchy, he undertook to organize some surveys by dog team and later with horses to assist us in location. But the dogs and horses proved too slow. We had to get our general lines laid out from the air. Once they were established we could send out ground parties to check our conclusions.

McCusker was put on the U.S. Army payroll and stayed until construction was well advanced. President Roosevelt later awarded him the Order of Merit for his contribution to continental defence.

When we arrived back at Edmonton Feb. 25, I left Capes there with Public Works Minister W. A. Fallow of Alberta to work out details with local people.

* * *

The visit of Gen. Hoge very much impressed a young reporter from The Edmonton Journal, A. D. (Peter) Elliott, who recalled:

My beat included the Alberta and Northwest Chamber of Mines. On Feb. 19, 1942, I encountered Hoge and his party there, very impressive in great quantities of gold braid. He was in consultation with Leonard Drummond, chamber secretary. I thus became one of the first reporters in Canada to become aware of the Americans' interest in construction of the Alaska Highway.

Much to my surprise, Hoge seemed quite willing to talk about what he was doing, where he was going and why he was there. This was a new experience for me because, having been on the military beat, I had been drilled for months to be careful what I wrote. Canadian Army officers were tight-lipped about their activities when the press was around. It was frustrating; I'd dig out a story about some world personality being posted to Edmonton. The censor would kill it on the grounds it gave aid and comfort to the enemy. It was extremely refreshing, therefore, to run into these Americans. They appeared never to have heard of censorship.

They were going to build a highway and they didn't care whether we or the Japanese or Germans or anybody else knew about it. Later when I went up and lived in the camps there was never any secrecy on their part. None of the copy I wrote about the Americans ever went to Wilfred Eggleston, the chief censor in Ottawa, although I believe some copy from other reporters was badly chopped by him.

Anyway, the story I wrote that day made a big front-page headline. What really floored me, though, was Gen. Hoge's promise to phone me on the way back from Fort Nelson, which he did Feb. 25: a big wheel phoning a small-time reporter. It made my day. The story I wrote that day made a much bigger top line on the front page. He came right out and said the route was "entirely feasible." It seemed surprising he should have made a statement of this nature before he got back to Washington to report to his superiors.

Lieut.-Col. Mueller got Hoge into trouble with some information he handed out to the press and which was used in papers in Edmonton and Washington. Hoge recalled:

Mueller used no discretion. He handed out information on where we were going to start, how we were going to open the road and everything. All he said was true enough except that when he said it we hadn't yet completed a formal agreement with Canada.

We headed back to Washington on the Canadian National Railway. Arriving at Saskatoon early in the morning, a porter came along and told me there was an urgent phone call from Washington for me at the station. As I hurried along that long train in the freezing pre-dawn darkness I couldn't figure out why they wanted me. The deputy chief of staff was on the line giving me hell for allowing Mueller to spill his guts to the press. I had to get him shut up in a hurry.

* * *

Following Hoge's departure, talk and rumors around Edmonton about something happening in the North were rife, it was recalled by George Yakulic, a young reporter for the Lethbridge Herald:

The papers weren't paying much attention to these rumors so I was fortunate enough to get the first hard news break that definitely established the Americans planned to build the highway. I paid a routine call to the old Unemployment Insurance Commission office and W. E. McCutcheon, the manager, showed me a telegram he had received from the war department in Washington asking him to hire as many men as possible for construction of a military highway to Alaska.

I went back and wrote a 100-word story which, in turn, was eventually picked up by Associated Press of the U.S. We all laughed like hell that a whistle stop like Lethbridge had scooped all the big American papers on their own story. Washington had imposed a news blackout on the story — then I broke it. This was every young reporter's dream — a clean scoop on a story that had been top secret in the U.S. until then. Then all at once — boom — this story comes out because we, in our naivet, were not aware of its significance. This may have been responsible later for a news black-out on press coverage of the North.

Within a week one troop train after another started rolling through Lethbridge from Great Falls. The whole secret was out anyway, so I don't think I gave aid or comfort to the enemy, although Washington raised hell about the story appearing in the American papers.

* * *

One of the GIs on one of those trains was Ollie C. Willis of Miami, Florida, who was in B Coy of the 35th Engineering Regiment under Lieut. Milton Miletich. He recalled:

Because we had been training at Fort Ord, Calif., since December we were in an advanced state of readiness and reached Dawson Creek March 9 and damn near froze in those knee-high leather boots they issued us. We lost no time hitting the winter road, "walking" graders and Cats which had no cabs for protection from the cold.

They sent us out on that trail with no mechanics—just a bag of tools. The heavy machinery was never greased from the time it was unloaded from railroad cars at Dawson Creek. It arrived in Fort Nelson in pretty sad shape. There wasn't a hydraulic hose left intact to enable us to raise or lower the blades. It was fortunate Spinney had built "service stations" every 70 miles, consisting of barrels of fuel and a cookshack. We'd stop and pour in a barrel of Diesel fuel and keep pounding onwards. The cooks could turn out the best buckwheat pancakes in the North but the rest of the food was abominable.

* * *

When the advance party of 20 under Lieut. Miletich arrived at Fort Nelson airport late one afternoon, Alex Johnston was on hand and recalled:

Immediately a mutual admiration society was formed. Dressed in their unsuitable clothing and these leather boots, we considered the outfit had made what for them was a heroic trek. And I think they stood in awe of us having worked up there all winter keeping this airport working.

I was surprised at how soon this outfit arrived after Gen. Hoge had left. I was on hand when Homer Keith brought him in late February and we put him in the staff house.

It was a cold and hungry group. They were entirely out of food and wanted me to feed them:

"I'd like to feed you but I have no dishes."

"We don't need dishes; we have our mess kits," responded Miletich.

So our cook gave them meals. We thought no more about it till some months later a pilot walked into the cookshack one day:

"Where do you want the meat put?"

"I've no meat on order," I replied.

"Well, I've a quarter of beef for you."

"OK, I won't argue. Unload it."

When it arrived in the kitchen we found it was compliments of the 35th for feeding their men.

I got along very well with these soldiers. When they ran short of certain items I would trade them something I had in surplus — and vice-versa. They always returned better measure than they received. I would loan them half a keg of nails but they would send back a full one. They were very short of welding rods which they were glad to get. Later when truck parts became very hard for me to obtain I found they would trade a new engine for a bottle of whisky.

It was April 5 when the last of their equipment arrived over that 325-mile road. It was April 17 when the spring break-up made the road impassable. This was two weeks later than the 1941 break-up which had caught us short. They had almost everything they needed to make them self-sufficient for the summer. The only thing they ran out of was Diesel fuel. Four hundred and seventy-six barrels arrived by the Mackenzie River route.

The local people were simply flabbergasted to see the amount of the 35th's equipment (badly beaten up as it was) which was comprised of 20 large bulldozers, 24 light gas bulldozers, nine graders, six rippers, six earth movers, 2 1/2 dozen trucks, 25 jeeps, 10 command cars, a sedan, 12 pick-up trucks, a truck crane, two power shovels, concrete mixer, electric light generator, compressors, six plows and several drop hammers.

The locals were even more surprised later on to see 23 railway cars of new Cats and other equipment arrive from a Caterpillar Tractor Company factory at Peoria, Ill., on a supplementary equipment order.

After the 35th got the badly-beaten-up equipment to Fort Nelson, a group of mechanics from the Union Tractor Company in Edmonton had to be flown in to get the machines going again — mostly by cannibalizing. Later a Caterpillar tractor agency was established at Fort Nelson.

They were able to do a good job because, just as the 35th got into the construction season, heavy rains came along and bottled them up in Fort Nelson until near the end of June. Nothing moved and they repaired machines. After that there was mud, terrible mud, to contend with. It was so deep and sticky it unscrewed the drainage plug in the oil pan of a jeep grinding through it. The oil all drained out and all the rods burned out.

* * *

After the new road was holed through in September, the 35th drew a new assignment: assisting in construction of the Canol Road. This necessitated another equipment overhaul by factory representatives. However, there was nobody available in Peoria and Harry Garriott was sent up from Union Tractor Company in Calgary. He recalled:

The assignment made me one of the first Canadians to travel over the new road into the untapped wilderness.

When I arrived on the scene in Fort Nelson I was staggered by the immensity and scope of the project. I was familiar with some of the larger construction projects in Canada but was absolutely amazed by the number of machines the Americans had. It was almost more than I could conceive. I doubt if the people in Washington could visualize it.

My job required me to travel north of Fort Nelson to the advance units of the 35th and work back from there to Fort St. John, checking the equipment also of the 95th and 341st Engineering Regiments when I came across their units.

I flew into Fort Nelson and went north with a convoy taking supplies to the advance party. This included fresh meat which they had run out of. Some of the boys told me stories about being so hungry for fresh meat they went fishing with dynamite. One dynamite blast provided three tubs full of mountain trout for the mess.

Since mud made the road impassable in some locations, it took a week to make 275 miles, then it took me five weeks to work my way back to Fort St. John. Altogether there were 1,000 units to inspect, including scrapers and loaders and 105 D8 Cats, 137 D7s, 207 D4s and R4s.

This job done, they wanted me to order parts required. This was a task that could have taken me two months alone — but they assigned me some men and we worked out a system that allowed us to finish in seven days. The required parts for each machine arrived in a crate and came within a month.

* * *

Garriott was correct in his assessment that even Washington couldn't visualize the immense scope of the project.

Hoge recalled some of the difficulties he ran into with Washington when he came back to the field in Dawson Creek in March. Washington had failed to grasp the immensity of the Canadian North and the problems associated with road-building there. In that Cleveland interview with the author April 16, 1968, it was amusing to discover he was still irked about Washington bureaucrats in the war department being indifferent and ignorant.

He was short in stature, with grey hair combed straight back, militarily erect and correct. At that time a man of 75 (he died a few years later), he had a big nose, something like the movie cartoon character, Mr. Magoo, and a Swiss-type fedora.

At the end of the lunch, he went off down the street to do some grocery shopping: a long stretch from some 26 years previously when he had the power of life and death over 10,000 GIs ramroding a road through a trackless bush.

There were GIs like Pte. Harry Houtling of the 35th, a good man with a lot of friends who had never been outside New York City before. He was assigned to supply and his job was to bring up to the forward units such things as clothes and mess kits. He was forced to carry these on his back in a pack many days. Some days he would have to walk as far as 10 miles, fighting mud and mosquitoes all the way. Eventually this got to be too much for this city-bred soldier, worse than anything the enemy could throw at him because he couldn't strike back. He went out and blew out his brains one day. Other privates thrived on this outdoor life.

* * *

Initially they started us off with all the best wishes and promises of everything. But after we were up there a while they simply forgot about us. They had started the Canol project and there was the build-up for Australia. So they started to cut back on us. For instance, when they sent the 93rd Engineering Regiment into Skagway they only had three bulldozers. And they couldn't get more, Hoge recalled:

We wrote letters and sent telegrams but nobody paid any attention to us. Of course, there was some justification as they had so many other projects going at the same time.

Col. Theodore Wyman, Jr., the chief of the Canol project, rubbed me the wrong way. We had several fights about him being able to divert to his project's use a lot of equipment we badly needed. He was a ruthless man who tried to commandeer everything. He was back in Edmonton where he could talk to influential people in Washington who could get him everything. It irked me to think of all this equipment diverted onto Canol, a badly conceived project which I thought served no purpose.

The people in Washington had all sorts of queer ideas. One was about rations. Some fellow wanted to furnish us with guns so we could kill all our own food. Even if this had been practical, he didn't realize Canada had game laws.

Somebody else ordered a whole shipload of coal into Skagway for me. I needed it like a hole in the head. What I wanted were fresh vegetables and mosquito nets.

I ended up giving the coal to the White Pass and Yukon Railway. They piled it along the tracks.

Nobody knew or could realize in Washington how bad and terrible the mosquito problem was. When I tried to get head nets for the GIs the requisitions were ignored. One day I got mad and jumped into one of our planes and flew to Washington. Barging into the quartermaster-general's office I told him:

"I need 10,000 mosquito nets."

"Why," he replied, "there should be no trouble about that. We have a million of them right here."

"I know you've got them but I've got a million mosquitoes for every net you've got—and I can't get any nets. You people don't believe there can be mosquitoes in the Canadian bush because it is cold there; but not in the summertime."

He then arranged to ship a boxcar full.

The mosquitoes were so thick they appeared as a misty cloud over one's head. One could lie on his bunk and hear the humming of these miniature vultures waiting outside just for one sight of human flesh. We could never figure out how the mosquitoes, bred for thousands of generations in the thawing moss and living on plant juices, could figure out a soldier's blood was good. They were worse in that regard than the Japanese.

Then there were these no-see-ums. We were defenceless against them as they could get through netting to torture the occupants. We could develop immunity against them after a few days but not so with the mosquitoes.

* * *

I couldn't even eat at times because the mosquitoes were so bad, it was recalled by Lieut. Herman Engel of E Coy of the 340th:

By the time you had picked the mosquitoes off a forkful of food and were ready to lift it to your mouth, it would be covered again. You'd give up and say "to hell with it" and munch on some hardtack.

Face nets were finally issued in the light olive drab color. Unfortunately the people who made these never test-wore them. The light color reflected the sunlight off the little fibres of cloth. Consequently, the wearer couldn't see very far and couldn't recognize a person coming toward him. They were a real nuisance when handling surveying equipment.

I had my wife send me a few packages of black dye. The black color absorbed the sunlight, and you could see who was out there.

* * *

Some of the boys inadvertently found humor in the mosquitoes, among them Sgt. Speed Werkmeister of the 18th:

We had slit trenches for latrines. Beside each latrine were cans of Diesel fuel. A guy would finally get brave:

"Well, I can't hold it any longer."

As he walked toward the latrine he'd break off a poplar branch or two and throw them into the slit trench, toss in some Diesel and light a match to get them burning and throw oil on top. This ritual would produce a dense cloud of black smoke. He'd save one small branch to fan the smoke when he got his pants down. He'd choke and gag in this acrid smoke until he'd answered the call to nature. Even so those damned mosquitoes would sneak through the smoke and dive-bomb the exposed behind in a dozen places.

There were rumors around that mosquitoes fell dead after biting certain members of the officer corps.

In the tents at night we had to cover a hot stove with spruce boughs and let the stinking fumes fill the tent. It was often a choice of choking to death or getting bitten to death. Some of the guys chose the latter.

I never gave up eating because of them, however. In the morning the cooks would beat up pancake batter while trying to fight these damned things off. When we'd get the pancakes there would be little black things in them.

"What's in the pancakes?"

"Caraway seeds," the cooks would chorus.

"The hell it is," come back a chorus of GIs. "They have legs on them."
"Eat it, you bastards. It's plasma. That's all the fresh meat you'll get today."

* * *

Humor wasn't much aid and comfort in fighting lack of knowledge and misunderstanding in Washington, Gen. Hoge recalled, as well as weather on the job:

It was frustrating trying to keep contact with the whole 1,500 miles of the project. In fact, I found it was impossible as I would be grounded for a week at a time by bad weather. I came to the realization I couldn't control it all from one spot. I told Washington I had to have a deputy to take charge of the south end. They sent in Gen. J.A. (Patsy) O'Connor and he moved to Fort St. John. I went to Whitehorse June 1 to expedite things.

After a couple of more go-rounds of indifference, Sturdevant came up about half a dozen times at my request. When I'd get him out in the bush and show him what we were up against, he ultimately got us the help we needed.

And we finished the job.

Bush pilot Les Cook causes mock terror as he "buzzes" army camp "company street."

3

Les Cook Found New Route For Americans

On Dec. 4, 1942, a Norseman took off from the Whitehorse airport with three persons aboard. Immediately after take-off trouble developed. The plane was unable to gain altitude.

Although the pilot could have glided in for a crash landing in the settled part of town, he banked to bring the craft down in open ground. During this manoeuvre the wing caught on a power line and the plane went into a sickening cartwheel and crashed 100 yards from the hospital. It caught fire upon impact.

One of the would-be rescuers was Albert Beattie of nearby Carcross who, to his horror, recognized the pilot as Les Cook, a friend who formerly worked out of Carcross for Northern Airways but was now flying for Gen. William Hoge, the engineer in charge of the construction of the Alaska Highway. Attempts by Beattie to pull open the door failed and Cook, aero engineer Ken McLean and a man named Dickson perished.

* * *

Thus was cut short at age 34 the career of Leslie Albert Cook, a legendary Northern bush pilot who was given credit at the time for knowing more about flying in the Yukon than any other living person. He had intimate knowledge of the mountain passes and water routes throughout the territory. General Hoge recalled:

When we first went into the Yukon we didn't know anything about the country. The two people who helped me most were Les Cook and Herb Wheeler, president of the White Pass and Yukon Railway.

Herb was a great old Irishman who had jumped ship at Skagway before the Yukon Gold Rush and after it he joined the White Pass as a section hand. He practically built the first Whitehorse airport himself and his advice was invaluable.

The U.S. Army engineers didn't know anything about the country through which we were supposed to build the highway. Neither did anyone else — except Les Cook. Between the two of them we were saved hundreds of thousand of dollars and much time. Of the two, I think the contribution of Cook was the greater. He was the first pilot I met in the Yukon.

I remember trying to locate the best route from Watson Lake to Whitehorse. I put out a few enquiries for anyone — Indian or trapper — who had been across there. I couldn't find anybody. The trappers only knew the specific area in which their traplines were located.

The original plan had been to go over the top of the mountains, a route that would put the road close to the 6,000-foot level. Someone supplied me with a map. Cook took a look at this map and told us it was "crazy."

"Even the rivers on this and other maps north of Whitehorse show them flowing the wrong way," Cook pointed out. "Furthermore, south of Whitehorse you don't have to go over those high mountains. There is another route. I have flown it several times."

He had been hauling oil and spare parts from Whitehorse to a contractor who was working on the Watson Lake airport. He showed me the route that followed the Rancheria River. It came through the mountains in a pass that was less than 3,500 feet.

That was a great break for Col. Frank Pettit and me. Without it we would have had a helluva job locating the road between Watson Lake and Tenana, Alaska. Henceforth we always called the pass he showed us Cook Pass. To him goes much of the credit for the location. He was so skilful and resourceful that I always felt confident when flying with him for our safe return to our base.

Had Cook not been on the job we would have had to make the highway 500 miles longer than the final route. His route was through forest growth which had never been travelled before by man.

Some of the old-timers we had contacted weren't much help at all. To begin with, they flatly told us we couldn't hope to punch a road through in one season. They said muskeg would hold us back where mountain passes didn't. George Black, Conservative MP for the Yukon, simply told us we were crazy; that the road would have to be laid over hundreds of miles of muskeg which would not hold up.

With egg on his face when we finally proved him off base, Black pointed out a road was built from Whitehorse to Dawson City 40 years previously with horses, picks and shovels in one summer. However, that road followed an explored trail along the Yukon River. Maps didn't even exist for much of the terrain the Alaska Highway was to traverse.

We were very happy to see Canadian bush pilots flying alongside us — and kept two on staff to show our boys the ropes. Les Cook was stationed at Whitehorse and the other Canadian at Fort St. John.

In order for us to get around the job better I went back to Washington and requisitioned four single-engined planes. They sent me two Norsemen and two Beechcraft and two U.S. Army Air Force pilots.

We used those planes for reconnaissance as well as travel. I was on hand when the route was located to Watson Lake from Fort Nelson. Our first attempts were down the Fort Nelson River to where it joins the Liard. I favored this route (and still think to this day we would have been better-advised to use it) because I liked the appearance of the ground better and it seemed the Grand Canyon of the Liard could be bridged easily as it was narrow.

I was dissuaded from this route because we didn't know enough about the big streams we would have to cross nor did we have facilities to cross them. The route which we finally did settle on included a difficult crossing of Steamboat Mountain, a great deal of rock cutting along the shore of Muncho Lake and a major suspension bridge over the Liard further down.

A great body of mythology sprang up around the hair-raising flying we did when we went in there that summer of 1942. However, I'll tell you a true story.

I was on a survey flight to Fort Nelson with a bush pilot from Edmonton and a rented single-engine, single-seat plane. A Public Roads Administration engineer and I had to sit in tandem on bedrolls behind the pilot and I had my legs around the pilot and he had his legs around me. We got socked in at Fort Nelson for three days and I was getting edgier and anxious to get back to Fort St. John to look after 101 details. I persuaded the pilot to take off in fog the fourth day.

"If you can fly level," I said, "I can get us back to Fort St. John. We'll go down the Prophet River till we hit the Trutch. I know where it comes out of the mountains to join the Prophet, then we can go down that river a way till we hit the Blueberry."

To do this we had to keep level because the ceiling was only about 400 feet.

We took off. We got down the Prophet all right but we missed the Trutch going off to the left. The first thing I knew we were right in the middle of the Rocky Mountains.

Look up — and there was a solid wall of rock facing us. There was no room to circle to gain altitude.

Circle — and be confronted with another wall of rock.

We circled around in a canyon and finally managed to break out and hit the Prophet again and then the Trutch and finally found our way to Fort St. John. But we had our feet in the treetops most of the time.

We had to thank our pilot for being a damned good flyer. The PRA engineer couldn't do anything but sit behind me and swear out of fear and frustration.

I made another hair-raising flight like this — this time with Cook. We had gone to Burwash Landing north of Whitehorse and had gotten socked in again for three days. He made several attempts to break out but failed; couldn't see a thing.

On the fourth day, however, he took off and managed to reach Whitehorse by flying low following the Yukon River. Whitehorse airfield was socked in. We could see the river through the soup and we knew the field was right down there but we couldn't see it. We even went down into the gorge but no field came into view.

There was nothing we could do but turn around and go back. This was typical of a number of flights I made with him and other bush pilots.

One of the routine jobs performed by Cook and his contemporaries flying out of Whitehorse began in May, 1942, with the arrival of the 18th, 340th and 93rd Engineering Regiments. They flew crews ahead of trail construction to build temporary bridges. In one case the commanding officer of the 340th realized supply lines would be difficult so he had rations and fuel flown ahead and cached along the banks of lakes and rivers awaiting the arrival of the advance troops.

* * *

One officer using the services of Cook was Lieut. Herman Engel, Jr., of the

340th. He recalled:

After previously-despatched location parties had bogged down, I took out a party of Indian guides. They were good fellows but we made the greatest progress between Morley Bay on Teslin Lake and Watson Lake when Cook came on the scene.

On his regular food drops, he would take me up and circle around a few times so I could see the lay of the land ahead. He would suggest the best direction to go.

The way he would locate me was by flying in big circles in the area he figured I would be. I would go to the bed of a river or the shore of a lake or some other open space and build a smudge fire. Then he would land on the nearest lake and leave supplies.

Sometimes he flew in a bunch of mail but it had no priority. In the early stages of our tour of duty in the North we wouldn't have received any mail except for pilots like Les Cook who took pity on us and would leave it in a cache with other supplies. However, mail service depended on the pilots being considerate enough to see we heard from home.

For entertainment we had the bears. One time I got to a food cache and found they had broken into it, smashed the cans and knocked them into the water. All the labels were gone. We'd open a can for breakfast and find it was diced carrots or pickled beets — or grape jelly. That was amusing. Those were the things that made life bear-able.

In the way of amusement, I will never forget one flight I made with Cook. The water was so calm on a small lake from which we were taking off, he couldn't get the plane up on the step. Calm water will create suction and hold the plane down.

Usually when this happens a pilot will get somebody with a motor boat to roil up the water. But in this case this lake had never seen a motor boat.

Therefore, he asked me to sit out on the pontoon and drag my feet. He then circled and crisscrossed the lake several times to stir up the water. I climbed back in just as he was making his take-off run.

In those days I was pretty young and daring. I never thought in terms of being scared. Today, I wouldn't care to fly like this with anybody. They were all experienced flyers — Cook had 700 hours on flying boats, 3,700 on sea planes and 3,950 on skis and wheels — and I don't think they felt they were taking too many risks. Actually, they were a breed of their own.

Cook would fly over a mountain and skim the tops of the trees because they were flying at the maximum those small planes were capable of. When he wasn't doing this he took great delight in flying low over the "company street" in our camps. There would be rows of tents on either side of a clearing in the bush and he would drop down to tent level and pull flaps and knock kitchen tent flies over.

It was great fun to watch the GIs duck and run.

But for all the mock cursing and howls from the GIs for buzzing and other monkeyshines, they had nothing but praise for this great flyer. They knew their task would have been much more difficult had he not been there to show them the way. They knew he would be on hand if mercy flights were required. He was a minor hero who won their greatest admiration and praise. Word of his derring-do was passed by word of mouth among the personnel.

* * *

Cook's willingness to take risks won him the U.S. Legion of Merit, posthumously, April 15, 1943, signed by Gen. George C. Marshall, chief of staff, for a mercy flight he made Nov. 16, 1942.

A private in the 29th Survey Regiment at a camp at the White River developed a ruptured appendix the day before. Capt. Guardino, an obstetrics specialist, decided to move him to the emergency flight strip at the Donjek River (a rough strip from which the tree stumps and stones hadn't yet been removed) for an emergency flight to the newly completed hospital in Whitehorse, 167 miles from there. This involved carrying the sick man two miles in a litter and crossing the uncompleted bridge over the river, followed by a 30-mile ambulance trip to Donjek.

Maj. R. W. Norberg, chief medical officer of the 18th Engineering Regiment at Donjek, radioed for a plane. There was a delay but he was notified a plane would arrive at 11 a.m. next day.

The weather was so bad the only experienced civilian pilot refused to fly. Les Cook was in Fairbanks and could have stopped on the way back but didn't receive the message.

He arrived in Whitehorse late in the day after a very rough trip. Word was received from Norberg the private's condition was growing worse. Capt. William Joyce and Lieut. Eugene Moskowitz of the Medical Corps volunteered to fly to Donjek and Cook agreed to take them.

Because of the overcast Cook flew past the Donjek but finally recognized the White River through a break in the clouds. He turned back and was guided to the Donjek strip by lights of trucks lined along it.

The Donjek medics converted the front of the barracks into an operating theatre by hanging blankets on wires.

Although it seemed suicidal for anyone to fly those valleys that night Cook's plane dipped low over the camp and he gunned the motor as a signal to get ready. Ten minutes later Joyce and Moskowitz were there sterilizing instruments. The operation was successfully completed at midnight. The patient recovered.

As with all legends in their own time, Cook had critics. Some of the sceptics, who had doubted tales told by him about flying through the St. Elias Mountains with peaks 12,000 to 19,000 feet, began to regard him in a new light. He had frequently run into tremendous head winds in the passes. On one trip when crossing the range he had hit 100-mile-an-hour winds which had hurled his single-motor plane like a cockle-shell on a rip tide, slamming him upside down and back toward the peaks as quickly as he could right his craft. Only previous experience with these winds got him out of that one.

* * *

The fact he could go any place with a Norseman aircraft, dropping into lakes at treetop level, added to the legend. He also developed a reputation as a bit of a daredevil, too, although he took most of the chances when alone in the plane. Gordon Yardley, who arrived in the Yukon on the same boat with Cook May 18, 1937, and lived near him at Carcross, recalled:

He ran into trouble at the Carcross bridge several times by not allowing himself enough room to take off on Lake Bennett — but he always seemed to get out of jams.

I have seen him many times trying to get off with an overload. He'd roar up the lake for a mile and a half and not be able to get up on the step. Then he'd come back to the dock, throw off a quarter of beef and try her again.

On the next try he'd stagger off, swing around and come back over the town about 200 feet up and circle several times to get altitude to cross the mountains that surrounded the village.

For all his daredevilling and crash landings, it never seemed to worry him about a motor conking out and piling him up in the bush. He piled up his plane a number of times but always walked away. What did concern him was the possibility of a plane catching fire in a crash. He seemed to have a phobia about this and I remember him saying once he had hit the ground he would have to get the hell away from the aircraft very quickly.

It was ironic the gas-fed fire he feared most was the cause of his death. He might have had a chance had he not broken one of his primary rules that fateful Dec. 4. He took a chance with passengers aboard. He had worked with McLean and Dickson all day repairing the pitch regulator of the Norseman's propeller. Although it was cold work done under primitive conditions, the crew was a happy, bantering one.

The tactical error he made was taking off from the middle of the runway instead of using the full length for take-off. He took off and dropped over the edge of the high bench upon which the Whitehorse airport was built. Had he taken the full length he might have discovered the prop was in full fine pitch at the time. However, having dropped over it was too late for him to correct the pitch so the prop would grab the air.

* * *

Cook was born in Pincher Creek, Alta., the son of E. G. Cook, who later became a member of the Alberta Legislature. While still enrolled in the University of Alberta at Edmonton age 19 he was commissioned to the Royal Canadian Air Force.

Canadian military authorities had observed the effectiveness of the airplane during the First World War and had determined that an air force should become a permanent branch of the armed forces. However, because there was little encouragement for young men to take up flying as a career the strength of the RCAF kept going down. The government therefore went into a program of pilot training, offering commissions to young men in universities. The first class in 1927 drew only 13 candidates and, as this number was generally regarded as unlucky, Les Cook was persuaded to become the 14th student in the class.

He graduated in 1930 and was posted to RCAF northern operations for two years. He became hooked on the North. He left the RCAF and, after working around until 1937, became chief pilot of George T. Simmons' Northern Airways Limited for $7,000 a year.

He became a northern expert and advocate, opening new flying services under the most primitive communications conditions.

The extent of poor communications was starkly demonstrated when he established a trading post at Sheldon Lake in "the back country" at the edge of the Mackenzie Mountains in competition with an established post at Pelly Banks owned by Taylor and Drury of Whitehorse. He turned this operation over to his brother, Jim.

Jim was killed in an unfortunate accident. He was showing his wife how to set a bear trap in which the integral part was a gun a bear would trigger off and shoot itself. Somehow the gun went off and killed him.

Cook's brother-in-law from Atlin was there — and he had to walk out 150 miles to Teslin to notify Cook of the death.

Cook married in 1941, sold his interests and moved "Outside" to a sedate existence in Vancouver. That only lasted until spring. He was so eager to go north again he took a $1,000-a-year pay cut to go with White Pass Airways at Whitehorse. But he heard the Canadian Pacific Railway was trying to buy it and other small northern air lines and amalgamate them into its Yukon Southern Air Transport. He wouldn't go to work for the CPR as he didn't like the way it carried out plane maintenance and methods of operation.

Just when he was about to become unemployed, Gen. Hoge arrived on the scene and hired him as a pathfinder. He lived long enough to see the Americans start to put millions into creating the kind of aerial travel service in the North he envisioned — a proposal he had failed to convince Ottawa to bankroll.

During his years with Northern Airways, Cook was constantly agitating at both provincial and federal levels for improved aviation facilities for the development of the North because, as he saw it, this could be accomplished only by the use of the airplane. At his behest, Mines Minister W. J. Asselstine of British Columbia wrote a letter to federal Transport Minister P. J. A. Cardin trying to persuade him to spend some money on ground facilities for air service. But, alas, Ottawa had no money because it was fighting a war in Europe.

On Nov. 16, 1940, Cook received a rather curious letter from Vihljalmur Stefansson, the famous Arctic explorer, from Fairbanks, Alaska. Stefansson wanted his advice on an unusual problem. He had been sent north from New York to make a report on the feasibility of defending the North should it be attacked from the west.

Communications, he thought, would constitute a big problem. He wanted Cook's opinion on using homing pigeons as he had heard Cook and Arthur Burt, a former Northern Airways pilot, used to carry them to send back messages in case of forced landings in the days before there was much use of radio. Cook wasn't high on pigeons as they couldn't handle snow and storms in winter and weren't very reliable.

Cook was consulted for technical advice on the North by E. W. Elliott

Company of Seattle, management contractor in charge of transporting men, materials and equipment onto the job site for the Public Roads Administration. In April, 1942, he offered to assume full responsibility for setting up an airline service to transport personnel along the highway. He flew senior personnel over the various routes a number of times to acquaint them with the territory and the problems. However, before he could make a deal with Elliott he was snapped up by Gen. Hoge for reconnaissance.

Cook's advice was sought also by Washington for a survey that was so top secret the transportation corps of the U.S. Army didn't even tell him what it was for. At the behest of J. E. Floyd of the office of the chief of transportation at the Pentagon, he made a photography flight down the Rocky Mountain Trench, and reported May 22, 1942.

The trench is nominally a wide valley beginning at Prince George and running through to Whitehorse and Fairbanks. The highest elevation to cross along the route is less than 3,500 feet. He sent Floyd maps and photos.

Although Cook did not see how the information he gave him could be of much use, he was not aware at the time the Americans were investigating the possibility of building a railroad along the trench at the suggestion of Frederick Delano, an uncle of President F. D. Roosevelt.

Some route staking later took place on sections of this route but nothing ever came of a venture into railroad building rather than highway building.

Cook packed a great deal of productive activity into a short life. But like anyone else in the front line of battle, he became a casualty of war and somebody new was sent in to take his place.

4

Alsib Movement Had Its Ups And Downs

The cold war between the Soviet Union and the United States could have had its genesis in the wartime lend-lease project known as Alsib (Alaska-Siberian) movement of aircraft.

There had been a great deal of uncertainty and suspicion of the Soviet Union by the U.S. and Great Britain with the signing of the German-Russian non-aggression treaty in August, 1939. This treaty resulted in the U.S. beefing up its Alaska defence system from time to time.

However, the collapse of the treaty in June, 1941, brought an about-face by President Roosevelt. He immediately declared the Soviets eligible to receive war supplies on a lend-lease basis — an act tantamount to giving the Soviets war materiel gratis.

Within a month Lt.-Gen. Philip I. Golokov was in the U.S. outlining Soviet needs to Gen. George C. Marshall.

The immediate need was 3,000 fighter planes to throw against the Luftwaffe — and the Russians asked for 200 immediately. Although this meant "adjusting" allocations of planes to Great Britain, the British went along with the deal, agreeing to divert 141 planes.

The fastest way to get these planes to Russia in flying shape was via Alaska. The Soviets were to see that pilots and mechanics were sent to

Ladd Field at Fairbanks for familiarization training so the planes could be ferried directly to the front. However, five days later on Aug. 5, 1941, Soviet Ambassador Constantin Oumansky came back to report his government believed the plan impractical and asked the planes be shipped knocked down in crates via water to Murmansk and Archangel.

Then followed a series of intrigues almost the equal of the method Lockheed Aircraft Company of Burbank, Calif., used in forwarding Hudson bombers to Great Britain before the United States declared war on Germany.

The company was prevented from shipping them directly to Britain by the U.S. Neutrality Act so it bought a wheat field on the border between North Dakota and Canada. Teams of Canadian horses were hitched to the planes and pulled them — driverless and pilotless and not subject to any law — across the border to waiting British pilots who flew them overseas.

Although the Alsib route was 2,000 miles shorter and the safest from enemy attack, the Soviets persisted in using the Murmansk gateway and another through Abadan in Iran. They didn't want any Americans peering into Siberia which, at that point, was better-developed with airfields than northern Canada and Alaska and cities like Komsomolsk with 100,000 population.

The infrastructure had been developed by exiled intellectuals for years before the polyglot settlers arrived. It was not a boom-and-bust economy like Canada's North which was cursed by too many people with no real attachment to the community.

The other reason the Soviets banned the Americans — even after war was declared on Japan Dec. 7, 1941 — was they didn't want to become friendly with Japan after losing a recent disastrous war to that country.

No American mechanics and technicians were allowed. If Soviet mechanics couldn't repair lend-lease planes, they were shoved aside. New ones were always available.

The Soviet point of view was apocryphally stated in a conversation at Ladd Field:

"It would be more efficient for your mechanics to come onto our bases — but all our bases are secret."

"But we're supposed to be allies," replied an American.

"Yes, but where would the Soviet Union be today if we had shown the Germans our defence installations when they were our allies?"

On the other hand, Soviet officers and men "infiltrated" the U.S. and Canada as far south as Edmonton, Waterways and Great Falls. They were allowed to tour freely wherever they wanted. One visitor to Edmonton was Capt. F. K. Panamerenko, a Red Air Force hero who wore the Lenin and Red Star decorations.

Groups of high-booted, flat-capped Soviet pilots appeared in downtown Edmonton regularly. The first group to do so stopped a baseball game when they entered a park. They were loudly cheered. Under expert coaching, it wasn't long before they were yelling "kill the umpire" and "throw the bum out."

The only American to have a real good look at lend-lease planes in the Soviet Union was Capt. Eddie Rickenbacker, a First World War pilot who became president of Eastern Airlines. But he went there under a political cloud.

He was asked in April, 1943, by Gen. Hap Arnold, chief of the U.S. Army Air Force, to go to the Soviet Union to find out more about Russian activities and how they were getting along with the $1.5 billion in lend-lease planes. However President Franklin D. Roosevelt hated Rickenbacker because of his outspoken criticism of the administration. Even though the U.S. was fighting for his life, Roosevelt refused to give Rickenbacker his blessing.

Rickenbacker hit it lucky as at the Moscow defence command he ran into a Russian pilot he had entertained in 1937. He thus got places no other American could.

His great discovery was that with the help of U.S. planes the Soviet forces had developed from a Communist rabble into a great military machine that would defeat Germany.

Rickenbacker got to Prime Minister Winston Churchill of Great Britain with this message but Roosevelt refused to see him. This bullheadedness was later responsible for his failure to negotiate peace terms with Stalin.

Ambassador W. H. Standley was sent to see Stalin in April, 1942, to persuade him once more to take delivery of planes via Siberia — but Stalin was disinterested and used every excuse in the book. He suggested delivery via Greenland would be better — and planes were eventually delivered via that vastly expensive and dangerous route.

Next month Gen. Arnold, Gen. Dwight Eisenhower and several other big wheels put pressure on Stalin to allow the U.S. to use its own pilots to ferry planes to Siberia. Stalin would not go for the deal with U.S. pilots and Maj. Edwin R. Carr, USAAF historian, put it this way in 1964:

"It would take no special power of divination on Stalin's part to see that this could be the opening wedge to the use of Siberian air bases against Japan by the Americans."

It was a truly Machiavellian situation in which two unwilling allies — each fighting for its life — were holding each other at arm's length. While millions were being killed, the military leaders were jockeying with each other for a relative advantage. Only the most devious of schemers could afford the luxury of engaging in such byplay while facing the possibility of defeat from two separate enemies, Germany and Japan. The common enemies could have been dealt body blows by acceptance of assistance from each other.

Stalin finally did agree to accept delivery, with Fairbanks as the transfer point. Following this agreement nothing happened for a couple of months. Planes were sitting in storage against delivery orders. It got so bad Gen. Arnold sent an emissary to Litvinov June 20, 1942, to ask him what he intended to do with these planes. If they didn't want them the Americans could use them elsewhere.

This time the deal seemed off again. Soviet Ambassador Maxim Litvinov said airily the Russians were not interested in the Alsib movement unless more planes could be provided. This sort of devious, paranoid thinking was hard to accept. It was lucky that word of it did not get out in Dawson Creek. It was tantamount to the Americans forcing planes upon the Russians to fight the Russians' war. At that point the Yanks were a bit rattled as the Japanese had just invaded the Aleutians and, understandably, they were anxious to hit them in any way possible.

About this time the Second Protocol was being drawn up and Litvinov hoped to receive a greater allocation of planes. Under the new protocol the U.S. agreed to supply 2,544 planes for the year — or 212 a month. Everything seemed ready to go over the Alsib route July 18 following talks between Maj.-Gen. Follett Bradley and Gen. Bolyaev.

Although the people of Dawson Creek were not aware of the destination of the planes, the first actual delivery was made Sept. 3. Thus was born the secret air operation by means of which the Soviet Union was able to obtain 10,000 planes to smash the bomber strength of the Luftwaffe at the crucial period when the Germans were at the gates of Stalingrad and Moscow.

The United States Army Air Force invited a group of reporters to Ladd Field at Fairbanks to mark the beginning of the Alsib movement. But events there took on an air of unreality and mystery. The installations — hangars, fuel tanks, mess hall and theatre — were semi-underground. Despite the fact the First Protocol had been signed 1½ years previous, no planes had been delivered and Sept. 3 only five A-

20 light bombers came through. Several days later the first group of Russian pilots and mechanics under Col. Michael G. Machin arrived to take delivery. The five planes sat there three weeks before Machin's men began flying them as, without a word of warning on Sept. 19, the Russians sent word it had been decided not to use the route.

Then a few days later word was received the Kremlin had reconsidered and the route was reopened. It was thought this was a result of the visit of Wendell Willkie to Stalin.

* * *

One of the newsmen in for the ceremony was George Yakulic of the Lethbridge Herald and he recalled:

Standing on the apron with his legs apart and his hands in his back pockets was Gen. Ludson D. Worsham, top military man for the area. Looking at the two planes disappearing into the blue, he said:

"There's a couple of sons of bitches we'll have to shoot down some day."

The underground hangar was divided by heavy wire mesh netting. The planes were checked over and when the American mechanics were satisfied they were airworthy, a big gate in the mesh was opened and the plane towed through to the Soviet side.

A group of Russians began swarming all over it painting out the white star and decaling on a red star. What got me was that despite the fact they never paid a cent for these aircraft there was always hell to pay following the inspections. A Russian major would allege he had found a discrepancy, even one which had developed in the flight from California, and demand it be corrected. He even refused some planes. They were adamant in what they wanted and arbitrary in their demands and way of doing business.

If they were dissatisfied in the way senior U.S. officers were carrying out their duties, they would never try to come to an agreement. They would turn on their heel and say:

"Very well, then, we'll take it up with President Roosevelt."

They were convinced Roosevelt was on their side and that they could get anything out of him they wanted just by saying the word. This notion stemmed from disagreements over discrepancies in bookkeeping. The U.S. counted factory delivery as satisfying its lend-lease commitments. The Russians regarded a plane as delivered when it came into their hands. In the first months of 1943 the U.S. books showed commitments being satisfactorily met. But the Russians were able to prove the U.S. far behind because a great deal of sloppy and careless work on assembly lines in California had resulted in too many planes failing to be given certificates of airworthiness and thus couldn't be flown right off to transfer points.

Factory inspectors who spotted defects were vilified. For instance, all hell broke loose at Santa Monica over the head of a Canadian inspector when he tied red tags on seven planes one day.

Planes were sent out with poor hose connections, loose packing nuts, oil leaks and other carelessness. They were turned out by the same type of worker who sent Liberty ships to sea (to break in two) with bridge welds between steel plates rather than solid welds.

It later became a black joke among the Americans that the Central Intelligence Agency was even then anticipating the cold war and the military was selling them all these defective planes to sabotage any future potential threat! But American pilots were the ones who really got it in the neck.

The poor performance by the American workers could be laid chiefly at the doorstep of middle-class carelessness, uselessness and stupidity in the face of lack of direction and initial lack of knowledge of the characteristics of the terrain over which the aircraft were operated.

A love-hate relationship developed between the Russkies and the Yanks over these planes. In their defence, it must be said that when the Yanks found out how really bad they were they assigned dozens of mechanics to Edmonton, Fairbanks and Nome to repair them and modify defects. Towards the end of Alsib, the Russians realized how greatly improved the planes were and begged the U.S. for more. However, by this time the U.S. realized it had a problem on its hands. The Russians had practically defeated the Germans and now became a menace themselves. Therefore, Uncle Sam politely refused all requests for the improved models on the grounds he needed them himself.

Many fighter planes were lost en route to Moscow — mainly because the engines wouldn't run cool on the ground. If they didn't get off right away they would overheat. They had a lot of hairy times with those peashooters as the coolant fluid heated up and expanded so rapidly the relief valve would pop before the take-off, enveloping the pilot in a cloud of steam. It used to irk the pilots of commercial flights when the tower would get a flight of 15 or 20 of these off first and hold the commercial flight. As one pilot told me:

"A Russian has to be rather wild, crazy or don't-give-a-damn type (or a combination of all three) to fly them all the way to the Soviet Union — or have a nervous break-down."

Once they got the bugs out — and this took many months and new procedures that had to be started from scratch — the Americans made big grandiose plans. The Russians couldn't fathom their methods. They planned to expand deliveries to 5,000 a month in the spring of 1943 to counter the German push. They even went to the extent of asking the Canadian government for permission to establish a northeast staging route along the Mackenzie River route to Fairbanks to carry out their plan. Fortunately the Russians turned back the German push at Stalingrad and the Yanks scaled down plans to actual deliveries for the year.

Gas deliveries to the airports were erratic that first winter. At some, tanks were filled from five-gallon pails trucked many hundreds of miles on the preliminary road. The Canadian sector was one of the worst.

Some of the most elemental procedures, such as ordering spare parts, were imperfect. Great quantities of equipment were ordered but some of it was rendered useless when parts were smashed by careless workers. Records were lacking and much of the stock became buried under snow banks with no records to show which snow bank. Items not thought to be in stock turned up when the snow melted — after planes had been held up for weeks awaiting parts.

At Northway, Alaska, 991 ski poles showed up but not enough equipment to calibrate a bombsight.

* * *

The wild and weird way the Russians handled the planes and their fatalistic attitude toward life never ceased to amaze and annoy the Americans, it was recalled by Mrs. Ginny Hall, who was one of the few women ferry pilots in the USAAF and later ran a tourist lodge at Mount McKinley, Alaska:

The Russians knew little and cared less about "running in" new planes. We used to shake our heads when we saw them jump into a P-63 with less than 20 hours on it and fly it right away under full throttle. I later discovered the reason for this seemingly reckless stance. Most of them were war heroes — some wearing the Lenin Medal and Red Star — who were on "rest duty" from the front, quite a few with combat fatigue. They had been trained to scramble to get their fighters into the air fast against the Luftwaffe. They had a large number of women pilots who treated planes the same way.

The women were an eye-opener for us Americans. We had put women on a pedestal and kept them beautiful — and useless. The Soviets treated women on an equal basis with men in both highly skilled and non-skilled jobs.

Many of the women were inexperienced. I saw some with less than 10 hours in fighters who had little regard for airport safety regulations.

A gaggle of women pilots was taking off from Great Falls with a flight of fighters. One woman ran out of the latrine late. She kicked the chock from under the nearest wheel, jumped into the cockpit and spun the plane around a couple of times to shake loose the other and rode straight across the centre of the apron to get her plane into the air to catch up with the rest.

One Russian pilot, when admonished that planes wouldn't last long with that kind of treatment, replied:

"That's O.K. I don't think I last long, either."

Our boys used to think themselves quite the heroes for having braved the wilds to ferry the planes to Fairbanks. However, they had many "frills" compared to the Russians. The Russians had no search and rescue operations. If a plane went down that was tough — not because they didn't value human life but because their economy and war effort couldn't afford it.

When they took over American planes they tore out much of the armor plate, some of which was put in for the protection of crews. But it added weight to the aircraft and they would fly faster if it was removed. To the Russian general staff a dead pilot was just another expendable piece of cannon fodder.

Another apocryphal story illustrating the Russian attitude to military personnel relates how a Russian pilot took off at a northerly heading rather than west towards the Soviet Union.

"That pilot is heading the wrong way. He'll never reach Moscow," an American officer said.

"Oh," replied a Russian officer, "it really doesn't matter. He wasn't a very good pilot anyway."

The Russians stoically accepted the fact that one or two of their pilots in each flight would never make it home.

* * *

The empty bush-covered Siberian wilderness did not scare the battle-hardened Russian pilots as much as uninhabited forest and mountain terrain of northern Canada scared American pilots. Many U.S. pilots were kids who had never been outside a city. When they first started flying the ferry runs they were afraid of the country as they had been told a forced landing meant almost sure death. Few knew how to survive in the bush.

Although they were not able to stop crashes, the Americans out of humanitarian consideration took two steps to correct the situation over and above improving the airports and navigational aids.

One was to institute a search and rescue operation with para-medical rescue teams. The other was to build a series of emergency flight strips.

The fact the search-and-rescue operation out of Fort Nelson dropped dogs by parachute made it one of the most unusual operations of the war, comparable only to parachuting mules out of DC-3s to ground troops in Burma. Dropping dogs to downed pilots in northern Canada received little publicity compared to the mules in Burma, mostly because of official secrecy.

Although few, if any, rescues were effected by the trained dogs, it was another example of Yankee ingenuity. Proved workable, the concept was so beautifully simple it had sourdoughs walking away shaking their heads at the crazy fool Yankees.

The idea was that where a plane crashed in a location too inaccessible for a rescue plane to land, a medical team would be parachuted to the site and could order dogs and a toboggan dropped to evacuate the victim to a lake or other location where he could be picked up.

An American and a Canadian masterminded the plan. One was Dave Irwin, who spent the 1930s in Alaska and after the war lived in Scotrun, Pa. The other was G. C. F. Dalzeil, a noted bush pilot and experienced woodsman out of Watson Lake.

The USAAF had 300 dogs trained in Presque Isle, Me., for search-and-rescue work. Irwin and his dogs took basic training there.

There were some dog casualties at first in experiments with equipment. However, it was established that two dogs lashed together in a special harness and kicked out of a plane on a regular 28-foot red cargo parachute (for easy finding) was the best arrangement. Sent singly, the dogs struggled all the way and could be injured on landing; sent together, they drifted down quickly and quietly.

Irwin and Dalzeil developed a cradle for the dogs, with their front legs sticking out through holes in the canvas and their back legs hanging free.

Harry Marsh, an Alberta bush pilot who flew for the Americans, recalled one instance in which dogs were used:

On Nov. 5, 1943, Capt. George C. Dorris of Roundup, Mont., took off from Fort Nelson with an A-6 training plane bound for Fairbanks. He made an emergency landing at Trout Lake 100 miles north in a fog. The plane broke through the ice and turned over.

I discovered the overturned plane Nov. 10 on a trip to Fort Simpson. Although darkness was fast approaching, Maj. Joseph Westover, search and rescue master at Fort Nelson, despatched a C-47 Skytrain to the scene. A flare was dropped and it was confirmed the plane was the one Capt. Dorris was flying. Westover ordered Capt. William R. Jacobs of Lewiston, Me., a flight surgeon with 22 drops to his credit, to parachute to the wreck to render assistance. He was guided to the plane by three flares dropped by the circling C-47 after a rough landing.

He found Dorris dead but heard a dog howling inside the aircraft.

Dave Irwin in the rescue plane parachuted in with two dogs, a radio, food, tools and a tent. They rescued the dog, Sacktime, Dorris's pet.

Irwin asked for Dalzeil to fly into a nearby muskeg with a ski-equipped plane next day to fly out the body and other things worth saving from the plane. It was two days before he could fly in due to bad weather. Once he did get in, it was four days before he could take off again.

Sacktime joined the rescue dog unit at Fort Nelson.

At the end of the war Irwin's husky dogs met an ignominious end. Irwin could not take them all home with him to Scotrun so he sold the other 24 to a man in Dawson Creek, who nearly starved himself trying to feed them. They barked and howled all night and people got fed up with them and forced him to sell them to Indian trappers in the Great Slave Lake area.

* * *

To the Russians this humanitarian attempt was a sign of weakness. It wasn't proper for the military, they thought.

They even sneered at the way the Yank flyers swaggered in public in heavy sheepskin-lined boots which flopped open. They winced at seeing uniforms worn in public like golf attire, with buttons undone and scarves thrown carelessly around their necks; and those undisciplined Americans had their hands in their pockets and chewed gum like ruminating animals. These were the end-product of a largely volunteer civilian non-military type of service the Americans fielded to fight — and win — the Second World War.

The Russians who came to pick up planes were generally snappily dressed, probably on instruction. The Americans could never break through their reserve and suspicion. They'd come along in pairs as if they were a marine guard just off the parade square with absolutely nothing out of place in their uniforms and long coats. They clicked their heels going around corners and moved as if they were precision-drilling. They were smart young men who never let down for a minute.

While they were generally aloof, they'd bring bottles of vodka into cafes as they did at home. Although it was strictly illegal here, nobody minded much. They poured and drank it neat with a chaser, and offered the bottle all around.

There was a big dining room at Ladd Field with a wide aisle down the middle. The Americans sat on one side and 300 Russians on the other.

* * *

One of the biggest wartime international social events was a Christmas party staged for them at Fairbanks. This was a formal occasion. Their women took advantage of the fact there was no wartime rationing in Alaska to splurge on silk dresses which were not available in the Soviet Union or anywhere else at the time, it was recalled by George Yakulic:

However, an item of apparel Fairbanks storekeepers couldn't obtain for them was high-heeled dancing shoes. The foot size of these women of predominantly peasant stock was significantly larger than their American counterparts.

There were a few guarded snickers when the women showed up in elegant gowns wearing big boots a yard high and a foot wide. They did not present a stylish appearance. The women were mechanics, interpreters, stenographers and wives. Somehow, a few of the Russians were able to bring wives and families with them to Fairbanks.

They all wore fur coats. They couldn't understand why the Americans were not so equipped against the cold. A Russian general asked:

"The Russian armed forces requisitioned the furs of the civilians at Moscow, Stalingrad and other cities. Your women wear fur coats. Why are these furs not requisitioned to keep American soldiers warm in Alaska?"

It seemed alien to him that it was not part of U.S. government policy to requisition personal possessions from its own citizens.

They came with a plentiful supply of American dollars. However, most of the dollars were big, old blanket bills — four by six inches — about twice the size of the currency then in use. These bills had gone out of use nearly 30 years previously.

At first the merchants were suspicious of them and refused to accept them. Indeed, some of the younger ones had never seen them before.

"They can't be real money," they said.

But these bills turned out to be legal tender. They had been printed from 1900 to 1915 and were never officially withdrawn from circulation. When the merchants discovered they were still good, they were glad to take all they could get. They had appreciated in value as collectors' items.

No doubt the Communist government over the years had confiscated them in the hands of White Russians and other political undesirables. Hidden away in the Kremlin vaults over the years, they were made available to the pilots going to Alaska.

With no goods on ration in Alaska during the war, Russians as well as Canadians found that state a paradise for scarce items like champagne and shoes.

The shoe stores made a killing during the Alsib movement, which continued to Aug. 1, 1945. The Russians' motive for buying was to take them home to make a profit. Officers bought them by the carton. As they would pay premium prices, they somehow seemed to know about all the new shipments to the co-op department store in Fairbanks before we did.

One story — probably untrue — is that a Russian officer triumphantly carried away 15 pairs of shoes. When he left the store the clerks found they were all for the same foot.

Another quantity purchase by the Russians was French safes. We used to kid them a great deal about this but they would merely shrug and go buy another gross.

Last of all, some of the booksellers made fortunes selling technical and language books to them. They were avid for any reading matter (including daily papers) in any languages.

While Negro soldiers
showed no fear of the Japs nor the
bush, their fear for bears was
legendary.

5

Negro GIs Made Unexpected Impact

The U.S. Army came into Canada in 1942 before desegregation of the black regiments had been ordered by President Harry Truman. Truman had seen the magnificent contribution the blacks had made during the war and he also felt the sting of criticism from allies of the U.S. about sending them into battle in segregated regiments. He forced the army to become a more democratic institution.

A number of black regiments were used in Canada. Before they arrived, Western Canadians had had little or no contact with Negroes in the same concentration in which they came in to fight the Japanese. The chief previous contacts were as porters on trains and the small settlement of Amber Valley near Athabasca, Alta.

However, many Canadians were aghast at the rough time the Negro GIs were given: shoddy treatment, systematic insult, discrimination, humiliation and frame-ups.

A large percentage of the 100 persons interviewed for this manuscript made mention of their contact with these strangers who were conscripted in the warm balmy climate of the southern U.S. and were transported to a terrain almost as hostile and frigid as the gun muzzles of the Japanese on the war front. It was difficult to visualize the dire circumstances these young blacks faced in this war.

A regrettable gap in the research carried out in the early 1960s was not being able to locate and interview a single Negro, although several attempts were made. No encouragement was given by any regular source to facilitate interviews with Negro GIs and Negro sources seemed indifferent to having their effort recorded as part of their history. The alternative to actual contact, then, is a series of impressions of this Negro odyssey through white eyes.

* * *

In January, 1942, the Canada Department of External Affairs received an extraordinary request from the United States government. Washington asked Ottawa to allow it to bring Negro soldiers to Canadian soil to help punch through the preliminary Alaska Highway route.

Although External Affairs regarded it as an unusual request, it was granted without asking any questions.

What the Americans didn't indicate to Ottawa (and was probably the reason for the request) was they knew the Negro GIs would be in segregated regiments. As such, they would greatly out-number whites and Indians in small villages of northern Canada and potential problems could arise.

One of the most revealing British war cabinet documents is a minute in which the ministers made a decision to "educate" the British army and public to conform to U.S. attitude to black troops sent to aid Britain, namely that it was "desirable that the people of this country should avoid becoming too friendly with colored American troops."

For varying lengths of time there were 1,200 of them in the Fort Smith, N.W.T., area and there were 1,500 of them in camp around Dawson Creek (population 700).

At the time, few Canadians realized there were more than 7,000 Negroes in northwest Canada during 1942 and 1943. They came in three regiments and a task force. The engineering regiments were:

* The 95th, with 1,500, which arrived in March, 1942, to follow up the all-white 341st between Dawson Creek and Watson Lake.

* The 93rd, with 1,500, to work on the Watson Lake to Whitehorse segment.

* The 97th with 1,500, which was taken in through Valdez, Alaska, to work on the north end of the highway.

* Task Force 2600, with 2,500, to expedite freight and materials for the east end of the Canol pipeline between Fort McMurray, Alta., and Norman Wells, N.W.T., along the Mackenzie River system.

When they first showed up on the job, their deportment, generally speaking, was good. Discipline was good, they wore uniforms snappily, they were never out of place.

However, they found it difficult to endure the shoddy treatment by some of their white officers, they were lonely (some of them were two years in the North without a furlough as there was no way to move substantial numbers on and off the job quickly), out of their element in cold weather, scared to death of animals, especially bears, shunned by white men and women alike and quite alien to Western Canadians.

They quickly learned a new-found freedom here. They were not expected to be diffident to Canadians; to have to step off the sidewalk for a white person, especially a woman; to go to the back of the bus; nor were they excluded from churches or restaurants.

It did not take them long to start enjoying this freedom of movement and status — and they were quick to exploit it. They did a 180-degree turn in their deportment and abused their freedom in a manner which startled Canadians and was misunderstood by many with whom they came in contact.

Tales of incidents involving them began to circulate out of Dawson Creek and Fort St. John. As the tales were told and retold, it became hard to sort fact from fiction. Canadians stood aghast at tales of rape and molestation of women and shooting of blacks by military police. The MPs used violent methods against violent men.

Some of these rumors probably had their origin in a story by Constable Bill Lumsden of the old B.C. Provincial Police stationed in Fort St. John. A Negro soldier was said to have raped a nurse and MPs were out looking for him armed with submachine guns. They cruised around the streets in jeeps and would have shot him on sight had they found him.

The civilian police figured the MPs might get the wrong man and went out looking, too. They captured the Negro first and locked him up in the town cells. Then they demanded and obtained safe passage for him before they would turn him over to the MPs. He was flown out to a U.S. military prison to await a properly conducted trial.

In another incident, MPs were supposed to have picked up three Negroes who had an argument with a prostitute over the price and who had ended up raping her. She turned them in, a kangaroo court was held and they were put in front of a firing squad in the morning. Another version of this story is the three Negroes were shot — but not by a firing squad.

Several Negroes had attempted to enter the home of a farmer's wife who was there alone. She escaped through a window and went into town and notified the base commanding officer. He placed a squad of MPs on guard and called the GIs out on parade next day and told them this area was out of bounds.

They decided to "get" her and went back later with the intention of doing so. Three of them were shot on the spot.

It is true Dawson Creek was placed off limits to Negroes after this incident and the black GIs spent most of their time in the army compound.

The one incident which hit the papers in Dawson Creek concerned a nurse, Muriel Murray. She was walking along the road back to town from a small prefab dispensary the army engineers had built across the road from the army camp. She was attacked by two Negro soldiers. A vehicle came along and scared them off. However, during the struggle she bit one on the hand.

Finally, one of the Negroes, Capt. Evans, was forced to go to a doctor for treatment of blood poisoning in the hand, the Dawson Creek Star reported. He was charged with attempted rape.

He was court-martialled before Col. H. L. Twichell, commanding officer of the Dawson Creek railhead, March 25, 1943, cashiered out of the army and sentenced to 15 years.

* * *

In one camp the Negroes resorted to a lynching — a form of white atrocity where they came from in the southern U.S. It was witnessed by Lloyd Wilder, a trucker, who later became owner of Fairmont Hot Springs in British Columbia. He recalled:

One morning my brother and I pulled into a Negro camp just north of Fort Nelson, intent on getting some breakfast.

They had held a lynching the night before and had strung up two white second lieutenants on a tripod in the middle of the road. I guess they had gotten fed up with them and hung them both.

This cancelled our plans to stop there. When we saw this sight we didn't want to get mixed up with a bunch of ugly Negroes. It was an unnerving experience.

* * *

Then there was the story from another trucker who had been up until

2 a.m. with a crying baby. Suddenly, there was a knock on the door and there was a gigantic Negro highly intoxicated who wanted to come in. He was persuaded to go back to the barracks before he woke up the household. Not having a bad disposition, he apologized and left.

But he didn't go back to camp. He went next door, gained admittance without waking anyone, went upstairs and piled into bed with two young sons of the owner and flaked out.

In the morning, the neighbor's wife came down at 6:30 a.m. and taxed her husband with:

"Jack, what in the world do you mean by bringing home that huge Negro and putting him to bed with the boys? You must have taken leave of your senses."

The husband denied knowledge of any visitors. He went upstairs and, sure enough, here was this big Negro and the two boys still sound asleep. He tapped him on the shoulder. The Negro awoke and said in alarm:

"Where am I?"

"You're in my house and I don't know how you got here."

"Boss," he said, "what time is it?"

"Twenty to seven."

"How far is it to the camp gate?"

"About a mile."

"Boss, I've got to get inside that gate before seven or I get shot. I just got to be there. I'm in real trouble. I don't know how I got here and I don't know what I done to you by being here. I don't remember anything."

He came downstairs and the wife, who had been listening at the bottom of the stairs, said:

"Won't you have a cup of coffee?"

"Thanks a million," said the Negro. "You're such nice people — but I simply have to get inside that gate."

The last they saw of him was running down the street. The interesting thing, though, was everybody who met this guy liked him. There was nothing offensive about his manner and they didn't attempt to turn him in.

* * *

This was an innocent piece of byplay compared to the most bizarre practical joke in Canadian history perpetrated by Negro troops. It happened at several project locations where they were stationed. Paul Kaeser, one-time hotel manager at Fort Smith, N.W.T., recalled:

GIs in Task Force 2600 let it be known in the native community that a big jackpot would be given to the first Indian woman who had a child fathered by a Negro soldier. This sent every eligible woman over the age of 13 flocking around their camp looking for action.

During the year they were in Fort Smith area they left nine illegitimate children. The youngsters were easily identifiable by their kinky or curly hair. This is an ethnic trait not encountered in Indians. They have straight black hair.

The townspeople rallied around the first Indian woman who bore a half-Negro child. They took up a collection of $800 to give the child a start in life — a considerable sum then but nowhere near the huge sum the rumor mill had indicated.

At Lower Post, B.C., at Mile 620 on the Alaska Highway, where the 93rd Engineering Regiment was encamped, $10,000 was promised to the first Athabaskan woman. The band chief was very angry about the situation and there were a lot of hard words between him and the officer commanding the regiment. There was more indignation when the first baby did arrive but there was no $10,000. The regiment had long since departed for the Burma Road. About a dozen half-Negro children were left behind there.

* * *

Before segregation, the Negroes never had a chance of becoming senior officers, it is recalled by George Yakulic, then a Lethbridge Herald reporter and Time Magazine stringer, who toured the highway project many times. He recalled:

I can never recall seeing a Negro with a rank higher than lieutenant. And the white captains, majors and lieutenant-colonels in charge of them were held in contempt by other officers. In the officers' messes and clubs the brother officers spent much time riding hell out of officers commanding Negroes on the assumption they were poor bastards not worthy of commanding anything better. The battle of the Mason-Dixon line was fought night after night.

It appeared to me the Negroes had more empathy with Canadians than they did with their officers. They regarded Canadians without deeply-rooted prejudices against them. They would confide in a Canadian where they wouldn't even talk to a white American.

For my money, the best officers were those who commanded the blacks, understood them and knew how to get the best out of them.

If there were any dirty mean jobs to be done, it was U.S. Army tradition the Negroes got the first chance at them. They would put up with conditions white men wouldn't because they didn't have much choice. The Negroes were always sent in first. They also put up with privation because, frankly, they were tougher.

The Negroes accepted their inferior status but would only do the rotten work on their own terms. The first thing a white officer learned was not to push the black GIs.

When they decided in the middle of the afternoon to shoot craps, the smart officer damned well let them shoot craps. Ordering them back to work only resulted in surly troops who didn't get any real work done. He knew their game wasn't going to last for hours. They always had a pair of dice with them and when they got the urge they'd spread a coat in the middle of the road and hold up all traffic as they rattled the bones for five or ten minutes, then go back to work happy as hell. They'd really talk to "dem bones." They could be heard 200 yards away. They really worked hard. Here is what I mean:

One of their bridge-building crews was working on a swift stream. They had bridged it with a mud sill bridge and several bridges had been swept away. A tall, lanky colonel came along to find out what the difficulty was. When he arrived they were shooting craps. He called the major in charge:

"Get those black sons of bitches out of that crap game and back to work," he bellowed.

The major made it plain nobody was going to call his men dirty black sons of bitches:

"These men are American GIs just the same as any others and nobody is going to push them around," he declared.

The two whites had quite an argument but the major had made his point — and the colonel backed off.

* * *

Joe Irwin, A Canadian bush pilot from Rochester, Alta., relates another story about another colonel backing off:

Canadians became acutely aware of what racial segregation meant when 2,500 white and colored troops from Task Force 2600 moved to the "prairie," a staging area at the end of the Northern Alberta Railways steel between Fort McMurray and Waterways in the early summer of 1942. But friction soon became apparent so the whites were moved four miles away to Fort McMurray.

There was more than friction when the whites and blacks hit the beer parlor at the Franklin Hotel. To keep peace the army had to declare alternate "black" and "white" weeks in the hotel. This saw-off was backed up by military police.

Lieut.-Col. Theodore Wyman, Jr., officer commanding the U.S. Engineering District for Edmonton, came strutting in there one day with his hands in his breast pockets — a stance he often assumed. He barged into a black MP stationed at the dining room door with a rifle in his hands and an order to keep out all army personnel. The order for this had been cut by Wyman himself when he had shown up the week previously with his wife and found the dining hall crowded with Negro GIs. Not being aware of the saw-off, he figured the hotel had catered solely to Negroes and decided to get rid of them.

He looked up at the big MP and said:

"Out of my way, black boy."

"Begging your pardon, sir, but this here hotel is off limits to the Yew Ess Army — and you sure are the Yew Ess Army."

Wyman beat a hasty retreat — and the ban was lifted the same day.

When it came to dealing with them, Wyman was a tough cookie. In commenting on the work of Task Force 2600, he had said:

"When we planned the Canol project, we made the provision for 25% casualties. We haven't even had 1% yet, so why should any of them kick about the conditions under which they are living?" The conditions were pretty crude: uninsulated shacks and barracks later on through the cold Canadian winter. Some never came out for days.

Racism and segregation did not bother them as much as the cold and wild animals, their two greatest fears.

* * *

Their fear of bears was legendary. Conductor Ray Scott of the NAR recalled a time he was on a trainload of them going north to Waterways in the summer of 1942:

The train was delayed out in the bush and many soldiers got off to get some exercise. I told one of them to look out for bears.

"You-all say there's bear around here, boss?" he asked.

"Yes," I replied.

Whereupon word spread among them — and they all ran back to the shelter of the train in panic.

They were really frightened of bears. They almost seemed to blanch with fear at the mention. The train was not delayed by any stragglers at that stop.

* * *

Alex Johnston, a foreman for Western Construction and Lumber, working on the new Fort St. John airport recalled:

I had a top Negro catskinner who had quite a problem. None of the men would sit at the same table with him nor sleep near the same bunk.

However, that kind of shoddy treatment didn't seem to bother him as much as his fear of bears. He wouldn't walk in off the job at night. He'd drive his bulldozer right up to the cookshack door to stay clear of any wandering bears.

Cold was so foreign to Negro troops they had a difficult time handling it.

Many of them were bayou blacks from Alabama and Mississippi and they used to get so cold they'd be blue-black. Nothing in their previous experience in the South had prepared them for the Canadian North, its cold and its snow-capped mountains.

* * *

It didn't help matters any that when they first arrived the weather was pretty cold that spring and they had not been issued winter underwear and other warm clothing. But once they were issued with fur-lined parkas, they never took them off. Dick Panter, a superintendent for the R. Melville Smith management contractor of Toronto, recalled:

I was in the Dawson Creek railway yards on a hot day in summer when I was attracted to a work song being sung in harmony. Going toward the singers, I found a Negro section gang building a siding. Despite the heat every one of these GIs was wearing an army greatcoat and parka. Every last one of them was cold even with this heavy clothing.

They developed a fear of the North because people had told them a lot of myths about it in advance. The cold wasn't as bad as people tried to make out. But the myths made them afraid of it.

The fact that some of them froze to death didn't allay their fears of cold. But as was the case in tales involving Negroes molesting and raping women, the combined total of those who purportedly froze during the winter of 1942-43 was more than the number assigned to the job. It was, however, possible to nail down some case histories of them freezing while driving trucks. However, there were some deaths among whites for the same reason. Oscar Albanati, a Peace River homesteader-trucker, recalled:

I was driving into Fort Nelson from Dawson Creek and ran into a convoy of army trucks which was stopped. I walked to the truck ahead and asked the driver:

"What's wrong ahead?"

"I dunno," he replied, "I've been here more than an hour."

I was a little low on gas and figured I would run out if I stayed around there too long so I decided to hike up the line to find out how long the delay would be. If the motor stopped for too long I'd never get it started in the intense cold. I asked a couple of other army drivers to come with me but they said it was too cold.

I came to the stalled truck at the head of the line. There was a black swamper in the cab. I thought he was sleeping. The other had the hood up and was leaning against a fender peering into the engine.

"Boy," I said, "what goes on? What's the hold-up?"

I gave him a tap on the shoulder — and he fell over.

He had been wearing big mitts and was trying to repair something but his hands were so cold he was getting nowhere — but meanwhile getting colder and colder.

He was dead; frozen stiff.

Nobody had come along to offer help and I assume he froze to death standing there. The man inside was so cold he couldn't move. But he wasn't dead.

I spread the alarm and roused a couple of others into action. They shoved the stalled truck off the road and loaded the frozen swamper into another truck and quickly ran him into Fort Nelson.

The cold had simply paralysed the poor Negro driver as he tried to get the truck running again. That's the way it happens when one freezes to death. You lose your sense of reasoning and become drowsy and sleepy and don't feel the danger approaching.

I heard of another incident like this near the Emil Anderson construction camp at Mile 107 north of Fort Nelson. Four of them were sitting huddled on the bumper of a truck waiting out a delay and they were found frozen to death. There were heaters in the trucks but they hadn't been instructed on their operation. There was plenty of wood around to build a fire but they had never thought of it or were too cold to get it.

Lloyd Wilder picked up seven blacks and whites frozen to death on the road between McCrae and Whitehorse one night. They had evidently been forced to walk in 60 below weather by a truck breakdown.

Peter Inglis, a Vancouver Province reporter, saw a group of Negroes refuse to ride thirty miles in an open truck at 55 below zero. They were put on charge for mutiny and taken outside to military jails.

One particular make of truck had an outside valve on the gas line from the saddle tanks that used to freeze. Negro drivers didn't know what to do with it when it froze. They stopped the truck because they had no orders to do anything. They started walking and were found later with frozen lungs.

* * *

J. H. Vollans, NAR superintendent at Dawson Creek, recalled:

A lot of this business about cold was in their minds. They could take the cold as long as they didn't know what the temperature was.

I was standing on the platform one night with Maj. Elmo Schlei of the Quartermaster Corps when a troop train of Negroes from the South arrived. One of them walked over to me:

"How cold is it, sir?"

The station thermometer registered 58 below and I told him that.

That made all the difference in the world. This poor kid just stood there and began shivering all over. He let out a yell and ran back to tell the rest how cold it was. They all ran back to the coaches where there was steam heat.

* * *

The Negroes were in Canada at a time when no racial bias was implied in colloquially referring to them as "niggers" or "darkies." This fact was revealed by Rev. Yvon Levaque, a Roman Catholic priest at Fort Nelson:

I had a lesson in race relations pointed out to me by Capt. Edward G. Carroll of Washington D.C., a Protestant chaplain in the 95th Engineering Regiment. I called them niggers, as the majority of Canadians then did. He put me wise in a hurry that this appellation was an insult to his race.

"We call ourselves Negroes," he told me pointedly.

But despite the lesson of his reprimand not all of his people referred to themselves as "Negroes." There is a story which I tell — and which I have heard many others claim they originated. I was driving along when I came upon several Negro GIs trying to wrestle barrels of gasoline onto a truck. Despite the fact gas was scarce they were pouring it onto the ground to lighten the load.

"What are you doing, Sarge?" I called as I stopped the Chev.

"I'll tell you, sir," he replied. "Uncle Sam will have to make the niggers bigger or the barrels smaller."

They laughed like crazy but I made them fill up my tank before they dumped any more into the ditch. At that time gas was worth $3.64 a gallon there.

Their religious music was a new experience for me. I once held a service for 80 from the 95th Regiment before their regular chaplain arrived. After I had packed up my portable kit to go to the next camp they asked me if I'd mind them staying and singing some of their revival hymns. I told them to go ahead and stayed around to listen.

Hearing them sing and shouting "hallelujah" showed me they had a spontaneous faith. Everything was really jumping.

One thing that caused a lot of head-shaking was the callous manner in which they handled equipment and supplies. When a Canadian truck driver admonished a Negro driver for running a truck miles on a flat and ruining the rim, he replied:

"Oh, that doesn't matter. Uncle Sam has lots more wheels and tires."

* * *

True, Uncle Sam had but it shocked Canadians to see the waste. Oscar Albanati recalled:

I had a radiator spring a leak and had to stop at an army camp north of Fort Nelson for repairs. Afterwards the motor refused to start. Three Negroes in a big four-by-four wrecker offered to give me a tow to start it. They hooked onto me, laughing and joshing among themselves. They didn't give a damn for anything. Coming along in front of the officers' mess, they turned too short. Since my steering gear was stiff from the cold I couldn't steer out of the way of a jeep sitting there. My truck snagged the jeep and pulled it about 500 feet and smashed it up. They didn't see it and kept on going.

Once on the highway, they set a fast pace. My motor started in half a mile but they kept going. I couldn't make them hear the horn and putting on the brakes didn't get their attention, either. Finally, they stopped at the bottom of a steep hill. The driver came running back and said:

"By gosh, you're hard to pull."

"Look, fella," I said, "my engine has been going for a mile and I've been trying to stop you. You wrecked a jeep down at camp."

"Well, by God, we got you started anyway," the driver laughed. "Who cares about a wrecked vehicle?"

* * *

Their attitude to equipment is exemplified in an incident in which Harold Havig, a Stettler trucker, recalled:

I rode from the Lower Liard River crossing to Watson Lake with a Negro driver in a tandem-drive truck with dual wheels on the rear end. There were chains on the rear wheels and as we progressed the chains started breaking and hammering against the steel truck box. Imagine the noise they made! I could stand it no longer and said:

"Why don't we stop and fix the chains or take them off?"

"Mister," he said, "there's nothing in my orders that says I have to stop this truck and take the chains off," and he drove stolidly along.

It was late on an extremely cold night when we arrived — to be greeted by a very angry Negro sergeant. He had heard the truck coming for 10 miles and was ready for the driver.

Those flailing chains beat holes at least 16 inches in diameter in the box and they also beat to pieces several kegs of nails which spilled and littered the road for miles.

I don't think this guy had ever driven a truck before he got into the army. It sure would have been a happy day for him if he could have ever gotten back to Harlem. I suspect he, like many others, deliberately smashed up equipment in hopes of being sent back some place where it was warmer.

North of Watson Lake a unit of the 93rd Engineering Regiment wrecked every bit of machinery in camp, except a couple of jeeps. They were court-martialled for smashing up the last two D8 bulldozers. They had backed them up, opened the throttles wide and jumped off and let them come together in a grinding head-on crash. At the court-martial the president said:

"How much equipment did you have at this camp?"

A big black fellow got up and said: "Sir, we just had the two 'dozers and the jeeps left."

"What happened to all your other equipment?"

"Well, sir, the vehicles just run together somehow long before we got the D8s lined up."

The 93rd got its wish. They were shipped out all right. But they didn't go back South. They were despatched overseas and were in the vanguard of the Normandy invasion. The action was pretty hot and they were pretty badly cut up. Some of the others ended up on the Burma Road.

* * *

It was usually in the last days of their tour of duty the black troops became destructive. They resented being held over winter in the North for no good reason in substandard housing after they had completed their road-building work. But, when need be, they could take on extremely cold jobs. George Yakulic recalled:

The 340th was a white regiment which worked on the temporary pile bridge on the Upper Liard River crossing before the permanent cantilever-truss bridge was created.

Before they finished the pile bridge in the fall of 1942, needle ice began forming. New needle ice is as sharp as a razor and as it broke away and drifted down the swiftly flowing river it began to cut the piles at the water level, placing the bridge in jeopardy if it continued. It was necessary to place steel guards on the wooden pilings lest the ice cut the pilings off. Oil drums were cut in half for the shields and they had to be placed on the upstream side.

The Negroes of the 95th were ordered out for this job. This meant sending naked men into the water at well-below-zero temperatures.

The longest the poor devils could stand it was 15 to 20 minutes — when they would become paralysed and numb and another relay would replace them. Some were so stiff and cold they had to be fished out.

At first they built roaring fires on the river bank to try to get them warm but this wasn't good enough because they'd be roasting on one side and freezing on the other. They then developed a system of wrapping them in blankets and rushing them back to camp.

The few times official recognition was given to Negro regiments was when such praise could be used for favorable publicity purposes for the U.S. Army. A prime example came at the first crossing of the Sickanni Chief River. The job was nominally invested with the 341st Engineering Regiment.

When the river was reached, the 76th Ponton Company, which had not seen action for some time, wanted a crack at bridging it. But a 166-man crew of the 95th on the scene said they could throw a mud-sill bridge across in four days — much more quickly than the 76th could get into action. The professional engineers estimated it would take two weeks.

Word of the 95th's boast was carried to other outfits and monthly salaries were bet on the outcome of bridging the 585-foot-wide glacial river.

With almost 24 hours of daylight it was possible to work long hours. Half forded the river on rafts and they each worked towards the centre.

At high noon on the fourth day a black private cockily drove a command car across the river — 84 hours after the work was started. They had cut the wood in the bush.

Word of the competitive rivalry reached the base camp at Dawson Creek. Gen. J. A. O'Connor took the opportunity to take in a visiting press corps and speeches were made at a short ceremony. The 166 builders stood on the new structure and sang The Star Spangled Banner. Gen. O'Connor stated:

"Some day the achievements of these Negro soldiers — achievements accomplished far from home — will occupy a major place in the lore of the north country."

O'Connor's special assistant was Capt. Richard L. Neuberger, a Portland, Ore., newspaperman who later became a U.S. senator. He forwarded the story of the feat of the 95th across the States.

What the story didn't say, however, was the 95th was "put down" very neatly by the 341st. The ponton company was allowed to proceed with its floating structure right beside the 95th's bridge. It was used and the wood-sill structure fell into disuse.

Nobody seemed to be too much concerned about this duplication of effort. The official published history book of the 341st didn't make a mention of the Negro regiment's participation.

6

Hundreds Of Canadian Truckers Employed

There are two kinds of trucker.

One tries to make money by driving day and night for weeks.

The other finds he can make money driving day and night, then after establishing reasonable rates and reliable service, he finds he can make more money by leaving the driving to those in group No. 1.

E. J. Spinney of Dawson Creek was one of the latter class of self-made entrepreneur. He was a two-fisted non-smiling Nova Scotian, a pioneer in the Peace River country. Before the war he had worked on the Northern Alberta Railways as a section foreman and his wife did laundry for section hands for 25 cents a week. He did some farming, ran a government ferry and saved enough to buy an old White chain-drive truck.

In the fall of 1941, with the completion of the new runway at the Fort Nelson airport by Western Lumber and Construction Company, Spinney won a contract from Imperial Oil Limited to haul 500,000 gallons of aviation gasoline in there from Dawson Creek over the winter road which had been completed the winter before. To fulfil this contract he scoured the Prairies for farmers with dual-wheeled trucks and put them to work driving over that terrible road with overloads of six tons of 45-gallon drums of gas.

To break the boredom and hardship of this shuttle run, the truckers began competitions to see who could make the fastest time over the 325 miles. Gordon Wilson made it in 14 hours once. The usual return trip took a week but Paul Loiselle made one return trip in 59 hours.

* * *

Loiselle was another self-starter like Spinney. He emerged after the war with the biggest trucking outfit on the Alaska Highway — Loiselle Transport Limited — which later became a subsidiary of the White Pass and Yukon Route. He recalled:

I had moved to Dawson Creek with my father, Romeo Loiselle, to farm in 1937. He had been a farmer and rancher on the Little Smoky River near Donnelly. I drove his truck the first fall, then bought a two-ton truck of my own and went hauling grain, livestock and firewood for local people. I didn't make much money as the roads were poor with very little gravel. In fact, the main street of Dawson Creek was just a big mud puddle in the spring.

During the spring break-up I'd be off the roads for several weeks. Other work was scarce.The spring of 1939 the only work I could find was piling lumber for 25 cents an hour.

* * *

Don Menzies of The Edmonton Journal made a trip over the road with two Saskatchewan farmers, P. F. Tompkins and his son, Short (a nickname as he was lean and lanky). He recalled:

We took off Friday night, March 13, 1942, and arrived at Fort Nelson Sunday at 2 p.m. after the wildest, most exciting and exhausting trip of my life, a trip that would have shaken the gizzard out of a dinosaur. They drove day and night, spelling each other off.

The Tompkinses picked up their loads at one of the gasoline dumps in Dawson Creek or Pouce Coupe into which a steady stream of tank cars rolled to unloading standards for six weeks. Day and night seven days a week 45-gallon drums were filled by Imperial Oil and despatched in trucks with machine-like regularity. Although there was a shortage of drums, the company obtained a special priority order to turn them out by the carload at its drum plant in Sarnia.

Short Tompkins was only 18 at the time and he had been over the road 22 times without mishap. By the time I had negotiated the bumpy, winding, hilly trail for 30 hours bucking mud and snow, climbing 45-degree slopes and sliding down cliffs of greasy clay I was all shook up. I decided to fly back to Dawson Creek, not wanting to repeat the endurance contest. By the time I had reached Bellyfull Hill I had stomached enough.

Some of the hills were so steep the driver couldn't see the road in front because of the engine sticking away up in the air. Once coming up an icy incline the truck spun out and started to slip sideways. Short threw it into reverse and backed down over a makeshift bridge. The trick is to always keep the vehicle under control; never coast.

The road was a single track with no ditches. Most trucks had Fort Nelson decks — a narrower platform than usual that enabled them to squeeze past each other in narrow spots. The rule of the road was that loads had the right of way. This sometimes necessitated shoving an empty truck off the road to allow a loaded convoy to go through. The last loaded truck through would pull the empty back onto the road again.

* * *

Just about the time the Canadian truckers were finishing the Imperial Oil contract, the 35th Engineering Regiment arrived in Dawson Creek March 9 and took their equipment over the winter road to Fort Nelson. By that time the farmer-truckers working for Spinney had been over the road enough times they were regarded as veterans. Their services were quickly snapped up by the Yanks. In addition to Spinney, Gordon Wilson of Wilson Freightways eventually wangled a 17-million ton-mile contract from the U.S. Army, including supplying gasoline for Fort Nelson.

Army truckers had a great deal of difficulty getting over the road because they had governors on their motors. However, truckers like Archie Finlayson would wind up their trucks to get a run at a hill with the engine going wide open. The American trucks would power out near the top just when they needed power to give them a boost over the top. It wasn't long before they had the governors off after a few lessons from the Canadians.

Spinney was hired by Lieut.-Col. C.A. Mueller of the U.S. Army Quartermaster Corps to organize a trucking consortium to take a hauling contract for the Americans.

Mueller had previously tried to persuade John F. Wilcox, master mechanic, and Ace Comstock, station agent for the Northern Alberta

Railway, to quit their jobs and organize a consortium. However, when they went to the Canadian Bank of Commerce to borrow a few hundred dollars to get the business off the ground, the manager talked them out of it. He convinced them they'd lose the money plus their railroad seniority.

The attainment of security was so much ingrained in Canadians then that they turned Mueller down, whereupon he went to Spinney. On the strength of the fact he had a White truck and was willing to take a chance, he got the job. Using his military priority, Mueller got Spinney 16 new trucks from the U.S. in six weeks.

With these trucks and hundreds of others from Canadians who took subcontracts, the company made $1 million in the next year.

Many Canadians were at a loss to know how to deal with the big-spending Americans. Hanging onto the tail end of the Depression, many had never seen that kind of money before, especially those from the agricultural hinterland. They had been taught by the exigencies of the Depression to save money. Spending thousands seemed to make them feel guilty.

They had no idea of the gigantic effort the Yanks had mounted; few could comprehend its scope; many were actually suspicious of the Yanks; they just didn't know how to seize the opportunities that were presented to them, despite the fact the Yanks merely demanded they do what they were told, no questions asked.

As boss of this trucking empire, Spinney was a hard-driving, hard-hitting person of the type who wouldn't ask an employee to do something he wouldn't do himself. He had no mercy on slackers, incompetents or drivers down on their luck. His byword was:

"Tramp her into the bull-hole and cut her loose."

If a man couldn't do this, he was no good to Spinney. He drove hard bargains with subcontractors despite his personal knowledge of how hard it was to make a buck at the business. This is often the trademark of self-made men. For it they are usually hated. But he got things done on time. That was all that counted in the business of war.

Although he had a way of getting work out of his men, occasionally he relented in unusual ways. He would do such things as talk the U.S. Army into renting him a plane to airlift a group of truckers to Calgary to bowl for a couple of days.

This was the forerunner of the post-war gambling charters to Las Vegas.

Money and success brought him the curse of alcoholism. When the trucking business slackened off after the war, he bought the Roseberry, a downtown temperance hotel in Edmonton. It burned down shortly afterwards. He died at age 54 about this time.

* * *

Besides Spinney, there were a number of other management contractors with contracts for hauling gas and other materials. Cliff McLeod of Regina, then an employee of the old British-American Oil Company, recalled:

Glen Braden, B-A dealer and member of the Legislative Assembly for British Columbia at Dawson Creek, won large contracts — larger than he could handle. I was sent in to survey the situation. I recommended one of two courses of action:

1. The company revoke Braden's dealership and handle the contracts itself.
2. Send in extra help for Braden, who knew the business and could handle the contracts adequately.

The result was I was sent in to help him and brought in competent help. It was a double-barreled deal: to deliver gas from our Calgary refinery to handle the Public Road Administration's 250,000-gallon storage in Dawson Creek; and to deliver gas from storage to points along the highway.

My biggest job was trying to keep track of my tank cars on the NAR. Despite the fact I was bringing in five cars at a time — big shipments for those days — the railroad lost them with regularity. I had my own crew of five on hand. They knew how to take an engine and handle a movement in the Dawson Creek yards. They could help switching crews in whatever way the crews needed help.

Most of the shipments up the highway were rush orders on which we bypassed the storage depot and filled tank trucks directly from rail cars as soon as they were spotted. These rush shipments meant having truckers on call seven days a week 24 hours a day.

They didn't take drugs or keep-awake pills in those days. They drank whisky straight out of the bottle.

Good drivers were hard to come by. When we did get one we made an effort to hang onto him. For instance, I was paying a driver $1,000 a month to deliver gas to our customers around town.

Lieut.-Col. Mueller and Maj. Elmo Schlei of the Quartermaster Corps negotiated various contracts. I got more than my share because B-A had local men on the scene who knew local conditions. Our chief competition, Imperial Oil, on the other hand, brought in people from the East.

Not knowing our local conditions, one of the Eastern tenderfoots would run into an unsympathetic hard-nosed army type like Schlei — and that would be the end for him. I found Schlei hard-driving and tough, a real character, but a decent sort all told if you did the job he wanted done.

Although liquor was on ration, I made it my business to know how to obtain whisky by the case at the government liquor store at Pouce Coupe. When there was a deal in the making, you didn't need a bottle, you needed a case. There was no such thing as a public relations account then. But I had one of the largest petty cash accounts in the company. We got the business.

I also had to make it my business to know enough ropes to get things done under extreme odds. Like the time I went to the office of Beattie Bobiller, the boss of the Fort St. John airport extension job for Tomlinson Construction Company, to pick up gas ration coupons for 150,000 gallons Tomlinson bought from us.

"They are on the counter. Help yourself," said Bobiller.

I started counting and found only enough coupons for 15,000 gallons.

"Where's the rest?" I asked.

"You have them there. That's all I have."

"We're in real trouble then."

However, I was able to suggest a way to get us all out of that jam with the realization that Tomlinson was a relative of Defence Production Minister C. D. Howe at Ottawa. It had to be impressed upon Howe that Tomlinson was on a high-priority defence job.

At the end of our gas contracts only $5,000 was not approved by the United States General Accounting Office in Washington, compared to millions owed other companies. I knew enough ropes to settle most of ours by negotiation.

I often found it advantageous to go out of my way to suit the needs of a U.S. Army supply officer. If I came across one who was a Standard of New Jersey man in civilian life or a former Shell Oil Company man, I would often change the stencils on barrels to "conform with their needs." After all, the gas all originated in the same hole in the ground.

I liked the way the Americans operated. To them nothing was impossible. They had a positive outlook about everything — and would find a way of doing it.

We took a bit of pride in the "sight-unseen" dealings with the Americans. For instance, a foreman from John A. Roebling's Sons Company of Trenton, N.J., walked in one Saturday night. He wanted

100 barrels of gas delivered at the Peace River bridge site Monday morning (the company was supplying steel for the new suspension bridge being built there). We had never seen each other before. In only a matter of minutes we had completed the deal and arranged payment. The gas was on the job next morning.

In the spring of 1943 we had to stockpile a supply of gas across the Peace River to last a month at the various camps along the road to see them through the spring break-up when the roads became impassable. The break-up caught us early but we had prepared for the eventuality by stringing a two-inch pipe across the still-uncompleted Peace River bridge. It was impossible to cross the river by ferry during the spring flood as it was running 18 miles an hour carrying blocks of ice as big as a house.

I had asked Stuart McRae, manager at Imperial Oil, to go in on the pipe construction but he refused. Soon he came around hat in hand to ask for permission to use our line.

We pumped five million gallons across the river and kept enough on hand to keep things moving during the break-up. During this movement I was forced to store gas in tank cars in the rail yards for several weeks and ran up a demurrage bill of $5,000.

Other "biggies" with gas-handling contracts were Western Transport, which was organized by George Solomon, Vic King and Ted Gibbs of Regina; H and N Transport, organized by Harold Holman and Mike Newman; Figol and Fowler, organized by Pete Figol and Bill Fowler of Calgary, and George Schmidt of Dawson Creek.

Ray Jewell of Calgary, with 150 trucks, had a gas-hauling contract with Imperial Oil. He had started out small, hauling gas from Turner Valley field to North Battleford, Sask., to build up his fleet. He was one of those who sent in trucks to haul gas to Fort Nelson over the winter road in the 1941-42 winter.

Walter Parent trucked for Jewell and when Jewell closed out after the war he won a route franchise from Dawson Creek to Edmonton. He later merged with Roger Forsyth of Canadian Freightways.

Through these management contractors B-A had access to hundreds of trucks. At times there were 400 trucks on the road hauling to the U.S. Army alone.

One of the most controversial contractors was George Schmidt. From a technical standpoint he was among the best on the job. He was able to get plenty of equipment and was well enough organized he could get one and a half times as much work out of his drivers as the others. He had his own shop which was highly efficient, with a nightly schedule of work which saw overhauls completed in eight hours.

This happy state of affairs ended during a "special trip" with two airplane motors. All truckers looked forward to these special trips as they commanded premium rates. There was also an unwritten agreement that truckers who took them would be given special preference in future hauls. This agreement was usually forgotten, however.

Some confusion surrounded the succeeding events but one thing was clear. One of the motors went missing on the trip. The U.S.government sued him for $1 million in the ensuing flap. As reparation, he was required to relinquish 10% of the money for his hauling contract.

He was able to escape this obligation by selling his outfit to Roger Forsyth. Forsyth had started in a small way with a couple of old chain-drive trucks as Northern Freightways. It became Canadian Freightways in 1942. Before Freightways took over, Schmidt was always in financial straits. Many of his subcontractors were unable to collect all the money coming to them. That 10% he was required to rebate to the army was just too much for him to handle.

Pete Figol was pretty green when he started truck driving and gas hauling with one old truck. He was able to hire Harold Havig of Stettler, who showed him some of the fine points of hauling heavy loads on gravel that served as Alberta highways before the war. He eventually learned the theory and, after his contract work on the Alaska Highway with 575 trucks, organized a well-known transport out of Edmonton. The brains of the Figol company was Bill Fowler of Calgary who had the ability to negotiate contracts with the U.S. Army and carry them through.

* * *

A trucker who took contracts with Spinney, Figol and Schmidt was Oscar Albanati, a homesteader at Bezanson, 20 miles east of Grande Prairie. He had a one and a half ton B-30 International and he recalled:

We homesteaders were a resourceful and adaptable bunch. My farm was on the west side of the Smoky River. Nearby was the tortuous ferry crossing on No. 2 highway. One spring day I crossed on the ferry. Two hours later I found the river in flood and too dangerous for the ferry to cross because of big trees and other crap coming down.

I went back to Ed Manerow's place and found he had crossed the river in the opposite direction earlier in the day. He couldn't get back either. Since I didn't have a hotel to go to I stayed at his place three days until the ferry was put back in service and did the chores and looked after the farm.

I found he was doing the same at my place during my absence. There were no phones then.

Although we were used to the primitive road conditions of the area, nothing could prepare us for the "suicide hills"–especially the S-shaped one north of Fort Nelson.

One day Howard Wiegan of Claremont and I were heading back to Fort St. John. I had a Negro with me hitchhiking a ride to hospital. Wiegan was ahead and made it to the top on the far side of the river. Then we noticed a truck coming our way out of control.

"This is going to be it. I better hit the ditch," I yelled.

I headed for the edge of the road. I was just a bit late and he hit the back end of my truck and spun me around twice, causing me to run backwards down the road towards a steep drop of 200 feet. I hollered to the Negro:

"Jump! This doesn't look good."

His mouth was wide open. His scared eyes looked up at me in fright: "If you ain't jumping, I ain't jumping, either."

Fortunately, the truck came to a stop when a guard post caught it and held. We got down shaking. I walked to the edge. There were at least a dozen trucks piled up down there.

"Look, fellow, see those trucks down there? We'd have both been there had that post not held us. Why didn't you jump like I told you?"

"I thought I'd be safer with you," he replied. "And we are safe now."

This Negro was more fortunate than a Negro "swamper" working on a Fairbanks Freight run. Proceeding up the long drag from the Sickanni Chief River the truck spun out and the swamper got down several times to throw sand under the wheels. The driver got going and the swamper ran to climb aboard. He missed the door handle and fell but the driver didn't see him and kept grinding to the top of the hill.

The driver stopped at the top to wait for him. When the swamper didn't show up he didn't worry. He assumed he'd gone into the bush for a call to nature. He waited more. Later another trucker came along and they decided to walk back. They found him a pulpy mess on the road. He had fallen under the tandem drive wheels and had been ground to pieces.

Since the drivers were paid by the ton-mile, there was a tendency to overload and either speed or drive too long without sleep. Us older experienced drivers preached "gear down, gear down" — even into compound low — to greenhorns who were prone to miscalculate on the hills and then become scared when they couldn't control the rear end with the motor. Once this happened the brakes were almost useless.

Although the civilian drivers didn't travel in convoys, as did the army drivers, the army was always vigilant in checking out overdue drivers at the "Checkpoint Charlies." Patrols were sent out to search for those overdue, not only to assist them but to make sure they hadn't made off with tires or oil.

There were very thirsty GIs at the checkpoints; and these GIs proved hazardous to those with booze aboard. They were empowered to seize it and confiscate it, sometimes catching unwary truckers with offers of $50 to produce a crock then seizing it. Of course, some truckers had made a fortune peddling bootleg booze.

However, despite the risks of carrying booze, most had secreted a crock or two to keep them awake and to obtain repairs.

I pulled into an army camp at Fort Nelson one night with two bottles of whisky and an engine in bad shape. I left the whisky where it was easily accessible.

Next morning I found the old motor lashed to the rear end of the truck. A new one had been installed. The whisky was gone. Pinned to the old motor was a note:

"Cut the rope at Calamity Creek."

Here the old motor would fall over a high bank and be lost to sight forever.

* * *

Not only did Canadian truckers have to live by their wits, they had to be tough, it is recalled by George Sayle of Sexsmith, a pioneer Peace River country farmer who later became president of the United Farmers of Alberta Co-op:

It took a good man to install a broken rear axle on the road at 20 to 40 below zero. Most of the axles were broken as we goosed our trucks down the draws at break-neck speed to make the hill on the other side.

An ingenious friend had a clutch go out on the winter road to Norman Wells from Peace River. But he drove his vehicle home that way. He was able to do so because he knew how to change gears without touching the clutch just by easing up on the gas at the right moment. A lot of drivers used to do this as a matter of course when going downhill, especially in the lower gears.

The bottom line for all those rough times was the pay cheques. In the first three weeks I earned $700–and thought I was the richest man in Canada.

* * *

A trucker who saw more adventures than the average Alaska Highway trucker was Harold Havig, a native of Ponoka, who later became a realtor in Stettler.

When the Americans showed up in Dawson Creek, he was working as shop foreman for Canadian Freightways, which was an amalgamation of Chris Nicholson's Canadian Freightways of Lethbridge and Gordon Wilson Freightways of Edmonton. He asked to be reassigned to the Alaska Highway and recalled:

Arriving in Dawson Creek, I found myself working in the shop. Wilson had nailed down a contract in May, 1942, with the Public Roads Administration. The PRA was moving in old prefab Commodity Credit Corporation bunk shacks and cook shacks from the Western United States to the Northern Alberta Railways siding at Dawson Creek and it was our job to haul them to Mile 49 to house supervisory personnel and Canadian construction companies engaged in rebuilding the road between Dawson Creek and Fort St. John.

My arrival coincided with the big push when the Americans expanded the NAR railhead. I was on hand when the first car was unloaded from the extended trackage.

Wilson had only seven trucks on hand. They were a motley lot, including a big Diesel we used to have to block up the Peace River hill. The technique was to run her till she stalled then have a swamper jump out and put the blocks behind the wheels.

The driver would get her revved up again and jump ahead maybe six feet until she stalled again. And the performance would be repeated all the way up.

I lived in a small trailer near the Wilson garage and soon was on the go day and night as a dispatcher. I never had enough trucks and was constantly wiring Edmonton pleading for more help and at least 350 more trucks. But I didn't get them. Being at a distance, Wilson couldn't see what was going on and refused to believe me when I told him there was trainload after trainload arriving here and much of it was simply being dumped on the ground and somebody would have to move it. The hillside north of town was full of freight.

My situation became unbearable, what with another guy trying to get my job. This guy repeatedly told Wilson the job was too big for me; that I couldn't handle it. He claimed he could do things better than I. Of course, he couldn't; he didn't have the equipment.

When I did get fed up and quit, my critic did get my job. I was vindicated. Within three months the company had been forced to bring in 1,200 trucks to handle the contracts.

I went to work for W. J. (Red) Powell, a pioneer sawmill operator at Charlie Lake. He had a small fleet of trucks. The Powell home also served as a float and seaplane base.

One day in June a plane on floats made a forced landing at Powell's with a broken magneto shaft. The pilot asked me if I could repair it in Powell's small shop. I was able to do so and we got the plane going again.

"It's always customary for the mechanic to go for the first test flight," the pilot said.

So I went up. It was the first time I had ever been in an airplane.

In late July a pilot named Bob Calm landed there with a Fairchild on floats. A former barnstormer and Yukon Southern Air Transport pilot before the war, Calm loved flying, was a good pilot and always wore a pilot's uniform and cap at a jaunty angle. He had undertaken to ferry three Fairchilds from Seattle to a PRA base at Carcross, Y. T., for project work.

He was looking for a mechanic to accompany him through the mountains beyond Charlie Lake. Powell told him I was a good mechanic; I had overhauled that magneto. He approached me with an offer of $70 for the round trip and I quickly accepted. We took that plane through without any problem.

The next plane Calm took up in September was on wheels. At the Liard River the oil line broke and oil sprayed all over the windshield. We made an emergency landing on a sandbar. After repairing the line we were able to take off and complete the trip.

The last flight was Oct. 28 and, against the advice of Mrs. Powell, Calm took off into turbulent weather, ran out of gas at the Liard and made another emergency landing there. That adventure was a story in itself. Suffice to say we arrived at Whitehorse minus the plane.

In Whitehorse I met an official of Northwest Airlines who had a problem. (The company had a contract flying men and equipment on and off wartime projects.) The problem was to move a shipment of three-minute heaters to Whitehorse from Dawson Creek. (When the weather went to 40 below zero these heaters were supposed to warm up a plane motor to enable the pilot to start it.)

Due to unbelievable railyard congestion these heaters couldn't be offloaded at Dawson Creek. The Northwest man was moaning and groaning.

Back in Dawson Creek Powell came up with the simple expedient of offloading them at Pouce Coupe. He won the contract for trucking them to Whitehorse.

I set out with three of them in a tandem-drive truck and another driver had two. We each carried our own gas and food to see us through. (As mentioned previously, the U.S. Army had decided to mothball the road for the winter.)

I had trouble on a suicide hill 87 miles north of Fort St. John. This was the place where a driver from Saskatoon had rolled back and piled up in the ditch. Before he could get his vehicle moved 10 big U.S. Army trucks in convoy did the same thing and piled up on top of him.

Our other driver had bigger trouble than me at J-72. He spun out and put his heaters in the ditch. He took off, left his truck there and never reported back again. Just disappeared.

The heaters were undamaged and some GIs filched them to provide extra heat for their camp.

On the return trip I spotted the truck and piggy-backed it back to Charlie Lake. When I eventually reported to Northwest Airlines what had happened to their heaters they were mad as hell. They sent me there with an order to return them. Back in Fort St. John intact, they were dismantled and flown in pieces to Whitehorse.

Meanwhile, my troubles on the journey to Whitehorse were mounting. I thought the end had come 60 miles out of Watson Lake when the truck pounded itself out near the top of a steep hill. The grade was so steep the load went back over the centre of the tandems and the front pair of driving wheels could get no traction and began to spin and pound the ground. From midnight to noon the next day I made several frontal attempts on the hill.

Then I used an old trick that helped truckers get over a slippery road. I turned around and backed up the hill. By backing, I got traction on the front wheels.

The farther north I went the colder it got. The next night at 11 o'clock I was so exhausted from herding this truck along I had to stop and sleep. Because it was so cold I couldn't get the truck going fast enough to shift into high. I was shifting continuously all day and that exhausted me. I solved the problem by stopping at a Checkpoint Charlie and talked some GIs into giving me enough coaloil to replace the oil in the rear end.

When I awoke I couldn't tell if it was 8 a.m. or 8 p.m. as there were 16 hours of darkness at that time of year. So I really worried about how long it took me to make the trip. This upset me. I think it was five days.

I had more trouble at the frozen Teslin River crossing. The army was scared of ice and didn't think the three-foot-thick ice would support my 14-ton payload.

I know it was midnight Dec. 21 when I arrived in Whitehorse at the Whitehorse Inn Cafe. The staff was ready to quit and locked the door in my face. Just then a taxi driver pulled up:

"You hungry, mate?"

"I sure am," I replied. I had run out of food miles down the road.

"Well, come with me," he said, and led me around to the back door and through the kitchen and sat me down at the counter. A couple of RCMP constables were sitting there. The waitress said she was going home. The cook couldn't care less what happened.

The taxi driver donned an apron and cooked up a fried ham sandwich for me. Best meal I ever had.

It didn't seem to be within the capability of the waitress to realize I was probably the first civilian trucker to haul a payload over the new road.

Although Northwest Airlines had a hotel room reserved for me I wasn't able to stay in it. The rough road had worked a radiator hose loose and I had lost all my antifreeze. This meant I had to sleep in the cab of my truck to make sure the motor didn't stop and freeze up.

Back on the road home I encountered four men from the Canada Department of Transport near Watson Lake. They took me into their camp and fed me. In answer to my questions as to where they were heading, one of them said:

"Somewhere down this road there is a plane sitting on the Liard River."

"Yes," I replied, "I know just where it is. I was in it when the pilot landed there."

After that there wasn't enough they could do for me. They helped me unload my freight at Watson Lake and saw I got fed there. There was more excitement for me at Watson Lake as a telephone gang came along and my brother, Arnold, was with it.

They asked me to follow them. Along the way I had to stop and have a sleep. When I awoke the engine was stopped. It was 67 below. I went into the bush for wood and finally got a fire going and melted snow in a five-gallon can.

With a hand crank I managed to get the engine turned over and started as the battery had run down. Once the motor started the ice in the block quickly thawed out. I thawed the radiator out with the old mechanic's trick of running my hot water into the bottom hose. This allows circulation in four or five rods of the radiator core and circulation started. Then gradually the rest of the radiator thaws out. It is necessary to get the circulation started lest the water turn into steam and blow up the radiator.

When I reached the Liard crossing the four DOT men had found the plane, removed the wheels and installed skis. They had brought cold weather starting equipment, got it going and took off and flew it the rest of the way to Carcross.

This was Christmas Day, 1942. We had difficulty getting things done but they got done somehow.

Not only was there a pride in getting things done under considerable difficulties in the North but the North seemed to inspire trust and good will among people working there. This was demonstrated to me when I met a Northwest Airlines pilot and co-pilot at the Whitehorse Inn. The pilot had a beautiful muskrat cap he had brought in from Fairbanks:

"How much did it cost you?"

"Ten bucks."

I handed him $10 and told him the next trip in to pick one up for me and leave it at the airport at Fort St. John.

"I'm not sure what my schedule is but if I get back to Fairbanks I'll get you one. If not, I'll send you your money back."

The co-pilot exclaimed in amazement after surveying this handshake deal:

"Have you ever seen anything like this in your life?"

"What do you mean?" asked the pilot.

"Well, here's a fellow you've never seen before and he hands you $10. They don't trust you like that on the Outside."

I didn't hear from him again for a year. By that time I was in the Royal Canadian Navy out of Saint John, N.B.

A letter arrived from Minneapolis with the same $10 I had given the pilot. I don't know how he found out where I was.

I had joined the navy in August, 1943, after having been given the run-around by the air force when I tried to enlist as an aero mechanic. They said I didn't have enough education!

After the war, thieves stealing an army jail uncovered a secret: the walls were drywall with painted iron bars.

7

FBI And Military Police Saw Action In Dawson Creek

Two United States police organizations operated in Canada during construction of the Alaska Highway and Canol pipeline. One had a high profile in Dawson Creek, Edmonton, Fort St. John and Whitehorse. The other worked under cover and only a handful of Canadians knew anything about it.

The former was the military police; the latter the Federal Bureau of Investigation.

Because of the impossibility of local police to control streets overflowing with U.S. Army personnel and construction workers, the military police were charged with patrolling downtown streets just as they patrolled U.S. Army bases.

In the case of Edmonton, they accompanied constables on foot or in prowl cars. This dual policing went on for a year, at which time it was felt the need had ended. In Dawson Creek the MPs were the only effective police force because the small garrison of B.C. Provincial Police was inadequate to keep law and order.

While the MPs officially had no control over Canadians, hard-pressed town fathers didn't protest too loudly when roistering Canadians got pushed around a bit. It, in effect, was law by intimidation. What Canadian civilian was going to do much arguing when faced by a pair of big bruisers with riot sticks two feet long?

Whitehorse was the only exception to the wide-open jurisdiction of the American military MPs. Because it was policed by the RCMP, the jurisdiction came under the federal government. Ottawa realized it was going to have a real problem of law enforcement unless a strong RCMP detachment was set up to keep the lid on things. It therefore assigned H. H. Cronkhite, then in Lethbridge near retirement age who had spent many years in the Yukon detachment, to run the show.

His condition for doing so was a free hand because he didn't want to be referring to Ottawa for decisions all the time. He was told to go ahead and write his own ticket but to keep out of trouble. The ticket he wrote was a small force of big tough guys who ruled with a firm hand but didn't brook any nonsense from anyone, including the military police, who occasionally forgot they were in a foreign country.

Cronkhite showed up at the liquor store one day about 9 a.m. An altercation had broken out in the middle of the daily line-up. Liquor rationing was in force there and the store was open only 10 to 12 noon. Line-ups began to form at 8 a.m.

Two burly American MPs had grabbed a Canadian worker, who was protesting:

"No, I was in line. I was right here. I just went across to get a package of cigarettes. I asked the guy next to me to keep my place."

"Back to the end of the line," growled the MP.

"No, I've been here since 8 o'clock. I don't see why . . . "

"Back to the end of the line," the MP ordered. They grabbed him by the arms and started marching him back.

Cronkhite grabbed the first of these MPs, spun him around and let him have it — wop — and sent him flying. He picked him up and put his face to his:

"Now, by God, you guys can do what you like with your own troops but, by Jesus Christ, you leave Canadian civilians alone."

He then turned and marched off.

Soon after he arrived back at the barracks, he received a call from Col. F. S. Strong, top USED man in Whitehorse:

"This is Col. Strong. I'd like to see you."

"Fine, Col. Strong. I'm in my office daily from 8 to 5. I'd be happy to see you any time you'd care to drop around."

There was a bluster at the end of the line–but in 15 minutes Col. Strong walked in and said:

"I understand you had a bit of trouble with one of my men this morning."

"There was no trouble I am aware of."

"Well, wasn't there some sort of altercation?"

"I just want to make it clear," said Cronkhite, "to your MPs that their job is to maintain discipline in the U.S. Army. Canadian citizens are my responsibility and your men will kindly keep their hands off them. As long as both of us understand this, we will have no further trouble."

The Americans had a healthy respect for the RCMP and this was one of the things that helped to reinforce it.

MPs were experienced constables from city police forces. They never patrolled in less than twos. Often, depending on the situation, there would be fours and sixes on hand. Whenever there was a big bloody argument that looked as if it could lead to trouble, they waded in with these clubs, cracked skulls and argued later.

* * *

A small riot at the Royal Cafe in Dawson Creek was recalled by Harold Havig, a Stettler trucker:

I saw five MPs in action that night. Some of the boys had an argument with management and decided to pull the place apart. Two MPs went in and began grabbing troublemakers and shoving them through the big white door. Outside was standing a big Negro MP who looked like Joe Louis, the former world champion boxer. In fact, many of us really thought he was Joe and he didn't try to deny it. He was grabbing them by the collar, whacking them on the head with his club and laying them on the sidewalk. Two others were picking them up and flinging them into the riot wagon.

The big Negro was very calm about everything. He put on a performance I'll never forget. They stashed nearly a dozen guys in the wagon before they were through. Of course, the MPs had to be no-nonsense guys or they wouldn't have kept control.

* * *

Although the MPs were on hand to curb physical acts of those in the military, the FBI was called in to ride herd on spies, crooks, subversives and thieves in the military and construction forces. In many instances the top security and safety officer was a FBI agent. Despite the fact Canada was in an official U.S. war zone and nobody was held accountable for any equipment brought onto the projects, this did not excuse gross negligence or laxness in handling of stores.

In the latter stages of the projects there were rumors of FBI agents being brought in to investigate thefts and other hanky-panky in the camps but it was a fact the FBI personnel had been on the job all along–either in or out of uniform. The RCMP was called in where it became necessary to make formal arrests on Canadian soil. There were many prosecutions but few convictions.

One never knew where the next undercover man would show up. For instance, M. F. Tibbetts was a sergeant in the 843rd Signal Service Battery. His experience in the Southern Main Telephone Company as a lineman would normally have earned him a commission in the army but he was doing undercover work, being strategically placed as he was in the signal corps, and so was retained at a lower rank.

* * *

The FBI sent a man into the offices of the United States Engineering Division at Whitehorse, it was recalled by Mrs. Margaret Murray of the audit department:

After three months somebody blew his cover. He and several other FBI agents were pulled out. While they were there they had access to all the payrolls of companies in the area. In addition to running security checks on employees of these companies, they uncovered salary boosting (i.e., illegally paying cooks at shovel operators' rates) which we knew was going on but couldn't do anything about. A man named Hanson was brought in from Washington to clean up the situation. A great number of cooks quit but he was able to replace them with a group of Chinese. Had the FBI not been on the spot more crooked work would have occurred than ordinary.

The cockeyed inventory system of the U. S. Army was impossible for Canadians and numerous Senate investigating committees to figure out as it had more issuers than receivers. Most of the stuff going into Canada was written off as if it was shells which would never be returned. Thus it was possible for the army to say that of the 30,586 pieces of equipment brought onto the projects by it and the civilian contractors only 365 were not accounted for at the end.

* * *

Con Farrell, a noted bush pilot, RCAF officer and later a Canadian War

Assets Corporation administrator, recalled:

I represented the RCAF at the big official opening ceremony of the highway Nov. 20, 1942. Arriving at Edmonton, I was billeted with the U.S. Army Air Force. I didn't have a sleeping bag and made this known to them. When I returned to my quarters several hours later there was a brand-new eiderdown on my bunk. After the ceremonies in the Yukon I spoke to one of the officers:

"Where do I turn this in?"

"You'll have to drop it off at Edmonton on the way out."

On reaching Edmonton a colonel at the USAAF told me to take it over to stores. I went there but the top sergeant begged me:

"Man, don't turn it in here. We can't keep track of things like that. It'll throw out our books."

"What'll I do with it?" I pressed.

"Take it. We don't want it."

I had that $75 eiderdown for many years–and a great many others came back with them, too. Many armed services personnel left such items with Canadians when they left the North.

* * *

Because of this and similar accounting, the U.S. Army's books were away out in 1944–so far that Washington was led to the assumption there was widespread theft going on. Capt. Tom Rodie, Royal Canadian Army Service Corps troubleshooter from Calgary, was loaned to the U.S. Army at Whitehorse to put his expertise on accounting practices to work to determine how they were missing stuff but the Canadian Army wasn't. He recalled:

I discovered there was actually no stealing. They hadn't been properly entering the receipt of goods. Most of the shortages were the result of sloppy bookkeeping, not theft. I showed them where they had erred, but they didn't seem to worry too much about it.

As an example: I drove vehicles into U.S. Army camps several times for repairs. One time they put on a new tire for me.

"Where's your vouchers?" I demanded when it came time to make settlement.

"Oh, to hell with the vouchers," came the reply.

* * *

A Senate committee unravelled some of the army's puzzling accounting practices when it travelled over the road by car and found no serviceable equipment not in use or not in equipment pools at appropriate storage points. Although it found wrecked or cannibalized trucks discarded along the highway, these were regarded as "accounted for."

Several rumors concerning large numbers of idle, but serviceable, vehicles were carefully traced down–and found to be groundless. One such rumor related to a large guarded compound containing several hundred usable vehicles north of Fairbanks. Investigation revealed these were government-owned equipment which had been classified as obsolete and available for war assets disposal. Another rumor about thousands of pieces at a washed-out bridge at the Pelly River along the Canol Road was in the same status.

By agreement, no American equipment was allowed to fall into Canadian hands. However, Imperial Oil was an exception. It had the pick of everything at Norman Wells: boats, drill rigs (which it bought for $1), the refinery at Whitehorse (which it picked up for $1 million) and $40,000 Kenworth Diesel trucks for $1.

In 1964 Imperial Oil received permission from the Canadian government to auction much of the equipment it had acquired. At one sale a cement mixer that had never been used was sold. All it needed was some new wiring and a new battery and it worked perfectly.

Some of those who had seen these sweetheart deals given Imperial Oil had no compunction about "stealing" from some of the warehouses crammed with supplies at Norman Wells after the Americans moved out. They had left one full of new oil stoves. Carloads of walk-in refrigerators were there; also a barge load of refrigerators suitable for butchers. In many of them were hams and bacon bearded with age.

Under an acre of tarpaulins were accessories for bulldozers. In one of the boneyards was a whole flotilla of motor boats and river craft.

An airline agent at Norman Wells saw restaurant kitchen equipment simply waiting to be stolen. He did so and sold it for enough to start a restaurant of his own–also with stolen equipment from Canol.

One of the most noteworthy thefts occurred in May, 1946. A jail complete with locks and bars was spirited away from Fort Alcan. Miners and settlers had raided the abandoned camp for lumber and wiring. Then they grew bolder and stole the jail itself. Mighty locks on heavy doors were removed and two-inch steel bars were wrenched from the windows.

When the thieves stripped off the wallboard they saw Uncle Sam had a real sense of humor. It was revealed the patent wallboard was painted to look like iron!

The wallboard was all that stood between prisoners and freedom!

Despite its flimsy construction, hardened criminals were kept in this "jail." However, had they escaped there was nowhere to run but the bush anyway.

* * *

Almost as comical–but not so funny–was the Indian who "bought" the jeep from some GIs at Whitehorse, it was recalled by W. W. Bradley of Provost, Alta., an expediter on the Canol project:

It all started when this Indian, who had been working at a wood-cutting camp supplying Yukon River steamers, got drinking with some GIs. One of them as a practical joke "sold" the Indian the jeep for $5. All he had to do was go to the army base at Whitehorse and pick out one he wanted from the hundreds in the motor pool there.

So he did.

How he did it nobody ever found out. The Americans were too much embarrassed to reveal it.

Having picked up the jeep, the Indian surprised the GIs by showing up with it. The joke at an end, they told him he didn't have to work any more and made him a batman for the outfit and told him how to get gas for his jeep.

For the first 10 times he showed up at the army pumps nobody said anything to him. They filled his tank and he went merrily on his way. However, one day an officer happened by:

"What outfit do you belong to?"

"I don't belong to any outfit," the Indian replied.

"How'd you get this jeep then?"

"I bought it."

"Je-e-e-e-zuz-z-z."

He called in the military police.

The Indian told them the story. The police took him out and he identified the soldier who "sold" it to him. A court martial was set up and everybody tried to keep from busting a gut with laughter. The GI figured that the camp security forces would end the practical joke.

Smilingly, they acquitted the Indian; the army couldn't even get a fraud indictment against him.

Although stealing by those on the inside gave the FBI and RCMP problems during construction, large-scale thefts occurred after the end of the war before and during the period the Americans turned the road and pipeline over to Canadian forces April 1, 1946.

Much equipment had been stockpiled and it was difficult to protect it as Northerners had assumed the U.S. War Department had declared a potlach and they saw nothing wrong with helping themselves to goods and equipment that were going to be destroyed.

* * *

Ray Hide of Pibroch, Alta., a salvager working on the pipeline out of Johnson's Crossing, recalled how things were:

One of my workers, Jimmy Smarch, an Indian, came around one day and asked me to drive him to Teslin and he would make it worth my while. I had other things to do but he was persistent. About 10 miles from Teslin he said:

"Slow down at that corner." I did – and when we rounded the corner he commanded: "Now stop here." We did and he disappeared into the bush. He reappeared with a new wheel and tire worth $50.

He made the trip worth while as he said he would.

One laughable incident occurred when another employee I knew only as Frenchy salvaged a truck off the Canol Road quite legally. I told him he could have it for next to nothing if he could get it going. It had been there 10 years.

He did so and was very proud of it. He drove it to Teslin. I told him to run it into Whitehorse at night and buy a licence for it.

However, on the way to the licence issuer's he was stopped by a RCMP constable who refused to believe his explanation that this was his first opportunity to buy plates. His English was not too good. The cop charged him with failure to have a licence and he was hauled before a magistrate. I went with him.

Things looked bad for him telling his story to the beak in his broken English. I got up and testified on poor Frenchy's behalf. There was no way the truck could be licensed before the issuer's office opened.

The magistrate heard me out and ruled: "Not guilty."

* * *

That Senate investigating committee took an easy-going attitude toward the small percentage of equipment the army was unable to account for, it was recalled by Maj. H. F. Johnston, manager of the Dawson Creek tire plant:

Canadians had been a bit shocked by rumors too persistent to be ignored that truckers had been engaged in stealing and caching thousands of dollars worth of goods they had been transporting. They went undetected for some time by bringing back false receipts for delivery.

I had occasion to seek help at a farm south of Dawson Creek one night when my car slid off the road. The farmer seemed pretty agitated about my presence–and suddenly he blurted:

"I'm in a bit of trouble. You wouldn't happen to be from the FBI, would you?"

"No, I'm running a tire plant. I'm not from the FBI I can assure you."

He walked along a few minutes and then he said:

"I want to talk to somebody from the FBI."

"I can arrange that quite easily," I said. In the next bunk to me was a big fellow in plain clothes who had the title of safety engineer but I found out he was an undercover agent.

The farmer's problem, it turned out, was that he had been in trouble with the law for bootlegging and he thought he could get the heat off by turning informer on a bunch of truckers who were using his place to cache stolen goods.

When the "safety engineer" went down to interview him, the farmer took him to a large cave which was filled with thousands of dollars worth of supplies of all kinds. Some drills we had been awaiting at the tire plant for ages were there. So were some motors for K. O. Aspol, the Ford agent in Dawson Creek. This was not surprising as there was a big trade in reconditioned motors. More than 5,500 were shipped in to Aspol.

Those Ford motors never lasted long. Some of them made only a trip or two. I think it was their high speed. Aspol wouldn't even try to repair them. He'd just slap in a reconditioned job and chances are it would be worse than the one he had just taken out.

* * *

The boys driving gas tankers were the ones who made the money for the simple reason few of them ever bought gas, it was recalled by Oscar Albanati, Bezanson, Alta.:

"I've been trucking here over a year and I only had to buy one tank of gas–and that's the one I bought to get up here," one tanker driver told me.

Where gas was scarce he would sell it to the boys along the road at a cut rate. Nobody checked. He sometimes arrived with only 50 gallons left.

Later on, they began sealing the tanks. But that didn't cramp my friend's style. He installed a tap in the tank near the cab where it could not be seen. He said:

"They were suspicious of me quite a few times but never caught me."

It takes a thief to catch a thief, as Norm Leslie, superintendent of A. E. Jupp Construction Company of Toronto, proved.

He had on his payroll a man named Hill, a notorious Toronto criminal. Leslie didn't know what to do with him so he put him in charge of gasoline distribution. The company had been plagued with thefts from unguarded caches all over the place.

Jupp never lost another gallon after that. Hill knew all the theft angles from experience and took measures to stop them.

* * *

The American military always seemed to be on the make for a bit of larceny, it was recalled by Charles Butler, president of Butler and Hawkins, an Edmonton firm doing contracting and subcontracting for the USED at Edmonton:

I fought off a move by Charles Balfans, the USED auditor on our project, to pad the payroll with four or five names and split the take. Fortunately, there were no repercussions for my refusal.

Things like this seemed to be standard practice in the U.S. Army. For instance, army regulations specified the furnishings to which base commanders were entitled and they usually ordered to the limit. If a base commander was entitled to nine chaplains he would requisition for nine even if he only had two or three on staff. The extra would be divided among the whole office.

For a trucking subcontract I took with Coast Construction Company at the Namao airport, I ordered $40,000 worth of repair parts. But I only received 5%. I made some enquiries and found there was a bit of hanky-panky going on between Maj. B. M. Dornblatt, commanding officer of the engineering regiment on the job, and Coast Construction. Dornblatt was evidently receiving a commission from Coast for being kept on the contract in the form of supplies for Dornblatt which he was peddling on the Edmonton market through fences. Some of the stuff he was peddling turned out to be my parts.

I called in Capt. Caldwell, a FBI agent attached to the USED.

Caldwell had a record of every Canadian on my payroll; he knew more about some of them than I did myself. He had the right to suggest I move off the job any man he considered a security risk.

He pulled an inspection without notice and took Dornblatt with him. When he came to the warehouse I suspected, Dornblatt didn't want to open it. This didn't faze Caldwell even though Dornblatt was superior in rank:

"I'm making an inspection, major, and I have the authority. Are you going to unlock it? I don't want to have to go over your head."

Caldwell ordered all our pilfered parts taken out and delivered to me.

When Dornblatt found out I was the man who tipped off security to his little racket he tried to blackball me off the job. He put me on report to Gen. L. D. Worsham, the top man, for wasting thousands of hours in unloading cars of supplies for the airport. However, it was a situation not of my making (there were not enough men on hand to unload the lumber we were forwarding to Namao, with the result our crew did a lot of standing around at the railway siding).

I found out what he was up to and went to my friend, Tiny Burdick, in Worsham's office and told him what was going on. He told me to put Dornblatt on report. Worsham had the situation corrected promptly. Dornblatt was furious with me. After that, he spoke very friendly to me.

The FBI had thefts on a grand scale and individual thefts on a spectacular basis to deal with.

For instance, the auditors held up $2.25 million worth of vouchers by Bechtel, Price and Callahan officials who had spent wildly on non-essentials and entertainment. I received orders from Worsham to erect several 24x48-foot Nissen huts, clean out Bechtel warehouses and store the loot until it could be audited and checked. It was about this time a building near the Calder railway yards in Edmonton, where some vital records had been stored for safekeeping from spies and saboteurs, mysteriously burned one day.

This fire, along with a flight one of the BPC principals made to Washington to lobby some of his friends in the Senate to call off an imminent investigation, ended this attempt to nail BPC.

* * *

Then there was a U.S. Army Air Force aero mechanic who found a damaged plane in the bush near one of the emergency flight strips. He worked on it many months, cannibalizing other planes to get it back in running shape.

He went on furlough from his base, hitchhiked to the air strip, stopped overnight and took off next morning with the plane, complete with a new paint job.

* * *

After the war when the project was turned over to Canada, the RCMP made a half-hearted attempt at security, it was recalled by Con Farrell:

I lost one warehouse with 250 electric motors north of Whitehorse. Occasionally, however, they would nail somebody not able to afford a lawyer and make an example of him.

The people around Dawson Creek felt sorry for an old Swede who rescued a sleeping bag with a three-cornered tear from a dump into which the Americans were burning them by the hundreds. He was hauled into court. It seemed unfair that he could be prosecuted but when I tried to turn in my sleeping bag I couldn't even give it away.

* * *

Because of the inaccessibility to both projects by the Japanese, the risk of sabotage was considered remote, it was recalled by Herb Mowat of Toronto, a foreman for Don Construction Company:

There was one attempt in 1943 on the Kiskatinaw River bridge which we were building–and this was made by a Finn, one of a 35-man Finnish construction crew. I shared quarters with their leader, an interesting fellow named Oscar Parkala. Most of his spare time he read voraciously to master English. He had been called back from Canada to the Finnish reservists in 1939 to fight that winter campaign against the Russians. The Soviets beat Finland and a peace treaty was signed and the Soviets took over the Karelian Isthmus. Parkala escaped to Petsamo where he managed to get a boat to Britain and came back to his home in Canada.

Later when Germany attacked Finland in the drive against the Soviets, the Germans conscripted several battalions of Finns. This meant the Finns could now be Canada's enemies. However, the American security people told us they didn't anticipate any problems with the Finnish bridge workers; but they added we should keep an eye out for potential sabotage situations. The Finns had no more love for the Germans than the Russians. These ones were actually damned glad to be 7,000 miles away from Finland.

This crew had been working 12 to 14 hours a day seven days a week for about three months. We finally gave them a day off. They all headed for Dawson Creek, 20 miles away, and at 6 o'clock returned pretty well plastered.

I had suspicions about one big six-foot-two man with straw-colored hair who kept pretty much to himself and was close-mouthed. When he returned well liquored up and mouthing off like a Nazi, I called security and they ran him into a concentration camp. The next day we made an inspection of the area and found a bundle of dynamite sticks with percussion caps and wires to a set of batteries and a switch. This man had evidently planted the dynamite the day before and the trip to Dawson Creek had interrupted his plans to blow up the partially completed bridge.

This was a case where liquor was a constructive force. Had this saboteur not gone to Dawson Creek and bought the liquor which loosened his tongue at a critical time, many men might have been killed.

* * *

Although there were no proven cases of internal sabotage, the Japanese made their presence felt in North America between Nov. 1, 1944, and April 30, 1945, when they set up the most costly fire balloon attack in military history. They earmarked $200 million for 20,000 of the balloons. But only 9,000 were launched. Of these, it is estimated 1,000 arrived here on the jet stream, some being discovered as far east as Manitoba (296 were actually picked up).

A meteorologist, Hidetoshi Arakawa, sold the idea to the military, pointing out the jet stream would carry the lethal weapons at a maximum of 120 miles an hour at 40,000 feet.

For the military, the campaign was launched at a time when the Japanese had given up hope of defeating the U.S. It was a morale builder in which everyone in the nation could participate to kill the enemy. They were launched at Sendai with appropriate prayers that each would reach its destination. As incendiaries they were simple, ingenious, devilish, silent and mysterious and could have had a debilitating and devastating effect.

The Japanese made one logistical error. When the balloons were despatched the forests and other target areas were wetted down with winter rain and snow. Five months previously everything was tinder-dry and fires could have resulted in a holocaust.

In launching them, the Japanese were working in the dark. The Americans kept total silence on the attacks and that included a radio blackout in the Yukon and Alaska. The silence had the effect of convincing the Japanese their weapons had not reached America.

The Japanese also didn't know a faulty triggering device had rendered the majority kaput.

They were made of five layers of mulberry paper (about the thickness of cigarette papers) which were strong and water-repellent when glued together by thousands of villagers. They were 33 feet in diameter, with 19 shroud lines 45 feet long glued to them and gathered together to a steel ring like a chandelier. When filled with hydrogen they could carry 750 pounds. The load was 26 bags of rocks each weighing 15 pounds. The payload was eight 15-pound fire bombs and one 35-pound high-explosive bomb.

They could stay aloft a week and, as the hydrogen seeped out and took them down below their operational height, barometers would trigger a mechanism whereby ballast was dropped along with a fire bomb. This loss of weight would carry them aloft again and would be repeated until all the ballast had been dropped. Another device set off the bombs and this was the faulty one that reduced their usefulness.

One of the incendiaries recovered near Minton, Sask., is in the National War Museum at Ottawa.

Due to a shortage of cooks, carpenters were transmogrified into instant cooks (at carpenters' wages).
COOKERY for BEGINNE

8

Different Factions Fought It Out

There were displays of braggadocio and rivalry among the various factions engaged in the great fight against the common enemy, the Japanese. Assumptions of social or economic superiority were rife among the thousands of strangers from across the continent thrown together on this urgent mega-project. Perhaps the secret of success of any project of this magnitude is confrontation.

Most persons on the job could–and did–cite examples of economic disparity. There was a wage disparity between Canadians and Americans doing the same work. There was even wider disparity between well-paid civilians and dog-faced American GIs. There was also wide disparity between Canadian and American GIs, with the Canadians making only 60 cents a day.

Although the 60-cent private was the lowest on the economic scale, the lowest persons on the social scale were the Métis and Indians. This was a classic example of natives of a country being treated as foreigners on their own soil by two invading forces as it were.

There was professional jealousy as the civilians despised the military for its spit and polish and mindless regulations. Specialists drafted into the U.S. Army had career army personnel working under them who despised them; and the hatred was mutual.

The Public Roads Administration engineers from the U.S. liked to impress their Canadian brethren with their invincibility. But they made their share of mistakes, it was recalled by Herb Mowat, a grade foreman for Don Construction Ltd. of Toronto:

The south approach to the Kiskatinaw River bridge had to be backfilled with 2,000 loads of what the Americans called "select borrow." This was known in Canadian parlance as "pit run" gravel. In building this approach we were guided by a centre line the PRA engineers had surveyed for us. The centre line of the approach was supposed to meet the centre line of the bridge naturally.

I should explain one thing about the way the survey was done. When a centre line was staked out the heavy machinery would constantly mutilate or change the stakes. Therefore, the engineers and surveyors installed what were known as "offset" stakes in the bush, about 100 feet away from the centre line, where they couldn't be altered by anyone. Grade foremen like me would have to find these offset stakes and then project the centre line while the fill was being hauled.

When I came to do this I discovered the centre line of the approach was five feet out of line with the centre of the bridge. Everything was all right as far as the levels went but the centre line was not going to hit the centre of the bridge. I was busy re-checking these calculations when Ralph Agnew, PRA division engineer, came along.

"Ralph, is it very expensive to move a bridge five feet at one end?" I asked.

"What the hell do you mean?"

"Well," I said, "you haven't built the bridge on the road. It's five feet out."

"My God, that can't be. The whole thing was worked out on the drafting boards. It's perfect."

"All right," I replied. "Seeing is believing. You take a couple of men and a tape and see what you can make of these centre stakes."

He spent an hour checking it out and came up with exactly the same result as I. Somehow the centre line of the bridge had got moved five feet north.

"Well, I can't imagine what kind of a mistake that would be. I'll have to go up to the engineering office and check it out," Agnew said.

About two hours later a survey crew came down and changed the centre line of the approach.

"What did you find was wrong?" I needled Ralph.

"Nothing," he replied with a sly wink. "The records were lost on that."

* * *

Jack Griffiths, a grade foreman for W. H. Harvey and Son, was sore at a PRA engineer who accused Curran and Briggs and Harvey of gold-bricking simply because they had cost-plus contracts. He recalled:

The engineer, W. L. Lafferty of Denver, was resident engineer at Dawson Creek for the PRA. He was one of that hard-driving breed of American engineers who figured if people weren't running constantly they were gold-bricking. I agree we were scraping the bottom of the barrel in the labor pool. For instance, I was invalided out of the Royal Canadian Air Force with a kidney ailment.

Lafferty was sneeringly critical of the unskilled labor used by the Canadian contractors: viz., "most are inefficient and lack the incentive to do a good day's work. Many cared little whether the job got finished or not." A day's work at that time was 11 hours.

He bluntly stated: "25% of Canadian labor would have been fired off the job by American contractors."

The American contractors admittedly had more experienced men. Since that nation hadn't gone to war until 1941, a great number of the crews were pretty well intact when the Alaska Highway job came up. They were mostly men from Minnesota who had all worked together on the job and lived in nearby communities with their families. They came to the highway as homogeneous groups with their employers.

Lafferty added: "It seems the general characteristic predominating in most of the Canadian contractors is to succeed by producing with as little physical and mental effort as possible yet still be able to refer to themselves as successful contractors. There may be good reasons why the labor is inefficient but it also is evident most of the supervisory personnel are employed without any regard to merit."

He found difficulty in acquainting Curran and Briggs supervisory forces with various phases of the work and added:

"They are inexperienced and devoid of all knowledge in constructing a road from slope stakes."

In Curran and Briggs' defence, it might be stated their personnel were constantly being disrupted by requests from the Americans to take on supplementary contracts. The Americans were slightly hysterical in their approach to getting the job done because of Japanese advances in the Pacific.

Later when the Americans began putting millions of men in uniform they sent as many "dogs" to work for their contractors as were to be found in the French camps of the Canadian contractors. A grab-bag of all kinds of saints and sinners showed up, many having the idea this was a lark.

* * *

On the other hand, many civilians who went up there were appreciative of getting a job, it is recalled by Bobbie Hill of Missoula, Mont., employed by Dowell Construction Company:

I met one old boy on one of the fleet of boats the PRA had chartered to take us north from Seattle. He had lived for years as an unemployed derelict wandering from one hobo jungle to another in California all through the Great Depression, existing largely on hand-outs and sleeping mostly under railroad bridges. He was really enthusiastic about the fact he had signed up as a bull cook with Dowell.

"Just imagine me at my age getting a job at $300 a month and board after the hard years I've had behind me. That was a dream only a few weeks ago. I've never had it so good," he said with awe.

I guess a lot of us felt this way as we had fought the Depression and "hungry '30s" on relief cheques and public works programs or in cow camps at $20 a month in winter. It had been real tough going.

My California friend had great plans; figured out how much he could save and what he was going to do with it.

He never made it.

On my first pay day I made a trip from our camp near Champagne, Y.T., to Whitehorse for mail and supplies. I ran into this old boy on the street with a case of Hudson's Bay overproof rum under his arm. He was really loaded and we agreed to haul him back to camp.

Next day he was too drunk to work. He went and lay down on a bunk in the cookshack–and died with half a bottle of rum in his hand.

I felt sad about the incident but a hard-nosed construction stiff came in, took a look at him and lamented:

"What a damn shame to waste all that good rum!"

* * *

When the Americans decided to go ahead with this project, the war department and management contractors sent telegrams to W. E. McCutcheon,

Lethbridge, manager of UIC, asking him to hire all the unskilled men he could for construction of a military highway in Canada. As they also knew there would not be enough labor available in Canada, they asked for blanket permission to import their own work forces. This permission was granted. McCutcheon recalled:

When word of the telegram was published in Canadian and U.S. newspapers that thousands of jobs were available, I was deluged with letters from all over the U.S. asking me for jobs. But I couldn't give these Americans jobs with either Canadian or American contractors under our regulations. I was forced to put two stenographers to work telling these unfortunate people the only way they could get jobs was to sign up with U.S. contractors. The stenographers sent out these letters for weeks.

It all came at a bad time for us. We were smack in the middle of setting up one of Canada's greatest social experiments: national unemployment insurance, which was being introduced by the Mackenzie King government. It was an exciting and trying time for us–and routine reports were weeks late in reaching Ottawa, although I was never reprimanded for my tardiness.

No compulsory military call-ups for the Canadian armed forces had yet come into effect in the spring of 1942–and the Lethbridge office filled hundreds of jobs for the Ontario contractors: cooks, bull cooks, skilled tradesmen, truck drivers, pipefitters, storesmen and partsmen. We provided medicals and transportation. Imperial Oil hired many of them.

We allowed the Americans to bring in most of the men they wanted but there was a political reason for us to keep that knowledge away from the public: in Lethbridge the government was making $10,000 a month relief payments.

All in all, the projects were good news to labor on both sides of the border, coming as they did on the heels of the Depression which hit American labor harder in some areas than Canadians.

The reason the wire was sent to Lethbridge was the Americans had had contact with me previously in the employment of Americans in Alberta oilfields.

It didn't take Canadians long, frozen on jobs, to discover they were frozen at a much lower wage than their American counterparts. When Americans were permitted to bring in their own specialists they were required to pay them the same as that of their Canadian counterparts.

That didn't work.

* * *

One blanket exception to the unskilled labor freeze was students. It was thus that Clyde McMurchy, a University of Alberta student and later Alberta Department of Agriculture publicist, went to work as a clerk for the PRA at Whitehorse during the summer of 1943. He recalled:

I was given passage to Whitehorse but bad weather kept me grounded nearly a week. I got fed up waiting and joined 200 American civilian engineers ordered to go by rail to Prince Rupert, then by boat to Skagway and thence by rail to Whitehorse. Obtaining food along the way was a problem as no prior arrangements had been made and feeding 200 visitors was almost beyond the capability of some British Columbia towns already tightly rationed.

We were held at Port Edwards staging area at Prince Rupert five days awaiting a destroyer escort for the sea trip to Skagway.

Many Canadian Army personnel had been stationed there without leave for a year and were a bit bushed. They knew the civilians were carrying liquor. At least four times while awaiting embarkation NCO ranks (with no authority to do so) forced kit inspection on unsuspecting civilians. Each time they came up with a new haul of our precious rationed liquor, which they confiscated for themselves. We had to hide the remaining stocks. The worst blow of all, though, was right at embarkation. The camp commandant demanded we leave behind cameras, cigarettes and matches as we were going into a war zone.

Arriving in Whitehorse, we discovered the left hand didn't know what the right hand was doing, with the consequence nobody was prepared for our arrival. We had to be billeted in temporary army quarters until the PRA camp was made ready for us.

We quickly encountered the anomaly of Canadian workers of the same skills working beside Americans but collecting much less money. For instance, early in 1942 Canadian welders on the new oil refinery at Whitehorse received $1.25 an hour, which was 50 cents less than Americans. That wage was admittedly big money, compared to common labor which was paid at 50 cents an hour.

The motive for the government wage and job freeze was to prevent Canadians from accepting higher-paying American jobs — a situation which could create Canadian labor shortages and subsequent inflationary trends. The Canadian government did not want to find itself placed in the position of competing with the U.S. Treasury.

Naturally, hard feeling developed over this wage disparity despite the fact labor contracts were under the jurisdiction of an international wage ceiling board. The disparity proved not only a source of dissatisfaction and irritation for Canadian workers but a rather unsettling embarrassment to the Americans.

The result was the Americans made official representations to the Canadian government to remove the freeze on Canadian wages and bring them into line with American wages. Canada rejected the plea but later reversed its stand late in 1942. At that time Canadian employers received permission to advance common labor rates to 75 cents an hour — only to find the Americans had jumped theirs to $1.15; and this continued through 1943.

When I finished my tour in Whitehorse in September, I discovered they had a Greyhound bus service to Dawson Creek. Two other guys and I made the 54-hour trip.

We had several hundred cartons of cheap American cigarettes in a big box when we reached Dawson Creek, intending to sell them to smoke-starved Canadians in Edmonton at a profit to help pay our university tuition. We laid over at the PRA transient camp overnight and, the next morning when we left by train, the guy detailed to carry the box left it under the bunk. We had a helluva job getting him up and he simply forgot it in the rush. The next guy in the bunk made himself a fortune.

* * *

One person who had a good handle on the labor situation was Bruce Ballah, who was sent to Dawson Creek from the National Selective Service office in Edmonton.

(The Canada Department of Labor has changed the name several times but for the purposes of this book it is referred to by its best known name, UIC: Unemployment Insurance Commission.)

He opened the office June 1, 1942. Ballah recalled:

UIC sent me in there alone to ride herd and keep tight control on the labor situation. It was impossible. In the 2 1/2 years I was there 20,000 men went through this office. I estimate the Ontario contractors under R. Melville Smith management turned over the work force four times, despite the fact labor was frozen. A man leaving his job was supposed to obtain a permit to go to work for another employer. An employer couldn't fire a man without just cause.

Working for the government was no sinecure in those days, either: The hours were long (my usual working day was 7 a.m. to midnight — and almost every weekend). I was not provided with any help for a long time. I finally did get a clerk, Gordon McArthur, and a stenographer. I wasn't given a living allowance (I was maintaining my home in Edmonton) or expense account, not even for transportation. It was even left to R. Melville Smith to supply me with office space and a place to stay in the bunk shack.

I was so short of cash I couldn't even buy four building lots I was offered. These lots are now in the centre of Dawson Creek. They were selling for $25 a piece. Hell, I didn't have 25 cents to my name.

The hiring bosses got wind of my impoverished state and they would place temptations in my way to do them favors. Part of my job was to service Pouce Coupe and several other small towns off the highway. For this I had the use of a jeep made available to me by the army. I was thankful; I'd have had to hitchhike otherwise.

If the civil service was run on this basis in 1991, the government of Canada would be able to balance the budget!

At times Maj. Schreiber would attempt to use my poverty as a lever. He'd call me up:

"Come on up to headquarters."

When I got up there, he'd say:

"You like the jeep?"

"Yes. It's all right."

"Well, you know, we're awfully short of trucks. We might need that one.

"If you guys pull that back I'll phone Ottawa and tell them about it. You buggers agreed to let me have it."

"Oh, Jeez, don't phone Ottawa," he recoiled.

"Well, what'll I do? I can't walk."

"Can't you please get us some Canadian help? They work rings around our guys."

He'd evidently not come across the terrible report by W.L. Lafferty of the PRA.

"I know they can work," I replied, "but I can't. It's against our regulations for you to hire them. I'd like to get some for you but I can't — and you know it."

Ottawa regulations presented us people in the field with a complicated situation which labor on both sides of the border found hard to understand.

The PRA had a different kind of problem in supervising civilian contracts. It brought everyone in on nine-month contracts. Included were fare on commercial transportation and per diem and travel expenses from home in the U.S. However, the turn-over situation became so bad the PRA was forced to institute new regulations March 16, 1943, designed to control the turn-over. It made it mandatory for all employees to pay their way home for failure to stay the nine months. They were given free transportation back if they returned for a second nine-month stint. To their credit, many did return and many stayed right on without a vacation.

The PRA further ruled all mechanics and laborers to be reimbursed for travel only on the basis of coach fares. This didn't violate employment contracts and it saved $600,000.

* * *

This ruling nearly caused a riot at the Northern Alberta Railways station in Dawson Creek one night, it is recalled by Dick Panter:

A gang had arrived on a tourist sleeper and we couldn't put them up at the base camp as we had run short of blankets. I made arrangements with the railroad to leave them on the car all night.

Some of them turned a little ugly because they had been promised — by someone who didn't know the score — they would receive travelling expenses when they arrived at Dawson Creek. Under the new rules we didn't pay this money until they had fulfilled their contract. When they found out they weren't going to get their money they demanded to be allowed to sleep in a plush first-class car on the train rather than the sleeper. The porter said "no" as that would have run him short of blankets for the return trip to Edmonton.

I got a hurry-up call from the station agent. He said:

"You better get down here. There's going to be a riot. They won't have anything but this first-class car."

So I paid them a visit and a big bruiser stepped up to me and said:

"We want to sleep in this car."

"There's no bedding," the porter said.

"We don't care whether there's any bedding or not. We want to sleep in this car."

"In that case," I said, "you can sleep in it without bedding."

The threat of a riot ended right there — and they did!

* * *

Later on, the Americans brought in some real dogs, the dregs of society, it is recalled by William Tunny:

Most of these went to the Canol project or larger contractors outside the management contractors. But when the construction bosses found they had a dog or a freeloader on the job they'd get rid of him by keeping him on the move. Word circulated among the foremen a dog was on the way and he'd be kept a day or so then transferred.

The dog would spend time running up and down the road from camp to camp, travelling at night or 24 hours a day — or they'd forget to feed him and starve him out. He'd finally get sick of this and stagger out.

* * *

Not a few civilians had actually been sent onto the Canol project to avoid jail sentences back home, it was recalled by John Fisher, a Bechtel, Price and Callahan employee:

Some were draft dodgers. Some were escaping marital problems. We had a Chinese bull cook at Muncho Lake. He had been convicted of selling a love potion made of lizard tails and other ingredients. He was a dirty slovenly fellow who had been given a choice by a Los Angeles judge of going to jail or going to work on the highway.

One of the timekeepers came to me one night and said this Chinese had taken $50 off him during a dice game. He enlisted the aid of three of us to gang up on this man and win his money back in a game of ace-away. We duly organized the game and invited him to sit in. The outcome of this project was the Chinese won $60 more.

* * *

There was only one instance of prison labor being used. This was at Fort McMurray and it was kept pretty quiet so the American union workers wouldn't squawk. The prisoners were out of Leavenworth military prison. They were released on condition they go to work for Bechtel, Price and Callahan. They were lodged in an old-fashioned stockade made of rails and were a rough and tough lot. Many of them were engaged in boat building as there was an acute labor shortage there in the summer of 1943.

But not all were dogs. There was a carpenter from La Croix, Wisc., who had saved enough on his first tour of duty to pay the mortgage on his farm. He was going to make $3,000 on his second tour to buy out his neighbor.

A former Los Angeles garage owner was making $1,000 a month repairing trucks on the Canol project.

The job also drew a large number of serious young people who regarded this as the biggest adventure of their careers.

A Louisiana lawyer was getting $650 a month as a timekeeper's helper. He was one of the few in camp who could write well — and he was the official composer of love letters.

An unemployed California professor of mathematics at a camp on the Canol was happy to be earning $700 a month as a cook.

* * *

An American called by his draft board could be sent to do civilian work. In effect, many men employed there were civilian conscriptees, it was recalled by Bruce Ballah:

Whole trainloads of these fellows were consigned to American contractors. Paul Wirtz, personnel man for Metcalfe-Hamilton-Kansas City Bridge, used to come and use my facilities for processing them.

In return for such favors, Wirtz used to invite me around to their camp on Sunday when they served chicken. Hell, we were lucky to get stew on Sunday anywhere else. With rationing, we Canadians didn't know what chicken or turkey tasted like. Wirtz would sit me down to a big meal then beg me to supply him with Canadian help, especially girls. But I just couldn't let him have them.

Wirtz had a helluva time with some of the men they sent him. After riding across 1,000 miles of isolated countryside many refused to work when they arrived at Dawson Creek. They refused to get off the cars. So he'd order the cars put under guards and send them back home. When this happened, each man who refused to work was automatically barred from getting a government job in the U.S. for 20 years.

The thing that used to "get" me about the Americans was they'd use six men to our one. For instance, Wirtz had a staff of six and I didn't think he processed nearly the same number of men as I did.

The Americans' over-manned roster was recalled by Mrs. Florence English:

An anomaly of the Canol project was there wasn't what could be called a middle-class working group on the job. The people at the top of the organization were the finest to be found anywhere: good executives and able administrators. But from this upper class the personnel dropped to the circus class.

The wage disparity, class disparity and worker rebellion were mild displays compared to the violent dissensions I observed between the different factions — Canadians vs. Americans, GIs vs. civilians, PRA vs. the army and northern natives vs. the engineers. The dissensions built up largely because of the Americans' over-manned and over-organized, but fragmented, system.

* * *

The GIs and civilians were kept out of each other's way for a purpose, it was recalled by Sgt. M. F. Tibbetts of the 843rd Signals:

When Watson Lake airport was expanded, McNamara Construction of Toronto and Mannix Construction of Calgary won some of the contracts. There were plentiful supplies of electric power available but they had nobody around who knew how to string wire or build a pole line. I sent a Signal Corps crew to help out but this was the exception to the rule.

I'd find some civilian would invariably get a GI up a pole and rub it into him about low pay:

"Hello, sucker, how much are you getting this month?"

This would create hard feelings between the $75-a-month private and the $500-a-month civilian.

* * *

The pettiness of the various factions frequently proved to be laughable, it was recalled by Jack Moore of Calgary, a pipeline welder for Bechtel, Price and Callahan:

Although the projects were under one head there were too many separate and independent chains of command. When put together with predictable rivalries they had a monster which was fighting itself a great deal of the time.

Empire-building and the multiplicity of division of authority on the Canol project resulted in trouble, friction and rivalry among gang bosses and between the different forces involved in the work. For instance, we weren't allowed to take orders from the army. The civilian contractors didn't have too much regard for the armed forces. But the armed services looked down their noses at the contractors, the people who were actually building the facilities the army couldn't build itself.

* * *

The dog-faced GIs who were later stationed on the highway after the initial construction stage were held in contempt by civilians, it is recalled by William Tunny:

One Sunday afternoon I met the receptionist from Washington, D.C., in Capt. Bussey's office driving alone in her car in Dawson Creek. I invited her for coffee.

"It's rather unusual to see a young woman like you running around alone. I thought you'd have a convoy of GIs with you."

"They're not for me," she answered. "I don't consider most of those fellows to be soldiers. Most are just a bunch of riff-raff Uncle Sam sent up here to get out of his hair," she replied.

A pretty harsh indictment — but I think she had a point, knowing some of them as I did.

As time went on, isolation plus lower pay schedules caused enough friction that there was a larger turnover among Canadians than Americans on the north end. The Canadian turnover averaged 19% a month, compared to 10 for Americans. However, it reached 25% in some American camps.

* * *

Men who had worked a nine-month tour of duty on the Canol project were treasured, it was recalled by John H. Fisher of Valley Falls, Kans.:

If we were willing to stay on, they would give us a good job whether we qualified or not.

Before the war I was a wholesale grocer-dry goods salesman. As the war progressed I couldn't get tires and my sons and sons-in-law were all called to the army. I went to work with Bechtel, Price and Callahan as a payroll clerk, and timekeeper at Muncho Lake. After my first tour

I decided to rehire with another Canol contractor, E.W. Elliott Company, which had taken over maintenance of the Canol road. Men were hard to come by as they all wanted to go home. The highest pay was being offered for carpenters so my buddy, who had worked before the war in a loan-shark office in Minnesota, and I went to Elliott's hiring office in Whitehorse.

They hired me because I was carrying a hammer. My buddy didn't have one but I persuaded the hiring boss to make a carpenter out of him. He agreed. Just as we signed the papers the phone rang:

"Sorry, boys, it's all off. They are all filled up with carpenters."

We went outside and looked at a list of employment rates. We noted piledriver operators were being hired at 2 1/2 cents an hour under carpenters. We walked back in.

"Are you a piledriver operator?" asked the hiring boss.

"From the swamps of Louisiana," I replied.

I signed up for 60 days and stayed seven months.

* * *

The employers who found it almost impossible to get and keep staff were Canadians on non-war contracts, it is recalled by Bruce Ballah:

Mrs. Con Hergott of the Condill Hotel in Fort St. John came to plead for help. She had difficulty trying to pay waitresses a decent wage because of the price ceiling on meals. But she ran into extreme difficulties this particular day. Her husband, who was with a trucking contractor, and Joe Dill, the undertaker in town, had built the Condill Hotel. She was a pretty woman and was wearing a new fur coat, despite the fact it was a spring day on which a Chinook had come through and turned all the snow to mud and slush.

I was unable to help her. Most of the waitresses had been snapped up by Canadian contractors for their camps up the road. She then departed. I saw her walk down "the street." Then pretty soon I didn't see her. By God, she had fallen into a sump hole. Right up to her neck. A septic tank as big as a house couldn't keep up with the sump and the sump couldn't drain away fast enough.

Later Con came to me and said she was going to sue me.

"What for?" I asked.

"She came to that bloody place of yours and fell into that sump hole."

"Well, Con, you can't hold me responsible for that."

"Well, Jesus, if you'd have given us the help we wanted, she wouldn't have had to come to Dawson Creek."

There was nothing I could do to mollify them — but in later years we laughed about her misadventure.

I had many Canadians putting the pressure on me to go to work for the Americans. I recall a pair of old girls from Fort St. John who came in one day. One was Lizzie Smith. We called her Mrs. Smitty, a big stout lady and a real card.

"Yes, what can I do for you?"

"I'm going to work for the Americans," she said in a high nasal penetrating voice.

"Sorry, you're not," I said. She reached over the desk and grabbed me by the lapels and shook me.

"You're telling me, sonny, that I can't work for them?"

"You can't work for them. That's the law."

One day years later I spotted her on a street in Edmonton and tapped her on the shoulder:

"Hey, you still want to work for the Americans?"

She turned, recognized me, and yelled:

"My God, you: you dirty skunk! I could paste you one. I never did get to work for 'em — but the other girls did."

"Well, if they did they did it illegally," I replied.

In one instance in Whitehorse a number of waitresses quit and went to work in similar jobs for the Americans. UIC forced the contractors to discharge them and they were naturally forced back to their lower-paid Canadian employers again.

Pay was deplorable for waitresses. But this all ended one memorable day late in 1942 in Dawson Creek. They decided to go on strike. They were sick of making only $5 to $7 a week for 7:00 a.m. to 7:00 p.m. shifts seven days a week. There was quite an uproar when people learned of these poor working conditions.

The strike was successful. All went back to serve the evening meals with a substantial pay rise.

* * *

Likewise, it was impossible for Canadian employers to hire American personnel not registered for UIC, it was recalled by Tom Lauder, a Dawson Creek teamster:

I could have hired lots of American GIs to drive teams for me but the UIC wouldn't let them and they couldn't get Canadians for me. I had eight teams and I could have had 20 if I could have gotten drivers. We were so hard-pressed for help I had to press my daughter and daughter-in-law into service driving dray wagons for six months.

While they were working, the army privates, who needed the money and would rather drive than bum around, sat and watched. I'd hire a GI and he'd work four or five days and somebody would see him — and that'd be the end of that.

* * *

Bull cooks were very scarce, it was recalled by Anton K. Money of Santa Barbara, Calif., a former Canadian who was a straw boss with Metcalfe-Hamilton Kansas City Bridge, at McCrae:

The reason was the pay was only $90 a month. Nobody was willing to work for that. We got around that by hiring carpenters' helpers for $1.50 an hour and putting them in the kitchen. This was known as salary boosting.

The way it was: Many so-called carpenters' helpers came in, never having used a hammer or saw in their bloody lives. I'd be at Whitehorse airport when 25 new men would come off the plane and my job was to assign them to the different camps. We were short of carpenters, too. I sorted out the phoneys by requiring each to open his tool kit. If I saw a man was carrying a set of finishing tools, I knew he was a joiner and assigned him to an inside finisher's job. The next would have a hammer and square in one hand and a new saw in the other:

"How long have you been a carpenter?"

"Since 8 a.m. yesterday."

"All right, how about peeling spuds then?"

The majority were glad to work in the warm kitchen rather than nailing on siding outdoors at 20 below. I'd put them to work helping the cook at carpenters' helpers wages. We had spud peelers (bull cooks) making $600 or $700 a month. They all demanded overtime or they wouldn't stay on the job.

We had to guarantee carpenters, plumbers and other tradesmen 30 hours of overtime above their 40-hour union work week or they'd be gone. Of course some of the phoneys who didn't know a crosscut saw from a ripsaw got on the gangs.

* * *

While some Canadian employers had trouble obtaining help, others run-

ning low-priority businesses never seemed to lack men, it is recalled by Bruce Ballah:

We had a bit of trouble with the Alcan Club in Dawson Creek in this respect. Working as bouncers and flunkeys were eight men who had quit essential construction jobs. I couldn't touch them because the club had a federal licence. They had phoney UIC cards, it turned out.

The Alcan Club was quite notorious. It was operated by one Tony Anzio of Vancouver, a six-foot-six former heavyweight fighter who had been reputed to be a sparring partner of Jack Dempsey. Working for him was another six-footer — a hard-featured poker-faced guy with a pegleg whom nobody crossed up.

The club was located in a big old warehouse on the town limits. It cost 25 cents to join. Out front was a place where truckers could come in and flop on one of the chesterfields when they couldn't find a place to sleep. However, they had about 20 card tables in the back and there was always a game going.

They cleaned out many a pay packet. I recalled a construction foreman who was relieved of $50 one night. He came back a couple of weeks later with a stake of $500 and they took $250. They also cleaned out a trapper who had just sold his winter's catch for $1,200 and was on his way to Edmonton. He never made it past Dawson Creek.

When one of the construction companies blew the whistle on Anzio for employing essential workers, I got together with a friend from the RCMP named Burfield. He didn't charge Anzio with running a gambling joint but running a bawdy house, and I was to be the chief witness.

Anzio sent word to me he would give me $2,000 to "forget" my testimony. When I didn't pay any attention he came in to see me. I was prepared. I had Dick Panter from the R. Melville Smith Company sitting behind the counter taking the conversation down in shorthand — just in case — then I gave him the boot. I gave my evidence all right and those essential workers at the club went back to essential jobs. After that Anzio treated me with some respect.

* * *

There are always excesses in boom-town situations. The excesses originated at the top as well as with the lower-echelon scofflaws, it was recalled by George C. Andrew of Toronto, office manager for R. Melville Smith Company at Fort St. John:

Several of our engineers were working for $400 a month. They asked for $500 but C.F. Capes, chief construction engineer for the PRA, wouldn't approve them.

I was disturbed about the inequities of the salaries of stenographers and wrote my boss, J.L. Zoller, Smith vice-president:

"I think it is too much in this day and age to expect a girl to pound a typewriter or sort invoices from 8:00 a.m. to 6:00 p.m. and suggest as much work can be done if the hours were from 8:00 to 5:00, as is the case with PRA and our Dawson Creek office."

Three days later Zoller's reply came back from Toronto — typical of the employer attitude of these days:

"I do not think we should permit much slackness. You mention the hours from 8:00 to 6:00. I think you will agree very few are at their desks before 8:30 and there is little done after 5:30. This would correspond with the hours kept by PRA. I imagine there'd be a bit more satisfaction if we insisted on an 8:00 a.m. starting time. These girls are much better paid than they were before they left Toronto and they were certainly satisfied with the arrangements at the time they left. The ones who are out of line are those who got undeserved increases. It may be better to adjust them downwards and have one or two dissatisfied than try to have the majority adjusted upward and get nowhere."

* * *

One other wartime adjustment made Canadians mad at their own government, it is recalled by Florence English, Edmonton office manager for Bechtel, Price and Callahan:

Under wartime labor regulations, my salary was only half of the American officer I replaced. But the regulation that forbade us to buy cigarettes at American camp commissaries really upset many Canadians. In the early days of the project, all civilians were classed as foreign service war effort personnel. As such we could buy a carton of tax-free cigarettes a week. A pack of 20 cost 10 cents; a carton cost 98. The GIs could buy unlimited quantities in the PX for half that price. It, therefore, was a temptation for GIs making $1 a day to buy 100 cartons of cigarettes and retail them to civilians for $1 a piece.

At one time half the population of Edmonton was smoking these cheap cigarettes — and it almost ran Imperial Tobacco out of business. (Those who didn't smoke picked up cartons and sold them.) Imperial squawked to the Canadian government and the government, in turn, made representations to the U.S. government. This resulted in our purchasing privileges at the commissaries being withdrawn.

This and $50 fines didn't stop the trade in cigarettes as a black market sprang up. Dawson Creek became headquarters for the cigarette racket. The GIs would sell them to the truckers and people coming out on the train.

The authorities caught on to what was happening when they found the U.S. Army was ordering as many cigarettes for the base at Dawson Creek as were needed for the population of Edmonton and Calgary combined! Buck privates were swaggering around like millionaires.

* * *

The U.S. Army tried to control the situation by cutting down the supply to a carton a week a man and having the military police search those who came out on the station platform at Edmonton, it was recalled by Mrs. Irma Gray of Saskatoon, an office worker for the PRA at Fort St. John:

I was petrified with fear when I arrived at Edmonton one day late in October, 1943, because I had 12 cartons with me. The MPs were going along lines of people detraining and requiring them to open their suitcases. They nabbed two guys ahead of me — but they skipped over me and I got all mine through.

Another commodity in which a black market developed was booze. In Canada it was rationed by permit but everyone with $1 could obtain a permit. Booze was not rationed in the U.S. Therefore everyone who was lucky enough to travel to Skagway or Fairbanks was expected to return with all he could carry, no excuses tolerated.

Incongruously, Dawson Creek and Fort St. John, the locations where liquor was in the most demand, were as dry as a desert without a B.C. government liquor store. This was because the townspeople had voted against an outlet on a local option plebiscite before the war and there was no way of reversing the vote.

The thousands of people who wanted a crock were forced to travel six miles to Pouce Coupe to a small understaffed store. The road to Pouce Coupe liquor store was the most heavily travelled road in Canada at the time. There was much head-shaking over this ritual by the Americans who had more liberal liquor laws.

* * *

Joe Bealhne was the government liquor vendor, it was recalled by Bruce

Ballah:

He was a fine white-haired old chap with a French accent. I was in the store one day when he nailed me. He was beside himself because he couldn't hire any help. It was a Saturday and thirsty people were crowded in like sardines and there were only two clerks to issue permits and take orders.

"M'sieu Ballah, can you 'elp to get somebodee to work 'ere?" he pleaded, breaking away from the mob and rushing up to me. "I'm having one hawful time."

"Well," I said, "I'll see what I can do."

And, by the Lord Harry, if three weeks later a crippled fellow from somewhere in northern Alberta didn't come in to the UIC office! He wanted a job on the highway but nobody would take him as he'd never had any office experience.

"Do you drink?" I asked him.

"No."

"OK, I got a job for you."

I called Joe and took this fellow right down in the truck. Well, you'd have thought I'd given him a million bucks. The guy just loved it there and Joe loved him because he didn't drink. From then on I was Joe's white-haired boy. He tried to kill me with kindness:

"Anyee time you want a bottle you let Joe know because I have 'shrinkage.' You're my friend."

I turned down his gifts; anyway I wasn't drinking much then. I couldn't afford it. However, I was in the store a few months later and caught a big American filling his pockets full of mickeys and threatened to turn him in if he didn't put them back.

He promptly did so — but I might as well have saved my breath. A few nights later a couple of army trucks backed up to the liquor store window and cleaned out every bottle in the place. Nobody had any idea where it all disappeared — not even the RCMP whose barracks were three doors north.

To simplify things for the staff and customers Bealhne carried only one brand of rye whisky, King's Plate. No matter what brand the customer ordered it would come out King's Plate and it cost $3.50 a bottle.

* * *

The permit book "rationing" was recalled by Roy Robinson, a superintendent for Storms Construction Company of Hamilton, Ont.:

Although liquor was rationed to one bottle, a $5 bill slipped inside the permit book would get you two bottles. Since any resident could buy a book, the clerks never bothered too much with identification — which meant many books were issued in fictitious names. The most popular person turned out to be Ernest Manning, the newly elected Social Credit premier of Alberta, a well-known teetotaler. His name appeared on thousands of permit applications.

All the guys going out sold their permits to those who stayed. I recall one time having accumulated 150. When anybody died Joe Bealhne retained his permit book for "emergencies."

It seemed that Canadian contractors were always running into emergencies and could depend on old Joe to pull them out! When you got to know him you could come down to the back door of his house at night and he'd load you right up. But only in an emergency!

Any of the contractors who needed liquor for entertainment could write him a week or so ahead and tell him how much they wanted — and he'd tell them to have a truck at his back door before opening time and they'd get it.

Wallace Mackey of Weston, Ont., was one contractor who didn't put up with any of this permit book nonsense. A big tall, gruff, hard-driving old construction man with a white mustache, he drank a 40-ounce bottle of whisky a day and never wobbled; but if he didn't have that 40-ouncer he was no good.

The rest of his crew dutifully lined up at the liquor store with their permits but he'd not get in the line-up. He'd go round to the back door and say to old Joe:

"I need some whisky."

"How much?"

"Quite a bit."

Joe would riffle through his "emergency" permits, Mackey would get a case of whisky, put it in his truck and away he went.

* * *

Everyone tried to wangle a trip to Fairbanks, it was recalled by Mrs. Jack Murray of the USED office in Whitehorse:

On the last trip I made I picked up four bottles of liquor for a party we had planned. I left the package on the airport bus to Ladd Field in Fairbanks and it got away before I could catch it. I got in quite a flap because I figured somebody might pick up the parcel and get into trouble at customs. I told my story to the woman at the airport check-in counter; if the parcel turned up she could send a pair of shoes I had bought but she could keep the liquor.

Several days later a messenger came into the office paging me. He had a big parcel. By golly, the girl had retrieved my parcel and shipped it complete with booze!

Part of the attraction of Fairbanks was that nylon stockings had made their first appearance in the U.S. and were being sold there before they were available in Canada. Some Western Canadian women were the first in Canada to wear nylons. Men who took them home to their wives found themselves placed on a pedestal.

* * *

Wallace Mackey wasn't able to intimidate me as easily as he did old Joe Bealhne, it was recalled by Bruce Ballah:

"Look, kid," he said as he bulled through the door one day, "I've got to have men — and no goddam foolin' around."

"Wallace," I said, "you'll get them the same as anyone else. But you won't get any more than's coming to you."

"Christ, I need them."

"If you'd let the sons of bitches work regular hours you wouldn't need so many."

"By Jesus, they work when they come to my camp."

"I know they work for you. You work them hard, too. Maybe too hard." His men were putting in a great deal of overtime.

So one day a week later four guys drifted in and said they wanted to go to the Mackey camp.

"OK," I said, "but I warn you: it's one of the best-run camps but also one of the toughest. If you don't cut the mustard out there, you're out. The Old Man will really give you the gears. He don't take nuthin' from nobody. You'll wish to God you'd never gone there."

Three days later Wallace came rushing into my office and slammed the door:

"Watinell were you telling those guys about me?" he demanded. "About how rotten I am?"

"I didn't tell 'em how rotten you were. I just told them how tough you were. If they couldn't hold their own in camp there was no use of them going there. Isn't that true?"

"By Jesus, kid, did you tell 'em that?"

"You're damned right. There's no sense of lying."

"By God, I'll shake your hand for that. Come up and have a drink some time." The frown he had come in with was replaced by smiles.

I went up to his camp one day and had a wonderful time. Wallace thought life in the bush was wonderful — and so it was.

The warfare between the various agencies and factions involved on the Alaska Highway was fierce and astounding to Canadians, considering the importance and urgency of the job. This was a bit sad because they were both staffed by talented top men in their field. A PRA resident engineer named Lednicki at Teslin, a good construction man, really hated the army fellows. He said:

"I never saw so many brainless people as the army has attracted to its engineering staff. I didn't think there were so many in the world."

* * *

Inspectors issued a uniform and brought into the Canol Project found themselves in the centre of many confrontations with hard-bitten pipeliners and construction stiffs employed by the prime contractor, Bechtel, Price and Callahan. It was recalled by Jack Moore, a Calgary pipeliner:

Had the U.S. Army been able to recruit personnel from qualified firms of pipeline inspectors to oversee Bechtel's work, there would have been no problem. However, too many were not qualified. This was a rush-rush job and the army didn't have time to screen out some of the poor help. Many were political appointees who didn't even know pipe was hollow. They turned down hundreds of thousands of dollars worth of work which was done properly merely because of some procedural irregularity which didn't show up in the book.

A qualified firm of inspection personnel probably would have turned down just as much work but these old-time hardened pipeliners bristled when they saw a greenhorn. They were not backward in coming forward, so to speak, and couldn't disguise their contempt for some of the army inspectors. To get back at them, inspectors turned down a lot of work and hid behind the book. It was a lengthy procedure to challenge the book. This led to a lot of trouble.

The most obstreperous of the inspectors were whipped real good, put on trucks and sent out and told not to return.

However, despite the friction of disallowing $3 million on the $138 million project, the job got done — and rather quickly at that.

When they first came onto the joint projects, the Americans knew it was going to take strong men and determined women to jump off into the Canadian wilderness — parts of which had never been inhabited, even by Indians. To obtain the kind of men it required, Bechtel erected in its hiring halls a sign which became legendary. It read:

THIS IS NO PICNIC

Working and living conditions on this job are as difficult as those encountered on any ever done in the United States or foreign territory. Men hired will be required to work and live under the most extreme conditions imaginable. Temperatures will range from 90 above to 70 below zero. Men will have to fight swamps, rivers, ice, snow and cold. Mosquitoes, flies and gnats will not only be annoying but will cause bodily harm. If you are not prepared to work under these and similar conditions, do not apply.

Between the vicissitudes of weather and bugs, loneliness and the factional internal warfare that occurred on both projects, it is slightly amazing both were completed and served the purposes for which they were built in one way or another. For enduring these hardships for one complete tour of duty, employees of Bechtel were given an Award of Service suitable for framing. The PRA handed out similar Certificates of Merit to highway employees. The Bechtel award was signed by Van W. Rosendahl, a senior officer of the company. It read:

"Fellow War Worker: The first time you entered a Canol Project office, you were no doubt greeted with the sign which has now become famous: THIS IS NO PICNIC. In spite of this warning, you and many others signed contracts for nine months and headed for the North. To a few people it was an adventure, but to most it was a serious desire to assist in the war effort.

"Time proved that hardship, weather and homesickness were difficult obstacles to overcome, with the result that only a small percentage of the total number employed had the determination to stay with a tough job and complete their contracts. Our records show you were one of those who could 'take it.'

"The policy committee and the management of Bechtel, Price and Callahan realize that one of the important factors in the successful completion of the project was the contribution made by those who stayed and provided the necessary continuity of operation.

"In the years to come, you will undoubtedly reflect on your Canol service as one of the most interesting periods of your life. In appreciation of your valuable contribution, Bechtel presents you with the enclosed Award of Service and wish to take this opportunity to thank you for your part in the Canol Project."

The Ho-Lems worked overtime to dry-clean uniforms of the 95th Regt. ordered to a new battlefield.
HO LEM
DRYCLEANING

9

Two Truckers Lived In A Double Backhouse

In the summer of 1942, Dave Ho-Lem and his brother, Frank, were in Black Diamond, Alberta, not doing too well selling electrical appliances and teaching guitar. Dave heard from his brother-in-law, Lee Yuin of Edmonton, that the boom town of Dawson Creek at Mile Zero on the new Alaska Highway was short of dry-cleaning facilities.

He travelled to Dawson Creek and found the Americans had "invaded" the small town and there were 10,000 troops and civilian workers going and coming all the time. He recalled further:

There was no way of getting away from it: Dawson Creek was then a rip-roaring town, 100 boom towns rolled into one. There were knife fights and knifings as whites and blacks, soldiers and civilians mixed it up. But the Canadian police were respected. You'd see a kid from Texas pick a fight with a weather-beaten Saskatchewan truck driver. A cop would come onto the scene and the fight was off.

Townsfolk stayed pretty close to home at night. If a girl walked along the street good and fast in the daytime she was all right. But if she strolled along she was usually looking for trouble — and got it. Some women asked for the trouble they got into. These American GIs were no different than any other soldiers far from home — healthy, well-fed and on the make.

The U.S. Army encouraged anyone who could set up a dry-cleaning business to do so — and guaranteed him all kinds of business. We decided to do business with the army and bought a building lot a mile from the famous Mile Zero milepost.

There was only one hitch that prevented us from starting up immediately. We couldn't buy lumber and nails to construct a dry-cleaning plant as the army had priority on all building materials. We came home and, after a struggle, scrounged around, obtained what lumber we needed and shipped it up there.

To equip the plant I bought a machine in Blairmore that would handle three suits of clothes at a time. I also bought a two-horsepower boiler that Dad had in his knitting factory, and a press.

Bill Lee, a trucker, loaded eight tons of this stuff on his four-ton truck and we started off at 40-below February 10, 1943. The roads were slippery and we had trouble with one of the tires and had to stop frequently to repair it.

Somewhere in the wilderness the truck stopped again. I felt we'd had it this time. We couldn't see any other vehicles or houses. We huddled in the truck clutching each other for warmth, resigned to the fate of freezing.

About 5:00 a.m. Bill noticed some lights go on half a mile away. We decided to hike towards them. It turned out to be the Indian School at Joussard run by the Roman Catholic Church. When we reached the boiler room door we were so exhausted we collapsed after the janitor let us in. We slept near the furnace.

Waking up some hours later, we saw a couple nuns in their habits looking at us. We thought we had met our glory!

They fed us some soup and got us thawed out and we stayed there until the afternoon, at which time we went out and got the truck started again and went on our way. Had we not been so close to that school we might well have frozen to death.

We arrived at Grande Prairie February 14. We called on a friend, Bill Mark, who ran a restaurant there.

"There's no use going on. You might as well turn back. Last night Dawson Creek was devastated by an explosion and fire," he told us.

We didn't know what to do. However, we got the bright idea of wiring the Northern Alberta Railways agent there and he sent word our lumber and lot were OK. So we kept on. On arrival we saw things were in a shambles. It was an inauspicious start to a business. But we had a piece of luck when we ran into Dan Soo, who ran one of the seven Chinese cafes, the Empress. He had some friends who were carpenters and he managed to persuade them to stay around and build our plant.

Three days after we opened they pulled part of the 95th Engineering Regiment out of there. We were told these black troops had been in the bush nearly a year and needed spruced-up uniforms to go back home. We told them we'd do it for the 300 going out only if it was shirts and trousers. However, when they came in they dumped tunics and parkas and every other kind of clothing on top of us. We worked 48 hours straight getting that job finished. In the end we were so tired we had to shout and sing and yell at each other to keep awake.

It turned really cold — 55 below — and we were afraid the return pipe to the boiler would freeze. We took turns staying at the plant to make sure it didn't. This wasn't the most comfortable place as there was a lot of finishing to do on the building, and there were many gaps and holes. But Bill Lee, Frank Lung, another brother-in-law, and I spelled each other off every three hours and we kept the pot-bellied stove going to prevent the pipes from freezing.

There was all kinds of business. The officers of a unit would come in and tell us how many men they had and put us under contract to do their dry cleaning. Soon after we arrived our days were all booked. Each unit had a special day.

We were able to get as much as $5 a suit for rush jobs. Price was no object when a man was going out on leave and wanted his uniform cleaned in a hurry.

The army engineers at the railhead had a large number of secretaries. Friday was their day for dry cleaning. Just about closing time there'd be a line of women half a block long picking up their laundry.

Brothers George, Charlie and Jack later came up and opened up a steam laundry down the street as business was so lucrative.

After the big pre-Christmas rush in 1943 the pressure let up and we had planned a big celebration. The girls working in the laundry, dry cleaning plant and at the Shangri-La Restaurant, which George and some of our relatives owned, had pooled their liquor ration permits and had acquired extra permits and had filled the refrigerator with several dozen cases of beer and several cases of whisky, which they stashed under beds upstairs.

However, the celebration was not to be. We had a big fire in the boiler room. Firemen from Dawson Creek, the army and Fort St. John managed to save the building but not before $4,000 damage was caused — damage that shut us down two months.

We were so happy with the job the firemen did, we told them to help themselves to the beer in the refrigerator. This they did. They also found the liquor. They soon appeared on the street carrying bottles from our cache. Soon not a few of them were carrying quite a load. This was the end of our planned celebration as we didn't have enough permits to replace the booze.

After this, Constable Leo Bagallies of the B.C. Provincial Police came nosing around. I suspect he and others figured we were doing some bootlegging. However, they aborted their own investigation. We had a few cases of roofing tar in tins which we had not used. It had no labels on it and looked like canned beer the Americans had introduced to Canada.

"What's this, Dave?" Bagallies said.

I acted surprised as if he had caught me bootlegging. He took the can away to the police station and opened it. His face was very red when he found out it wasn't beer.

Having made their fortune in wartime Dawson Creek, George sold out in late 1944 and returned to Calgary where he opened a successful laundry and dry-cleaning business, Rosedale Cleaners.

In the two years the Ho-Lems ran a laundry business in Dawson Creek it had grown to 4,200 and was beginning to emerge as an attractive small city. When the first units of the U.S. military arrived there in March, 1942, it was described as a "down-at-the-heel, beat-up little place of 700."

* * *

Despite the fact it was important as the northern terminus of the NAR the village's progress had been held back by politics.

It had been the original intention of the NAR in 1930 to build the terminus at Pouce Coupe, the county town, chief trading centre and fur trade centre for the B.C. side of the Peace River block. However, a local farmer demanded $30,000 for the terminus site. This was more than the NAR was willing to pay so it bridged the Pouce Coupe River and carried the line seven miles further to the small village of Dawson Creek, where the land was available for $10,000.

Although it had gained the railroad terminus and other services that went with it, Dawson Creek didn't have enough political influence to persuade the provincial government to move its regional offices there — for many years even after it had become apparent Pouce Coupe's growth had been permanently stunted by the wartime emergence of Dawson Creek as a city. The rivalry between the two towns never evaporated.

With the 1942 influx of thousands of troops and construction stiffs, sanitary conditions became deplorable. J.N. Bond, secretary, and George Bissette, chairman of the village commission, finding themselves faced with a water shortage, tried to persuade the engineering troops that one bath a week was enough. But the Americans wore layer upon layer of windproof garments and they were convinced they needed more than one bath.

The big problem faced by the whole area was lack of groundwater. The few wells drilled around town were overtaxed.

* * *

But while there was a lack of water for drinking and sanitary purposes, there was no lack of mud on the streets. The main street was often a big mudhole. Even the board sidewalks were pushed into the mud and almost out of sight at times, it was recalled by William Tunny, a carpenter who arrived March 4, 1943, a year after the U.S. military pulled into town:

We'd be walking up the street and see a lady looking to see if she could pick her way across.

"Do you want to go across the street, lady?"

"Well, yes, I would . . ."

And you'd pick her up in your arms and walk across.

"See you sometime. Goodbye."

You didn't know who she was. But it was the proper thing to do; we were all working at the same job.

One day I saw a U.S. Army lieutenant walking very properly up the street, nicely dressed in his uniform, and a young woman with him. They came to a crossing and he picked her up and started across through ankle-deep mud. He slipped and sat right down with the girl in his lap. We had quite a laugh; his face was very, very red.

The village commission couldn't begin to take care of the paving of streets or expansion of water and other badly needed civic services because the amount of taxation it could raise was limited by provincial statute. The commission even resorted to collecting $5 poll tax on the payrolls of civilian contractors which had set up in Dawson Creek but even this "quickie" money didn't raise enough taxes. It merely made itinerant workers mad.

As a protest measure the commission resigned in a body and the Province of B.C. was forced to step in and take over the administration.

The B.C. government went to the military and asked it to take a hand in the provision of more services. The military pointed out it was already assisting with policing and was supplying most of the water from a water point at Pouce Coupe constructed by E. Company of the 341st Engineering Regiment. From this point the army pumped 30,000 gallons a day and private contractors hauled it to camp and to the townspeople. One of the contractors was Tom Lauder of Stettler. He recalled:

In the first few months I was there following my arrival in March, 1943, I hauled water with teams and tanks. I had eight tanks going all the time. The army was thirsty for water. They wanted it in a hurry. They wanted it now. They wouldn't take no for an answer.

I worked 36 hours at a stretch hauling for them. They wouldn't haul it for themselves; I could never understand why.

My wife and I found a little cabin. There was nothing else. Later a trucker friend came in and he had no place to stay. I gave him the cabin and undertook to build a shack. I expected to have it done in a week but it took a month as the army kept hounding me to haul water. During that time we were sleeping under a tarpaulin right out in the open. It was pretty rough as there was a great deal of rain.

Housing was short for beast as well as man. The only place I could find to use as a horse stable was a roofless shed. I picked up a tarp from the army and used it for a roof. Later I bought some scarce lumber and built a stable on a three-acre piece of land near the town limits.

My standard day was 6:00 a.m. to 6:00 p.m. When I was building the little cabin I used to knock off about six to work at it for an hour or two. But no sooner than I got to work when officers came along with:

"What are you doing here? Where's your team?"

"In the barn over there getting a little rest and feed. I went for 12 hours."

"You gotta go again."

"Lord, give me a chance," I said. "I'm trying to build myself a little shack so we can have a decent place to sleep."

"No, we can't spare you. You gotta go to work tonight."

So I went and got something to eat and went back to work until seven o'clock next morning. They made it so a person couldn't refuse them.

They asked me and my men to work 24-hour shifts many times. Then the men got a bit independent and refused to work overtime. I was forced to do a lot of it myself. A team of horses drew $2 an hour for a standard nine-hour day. Out of this I paid the driver 75 cents an hour. Overtime was time and a half and double time on Sundays. That was good money and I could pay for a team in 10 days.

We worked most Saturdays. We went Sunday the same as any other day. I'd see men going to church in their work clothes and come out and go back to work.

We were paid every Saturday at 4:00 p.m. in U.S. dollars. The paymaster came to us. We never had to go looking for him or line up at a wicket.

In addition to hauling for the army I acquired a permit for supplying 500,000 gallons of water over six months to the town. We were paid 10 cents a pail or $1 for a 30-gallon barrel. Women used it three times before finally washing the floor; that was the last use.

The contractors based in town were required to find their own supply sources. Many construction superintendents had to spend time scouring the hills south of town for springs.

The water had a high mineral content — iron and alkali. The army doped it heavily with chlorine. It was awfully hard on horses and many almost died before they got used to it.

I hauled a lot of water with horses. Finally we had to get an old four-wheel-drive truck with a tank on it.

One winter night this truck lost its brakes on a hill with a load of water. Bruce Ballah of the Unemployment Insurance Commission and a couple of other guys were sitting on a chesterfield in the bunkhouse at the R. Melville Smith camp when it rolled out of control through the building. Fortunately, Ballah heard it coming and threw the others 10 feet across the room. The truck flattened the chesterfield, went through the floor and stopped.

Everyone sobered up very quickly.

Although the most obvious part of Dawson Creek's wartime life was trucks, it may have seemed incongruous to a later generation there were so many draymen and dray horses on the scene.

My son, Bob, was a trucker on the old Fort Nelson trail and later did a lot of work for the U.S. Army. From him I learned of the desperate need for choring and roustabout teams around the camp and construction sites.

I brought in all the horses and harness I could find from the Innisfail area. Later the U.S. Army shipped in a bunch of harness and horse shoes. We could get anything from the army. It even offered to buy us horses to help with all the work they threw at us.

Bill Simpson had also come in from Innisfail with 100 head of horses and located 100 miles northwest of Fort St. John. He rented the horses out to survey parties at $15 a day and made a lot of money.

Tommy Wilde had originally come in from Cochrane, Alberta, to take a Brewster pack train of hunters out and couldn't get out. He had spent the winter there and later squatted on a piece of property near the Peace River bridge. He rented out dozens of horses for surveys and packing along the Canol road.

The horses didn't do well due to lack of timothy hay and good pasture and it took a lot out of them at first. We had to bring in supplementary hay and oats. The mud made them lame. They developed sore shoulders and necks from harness chafing and we had to ship many out after three or four months on this tough job.

A couple of business practices taken for granted today had their genesis at Dawson Creek — out of necessity.

I'm sure someone who saw the little grey team I rented out by the day at the army camp for choring around picked up on the idea for the rent-a-car business. I'd take the horses down there in the morning and leave them standing on the company street. Anyone needing a team would pick them up and do what needed to be done and pay me later when I went back at night. They didn't work half the time but some days when they did work they made me $40.

The officers and girls from the office drove them all over, spoiling them every way and feeding them sugar. Later I had them on a street job in Dawson Creek. Every time they'd see a soldier they'd take off and go over and nuzzle him for a lump of sugar.

I know somebody used this idea and profited with cars.

Dawson Creek also had the first self-serve food store I ever saw. It also came about by necessity. There just was not enough clerks to serve the crowds. To get any service one had to pick up what he needed then took it to a clerk and asked him to take the money.

And somebody picked up on this.

There was a lot of "self-serve" going on around the NAR yards but it didn't draw jail terms as it would have anywhere else. Hundreds of cars of merchandise followed the Americans. At first much was unloaded and piled for a mile alongside the track and left unguarded so the empty cars could be taken away.

There were oceans of oil and gas in drums and all kinds of flour, sugar and meat. We just couldn't see these commodities going to waste with rationing on. We made sure they didn't, too. The result was that we were able to take care of the large transient population without the necessity of extra ration stamps.

Most of the town's businessmen kept their places open round the clock in those rush days — only closing long enough to allow staff to eat.

There were plenty of inconveniences. But there wasn't much grumbling as there wasn't time for that luxury.

The government finally convinced Col. Albert Lane, commanding officer of the 341st and later of the Dawson Creek army base, that the military should assume more responsibility in providing essential services for the town. Since lack of water and sewer and other facilities made for unsanitary conditions in town, the town was out of bounds a great deal of the time to the GIs. It was to the army's advantage to assist with civic services as the army had increased the need.

* * *

Troops from the 35th, 341st and 95th Engineering Regiments all carried sidearms when they blew into town in March, 1942, Floyd Wilson, a grocer, recalled:

Regimental braggadocio and rivalries overflowed in their first engagement in the pub the night they got off the train. A shooting incident was narrowly averted. After the incident, all GIs were forbidden to carry sidearms in Dawson Creek. The strong 14% Canadian beer (U.S. beer was only 2%) made them trigger-happy and boisterous.

* * *

The Americans found all goods cheaper than back home; U.S. dollars commanded a 10% premium. The editor of the Grande Prairie Herald Tribune recalled:

The first party of American GIs to arrive walked into a pub and tossed down a U.S. $10 bill for a round of drinks — worth $1 Canadian. They received a $10 Canadian bill in change.

"Hey, we're paying for the drinks," one guy exclaimed.

"Yes," responded the barkeep, "you've paid and the Canadian $10 bill is your change."

* * *

When it was explained to them their money brought a premium it was hard for them to get rid of that plutocratic feeling. With their vast purchasing power they had stripped all the towns from Edmonton to Dawson Creek of clothing.

Tommie Gregg, a NAR engineer, recalled:

We couldn't buy any new underwear the first year they came in here. Money meant nothing to them. It made some of us a little sore on occasions when they tried to lord their dollars over us.

A Canadian construction company superintendent who arrived in Edmonton late in 1942 to work on the Peace River bridge told me winter clothing was all gone in that city, especially the medium and large sizes. All the merchants said the U.S. boys were taller and heavier than average Albertans.

* * *

Roustabouts, hangers-on, sharpies, swindlers, gamblers, the criminal element followed in the wake of the boom. Jack Moore, a pipeline welder for Bechtel Price and Callahan, recalled a brush with a hood:

I stopped in Dawson Creek overnight waiting to catch the NAR Muskeg Special to Edmonton. I had been paid off after nine months and had $3,000 on me. My buddy, a shovel operator, had $2,000. We got into a game in the New Palace Cafe building, a place run by a well-known Calgary gambler. My friend was a blabbermouth and the gang around there soon knew we had money. I left early and went back to the Dewdrop Inn.

The hall lights were all out. There were no locks on the doors. That was then usual in the North. I reached for the drop-cord from the ceiling to turn on the light. I heard somebody come in behind me and tell me to stand against the wall. A couple of drinks had given me a false courage and I let a punch fly at him. I connected and a .45 automatic flew out of his hand and we grappled on the floor. I had seen him hanging around the game and he knew I had a roll.

With this there was a great thumping down the hall and in pops Wilfred Michaud, the proprietor, a man in his 60s in a long nightshirt and a tasseled nightcap. When he saw the gun on the floor and this fellow bleeding at the mouth, he turned and ran so hard he ran up his nightgown — ran right up the front of it and ripped it almost off himself.

Michaud regained enough composure to call the B.C. Provincial Police. They came up and took the guy into custody. The gun had been stolen or bought from a GI. He was an escapee from the New Westminster Penitentiary.

Another incident was recalled by Henry Wright, a mechanic with Dufferin Paving Company:

There were thieves about during my first night in a PRA bunkhouse in Dawson Creek. Thirty men had all hung their trousers on hooks on the wall. Next morning 29 had been cleaned out of every cent they owned.

But they missed me; my wallet remained intact. I felt many suspicious looks that day.

This was typical of the times. It was a wide-open town full of fairly wild characters. You had to watch your step where you placed your money where you slept. You didn't have to look for trouble; it was there all the time.

* * *

Roy Robinson, a foreman with Storms Construction Company of Toronto, recalled:

Jack West, the superintendent, and I were in Dawson Creek over Christmas, 1942. Since we knew all the girls there, we got a room over the Empire Cafe, and had a Christmas tree and all the trimmings.

We discovered Ernie Swanson, a hard-boiled pal of Jack's from Sudbury, was in town. We avoided him when he started to drink hard because he got wild and crazy. We were in bed one night when there came a loud pounding on the door and this Ernie hollered:

"Robinson! Jack! Wake up!"

We never made a move.

"Wake up," he roared, "and get the door open or I'm coming through her."

"No, Ernie. We're too tired. Slow down and go to your room," we said.

"I'm comin' in if you don't open her up," he slurred drunkenly.

By this time we were out of bed — and Jack knew he would hit the door. So when we heard him running for it he pulled it open. He came into the small room fast — and he went out just as fast: right through the window. And he took both halves with him.

Luckily, there was about five feet of snow below and he didn't hurt himself. All I could hear him shouting was:

"You dirty sons of bitches, and me your friend, too."

We hung a couple of blankets over the broken window and went back to bed.

* * *

Until the army got rolling and organized the canteens, there was a marked lack of recreational facilities. There was only one 250-seat theatre and there was a two-block line-up every night. When the dances at the canteens got going the procedure was to pick up girls in town and run them out in army carry-alls. They were unloaded at the door of the hut and marched inside and the chaperones didn't allow them to leave until the carry-alls called for them again. The men-women ratio was 20-1.

* * *

Although food was cheap, thanks to the Wartime Prices and Trade Board profit ceilings, eating was a problem, it was recalled by Bill Porterfield, a NAR accountant; Don Leach, a tire store operator, and Tom Lauder:

A meal of soup, pork chops, potatoes, bread and butter, pie and coffee cost 45 cents.

There were seven Chinese restaurants. They were all small and they ran 24 hours a day along with nickel-a-play juke boxes playing Kate Smith singing "God Bless America" for 23 hours a day. It became a trade practice to fill up a place, lock the doors and feed the diners then bring the next corps of hungry people. But it was common to see the places so jammed the waiters couldn't get to the doors to lock them. Even without locked doors you couldn't get in for hours. Many railroad people would go to the grocery store for biscuits and cheese and take them back to the job.

When the Ho-Lem family first came to town to run dry cleaning and laundry businesses, they found the best means of getting something to eat was to help wash dishes at a friend's restaurant, then eat with the staff. The restaurant couldn't hire enough staff and were glad of getting dishwashers.

To order a meal of one's choice was next to impossible. There was a menu some place. We seldom saw it, though. If you were fortunate enough to get a table the waitress dropped some bread and butter as she went by and, occasionally, a bowl of soup. Then she would bring you whatever "special" the cooks had made for the day — stew, pork shops, Swiss steak and other meals that could be mass-produced in large kettles. You ate it and liked it. The staff had very little chance to clean up.

Army medical inspectors were around town every week. They inspected every solitary place: restaurants, lanes, yards and even houses. When they discovered a restaurant that was pretty filthy, they'd walk in, place armed soldiers at front and back doors and tell the Chinese to clean it up before they would allow another GI to come in there. They'd order everyone out and military police would stand guard until they scrubbed the place from top to bottom and it was shining and spotless. If the Americans were going to send GIs into battle to get killed they wanted healthy GIs sent in.

Besides providing an upstairs room for a spot of gambling, the Chinese restaurateurs were prone to engage in a few tosses of the dice themselves. Thus at any particular time it was not possible to establish ownership of a cafe.

* * *

Cecil Mah had the Alaskan Cafe at the east end of town. He went into the unemployment insurance office one day for help. Bruce Ballah, in charge, recalled he heard a voice:

"Mr. Ballah. Mr. Ballah?"

I couldn't see anybody. He wasn't five feet tall and I couldn't see him standing below the counter.

"I can hear you but I can't see you."

He made a jump and I saw his head bob up and down.

"Oh," I said, "Cecil. It's you."

"Yes. I need some help badly."

"Well, I'll do what I can."

I sent a couple of waitresses to the Alaskan. The next day he came back.

"Have you got a place for a couple of waitresses?"

"Why, Cecil?"

"I lost the cafe gambling last night. I got to start over from scratch."

"That's normal for you. Where are you going?"

"I dunno. Can you get me a job, too?"

"Sure," I said, and sent him down to cook for old Hart at the hotel at Pouce Coupe. He did very well there. It was not long before he came back to Dawson one day:

"Well, I'm back in business. I have another cafe. Can you get me a couple of waitresses?"

* * *

The most difficult part of Dawson Creek's wartime reality was the housing shortage — an acute shortage. A tarpaper shack was a king's palace. Ten men could be living in such a place, it is recalled by Paul Louiselle, a trucker who became manager of Loiselle Transport Ltd.:

They were lucky. Some built homes out of packing boxes. Others lived in holes in cutbanks. Every old broken-down or deserted lean-to or barn within 20 miles was "drug in," repaired and waterproofed.

I knew a couple of truckers who were living in a big double backhouse.

Somehow a place was found for everyone to bunk even though some places were crude and shacks sprang up in the most unlikely places. This was before the Third World was ever heard of. Dawson Creek was the Third World.

Young fellows coming to town went forlornly from door to door asking for a room for themselves or a place to bring their wives. Housewives took pity on them and moved their own families into unfinished upstairs rooms. Somehow the booming voice of Lorne Greene (later the star of television's Bonanza) reading the CBC news seemed to boost their morale; he could only be heard in a living room on a big old console radio.

One of the sources of Dawson Creek housing was Pouce Coupe. Some houses and businesses were picked up and moved bodily. This was a sore point with Pouce, which was desperately trying to maintain its identity as the chief county town. But Dawson Creek and its citizens took great pleasure in getting back their own with this exodus of buildings.

* * *

Even some government officials had difficulty providing accommodation for their families. Bruce Ballah recalled:

In the summer of 1942 my wife and four-year-old daughter came to stay with me. There was absolutely no accommodation so we had to live in a tent for six months. Somebody loaned us an old set of army bedsprings and we put blankets on them for a mattress. You couldn't buy a mattress there then. When it got pretty cold in the fall, they had to move back to Edmonton.

A major highway is not built without attracting heavy traffic. Dawson Creek became a major truck centre with its streets full of vehicles at all times.

Stand on any corner and one could see trucks from the U.S. Army, Canol project, Fort William, Saskatoon, Hagersville, Ont., Kingston, Kenora and Calgary. They were hauling oil and gas, lumber to build camps, frozen beef, potatoes, canned milk and vegetables, human cargoes of carpenters, laborers and soldiers all over the place.

They came singly and in large convoys of as many as 20 for protection in case of trouble. By spring everyone had begun to hate trucks and truckers and their incessant noise. In below-zero weather the motors were never shut off (this was before the days of block-heaters). In real cold weather watchmen were on the job driving trucks around three or four blocks all night one at a time. At times watchmen would jack up the rear ends, put them in gear and keep them idling all night, thus adding to the racket.

True to superstition, fires always occur in threes. This happened in Dawson Creek at the 1942 year end: the Ho-Lem dry-cleaning plant fire, the jail burned down and then the big dynamite explosion and fire.

* * *

The town jail burned December 26 when the stove blew up. Albert Langdon, an employee of Miller Construction Company, a prisoner, was burned to death, it was recalled by Oscar Albanati, a trucker:

About 12:30 a.m. police were called to the Dawson Hotel, where Langdon was on the roof raising hell and firing a gun. He was taken to the town lock-up and lodged in the single cell. While he was being processed, Ray Hunter of Okes Construction Company came in a battered condition and said he had been robbed. Four B.C. Provincial Police and Sgt. Bartlett of the military police went out to track down his assailant and left Langdon in the cell. It later turned out Hunter had been drunk and fell into a ditch and lost his money.

The police did not return to the lock-up but went out to a party at the Public Works Administration quarters at the east end of town.

I first became aware of the fire when Wiegan, my partner, and I had returned from a road trip and were down at the shack cooking up a late supper. We heard shots and noises:

"What the hell goes? Are the Japs here?" I yelled.

When we saw the fire's reflection, we went downtown to see what we could do. The scene was terrifying. Men were running around frantically trying to find the cops and get the key to allow Langdon to escape.

We tried to break down the door but we couldn't get in. Some guys got the idea of trying to ram down the door with an army truck. They took a couple of whacks at it but were driven off by the heat. The chemical fire engine was out of service that night because the tanks had been sent to Edmonton for recharging. The GIs tried to get a chain on the cellblock and pull it out but it was too late.

We almost went crazy trying to get Langdon. It was painful to hear his terrified yelling. But the heat drove us away. Langdon finally crawled under a bunk and when they finally did get to him he was just charred flesh.

An official enquiry was held but no blame was attached to the police. The official reports indicated they had gone to a restaurant for coffee. It was established they were within their rights locking up a drunk. However, instructions were given to post a guard in future on all prisoners.

Langdon's father from Idaho brought a charge of criminal negligence against police but official records don't indicate the outcome.

10

Canadian Surveyors Become Golden-Haired Boys

When the 341st Engineering Regiment arrived in Dawson Creek, May 1, 1942, its task was to build a preliminary road 275 miles to Fort Nelson from Fort St. John. The GIs pushed off into dense bush country over high rolling hills and mountains and deep valleys cut by numerous creeks, rivers and muskegs. The job had to be done yesterday in wilderness that had never been opened for settlement.

The army was required to follow a route surveyed by Public Roads Administration location and surveying parties sent into the field a month and a half before it arrived. The PRA had seven location parties spaced six miles apart whose job was to locate half a mile of final line each day.

Back home, PRA survey crews had been used to laying out roads in federal parks where accurate detail and contour maps were made in advance. This was impossible in British Columbia as no such maps existed for this area. They thus had to revert to the old orthodox method of locating: foot reconnaissance and numerous aerial flights over the area. It was impossible for the survey crews to make their half a mile a day.

The PRA was required to be meticulous about recording the location of the highway to allow it to file plans of it in the registry offices of

British Columbia, the Yukon and Alaska. Eventually the road had to be turned over to these jurisdictions and border crossings accurately tied in.

In no time at all the 341st had caught up to PRA road locaters with their bulldozers. They were equipped to build 2 1/2 miles of road a day but were not making it, the greatest hold-up being lack of knowledge where to build the road. At that point the 341st figured that if it was to get the job done it would have to go into the business of projecting its own location.

In making this move, Lieut.-Col. Albert L. Lane and 341st top brass had been informed of a newer, faster method of locating the route by R. Melville Smith, deputy minister of highways for Ontario and one of the PRA management contractors brought in by PRA to undertake construction of a section of the permanent road. The new procedure had been successfully used to locate highways in northern Ontario (including the Trans-Canada Highway) in bush terrain similar to that the U.S. Army was now trying to push through. It was largely unknown outside of Ontario.

* * *

Smith told the army brass he could send in a team of surveyors from Ontario who could pick the route right off aerial photos "with no trouble at all." One of the team was R.N. Johnston of Toronto. He recalled:

Lane reluctantly agreed to try the new aerial mapping procedure. His officers' adoption of our revolutionary new technique (which proved invaluable all up and down the highway) got off to an uncertain start, principally because some of them had difficulty grasping it. However, once we got the photos we needed and they had caught on to what we had to offer, nothing was too good for us. We could practically write our own ticket as road locating speeded up to 10 miles a day.

Previously, I was forester in charge of aerial surveys for the Ontario Department of Lands and Forests, and when I retired I was director of research. The technique was pioneered in the 1920s when the department was engaged in mapping and building fire and access roads in northern Ontario wilderness.

In an endeavour to speed up road location through bush country, Holly Parsons and I discovered we could make use of aerial photos. Stereoscopic images of aerial photos, when well taken, give a reasonably accurate three-dimensional image of the ground. With the use of a simple stereoscope it was thus possible to mark the best route on a map in advance of sending a ground location party stumbling around in the bush to find a route. Only the most extreme ground conditions, very poor photography or some combination of these two could mislead an experienced location engineer.

From these photos, formline maps — which were a type of rough contour map — could be produced. A rough line of the route could be marked on the map and the map sent out with a field party. The trick was to locate the selected photo line on the ground.

In 1932 Parsons and I carried out a trial survey of this type north of Parry Sound, Ont.

In general, we found it was possible to follow any marked photo-line, provided we first oriented the photo and used a surveyor's compass. By training ourselves to view photo pairs stereoscopically in the field, preferably without a stereoscope . . . what the aerial stereoscopic images contributed to the whole location problem is a line which is known to be most desirable to starting field work. In other words, ground trial lines are not necessary.

Having developed this procedure without anyone else having generally become aware of it, the Department of Lands and Forests carried on some years until the old Department of Northern Development engineers ran into trouble pushing through some colonization road locations in rough country north of Sault Ste. Marie. The Northern Development engineer in charge of this operation kept writing to his deputy minister, Charles Fullerton, in Toronto noting the country was exceedingly rough and that he needed extra money for the work.

Fullerton figured the engineer was trying to stuff him to get additional allotments for more elaborate surveys than were needed; or that his field parties were deceiving him. He had looked at the map of the shoreline of Lake Superior and noted it is fairly regular and does not have many abrupt points or deep bays and simply couldn't understand what the difficulty was.

He happened to mention the problem to E.J. Zavitz, deputy minister of lands and forests, and a close friend:

"Oh, my aerial survey people can tell you exactly what the situation along the Lake Superior shore is by the use of vertical photos and stereoscope images."

Fullerton decided to give the surveys a trial. They were so successful the first field party from Lands and Forests succeeded in locating the Trans-Canada Highway from Batchawana Bay to just north of the

Montreal River in this way. That is still the route of today's highway. The Northern Development Department continued using the surveys until its road-building section was taken over by the Ontario Department of Highways under R. Melville Smith. He, in turn, became one of its biggest boosters. Selling it to the armchair boys in Toronto was hard work but once the highways department personnel saw it worked they became its advocates.

Smith asked me and one of his own highways department location engineers, Ken H. Siddall, to go to Fort Alcan at Fort St. John June 1 to introduce our method to Lane's chief of reconnaissance, Maj. M.E. Erdofy, a politician from New York, and Capt. Harold E. Nelson. When we arrived we found things in a turmoil and ourselves on the hot seat.

Siddall didn't help our situation at times. He was a big strong husky fellow eight years younger than I with a history of three heart attacks but he wouldn't slow down and look after himself. He had never graduated from high school but he had the brains to succeed in his field and didn't care for ceremony or rank.

One night Col. Lane was giving the crew a briefing on the work for next day. Siddall had gone to bed but he could hear him through the tent. Lane said something he didn't agree with, whereupon he jumped out of bed and burst into Lane's tent:

"Colonel, you can't do that."

You didn't do that to three-star generals — but Lane took it in good part.

Another night he arrived in an army survey camp late and hungry. Their amateur cook was roused to get us some grub. He started dumping a bunch of canned food into a big pot.

"Hey, what's that stuff you're putting in there?" demanded Siddall, risking a knife in the guts. To which the cook didn't take offence but mildly replied:

"What do you care as long as it's food?"

We found the army had had considerable advice from local non-military types on where the highway should go and how the location should be carried out. Most of the advice was not helpful.

So the army staff figured we were just another pair of gold bricks — Canadians with some influence who had to be endured for a time at least. The army engineers are a proud organization and the idea that outsiders could show them how to do their work was not welcomed, particularly when the outsiders were foreigners. They were able, competent engineers but they were slow to accept our new aerial location technique — just as the Ontario Department of Highways was skeptical about it a decade previously.

Aerial photography was not new to them. It was just that photographs with contour lines on them didn't mean anything to them. They were used to something else and they resisted the new.

We were in trouble because their people competent to take aerial photos for map making had been sent to the Pacific campaign and only greenhorns were left who knew little about plotting photos and they had difficulty getting the kind of photos we needed. When they finally did do what we asked the film had to be flown 1,000 miles to Seattle for processing, resulting in delays. Then we, ourselves, caused a further delay because it took us more than a week to find an identifiable object on the ground.

Erdofy and Nelson began to talk within our hearing about where they expected to be assigned after they were turfed off the job due to our incompetence.

But then a miracle occurred. We finally — just when they were ready to ship us home — were able to locate a muskeg shaped like a postage stamp and we were able to use the photos in the way we described.

Talk about the fortunes of war! From the camp pariahs, we became the golden-haired boys overnight. We were taken on strength as special corps majors, became senior Fort Alcan staff officers and enjoyed the novel and pleasant sensation of having Gen. Patsy O'Connor, an ex-Philippine Corregidor commandant, accept our recommendations without question. We were much flattered later when we were asked to go out and do the same job on the Burma Road but when they couldn't give us the assurance of working for them we didn't make any commitment.

Our technique eliminated the uncertain, tedious and slow process of putting out try lines for location. By the use of the photographs we could say:

"This is definitely the easiest way you can go through here."

The experienced interpreter could distinguish the different types of vegetation in the area: poplar growth denoted good dry ground but alder, willow and buckbrush were interpreted as wet ground; jack pine indicated sand and gravel, also well-drained; dense growths of small-size spruce and tamarack usually meant muskeg country and large spruce were indicative of fair ground conditions.

With the use of parallax bars it was quite simple to calculate the differences in elevation of hills and ravines.

For a while, Ken and I were the only two able to do the interpretation work on the aerial photos with the stereo pairs. We later taught several others to use them — but it wasn't a simple task. It required a bit of practice.

Capt. Nelson was assigned to work with us. He was quite a go-getter, an ambitious sort of fellow. We showed him how to use the stereo pairs. He said:

"Oh, yes, I see that. It's fine."

We thought he did. But we found out he didn't. Only about three weeks after that he got into a little trouble in deciding we should go through several muskegs. It was then I learned Nelson hadn't really grasped what I had told him and was getting by with guesswork. Some people will do that. You'll show them something and they'll say, "sure, I see it," but they don't. Siddall and I did about 95% of the actual location work between Fort St. John and Fort Nelson.

The routine we set up for our location work went like this:

We'd get in a bunch of aerial photos taken in the direction the road was supposed to go. In the Fort St. John office we would lay out a line on them as it was the only place we had a large enough desk space. We'd take the marked photos and go out ahead to the location party. This involved travelling by jeep and pack horse. Neither Ken nor I had ever ridden before but the horses were quiet. Along with the leader of the party we would mark out a line on the ground that we had marked on the photos by blazing trees.

The rest of the party followed, knocking down a few trees so the bulldozer operators could see the line. Then after a few days we'd go back to the office where another batch of photos would be awaiting us.

We found out later Col. Lane had personally tried to establish a location before we came. He had joined Erdofy's reconnaissance party and attempted to do the work with a compass sitting on a bulldozer to get the angles. Using a compass was a terrible thing to try to make a road location with as it would double back on itself and everything. Sitting on a bulldozer was equally bad as the compass always points to the dozer. So he'd have to get off and walk when warned by the surveyors about this. He did quite a few miles this way and we'd often come across his marks while doing work farther on.

Because the road had to be pushed through in a hurry, it was imperative to select a route with a minimum of river, stream and swamp crossings and with as little dirt to move as possible.

The aim of the locaters was, further, to keep to the top of all ridges and to make all wooded sidehill and riverbank cuts with a southern exposure as the sun's rays always penetrated them first in the spring and thawed out the road faster. However, there were some exceptions:

like the Prophet River.

The Prophet is a main river in the area and is subject to violent flooding. The trappers and Indians who knew the area advised the 341st to build a 300-foot bridge across it, taking the road to higher ground on the north bank. From previous experience, the 341st location engineers were inclined to agree, pointing out that taking the road along the south bank would mean putting it through a generally swampy "impossible" route.

However, as the result of our technique a new investigation was done, which showed the "impossible" route on the south side traversed shallow muskeg which could be easily dealt with. This speeded up the job considerably and avoided a costly bridge.

Originally it was planned the road would swing generally northwest to a point near Pink Mountain, seek a favorable crossing of the Sickanni Chief River and thence 100 miles along the Minnaker and Prophet Rivers to Fort Nelson. Aerial reconnaissance by Siddall and me turned up a better route and plans were changed. At Mile 90 from Fort St. John, the road turned north abruptly, crossed the Beatton River at Mile 100 and 15 miles further the Sickanni Chief.

Because of our close connections with the 341st as officers, we developed considerable respect for the GIs.

One of the things that struck me was many of the younger ones had come from President Roosevelt's Civilian Conservation Corps camps. They thought getting into the army and away from CCC drudgery was wonderful because they could now accomplish something useful for the nation. Many had run away from home to join up.

Others had been unemployed for years and had felt rejected by society. Now they were in the army where they were doing something that everyone praised them for: accomplishing a project foremost in the annals of engineering feats: pushing that preliminary road through in record-breaking time. The U.S. Army was proving to the world it could accomplish what was justly thought impossible in such a short space of time. It necessitated officers often working 24 hours a day. Their morale had improved and they worked like the devil. They learned what it was like to go full out for something.

Most of them were happy with long hours and strenuous jobs — much happier than they had ever been previously.

My impression of the engineer corps GIs was they were much more strict in rules and regulations when on duty than the Canadian or British armies. Off-duty, however, GIs and non-commissioned officers mixed freely, i.e., there was an army distinction between ranks but no class distinction.

* * *

Another point about the 341st was that prior to being activated March 6 at Fort Ord, California, only the top brass could be classed as engineers. The majority of the 1,200 men on strength were enlisted men with mostly other skills.

When they reached Dawson Creek in the middle of the night of May 1, it was below freezing and they were dumped off the train at a siding, with no tents or blankets.

The first work on the new road started at Charlie Lake, eight miles north of Fort St. John. The initial task was to drain, clear and corduroy a 500-foot stretch of muskeg out of camp. Corduroying consisted of cutting small diameter trees and laying them crosswise to form a roadbed. The bulldozers and other machinery had been delayed in transit.

Some of the young GIs got the reputation of being lazy when ordered to do this hand labor. This was not the way to do it. It was inefficient and those kids knew it. Therefore the sergeants had quite a job keeping them working with shovels, axes, brush hooks and machetes. As soon as their backs were turned, all work would stop and beefing would start. However, with the arrival of the bulldozers, it was a different story. They took hold and began to build roads. They'd even fight to get on these machines — and they'd work 18 hours a day.

* * *

When the 341st came on the scene and roared into action, the PRA had to change its plans because it was falling behind, it was recalled by L.J. L'Heureux, then a University of Saskatchewan second-year engineering student and later chief superintendent of the Canadian Armament Research and Development Establishment at Valcartier, Que.

The PRA changed its survey method and despatched an advance party to run a stadia line or rough survey. Walter Polvi, another engineering student, and I were members of this party.

Polvi had serious doubts about ever making it into Fort St. John this day in the middle of May on the first plane flight either of us had ever made.

We arrived in Edmonton from Saskatoon by train. Before flying out at 2:00 p.m. we had big steaks for lunch; a mistake, as we found out later. But this was the custom in the West and we ate steaks.

The aircraft was a 12-passenger Lockheed Lodestar. Although it was terribly rough I was sitting there rather enjoying it. I thought this was what flying was supposed to be and didn't know enough to be scared. We had seat belts but it seemed as if I was at the end of the belt half the time not touching the seat. My feet hit the ceiling a couple of times. I didn't throw up but I felt very badly with this big meal inside me. The passengers were all sick, including Polvi, the stewardess, even the co-pilot. The pilot was too busy trying to fly the plane to get sick. I said to him on landing at Fort St. John:

"We hit some pretty rough weather."

"Yes, it was rough. At one spot we went up 2,000 feet on an updraft and came back down 3,000 feet on a downdraft. It was one of the roughest flights I ever had."

The next day we were solidly on the ground on pack horses and started surveying from the first benchmark. Transportation was provided by a dozen pack horses owned by Don McDougall of Fort St. John, along with a cook and horse wrangler.

Besides Polvi and I, the party comprised Donald W. Ferguson, 35, a civil engineer from San Francisco, who had a lot of experience in Eastern jungles; W. Keith Bothwell, University of Alberta engineering student, with whom I alternated as recorder and marked all stations on the trees, and G. Harvey Maloney, who had spent three summers in a relief camp working on the Edmonton-Jasper highway.

A day or two ahead of our party were two engineers whose job was to blaze trees where we were to pass the stadia line. These were Carl Shubert, an experienced PRA engineer, and Lieut. Charles Neesom, Jr., of the 648th Engineering Regiment. They were accompanied by a couple of old-time packers and surveyors from Fort St. John.

We were accompanied by 60 soldiers from the 341st with axes instead of rifles, under the command of Master Sgt. Raymond Hallowell.

Thirteen GIs of Company B started out trail blazing May 19. The rest of the company didn't see these men again until August 20 when the job was finished.

Initially the work went quite well. However, it slowed up when we got into rough terrain, packers failed to bring enough food and attacks of infectious hepatitis began knocking out soldiers. This cut our progress to less than a mile a day from 10 and that was maintained only by us taking to the bush and helping GIs cut trees. First thing we knew, the lead bulldozers of the 341st had caught up.

After the aerial location was introduced, progress picked up again but the PRA's job became just recording a legal description of where the road was.

Besides the sickness among the GIs, another delay was caused when a master sergeant with Shubert got lost. We looked for him three days — to no avail. Then a group of three soldiers from New York volunteered to look for him — and they got lost. So we had to stop and look for them, too.

Some experienced tracking Indians were brought in and, after two days of following his trail, found him beside a creek. He was attempting to spear fish. They brought him out to an engineering troops camp behind us. He wasn't in good shape as it had been raining three solid days. His matches got wet and he couldn't make a fire. He was still walking but weak.

Shubert had left the sergeant at a certain point while he went ahead to investigate a slope. There was a mix-up and when Shubert got back the sergeant was gone. After he was found strict instructions were given that nobody was to leave the trail.

This sergeant was lucky. One guy wandered away and was never found. A few stories got around about soldiers who took off from camp and were never seen again. It was said they had shed their uniforms, acquired civvies and made their way back home to the U.S. The veracity of these stories was rather doubtful. I only knew of one GI who tried it. He was from the South and had resented the fact he had been drafted. He didn't want anything to do with the military and hated the rough life. He was a pretty good soldier all the same. He made one and one only attempt to go over the hill. He left camp and got out in the bush one night alone and thought that was tougher than the army so he came back quickly.

It was easy for the experienced and inexperienced to get lost. In forests north of Fort St. John burned-over spruce comes back in very thick, so thick a man can hardly push his way through it. There was a growth of it on the way to camp and the trail back went around it but one day I said to a couple of GIs with me:

"Let's cut this corner this time and walk through it."

It wasn't long before we were turned around and completely lost. I couldn't get my bearings. The only thing left to do was put our heads down and push our way through with these boy-scout-type felt hats we were wearing. By the time we finally did push our way out of this small grove, the rest of the party had stopped and was looking for us.

Once the joint PRA-army effort at road location and building got organized and under way, there was no respite from work. I was in there for three straight months of seven-day weeks from sun-up to sundown — and that made the work day from 15 to 18 hours. Although we had horses available to get us around a bit we covered immense distances on foot. There were times when we had to walk eight miles from camp to start work. We walked an average of 25 miles a day, including to and from the job site.

We encountered everything in the way of weather. At one time 4½ inches of rain fell and shut the job down two weeks because of mud. The bulldozers couldn't move because fuel deliveries couldn't be made. At other times it was stifling hot with black flies and horse flies making life miserable. After the middle of August we encountered two feet of snow. It appeared without notice one night, covered the trees and then started melting. For three days water was pouring all over us and, as we had no raincoats, we were soaked all the time.

While the GIs were quartered in bell tents most of the time in the field, our only shelter at night was a tarpaulin which we threw over spruce boughs and hung mosquito netting over it. During the night it became very cold and we'd wake up in the morning and find our hair caught in the ice.

We took this and other rough outdoor life in stride. Working on this job was of inestimable value to my training as an engineer. Because there was no way to get out and spend money, I came out of there with $700 — and back at Saskatoon was one of the richest men on campus. I felt like a millionaire after having had to get by the previous two years on $400 a year.

When I left Fort St. John and plunged into the bush and muskeg in May, it was a one-restaurant, one-hotel, one-general-store village. When I returned 3 1/2 months later — this time along a new 275-mile road from Fort Nelson in a staff car as big as a Cadillac — it was almost impossible to believe the transformation. We in the bush didn't realize what had been going on in "civilization."

There were now seven restaurants, enlarged beer parlor, gas stations and a boom-town population of 5,000. There were even girls — a big event for me after having lived in isolation so long. There was also a shuttle bus service to the army camp. The most interesting place to me was a weather-beaten log building with a big sign on the outside: EAT.

The morale of the GIs was much higher than the week I arrived. I flew in at the time of the greatest tragedy on the construction of the highway: 12 GIs drowned in Charlie Lake.

Rains had mired down operations at the west side of the lake and a 341st unit was ordered to move construction machinery nine miles across the lake by ponton raft to work on high ground on the other side to keep the job going. These rafts were made of airplane-type floats lashed together, surmounted by planks and powered by heavy outboard motors. The sat very low in the water but they could carry a truck or bulldozer.

Maj. John Turvey of Houghton, Mich., was in charge of the movement May 15, utilizing an experienced sergeant and GIs from the 74th Light Ponton Engineering Company attached to the 341st. Turvey was a fine, efficient young officer who took his job seriously and treated it as if he was in a war zone.

That day the lake was a bit choppy and the sergeant advised Turvey he was overloaded for the condition of the lake. Aboard were a bulldozer, a radio and Turvey's jeep. In a moment of anger at having his authority questioned, Maj. Turvey told the sergeant he'd damn well do what he was told or he'd be court-martialled. Famous last words. Turvey was drowned when a sudden squall and the choppy water flooded the outboard motor. With no power, the 17 persons aboard attempted to paddle ashore but the pontons filled with water and the raft turned turtle. Eleven others loaded down with heavy parkas, boots and packs also succumbed in the near-freezing water.

Gus Hudin, a trapper living on the lakeshore, rowed a mile three times and managed to get five ashore alive. He was later given the Humane Society of Canada medal for bravery as he put his own life in danger approaching those desperate men in his small boat.

That night as the 341st dragged the lake for the bodies of their companions, they were confronted by a brilliant display of northern lights, the only such display in the 15 months they were there. The eerie greenish patterns in the sky added to their already deep feelings for the dead.

At a military tribunal, a case was made that Turvey had exceeded his knowledge and used his authority as if he was in a war zone and that he and the men with him had drowned unnecessarily under those circumstances. Because those northern lakes were tricky and several other ponton rafts had sunk, they were all ordered boarded over so the water couldn't fill them.

* * *

Eighteen months later — October 26, 1943 — another accident with some similarities occurred on another northern lake. At that time 14 died at Carcross, Y.T., on Bennett Lake. The tragic incident was witnessed by Gordon Yardley, who was shingling the roof of his home in that small Yukon settlement:

A B-19 bomber had been in for repairs at the Whitehorse airport. Capt. McWilliams and co-pilot Borey, who were not entirely familiar with the characteristics of this aircraft, took it up for a test flight. Although it was against the regulations, 15 men hanging around the hangar piled in for the short flight to Skagway 100 miles away.

On the return trip two engines conked out as the de-icers on two carburetors had not been hooked up. The two good engines weren't performing well, either. McWilliams elected to try to reach a landing strip at Carcross used as a home base by George Simmons for his Northern Airways.

I could see the crippled plane coming and realized the pilot was going to try to make a landing as he kept dropping. When he was 20 feet above the lake he cut the engines and made a bellyflop into the lake. A big wall of water sprayed over the plane. The doors opened and 17 men climbed out onto the wings.

All the locals' boats had been pulled out of the lake for the winter except mine and it was quite a way across an inlet. George Simmons and I finally got this 18-foot motor boat under way. Cpl. Bolger and Constable MacDonald of the RCMP ran and got their boat out of storage, couldn't get the outboard started and rowed out.

As we got underway, the plane had started to sink and the men were all in the water. The situation was all the more disastrous because they were all within 30 feet of comparative safety. The craft had hit the water near a ledge jutting out into the water with only three feet of water covering it. It dropped off sharply into deep water at that point. They could almost have jumped off the wing onto the ledge and waded ashore. Of course, they didn't know the bench existed and the people on shore had no way of making them hear that safety was so close at hand.

The other shore looked closer and some of them started swimming for it, doing the Australian crawl. They were good swimmers but they quickly became paralyzed in the cold water and none made it.

None but McWilliams and Borey took their seat cushions with them as life jackets. Neither were they aware there was an inflatable life raft aboard big enough to float the whole bunch.

Simmons and I managed to grab four. I pulled one in by his broken wrist. The Mounties picked up two. Borey was saved but McWilliams wasn't. They were treading water with their seat cushions. Borey said to him:

"How are you doing?"

"I'm doing all right but I wonder how the rest of the boys are making out?" McWilliams asked.

Borey looked around to see. He turned back to say something to McWilliams. The seat cushion was there but McWilliams wasn't. The severe cold water must have stopped his heart. They were almost shoulder to shoulder but McWilliams disappeared without a sound. It was that fast.

We picked up one more. The Mounties managed to save two. When we got them to my place they weren't complaining of the cold. They were complaining about burning skin caused by aviation fuel which soaked their clothes.

They were all wearing web belts — some kind of army issue. The belts had shrunk in the water and tightened up around their bodies. We had to cut them off with a knife.

After we got the guy who nearly went down undressed (I saved him by going overboard while Simmons hung onto my feet) he came to. The first thing he asked for was a drink of water — this after he had swallowed half the lake! Then he asked for another glass; he said he was awfully dry.

Before we brought the six survivors ashore somebody had phoned Whitehorse to notify the U.S. Army Air Force. In no time at all they had a doctor aboard a Norseman plane and on the way to Carcross.

Nobody told the Mounties the doctor was on the way. One of the men they picked up was semi-conscious from exposure. They decided to move him to Whitehorse hospital; all he likely needed was to be warmed up. They commandeered an old car and bundled him into the back seat and took off 70 miles to the hospital. He died on the way. For this action they received an official reprimand. All the rest of us received official commendations from the U.S. War Department.

By the time the doctor arrived all were conscious and sitting around smoking. Two were in bad shape and the doctor ordered two ambulances to Carcross to transport them, although I didn't think there was any need for that. One of the ambulances crashed over a bank and was wrecked beyond use.

The doctor decided to drive the two to the hospital, leaving the young sergeant behind to fly home by the Norseman the next morning.

I heard them taking off from the airstrip the next morning at 8.

Suddenly the roar of the Norseman stopped. There was a big explosion and flames shot 150 feet into the air. The Anglican minister and I sped to the airport in his car.

There we found the pilot had lost control of the plane on the gravel strip and it had veered off towards the hangar. I guess he figured he could lift over the hangar so he never cut his power. But he clipped two feet off the tail of a plane on the tarmac. The impact swung him into the big A-frame used by Simmons' mechanics for lifting motors out of planes.

We had a terrible sight to face. The burning Norseman was hung up in the A-frame and the pilot and sergeant burned to death strapped into their seats.

This was truly a black day for Carcross, with 14 lives lost in this tragic series of events — events that brought the war close to home.

* * *

Maj. John Turvey of the 341st took his lead from Gen. J.A. (Patsy) O'Connor, who regarded the project as a strictly military operation — and ran it as such. If lives and equipment were lost that was the fortunes of war. R.N. Johnston, who was in O'Connor's headquarters at Fort St. John, recalled an incident which demonstrated this:

The bulldozer at the head of the line came to a big muskeg one day and the driver started into it and it began to sink. There was no other way. The crew would have to go a long way around the staked route.

The officer in charge radioed O'Connor for instructions. O'Connor got on the blower and asked them:

"Is there any possible way to go around?"

"No," came back the answer.

"Well, give her another try," he said. They did and about an hour later called back and still maintained they couldn't make it.

"How far is it you have to cross?" demanded O'Connor.

"Oh, about 350 yards," the radio crackled.

He told the caller to run the bulldozer into the muskeg and put fill over the top of it if need be. They demurred about this — and it nettled O'Connor.

"Look," he said, "you're holding up an operation that concerns 10,000 men. I don't care if you have to drive four or five bulldozers in there and lose them. Now go ahead, drive them in. They're dirt cheap to us."

They finally drove in a couple of machines and they discovered it wasn't as deep as they thought. When they first went in it was apparently pretty deep but it got shallower towards the middle and they were able to scoop out the muck and fill it from there on.

Using the bulldozers for fill enabled them to get through. The old rascal was right. It sounded crazy but they were holding up a vast military operation. They couldn't move and they had to get through. And they did.

Once they got their bulldozers moving in high gear the 341st was able to clear a 200-foot right-of-way at an average of three miles a day.

* * *

The next job to which they were assigned after reaching Fort Nelson was improving the road north of Fort Nelson. Two of the chief obstacles with which they had to contend were the road location past Summit Lake and Muncho Lake. In both these locations the road had been taken up over a mountain rather than on a bench at a lower level. The grades were so steep and dangerous it was only safe to negotiate them in four-wheel-drives. In wet weather even these vehicles needed help from bulldozers.

The 341st brought in 1,600 cases of dynamite to widen a narrow ledge along the shore of Muncho Lake. It was a temporary job. Many trucks had slid off into the lake and lives had been lost.

Next season a contract was let to Wallace Mackey Company of Weston, Ontario, to blow off the entire cliff along the lake to widen the road. A specialized construction technique — a costly one — was to drive in coyote holes at an angle with dead chambers right-angled at each end. They would then be loaded with tons of dynamite which would lift the side off the mountain. The army ordered this work abandoned late in 1943 as the war in the Aleutians was quietening down. The holes may still be found there.

Later the road was widened by chipping away further at the cliffs.

It was the same story at Summit Lake, except the grade was steeper and more dangerous and the cliff face had to be blown off to construct a bench. This was a more urgent job as it was impossible to carry the road along the water's edge since the lake at this point was in a narrow canyon three-quarters of a mile long.

Civilian contractors were brought in November, 1942, to reroute the road behind the mountain on a less-severe grade. Emil Anderson Construction Company of Fort William, Ontario, later of Hope, B.C., was awarded a contract for blasting and removing 300,000 cubic yards of rock. The crews drilled coyote holes 200 feet deep. Into these they placed 107 tons of dynamite.

Some trouble was experienced in getting the dynamite to the site because in the middle of the haul the Dawson Creek explosion occurred and government officials became edgy about the way dynamite was being handled off rail through town.

On a Sunday afternoon at the end of February, they blew it. It was a tremendous explosion, one of the larger construction blasts in Canada at the time. It really wrecked that mountain, tearing away enough for a bench to carry the road.

* * *

On July 10, 1943, a cook in Anderson's camp was the patient in a dramatic mercy flight off Muncho Lake, it was recalled by Roy Robinson, a foreman for Storms Construction Company of Toronto:

The cook had a ruptured appendix. It was essential to fly him to Whitehorse Hospital. The nearest lake where a float plane could put down was Muncho Lake 70 miles away. The cook was loaded in a 843rd Signals Batt. truck with Anderson's nurse and started out. However, because of heavy rains the MacDonald River had flooded and washed out a bridge. They called our crew to throw a line across the river and string a cable so they could move the patient and nurse across in a boat. I was afraid the cable would break so I made a test run across in a boat. It held. I came back for the pair. I reached for the cable to pull the boat ashore. I'll be goddamned if the bank didn't give way and I went down into the fast-moving water with a pair of waders on. The boots quickly filled with water and I'd have been drowned had not the boys pulled me out. They kidded me for a long time about that:

"The first woman you see in a long time — and then you have to go and fall in the damned creek."

The patient was flown to Whitehorse and came through all right.

Bill Lee, NAR conductor, climbs
telephone pole to report stalled
engine — then collected demerits!

11

Northern Alberta Railways Becomes Strategic Route

Gen. W.M. Hoge, the first U.S. Army officer commanding the Alaska Highway, was still angry 25 years later when he discussed the problems he had with Washington.

Exasperation was evident as he recalled how deskbound bureaucrats tried their damndest to thwart his immense wartime project in the Canadian North:

I was given seven regiments of engineering troops in March, 1942, and in getting them to the job site I was aghast at the rundown condition of the frontier railroads.

They were the Northern Alberta Railways, White Pass and Yukon and the Alaska Railway. They had all come out of the 1930s depression in bad shape. Some were almost derelict. We had to make do with three of the most decrepit and rickety pikes in existence.

Yet, despite the severe limitations, they eventually proved to be vital links that enabled us to move in thousands of tons of the materials we needed.

However, once my troops reached Canada and were sealed into the wilderness, Washington forgot all about us.

I began a barrage of criticism aimed at Gen. Brehon B. Somervell, chief of supply services for the U.S. Army, over his failure to deliver me the supplies I needed.

Somervell was an empire-builder who couldn't stand criticism. He flew to the job to see what I was raging about. One of the results of the visit was that it was decided the army would have to take over the operation of all three. This happened in the case of the White Pass and the Alaska Railroad. Railway operating battalions were moved in to assist the local forces.

The White Pass was a toy narrow-gauge (36 inches) railroad running 110 miles from Skagway in Alaska through British Columbia and then the Yukon to Whitehorse, crossing the precipitous Coast Range. The track was difficult to maintain under heavy traffic.

Gen. Somervell found the White Pass had seven engines of indifferent parentage and 100 cars. He saw to it more engines were brought in from Kansas Central, Silverton Northern, Dunsmuir Diggle and Co., one from a logging railroad in Oregon, one from a Hawaiian sugar operation and some that had been built for Iran and Iraq but not delivered. In addition three powerful decapods were ordered from Baldwin Locomotive Works. Thus at the height of the wartime boom there were 36 engines.

The U.S. government was able to divert a number of 36-inch gauge steel boxcars destined for South America. Eventually a fleet of 365 units of rolling stock were built up, including 26 passenger cars.

The army made arrangements to lease the White Pass October 1, 1942, but the move was illegal at the time. The reason was that it was against the law for a foreign government to do business on Canadian soil. But the federal cabinet of Mackenzie King passed an order-in-council under the Emergency Measures Act to make it legal.

The 770 Railway Operating Battalion of Clovis, N.M., with 402 men on the roster under Maj. John E. Ausland was sent in to run the railroad and improve the track. At full strength the battalion had a roster of 730.

The little railroad had averaged only 475 tons a week before the war. From October 1 to December 31, 1942, the same amount of tonnage was handled as in an average year. In the calendar year of 1943 tonnage went up to 281,000, dropped to 133,524 in 1944 and back to 38,000 in 1945.

On the peak day of operation, Aug. 4, 1943, 2,085 net tons were moved on 14 northbound and 23 southbound trains. Since this was more trains than there were engines, some engines obviously made several round trips.

* * *

As with the White Pass and Yukon, the Americans had designs on buying or leasing the Northern Alberta Railways, sending in few railway operating battalions, rebuilding the line with heavier rail and extending it to Whitehorse and Fairbanks. The NAR management haggled over an agreement (they were within $10,000) when the Americans decided to pull out of the negotiations. The railroad carried on without American input.

Reason for dropping negotiations was they had run a secret railway survey out of Prince George up the Rocky Mountain trench. This survey showed a more feasible route than the line to Dawson Creek from Edmonton. If they were going to get into the railway business, why try to upgrade a limping outfit like the NAR when they could have brand new trackage on the easy grades of "the trench?"

The man behind the "trench" survey was Col. Frederic A. Delano, chairman of the U.S. National Resources Planning Board. He was an uncle of President Franklin Delano Roosevelt and a railroad engineer who had been a former railroad president.

The railroad was to travel 1,200 miles straight up the trench between the Cascade and Mackenzie ranges. The trench was 7 to 15 miles wide, with plenty of gravel for roadbed and was, in fact, a site locater's dream.

With Prince George as the southern terminus, it would proceed to Watson Lake, Frances Lake, Pelly Banks, Carmacks and Fairbanks.

This was a hush-hush wartime survey very few Canadians ever heard about. Those who found the grade stakes around Watson Lake were told to keep their mouths shut.

Despite its perfect location, the Delano plan fell through. It had one big flaw. All the main population centres along that route were frequently fogged in, thus rendering it useless for air traffic. As there was a desperate need for airports, all work was abandoned on orders from James H. Graham, special assistant to the under-secretary of war after $2 million had been spent on engineering and surveys.

Before the arrival of Gen. Hoge and his engineering troops, the Northern Alberta Railways was a pioneer road handling mostly grain and hogs. Its main line ran from Dunvegan yards in Edmonton 500 miles northwest to Dawson Creek. Another line ran to Waterways and there were several branches.

The NAR became an important defence link as it put the Americans 500 miles closer to Alaska than any other land system. It enabled them to move supplies by the train-load — something they could never have accomplished as efficiently by truck as there were no paved roads into that country in 1942.

After the lease deal fell through, it proceeded on its own steam, as earlier explained.

* * *

The man who had the best insight into operations during the war was J.H. Vollans. He recalled:

J.M. McArthur was general manager. I had worked for him on the Canadian Pacific Railroad in Vancouver before he went to the NAR in 1935. He sent for me to come and take over the post of yardmaster in Dawson Creek January 1, 1943. Charles H. Dominy was superintendent there and he was three weeks behind in his sleep.

The NAR lines had been built by various entrepreneurs and were taken over by the province. The province tried to operate them but failed and the CPR and CNR bought them and operated them jointly from 1928.

When I arrived I found the NAR snowed under with the volume of traffic which had been thrown on it practically overnight. They had had no previous experience handling such volumes. Before the Americans arrived, 16 locomotives could handle the 24,000 cars of freight per year they moved, the twice-weekly passenger run to Dawson Creek, the twice-weekly mixed train to Lac La Biche and weekly to Waterways.

By 1943 we were handling 47,000 cars, by 1944 54,000. We had to schedule four freights daily to Dawson Creek and increased passenger frequency to daily.

The parent railroads had to send in 25 locomotives. We inherited some old CNR 2-10-0 decapods, which could get out of the Dunvegan Yards with 2,300 tons, and some ancient CPR 4-6-0s.

The master maniacs of the parent roads went through their rosters and palmed off all their lemons on us. How they must have rubbed their hands with glee at handing over to Charlie Stewart, our master mechanic, and Ted Faust, road foreman of engines, all those clunkers with steam leaks, flue troubles and other mechanical failures.

Stewart and Faust and all supervisory personnel were constantly on the road trying to keep those engines going. They just couldn't stand up under the continual pounding to which they were subject in extremely cold weather. There was no armchair railroading in those years.

NAR company policy was not to ask for deferments for any of its employees in the running trades called up for military service. Experienced men were let go and their places were taken by inexperienced engineers and firemen from the parent railroads.

The NAR track was all light (60-pound-to-the-yard) rail with a little 72-pound scattered around. The only heavy rail was 20 miles of 85-pound on the Smoky Hill. The whole line was built of old rails from other locations.

The ties were widely spaced and more than half needed replacement at the beginning of the summer of 1942. No tie plates had been used, not even on curves, tangents or bridges. This resulted in spread gauge and tipped rail which, in turn, caused many derailments.

The trestles — mostly of wood — were designed for 40-ton loads. It became necessary to move 60-ton loads over them. This was accomplished by reducing speeds to three to five miles an hour.

The engineers used to allege the trestles were so far out of line they had to climb up one side and down the other.

While the master mechanic dreaded the winter, the roadmaster looked forward to it. Cold worked in his favor as it froze the roadbed solid over the soft spots and he could move heavy loads on them.

However, the cold had its disadvantages. One 50-below night a crew pulled out of Grande Prairie with a car with a flat wheel. By the time he reached Dawson Creek the car had cracked 128 rails. For weeks trains were derailed until all the broken rails could be located and a supply of new rails could be brought in to repair the damage.

With the arrival of the spring thaw the roadbed became so bad in places the track sank almost out of sight. In Dunvegan yard we had to stop men from riding on the footboards of switch engines as the tracks had sunk below ground level and the engines were kicking up dirt.

Operating under the most adverse conditions imaginable, the crews were doing a tremendous job. Top speed for both passenger and freight trains was 30 miles an hour. West of McLennan it was 20 and, in addition, whole subdivisions were plastered with slow orders.

Ordinarily it required 24 hours to move a freight train the 220 miles between McLennan and Dawson Creek. However, at the peak wartime traffic periods it required four days. This was due to scheduling meets with many other trains and sidings jammed with freight cars. Usually a crew leaving McLennan with a heavy train had to pull half up the Smoky Hill at a time. Thus by the time they made the 90 miles to Rycroft, they'd have 12 hours in.

Maj. L. George Horowitz, a troubleshooter for U.S. War Department, made a trip over the line to Dawson Creek in mid-February, 1943, to make a report on the facilities available for movement of construction materials. He was appalled the NAR didn't have sufficient labor available to maintain the track even in its questionable condition. He questioned their ability to move more than 2,000 tons a day during the summer or 200,000 tons in an operating year.

He said to bring the capacity up to 4,000 tons a day, which was the capacity of the average single-track line, it would be necessary to import railway battalions and spend large sums.

Horowitz, it turned out, was too pessimistic. We overcame all the operating difficulties, spread gravel in appropriate places, extended passing tracks, laid additional trackage in all division point yards and added heavier rail. Much of this additional trackage was lifted after the war.

When I arrived at Dawson Creek it was very cold and everything was in a chaotic condition. There was traffic coming; traffic going; troops were on the move all over the place. The U.S. Army and the civilian contractors gave the appearance of not knowing what they wanted. They seemed to have no master plan.

The NAR yard had a capacity of 230 cars. The army's "temporary" railhead yards to the west of us (where the British Columbia Rail Road is now located) held 150. Both were jammed all the time. The problem was to make room for incoming loads. We always had to figure how we could get a train or two of empty cars out to make room for the incoming loads.

The U.S. Engineering District had built this large "temporary" yard on a sidehill. It was considered "temporary" because a permanent facility was in the works south and east of town. Thus, very little organization had gone into this railhead. Even so it was huge and elaborate by any standards then known in Western Canada.

John Wilcox, NAR master mechanic, was having a terrible time as there had been a fire in the new roundhouse. So he was back to "pulling" steam locomotive fires in an outside pit. The only other roundhouse on the railroad was in Edmonton and it was also hopelessly overtaxed.

To relieve the pressure, the Quartermaster Corps brought in some small Diesel locomotives capable of handling a couple of cars at a time, plus a couple of steam yard goats. Bechtel, Price and Callahan, management contractor on the Canol project, also brought a couple of Diesel switchers to their Waterways staging area.

Dawson Creek and Waterways thus made history by having Diesel switchers a couple of decades before Diesels replaced steam engines on

Canadian railways.

At Dawson Creek the army switching crews were inexperienced at first. At one point things got so badly bogged down (they couldn't move big enough cuts of cars with those little Diesels) they had to come over and ask a few of our off-duty brakemen to help them locate and switch out loaded cars. They took in a big yard hog and sorted out their yard.

When freight from the first supply trains arrived in Dawson Creek there were no freight sheds or unloading docks. Cars had to be unloaded along the tracks in the open until the freight could be moved up the highway. The U.S. War Department therefore bought 160 acres of land and ordered the USED to build a temporary unloading dock.

The USED called in E.W. Elliott Company of Seattle, Curran and Briggs of Toronto, engineering troops and NAR forces to extend the tracks and build platforms for the Quartermaster Corps so that, at least, perishable stuff could be stored off the ground. Some warehouses were merely platforms roofed over.

* * *

These installations quickly proved be too small, it was recalled by Dick Panter, superintendent for the R. Melville Smith management contractor:

Shortly after I arrived in July, 1942, I was contacted by Lt.-Col. Harry A. Schuppner, Dawson Creek division engineer for the USED, to expand the railhead facilities. He made it plain, first of all, the job would have to be done to army specifications and standards.

That was dandy but he didn't realize it would have taken nine months to get the lumber and hardware to do it his way — and he needed that facility and camp facilities nine months ago, not nine months into the future. I didn't argue. I said:

"OK. I'll build to your standards."

I used any lumber I could get my hands on. We managed to buy some locally. We had a small sawmill north of Fort Nelson turning out green lumber. I was able to buy some of the finest lumber in Washington State. But it wasn't enough and one day I had to call in a bunch of truck drivers:

"Go to any place within 100 miles of here and buy up all the dimension lumber you can get your hands on."

They did so and charged it to the Smith company and we, in turn, charged it to the USED.

At the same time we had another annoying problem with the USED to sort out.

The USED supervising engineer was Maj. E.M. Erdofy, an awfully tough sort of boy who wore one of those campaign hats. I think he'd had his face lifted. He handed me a set of plans and said:

"Build it."

Erdofy's plans called for a warehouse, two tracks, a warehouse, a road, a warehouse, a warehouse, two tracks and so on all the way along. I had Roy Mingall laying out the site. He was an instrument man who had done track work with me on the Canadian Pacific Railway. After the first day he came in and said:

"We can't lay it out the way they want it."

"Why not?" I asked.

"Well," he said, "it's on a 4 per cent grade and these warehouses are supposed to be on the same level across the yard."

I went in to see the USED. I started to explain to an engineering captain why we couldn't build the railhead according to Erdofy's plan. He said:

"I was an optician all my civilian life. I don't understand what it's all about. Will you meet the major at 10 a.m. tomorrow and explain this to him?"

I met Maj. Erdofy at 10 a.m. the next day:

"We can't do it according to your plans . . ." I started to say.

"Why not?" he demanded. "I did it at Baton Rouge. Why can't I do it here?"

"Because Baton Rouge is flat and this place isn't."

We walked out and took a look at it.

"See that? The land is rising on a 4 per cent grade and you can't keep them all at the same level".

He gave me a resigned look and said: "Well, go ahead and fix it up yourself."

We threw it together for them. They agreed to supply help for track-laying and the NAR supplied supervision which consisted of section foreman and helper. It was a full-time job for an army captain to pry enough troops out of hiding to lay track.

We finally got a good warehousing set-up out of it — but it wasn't to army standards. Neither were other buildings in the railhead complex which Schuppner called on the Smith organization to build.

After we finished it they sent out their architects with their slipsticks and tapes; they counted the boards and the number of nails in the boards. When they found it wasn't built with standard materials they were mighty annoyed and gave us a hard time. When it came to paying, the Americans said:

"Oh, we can't authorize payment for this. You haven't supplied us with three copies of tender."

"What do you want?" I asked. "If I'd taken the time to call for tenders we'd never have gotten the job done. You couldn't have put this out to tender anyway because we bought everything in a 100-mile radius."

They eventually came to the conclusion our way was right; but it shows the kind of difficulties we ran into.

They gave me a bad time about another building in the railhead complex. This was an ungodly long arena-shaped truck repair depot. It was so long we dubbed it "the Tunnel to Pouce" — supposedly because a truck travelling through it would emerge at Pouce Coupe.

It was operated so that a vehicle from a pick-up to a White Diesel could be driven in one end at night and a crew of 70 would have it out on the road next morning with a complete overhaul if necessary.

Specifications for the building called for a 50-foot clear span inside. Lack of materials stymied us until one of the superintendents of the Harold Harvey Company of Kingston, Ontario, came up with the idea of building arch ribs by laminating the shiplap our truck drivers had brought in. We prefabricated the arch ribs on the ground and swung them up with a crane.

Despite our ingenuity, Schuppner was ready to withhold payment. However, the only thing I can say is the "tunnel" served the purpose for which it was built and was still in service more than 25 years later as a school bus repair garage — long after many of the other buildings built by the army were torn down.

It was frustrating but we learned to be philosophical about solving our problems in those hectic days. We'd get word of 50 new construction men coming in on the train that night. Then I'd be faced with the problem of where to put them. One of the supply men would rush in with a plaintive plea:

"There aren't enough blankets."

"It's all right. Something will happen," was my philosophy.

By sundown another rail car would be opened and there'd be some blankets in it.

When War Department Troubleshooter Maj. Horowitz came through in February, 1943, he found the large temporary railhead at Dawson Creek had facilities for housing 2,000 people. Plans called for facilities to house 5,000, a hospital with 200 beds and facilities to handle 28,000 tons of freight a month.

However, he also found better facilities were required at Whitehorse and Fairbanks and he had the Dawson Creek expansion killed. The "temporary" railhead we built became a permanent one.

* * *

J.H. Vollans was only at Dawson Creek three months. He was then assigned to Dunvegan yards at Edmonton as superintendent of operations. It was chaotic. He recalled:

The Americans had many experienced railroad men in their transportation corps. Although some of them had held top jobs with big U.S. railroads — Lieut. Zimmerman, for instance, had been a yardmaster on the Southern Railroad from somewhere in Georgia — they never tried to push us around. They knew what our problems were and they helped us break a lot of rules getting that traffic moved.

Although they may have damned the NAR for its inadequacies many times, we heard many compliments from senior army personnel.

The entire operational problem was different at Dunvegan Yards than at Dawson Creek.

Maj. Fouchier and Capt. Donovan of the transport corps would show up at Dunvegan Yard with lists of cars several times a day. It was our job to locate these cars in the yard, switch them out and make up trains for Waterways, Dawson Creek or Peace River. They always wanted it done instantly.

It was usually impossible to work to the lists they supplied. Very often we wouldn't have half the cars as there was a tremendous back-up of cars on every siding on the parent roads as far back as the States.

We'd try to locate as many of these cars in Edmonton as possible and in other rail yards (and if not found we'd order them to Edmonton) and, what with 200 to 300 cars in our own yard to go through, it would take us hours to snake out 15 or 20 cars to get them moving north.

They wanted only the cars on the lists although there were cars with similar materials readily available on storage tracks.

If we had forwarded cars north from Edmonton and they didn't arrive at Dawson Creek, they would send out an expedition by road in a jeep or by railway on a track car to look for them in sidings or division points.

Expediters went to work fast April 2, 1943, when a crisis arose in the construction of the suspension bridge across the Peace River near Fort St. John. The river had started to thaw while they were erecting steel for the north tower from the ice.

Two cars of steel for the tower went missing on the NAR and, if not found right away, could shut down the job if the ice went out.

Rush wires were despatched. It was established the cars had left Pottstown, Pa., Feb. 22 and 24. They had passed through Edmonton March 30.

A frantic search was started up and down the line. April 3 somebody found the desperately-needed cars at McLennan. After some extremely competent talking on the part of the bridge contractors, the cars were rushed to Dawson Creek by special train April 4. The steel was rushed to the bridge site and the following day the tower was completed before the ice went out.

It was the army's theory it could load thousands of cars and hold them on sidings, paying demurrage, of course, and have them hauled north at will. It didn't work quite that simple for us — and resulted in a big state of confusion.

Some cars didn't turn a wheel for six months. Eventually an embargo had to be placed on the movement from the U.S.

Passenger service was just as hectic. A construction engineer who arrived in Edmonton in December, 1942, via the CPR found the NAR train 10 hours late, the station crowded with men sleeping on the benches and no hotel rooms available.

He found all trains crowded beyond St. Paul, Minn., with men coming to work in Edmonton and north. Some passengers even had to wait two or three days for a coach seat.

Those with duffel bags were the only comfortable ones as they were able to bring warm clothes with them. Others froze until warm clothing arrived in checked baggage.

As an example of the fact too much stuff was coming in and nobody knowing where it was required, there was that famous car of dynamite. Destined for the Canol project, it was ordered to Waterways. On arrival there it was ordered back to Edmonton and sent to Peace River. After a couple more moves it wound up in Dawson Creek. I understand it finally cost them $30,000 in transportation and demurrage charges before it was finally unloaded.

We ran a great many extras, specials and troop trains. In 1943 and 1944 we had 12 through freight crews working out of Dunvegan Yards and 16 out of McLennan plus passenger and wayfreight crews.

Not only did we lose cars but in cold weather, we used to "lose" the odd train. There were no telephones, block signals or short wave radios for despatching trains. All we had to depend upon was the telegraph.

A train on the run to Dawson Creek from Grande Prairie in zero weather would have engine failure — lose steam or run out of water — and not report in for hours. This meant we couldn't move another train till he reported in.

I was in the Dawson Creek station one 50-below night when the operator reported we had lost a train out in the bush somewhere near Hythe.

We began to hear a strange clicking on the wire. Finally the operator was able to read enough of it to find out that it was being made by Conductor Bill Lee. Bill had learned a bit of Morse code. He reported he had an engine failure.

To report the failure he had climbed a pole in this weather and had managed to cut one of the train order wires. He then worked the cut wire against the other and was able to tap out the message which gave us the location of the stalled train.

Bill didn't get any credit for using his ingenuity and knowledge to report his train out of action. The communications department took a dim view of him cutting the telegraph line.

The result was that instead of praise poor old Bill got 10 demerit marks on his record.

One of the reasons for failure of engines to produce steam was lack of good steam coal. The Americans were shipping in thousands of tons of coal from Seattle because miners here were far down on the selective service priority list and Canadian supplies were thus not dependable. However, the NAR had a policy of using as much domestic coal as possible, despite the fact this worked to its disadvantage in some cases.

It obtained some coal from the Gething mine at Hudson Hope, 80 miles west of Dawson Creek, but this was too "hard" and proved unsuitable for firing railway locomotives. It was necessary to mix sand with this to make it work.

At the same time the RCAF had hauled thousands of tons of softer Souris steam coal from Estevan, Sask., to nearby Fort St. John. It proved to be poor fuel for the boilers used at the airbase there.

The simple solution would have been to use the Hudson Hope coal at Fort St. John and the Souris coal at Dawson Creek on the NAR. But this never happened.

Things were busy for at least a year after the highway was completed. Both the military and civilian contractors took a great deal of equipment back out. A trainload of 25 flat cars loaded with jeeps, station wagons, cars and bulldozers left Dawson Creek every day for four months without any publicity. These vehicles were taken out for rebuilding and use elsewhere.

Before leaving, every vehicle had to be thoroughly examined by the NAR and a report made on its condition, otherwise the army would put in claims at the other end for every broken headlight and dented fender. One long day for inspectors was when 86 flat cars loaded with army vehicles left.

NAR passenger train crews were always a lusty group ready to assist a passenger keep whisky from going rotten in the bottles or assist drunks off the train or break up fights. Drinking and fighting aboard trains were so much a part of the scene nothing was usually done until a passenger complained.

If, for instance, a woman found a group of Indians were holding a drunken party in the women's washroom, the crew would feel constrained to form a flying squad and throw the offenders off at the next stop. Except sometimes they forgot to tell the engineer to stop!

Crews had trouble with drunks coming onto the property in other various manners.

One night a passenger train stopped with a terrific jolt. A Pullman porter running ahead to find out what happened met a brakeman who said:

"We hit a shack crossing the track."

It wasn't a shack but an old-time "caboose" used by threshing crews. It had stalled on the track while being towed to another set-up.

From the remains of the vehicle the train crew extracted eight occupants, all of whom were dead — drunk.

But uninjured.

For most Canadians the Second World War came to an end August 8, 1945, with the defeat of Japan. But for the accounting and auditing unit of the NAR the battle continued another 15 years — a battle with the U.S. government.

Because of its strategic location, the NAR became doubly important because great quantities of top priority rail freight could be routed right through from the U.S. without trans-shipment.

The way it performed drew this comment from the Toronto Star Weekly:

"The NAR has performed what almost amounts to a miracle. It has become one of the world's few strategic railways. The full story of its accomplishment will be told only after the war."

* * *

Shortly after the heavy movement began, the NAR found itself embroiled in a series of rate litigations.

Since the NAR was the destination carrier, it was its responsibility to collect all freight charges from the U.S. government and rebate proportional amounts to the originating and intermediate carriers.

Charles Anderson of Edmonton, auditor and long-time NAR employee, recalled what happened:

We suddenly found the U.S. General Accounting Office was making arbitrary deductions from passenger and freight bills we submitted. Inquiries revealed the deductions were land-grant freight discounts to which Uncle Sam claimed he was legally entitled. Because the land-grant deductions applied only to some U.S. carriers, the system had produced an extremely complicated rate structure.

In the early days the U.S. government, in order to encourage railways to build through certain unsettled territories, gave them permanent leases of public lands rather than sell them outright. (Evidently far-sighted legislators foresaw the day when railroads might curtail services or cease to operate over these right-of-ways but the right-of-ways might become valuable real estate after the railway left. They were a great deal more astute in dealing with their railways than the Canadian government was with the Canadian Pacific Railway.)

In consideration for the permanent leases, the railroads agreed to carry freight for U.S. government agencies at reduced rates. In order to compete for business during the depression, railways which did not have land grants offered lower rates or equalization to obtain government business. This made for a complicated rate structure; some of the tonnage rates had to be carried out to three decimal places.

The U.S. carriers contended the land-grant reductions did not apply to the U.S. Army, the PRA and other U.S. government agencies for the movement of freight out of the country onto a job in Canada. They therefore billed the freight at full rates.

The U.S. Army contended Canada was within the orbit of the continental U.S. and that the reductions should apply.

It was easy to see the NAR was caught in the middle because there were thousands of cars of freight and thousands of passengers for which the U.S. government began making these arbitrary deductions. Had we been forced to remit the full amounts to the originating and intermediate carriers, we would have lost a lot of money. Fortunately, we were able to make special arrangements with the railroads involved to deduct the amounts of the arbitrary deductions from their accounts pending resolution of the whole issue. We found out later this situation had existed right back to the time of the building of the Panama Canal in 1889 by the U.S. Army engineers and had been unresolved over the years.

The NAR continued to render bills on full tariff basis but the U.S. government continued to make arbitrary deductions. The only recourse for the NAR was to accept payment under protest, pending resolution. This meant a most meticulous system of record-keeping on bills of lading for this freight had to be set up and retained so the NAR could either recover the monies from the U.S. government or persuade the U.S. carriers to drop their claims.

* * *

Bill Porterfield, who came to the overloaded Dawson Creek yard from the Canadian Pacific at Prince Albert, Saskatchewan, January 1, 1943, recalled some difficulties:

The company auditor at the time was F.J. Kavanagh. He had us file every document connected with the movement of U.S. government freight and this included ladings for private U.S. contractors. All their freight was coming in under auspices of the PRA and USED. Some of the railroads figured these contractors were not eligible for land grant deductions — and we kept accurate records of this movement in case of dispute, too.

The recording job was made difficult in Dawson Creek by the labor shortage. I know I was working for at least two years without a let-up from 8:00 a.m. to 12 midnight. When I first arrived there was no living quarters except a bunkhouse the NAR had built for its employees. There was little or no male help so we hired waitresses and high school girls as bookkeepers and tried to teach them enough to get by on. But somehow we kept ahead of the paperwork.

* * *

Charles Anderson came onto the job about the height of this dispute, and recalled:

I was on the job in 1947 when the NAR entered a claim in the U.S. Court of Claims (which corresponds to Canada's Federal Court) to recover from the U.S. government the amount which had been arbitrarily deducted from payments and which we were supposed to rebate to the U.S. railroads. Preparing our case became a full-time job for me and several other accountants in head office in Edmonton for many months. The papers and documents involved filled 50 filing cabinet drawers. It was painstaking and detailed work.

In the end the case never came to court. The U.S. government prevailed upon the U.S. carriers to drop their claim and we didn't have to rebate them.

I don't know what kind of subtle forms of pressure Uncle Sam used. In a way it was blackmail. However, the government made a concession: it agreed by an act of Congress not to enforce its legal right to claim land-grant reductions on passenger and freight traffic after 1945.

The last of these settlements — totalling some $2.3 million — was made to the NAR and the U.S. carriers after 1958.

When it was all over, troubleshooters from Washington involved in the case congratulated the NAR audit department on the accurate and comprehensive accounting procedures — procedures which it had been unable to assail.

The PRA won a minor rate skirmish with the railroads when it sent R.H. Helmintor, its administrative officer, to negotiate for an agreed charge on contractors' shipments. PRA fiscal agents had discovered the NAR, CPR and CNR were using a rate structure designed for sparsely-settled agricultural districts.

The new tariff Helmintor negotiated did not apply to inbound shipments of machinery to Dawson Creek but did apply to outbound shipments (when the contractors sent their equipment back home) from September 4, 1943. Thus rates on carload lots to the midwestern states were reduced to $700 a car from $1,200. On the 1,000 cars of machinery shipped out the PRA saved $500,000.

While the Franceschini brothers of Toronto were in a Canadian internment camp, one of their companies worked on the Peace River suspension bridge.

12

R. Melville Smith Shot First, Asked Questions Later

Most Canadians continue to believe the construction of the Alaska Highway and the Canol Project was accomplished by American army and civilian construction forces. In the case of Canol this was true. In the case of the Alaska Highway, Canadian construction companies based in Ontario did about a quarter of the work.

When all the accounts were settled in 1945 the Canadians had received $29 million under their contracts done for the U.S. Public Roads Administration plus $816,000 in fixed fees. The total paid all civilian contractors was $109.4 million plus $5.1 million in fixed fees. Other costs ran the job up to $148 million.

Another fact is interesting in these days when conflict of interest is outlawed and virgin purity is demanded in government: R. Melville Smith, deputy minister of highways of Ontario, formed a private company to act as management contractor for all the Canadian construction forces.

The events leading up to the heavy Canadian involvement began early in 1942 and were set in motion following the initial shock of Pearl Harbor Dec. 7, 1941.

Although the project was a U.S. Army show, the army had to draw heavily on civilian contractors to do the work. Whereas it had sent in seven regiments of engineering troops to survey a route and bulldoze a rough preliminary road, these regiments were needed elsewhere in the war effort against Germany and Japan, and most were pulled out after the first construction season before the road was built up to all-weather standards.

The U.S. Public Roads Administration was selected by the war department to work closely with the army and supervise the civilian contractors it brought onto the job.

The PRA was a federal government agency charged with locating and constructing roads in national parks. As the Alaska Highway was decreed to be a road of approximately the same standards as national parks roads, which were set by the federal government, it was the most appropriate agency to recruit. The specifications: a road capable of handling 70-mile-an-hour traffic, all brush gathered and burned, borrow and gravel pits to be screened from right-of-way and backslopes trimmed.

* * *

These specifications later proved ridiculous, it was recalled by Bobbie Hill, a construction stiff with Dowell Construction Company of Seattle:

It would have been 10 years before the road was finished. The army wanted it right now. The Japs were upon us.

For instance, PRA enforced a regulation that every bit of wood on the right-of-way was to be picked up and burned or buried. The army had to step in and put a stop to this time-wasting exercise. The PRA got into a panic in December, 1942, when a bunch of senators toured the road on an inspection trip. The senators would see those piles of trees beside the road. They sent a crew, including me, to clean up those piles of green trees by burning them. No matter how much diesel fuel and gasoline we poured on them they wouldn't burn. Piles of black butts remained.

After all that wasted effort the senators never did see them. A big snow storm came along and buried them!

* * *

By August, 1942, PRA realized the standards could never hope to be maintained if the road was to be available for winter traffic. Therefore, the plan was altered. The Alaska Highway never did come up to national parks roads standards designed to handle large volumes of tourist traffic through scenic country. Ironically, this was exactly the kind of traffic it was forced to handle after the war when thousand of tourists began using it and grousing about the dust.

The PRA had to do things in days or weeks that, under less rushed conditions, would have taken months. A plan was evolved to get things into high gear by dividing the road into four sections and assigning each to a management contractor. A fifth management contractor was appointed to provide transportation of machinery and equipment onto the job site. The management contractors were:

• R. Melville Smith Co. Ltd., Toronto, which relocated and reconstructed the 50-mile provincial road between Dawson Creek and Fort St. John and later built sections of permanent road between Fort Nelson and Watson Lake.

• Okes Construction Company, St. Paul, Minn., which built road between Fort St. John and Fort Nelson.

• Dowell Construction Company, Seattle, Wash., which built road between Watson Lake and a point north of Whitehorse.

• Lytle and Green, Sioux Falls and Des Moines, Iowa, which built roads inside Alaska.

• E.W. Elliott and Company, Seattle, which operated as transportation contractor and camp builder and took on a piece of road between Whitehorse and the Alaska border along with Utah Construction Company of Salt Lake City

* * *

One of the independent contractors which signed a contract with the PRA directly was Dufferin Paving Company of Toronto. Dufferin was called in nominally to do some work on the concrete abutments for the suspension bridge built across the Peace River at Taylor Flats, plus some work on the approaches to the bridge, it is recalled by Walter Wright, its chief mechanic:

PRA had accepted bids from Dufferin on this and two other strategic jobs despite the fact two of its principals, James and Leonard Franceschini, were in a Canadian internment camp. The other work Dufferin did was two five-mile contracts in the Fort St. John-Charlie Lake area (when one of the contractors under R. Melville Smith had been unable to move onto his section) and in the 1943 construction season moved part of its outfit 98 miles north of Fort Nelson to improve the army road in the Summit Lake area.

The first inkling I had of the Alaska Highway was a newspaper story that Okes Construction had been awarded a management contract. I was frozen on a job at Welland Chemical Works at Niagara Falls, Ont., by the Unemployment Insurance Commission. My brother, Henry, was working at Decew Falls. We had both been heavy equipment operators but when I contacted Okes they said I should apply to a Canadian company as they couldn't hire any Canadians.

Some weeks later Jim Pickard, a drawling Oklahoman, one of Dufferin's job superintendents, approached us and asked us to return to heavy equipment work on the Alaska Highway. He figured the job would last five years. We didn't waste any time quitting our mundane jobs to go north to this exciting wartime project.

The company was founded by the Franceschinis, who were of Italian descent and had become wealthy in road and ship building. They had run afoul of public opinion because they had given one of their prize racehorses to the Italian dictator, Benito Mussolini. The authorities had succumbed to public pressure and put them behind barbed wire in 1940. However, their vast construction empire had been kept operating on government war contracts by men like George Morris, the general superintendent.

Many thought they had been wrongly interned. One was John Diefenbaker, a Conservative member of Parliament, who later became prime minister. He forced the Mackenzie King Liberals to reveal February 8, 1941, that Dufferin Paving had received a government contract for $447,000 at the Swift Current, Sask., airport after James Franceschini had been interned. The government sidestepped the issue by showing the company had not been owned by him but was a subsidiary of a company in which he had an interest. Later the Hyndman judicial commission determined Franceschini had been wrongfully interned. He was released on the compassionate ground that he was dying of cancer (although he survived for six years).

Following the completion of the preliminary road by the U.S. Army in 1942, the PRA asked Canadian civilian contractors to move north of Fort Nelson to improve it to permanent road standards. Pickard flew north and decided we could handle a contract near Summit Lake. He radioed me at Taylor Flats and told me to line up a convoy and start north immediately. We had the convoy all lined out September 20 in dry, sunny weather. It was a sorry-looking outfit of 30 tractor-trailer units and other trucks. In actuality, the whole outfit was a bunch of dilapidated green wrecks.

We didn't have much left when we arrived at the job site 198 miles north of Fort Nelson. We walked the bulldozers until the tracks fell apart. Wheels fell off many of the tractor-trailers. The brakes went out on the rest.

The first break-down occurred north of Fort St. John when the rear end of that old Leyland tractor we had borrowed from A.E. Jupp seized up. It was pulling a lowboy with a 1 1/2-yard shovel on it. Pickard couldn't find a substitute so we had to leave the shovel there and carry on without it.

A blond fellow from Fort Frances, Ont., driving a dump truck with seven tons of material in it, tore out the clutch when he tried to gear down on the suicide hill at the Sickanni Chief River. He sat solid to the bottom on the brakes and managed to burn them out. We had a big Corbett four-by-four loaded with fuel, gas and oil we used for a wrecker. I instructed the driver to push the dump truck to the other side of "suicide," but I warned them:

"Be sure and chain the dump truck to the Corbett because when you get up there a few miles you will be at the top of the hill which lets down to the Sickanni Chief. It's a bad one."

Of course, they disregarded my orders and never chained the trucks together. When they reached the top of the hill, I saw the brakeless dump truck break over and start down what was five miles of goat trail. For about two miles this blond kid gained speeds up to 60 miles an hour. He was starting to worry that he would miss the bridge at the bottom as he was freewheeling. He was lucky. About half-way down there was a gravel pit and he ran into it. After about a quarter-mile he got the vehicle stopped. They continued chained together after that close call.

We camped along the road several nights before we hit Fort Nelson. It was identified by a 35-barrel cache of diesel fuel and a sign: Mile 300.

Upon arrival at the job site with no decent equipment, we had to have some bulldozers to level off a campsite and build some road. Another chap and I took off up the road to steal some equipment the U.S. Army had abandoned between there and the Lower Liard River. They had abandoned a fair number of pieces of rolling stock as they were short of good mechanics. When anything went haywire they merely left the machine by the side of the road and kept on going as they had a lot of new equipment at their disposal.

I found half a dozen D-7 and D-8 Cats. Within a few hours I had two good D-8s ready for the road. We walked them back to Summit Lake.

By spring we had repaired and brought to camp more army bulldozers — our own and some 16 and 24-yard Letourneau earth movers.

We had only one casualty on the job. He was a guy named Scotty who had taken out a bulldozer with which he was not familiar and put it over the edge of the road on a high bank. He and another inexperienced man were attempting to get it back when something went wrong and it turned over and crushed Scotty to death, then turned over again onto its tracks and took off through the bush like a bull moose — with the blade up. It roared on for half a mile before being stopped by a stream.

The job didn't last the five years that Pickard predicted. At the end of the 1943 construction season it was pretty well all over for the civilian construction stiffs. However, I went to work for the U.S. Army Engineering District (USED) as a mechanic in Dawson Creek, later went into business and stayed there.

* * *

Few of the Canadian civilian construction workers were discharged outright, it was recalled by William Tunny of Mayerthorpe, Alta.:

After my stint with Dufferin Paving, I was permitted by Unemployment Insurance Commission to sign on as a carpenter with USED in October, 1943. The USED assigned me to Dawson Creek to build chart cabinets for airport control towers along the Northwest Staging Route, Alaska and the Aleutians.

Later they had me making packing cases for USED personnel to ship out in. At that time also some of the civilians working for the army had a problem with their luggage after having been there 2 1/2 to three years. Many had arrived with a single suitcase, and in the intervening years, had acquired more possessions. It was impossible to buy a suitcase in Dawson Creek as they were scarce and the merchants didn't have any.

They'd come around asking me to make what the Americans called "foot lockers." These were plywood boxes 36 inches long, 20 wide and 16 deep. Capt. Bussey gave me work orders to make one per customer because he realized the women couldn't dump their toilet sets into a gunny sack. Two men worked two weeks on these.

I was never really discharged. In July, 1944, when the USED decided to close down Dawson Creek, they told me I could transfer to the new Namao Airport at Edmonton. They knew, however, I didn't want to move there.

"Look Bill," said Capt. Bussey, "I'm not going to terminate you. If you want to go back to Mayerthorpe, I'll give you an extended leave of absence and if you ever want to do so you can come back to work for us without any red tape." I had gone to work at age 13 and I thought that was one of the best deals I ever received from an employer.

* * *

Another man who stayed on after the job was finished was Jack Griffiths of Grimsby, Ontario. He recalled:

I ran a gang of 70 on maintenance for the USED when it took over the road from the PRA at the end of 1943 and stayed until May, 1944. I came onto the job in 1942. I was then surveying a route for the Ontario Department of Highways for what was to become the four-lane Queen Elizabeth Way. The department asked nine of us to go to work on the Alaska Highway. I was given a job as grade foreman by Arthur M. Mills, a former department engineer who was superintendent for W.H. Harvey and Son. I arrived at Dawson Creek early in July about the same time as 22 carloads of our equipment started arriving.

Management contractors like R. Melville Smith were picked by the U.S. War Department for their engineering capabilities and familiarity with the business end of large road-building projects. They were paid a fixed fee for recruiting consortiums whose combined assets were not less than $10 million. It was their duty to assign the construction firms to specific stretches of road, move them onto the job, provide subsistence, repairs and other services on the job and keep records of the actual costs and labor on which payments to the companies were based.

A stipulation of the R. Melville Smith agreement was each company which took a contract was required to have a top executive on the job at all times.

Although the army engineers received most of the credit for punching the preliminary road through, the record shows that within eight weeks after receiving the go-ahead, the PRA had the first of 47 contractors on the job. By the end of the season 7,500 civilians were on the scene.

In 1943, 87 contractors with 15,000 men were at work improving the road.

If the contractors brought their own equipment in addition to labor they were paid a rental that was equal to 40% of the purchase price of a truck in a year if run eight hours a day. The rate was 25% on tractors. For many contractors, the government supplied some or all of the equipment.

The fixed fee was negotiable, depending upon the length of road to be built, remoteness of work, character of terrain and other factors. Dowell drew one of the worst sections. Conditions changed very often. There were difficulties in transporting equipment to the Watson Lake area. Others had to jump in and assist Dowell.

* * *

One of the smartest ideas of the whole project was when the PRA drew on the Civilian Conservation Corps (CCC) for instant housing for the initial assault on the wilderness. The CCC was a depression relief organization which created jobs for young men. With the onset of war, defence jobs and armed forces call-ups, it was liquidated. Forty CCC camps were dismantled and shipped to Canada with kitchen equipment and barracks for the workers. Bobbie Hill of Missoula, Mont., a worker with Dowell, recalled some of the buildings:

The biggest trouble ensued when coal-burning stoves were sent into country devoid of coal. They had to be converted to wood or oil.

We lived the first winter in old CCC barracks. They had wooden frames with tent roofs; there were four men to each room and the stoves converted to wood had to be kept going all night. Before the barracks arrived we lived in tents. They were quite comfortable. In fact, they were warmer than the CCC barracks at Camp 2W out of Whitehorse.

As for the CCC equipment such as 55 power shovels, 85 portable repair shops, 200 electric light plants and 1,000 trucks, much of it was ready for the junk heap. Also, there were delays in transporting the junk to the job site.

* * *

R.N. Johnston, Toronto, former head of research for the Ontario Department of Lands and Forests and an aerial route surveyor from June through August, 1942, recalled the audacity which won R. Melville Smith his management contract:

Besides being deputy minister of highways for Ontario, Smith was a founding member of the Ontario Good Roads Association. These two positions gave him a great deal of authority and for a number of years he ran the department practically single-handed.

Through these two positions, he became well-known in highway construction circles in the U.S. and even more so through his connection with the Alaska International Highway Commission, the peacetime group which had investigated the feasibility of building a road to Alaska through Canada.

Although he had never been to northwestern British Columbia, he knew a surveyor on staff who had done detailed work in that province. With coaching from this surveyor he went to Washington with the commission to lobby for the road. He made a great impression there when he was able to reel off with authority names like Pouce Coupe, Fort St. John, Lower Post and others nobody there had ever heard of. The American members of the commission thought it wonderful he knew the country and route so intimately.

When the war came along and the war department decided to build an instant road through the area, Smith was in solid with the PRA and other government agencies which worked on the project. The PRA asked Smith to line up a consortium of Canadian contractors to build a section of the road. He went one better. He got Ontario Department of Highways authorization not only to organize a consortium but became president of the management company.

It was an amazing thing that, as a civil servant, Smith should be allowed to operate with impunity and no questions asked in the Ontario Legislature about a private business which eventually did $30 million worth of business with a foreign government on Canadian soil.

But this was a wartime emergency and Smith did things no deputy minister has done before nor since. He was a remarkable man, away ahead of the pack which would be yapping at his heels with charges of conflict of interest. He was out to help win the war on a shoot first and ask questions later basis.

Kenneth Siddall and I had personal witness of the kind of authority he wielded during several briefings before we left for Fort St. John to do aerial surveys for U.S. engineering troops. An Ontario Treasury official phoned Smith to inform him construction approval for a certain piece of Ontario road would have to be cancelled due to lack of money. This official began to talk in a positive but critical manner of the impropriety of Smith's request for funds in the first place. Finally he stopped and this gave Smith the opening he was looking for:

"Look, Walter, I don't give a goddam where you find the money for this road — but you better find it because I am going to build it."

He then hung up. That's how he got things done.

It is very unusual for civil servants to talk in this manner or argue with Treasury officials. But, then, as I said, R. Melville Smith was a very unusual man.

He was equally forthright with the PRA when it began preparing cost estimates. He pointed out they were away low for the kind of terrain they were up against in the unsettled North. This was based upon his experience in building roads in Northern Ontario, including sections of the Trans-Canada Highway. The American engineers had estimated their costs for a completed road lower than he figured it would cost to build the preliminary road alone.

* * *

He wasn't the typical hard-driving active outdoor man who got out and roughed it and bulled jobs through as do so many construction bosses. Although a capable administrator and a good engineer, he was more the office type, it was recalled by Dick Panter, Smith's Dawson Creek camp superintendent:

Smith went to Dawson Creek in the early spring of 1942 but suffered a heart attack and they had to take him out. On doctor's orders, he wasn't on the job very much after that. In fact, he had to retire as deputy minister June 1, 1943, and was in ill health until his death in 1950.

George Porter was sent in to replace him as general superintendent, but Porter had a heart attack, too, and had to be taken out also. Fred Francis was sent in to run the job. He was there when I got there, then he went to Fort Nelson — and I joined him there.

The mountainous country is not easy on older people who have always lived at lower altitudes. There were all sorts of people who were collapsing under the strain. At that latitude the days in summer got to be too long. Twenty-hour days created a strain as contractors' bosses worked all day then drove into base camp to do business with me at night.

Because we were working on double daylight saving time, the sun didn't set until 12 midnight. I used to wish maybe one night a week they'd pull in the sun early. It was quite common to have supper then go back to work again. When it began to get dark you'd imagine it was time for supper. Then you'd realize you'd had supper four hours ago.

Another thing that caused stress was the dilapidated and run-down old equipment inherited by the PRA and handed out to the contractors.

The Alaska Highway was probably the first road which saw much of the equipment brought in by a fleet of ships owned by the project supervisor. In this case the PRA scoured the West Coast from Vancouver to San Francisco and commandeered a fleet of five steamships, a motor ship, five yachts (which were converted to freighters), 14 barges, 10 tugs and a 75-year-old sailing vessel, which was converted into a tug and made 13 trips to Valdez, Alaska. The "fleet" was hidden away in Lake Washington and Lake Union near Seattle and was taken over by the E.W. Elliott Company to move supplies north.

Amassing this fleet turned out to be another of the smart pieces of thinking that got the road built. Hauling thousands of pieces of equipment thousands of miles overland and distributing it to thousands on the job would have defeated ordinary contractors.

There seemed to be much against the highway's successful completion. But with these small strokes of genius by the PRA, headed by commissioner Thomas H. MacDonald, a native of Goderich, Ont., many of the roadblocks were overcome. There were tales of woe about the old equipment on a job so far from sources of repair parts. However, even with inadequate repair facilities, the contractors gave a remarkable performance; headaches and cannibalization were the order of the day.

Despite several shipwrecks and loss of life, the PRA fleet worked well but port congestion was an aggravation. Skagway was the worst offender. Until slips were excavated, barges and towed schooners were pulled in at high tide, which was 20 feet at that port, and beached to be unloaded by crawler cranes moving out on the mud flats beside them at low tide. The extent of the congestion was seen when one vessel chartered by the PRA arrived in port in December and wasn't able to clear until February.

The first Ontario contractor under the Smith umbrella to arrive on the job in Dawson Creek was Curran and Briggs of Toronto. Personnel and equipment began drifting in June 6. They worked under difficulties as the PRA and the army kept pulling them off the job for supplementary contracts for railhead and airport work around Dawson Creek. To keep up with all the work they were able to rent a few trucks locally but these were down half the time. They were unable to secure PRA trucks on a permanent basis.

A month later a person looking out his window in Dawson Creek might think he was in Ontario. On hand were Storms Construction Co., Don Construction Company, A.E. Jupp, Dufferin Paving Company, Campbell Construction Company, McNamara Construction Co. and Bergman Construction Company, all of Toronto; Wallace A. Mackey, Weston; Rayner Construction Co., Leaside; W.H. Harvey Co., Kingston; Bond Construction Co., Kenora; Emil Anderson, Fort William; Caswell Sand and Gravel Company, Kirkland Lake; D.O. Johnson, Brantford; McGinnis and O'Connor, Kingston, and Highway Paving Company and Harold Harvey.

Many contractors had pulled crews off the sections of the Trans-Canada Highway which was then under construction in Northern Ontario. There were so many personnel from the Ontario Department of Highways in Dawson Creek one writer asked: "I wonder how the department was able to function back in Toronto without them?"

* * *

Roy Robinson of Delmar Contracting in Hamilton, Ont., recalled:

I was with Storms Construction Company, having come from a construction family. My brother, Manfred, had an asphalt plant which he packed into Anchorage to build the first paved runways at Elmendorf Air Force Base. I had worked at the airport at Debert, N.S., on the Trans-Canada Highway and was at Beauharnois, Que., in the spring of 1942. In early July they called me back to Toronto, gave me two office boys, a bunch of truck drivers and a gang of carpenters and sent me to a location north of Dawson Creek to build a camp.

In a typical camp layout (usually with a mountain backdrop) a level area off the highway was cleared and a fence with a couple of gates was built along the road frontage. There was a compound in the centre with a row of tarpaper shacks down the right-hand side. In the centre of the bunkhouse was a cookshack and dining room. On the opposite side was the office and commissary. Behind the office was a warehousing area. On the left-hand side was a big garage and gas pumps. There was usually rank after rank of trucks awaiting repair in front. Between the garage and office was a timekeeper's shack.

As there was no running water, the camp was equipped with outdoor privies. They were located in a strategic place adjacent to the office. I earned the sobriquet The Bad Toilet Builder. The men and women in the office thought these structures were lovely until the first wet day.

There were no roofs. Jack West, the superintendent, gave me hell: "Of all things. You forgot the roofs."

My only alibi was the first latrines they had built at the army bases had four sides, no roof and no seat — just a 2x4 to sit on. (Many a guy with a skinful of booze fell into these at night and his piteous pleas would bring people on the run to pull him out.) We could built a road better than we could build backhouses.

The housekeeping varied from camp to camp. In an outfit like ours or Jupp's, where we brought in our own crews intact, things were orderly and vehicles kept painted compared to those who had to depend upon transient labor.

Although the Canadian contractors tried to keep a cadre of skilled people and foremen around them, this was practically impossible. We'd been at war since 1939 and most of the fit and able young fellows in the industry had become directly involved in the war effort. That meant for the most part we had to depend on medically unfit or older men and unskilled help. The Unemployment Insurance Commission, which had recruited all over Canada for the Alaska Highway, brought in 500 unskilled men from Quebec who found themselves out of their element in both weather and living accommodation and out of sympathy with "another British war."

To ensure that we had all our equipment on hand before the spring break-up on the new contracts north of Fort Nelson, we convoyed our equipment up during the winter. I was in charge of the last convoy in January, 1943. We were 13 days en route and spent most nights sleeping in the trucks.

Somebody had foisted off a bunch of Thornton-drive Marmon Harrington Ford trucks on the contractors. They were six-cylinder jobs built in Flint, Mich., and cost $8,000 apiece.

The Thornton drive comprised two driveshafts, one to the rear and one to the front. They weren't worth a damn in cold weather principally because of the heavy grease in which the rear ends were packed. It burned them out. I counted 50 down on the road with turn-out rear ends. Some of them belonged to Dufferin Paving. They started out with 140 and three months later only six were in service. When we accidentally discovered they'd run if the grease was removed and replaced by No. 20 engine oil, we sent back and picked up a bunch of them.

A. E. Jupp had trouble, too, on the move north. They were told if they needed oil to help themselves at American army dumps. Unbeknown to them the oil was detergent oil, just being introduced to the trade.

The proper method was to drain all the old oil out of the crankcases and refill with the new detergent. They didn't know this and mixed the two. This took the bearings out of 18 trucks.

Storms started out with 13 Marmon Harringtons, a few White diesels, some General Motors stake trucks, some four-wheel drives and two right-hand-drive Fords. George Prince of Saskatchewan was our master mechanic. He used every trick in the book to keep his fleet going, even removed connecting rods and ran some on five cylinders. This would work on those old long-stroke engines and keep a truck running for a while until new parts could be ordered and installed. But the engine vibrated terribly.

We arrived in camp with a double piggy-back: a Marmon Harrington atop a four-wheel drive and a right-hand-drive Ford atop that. Someone had put up a big sign on the derelicts:

"Watch The Fords Go By" — a famous Ford Motor Company advertising slogan.

* * *

At a few camps on the Canol Project, where he was stationed with Bechtel, Price and Callahan, rumor mills were started — complete with employees — it was recalled by John Fisher of Valley Falls, Kans.:

The job of the mills was to manufacture rumors to see how far they could go and how many people would believe them. One of the best rumors we manufactured got us into big trouble with Washington and the U.S. Corps of Engineers. The rumor was that rival crews laying pipe from the east and west ends were so intent on their job they had missed the meeting point in the Mackenzie Mountains and had laid 100 miles of pipe past each other.

The army engineers were furious and tried to find out where it was manufactured. Our rumor mill had to go underground for a while.

As a practical joker, I started a miniature gold rush at Camp 78E on the Canol Road. I had a broken crosscut saw and fashioned a hunting knife out of it. Jack Holzer, an ex-gold-miner of Wiseman, Alaska, was there and a gold filling fell out of his tooth. We soldered the gold filling onto the knife.

I then showed it around camp and, of course, the boys wanted to know where the gold came from. I let drop a couple of hints I had picked up the nugget in a nearby stream. When word got around a minor gold rush was precipitated as the whole camp went out to pan gravel. No gold was found — but it was great fun for us guys.

* * *

It was natural they went out to pan as there are showings of gold all over the North, as was attested by Bobbie Hill of Missoula, Mont., a laborer with

Dowell Construction:

My buddy, Les Stone, and I were installing culverts near the Takhini River near Whitehorse. He was a mucker in the Klondike Gold Rush and had signed on with Dowell at age 65 and had come up from California. I stuck my shovel into some gumbo created by meltwater. I washed it off and found a bunch of gold nuggets on it, just like a string of beads. Stone was excited. It was one of the best showings he had ever seen, but the deposits were so small they couldn't be mined economically unless the price rose to $400 like it is today. The gold is still there.

But there is also steel. Tons and tons of steel culvert pipe were trucked in and we couldn't find a place for it. We were told to bury it in the fills where we discovered the gold.

I found myself on the way to the Yukon on Labor Day, 1942. I had been working on the Canadian rodeo circuit trick roping and clowning, having "graduated" from spending the depression years on big cattle outfits in the Cariboo and Chilcotin areas of British Columbia.

With this experience I tried to get into the U.S. Border Patrol which had reverted to horse patrols during the war. However, at age 38, they said I was too old.

I ended up by signing on with Dowell Construction in Seattle. They equipped me with badge No. 658 — one of the originals — and shipped me out to Skagway on the Canadian Pacific boat, Princess Nora. It was a comforting sight to see a Canadian gunboat escorting us across the open sea north of Prince Rupert.

Dowell management was given the longest contract on the road by the PRA: 480 miles. To Americans this was an amazing distance: equal to that from Chicago to Kansas City. Contractors under Dowell ultimately had 1,500 pieces of rolling stock on the job. Some of the 260 bulldozers and 60 power shovels had been brought in to job sites from Whitehorse on Yukon sternwheel boats.

I normally would have gone home at the end of the 1942 construction season but Slim Strum, the grade foreman, persuaded me to remain on a standby and road maintenance crew overwinter; he would make it worth my while. At camp 2W near Whitehorse I was one of 60 men kept busy overhauling army construction equipment. There were seven Bobs in residence, counting the big police dog.

At the end of March I received word my mother was ill in California. Strum was as good as his word. He arranged a hard-to-get seat on a plane for me to fly out and stay for a month.

On my return, I spent several months convoying trucks from Edmonton to Dawson Creek. Because of a shortage of rail transport, Dowell convoyed many of its vehicles from Seattle to the job site in the spring of 1943 via Dawson Creek. I was then assigned to Morse Bros. and Associates of Rochester, Minn. Morse worked in the Watson Lake area and had a helluva time getting their equipment to the site. They even resorted to walking 10 scrapers and 25 bulldozers all the way from Whitehorse. However, by September 1 they were building a mile of road a day and hauling 20,000 cubic yards of gravel.

In the summer of 1943 we were privy to two of the best-kept secrets of the war — and this secrecy was made possible because of the strict censorship in the northwest Canadian theatre of war. The first was that most of the summer 150 miles of road between Whitehorse and Fairbanks were closed. It had sunk into the muskeg. The second was that following the famous "holing through" ceremonies the previous November the road was not open to through travel.

* * *

There had been much hoopla when members of the 97th Engineering Regiment and the 18th Engineering Regiment met each other at Soldier's Summit Nov. 4, 1942. On November 20 the U.S. military brought in 200 invited guests and the Canadian Broadcasting Corporation to do its first remote actuality broadcast from the Yukon. J. Frank Willis and Peter Stursberg later fed it out to the Mutual Broadcasting System in the U.S.

As a piece of window dressing, a convoy of army trucks loaded with strategic war materials roared off toward Fairbanks after the ceremonies. But they never reached Fairbanks that day. They stopped around the first bend because the bridge across the 1.5-mile-wide White River had then not been completed.

(It was so cold that day that broadcast equipment began picking up strange clicking sounds. Willis and Stursberg frantically checked the equipment for a loose connection. They at last found a microphone in front of Health Minister Ian Mackenzie of Canada was the culprit. He was shivering so hard his false teeth were chattering. A public relations flak on his staff had persuaded him to divest himself of his big coonskin coat for the benefit of photographers. He didn't want the minister to look like a backwoods rube.)

The 97th had holed through only a lightly gravelled winter trail after freeze-up in late September. The trail handled limited traffic during the winter but next spring the bottom dropped out of it and it became a permanent quagmire. Army vehicles which had been caught there in the spring thaw stayed in the muskeg all summer.

* * *

Soil conditions did not always contribute to construction snafus. Rivalry, friction, and competitive spirit between various factions also contributed to some. Dick Panter, a superintendent for the R. Melville Smith Company, recalled coming out on top of one of these endless bouts:

The spring break-up of 1943 wiped out the Kledo River bridge, 32 miles north of Fort Nelson, as well as many others. I came along trying to get things moving again as the Americans had to open the road to move out the 341st Engineering Regiment.

Working out from the south bank, the Dufferin Paving Company of Toronto had started to replace the structure by driving piles out to the stream. An American contractor, Dunnigan Construction Company of Minneapolis, camped on the north side, hadn't made a move. I crossed the Kledo on a breeches buoy and told Dunnigan's foreman to get moving and drive piles out to meet Dufferin Paving. He refused to move until he got orders in writing. I had no authority to give an American contractor anything. We stood and argued for a while and at last I walked away, saying:

"Well, starve then. How are you going to get food in if you don't get a bridge in?"

He got the message and began driving piles. But he knew the U.S. Army better than I. Col. William Leonhardt came along and ordered them to stop driving piles and rebuild the bridge on mud sills as it was quicker this way now the river had receded back into its normal channel. The Kledo was a small creek normally but what the colonel didn't realize was it would flood again in July when the snow in the mountains melted. Sure enough this happened; the highest crest in years. It not only scoured out the sill on the riverbed and tipped over Leonhardt's bridge, it nearly floated Dunnigan's whole camp away. The piles Dufferin had driven remained intact. PRA's Fred Capes thought this was a dandy. In fact, he was quite happy and tickled when the bridge went out just because he could show "those military bastards." But Leonhardt was not there to see the mess. He was long gone from the scene.

* * *

All Americans weren't like Leonhardt, especially those big Texans and

Oklahomans, it was recalled by W.W. Bradley, a Provost, Alta., farmer:

They were a bunch of tough fighting buggers but they knew how to ramrod trucks of pipe through to the Canol project. I had been in the U.S. Corps of Engineers during the First World War. When the Canol project came along they got in touch with me in Canada and put me to work as an equipment expediter. I got along well with the Americans because I could get bourbon. None of them could stand that Canadian rye whisky.

Although I was tough, I won their respect. The Christmas of 1943 I was trying my damndest to get the last shipments of pipe for Canol over the highway. We were working Sundays, holidays and overtime. A bunch of them wanted to lay over at Whitehorse for Christmas Day — and I told them they just couldn't do it.

"Look here," I told them, "you're just going to stop here for inspection and something to eat and keep right on going. You're not due to book rest."

However, they got some whisky from somewhere and all got drunk and that put a stop to the trip right there. They couldn't go on. I was mad as hell.

"The whole bunch of you are going on charge," I shouted — and took off for the officers' mess.

Later that night, there was a call for Lieut. Bradley. I reported and there were five drunken truckers with a big box all wrapped up in Christmas paper with a big ribbon on it. They'd gone to town and bought me a big mackinaw, which I treasured for a long time — until somebody stole it. Attached to the present was a card:

"To the best boss in camp."

That saved them all from going to the jug. They were smart enough to know I would relent.

The U.S. Army had complete control of all convoys going over the highway. The checkpoints were all-powerful, officious and a bloody nuisance. Their job was safety primarily. I'd be shepherding a convoy through a checkpoint when some dirty-nosed lieutenant with 10 times less seniority than me would order all the tires stripped off a truck. They'd be thrown in a big incinerator and replaced with new 10-ply tires. There might be a Canadian trucker across the road with a flat and couldn't move — but they wouldn't let you give him a tire.

* * *

The North impressed many Yanks. Some of them kept up friendships with

Canadians for years afterwards. One of them was recalled by Bruce Ballah:

Sgt. Joe Simpson from Brooklyn had a few drinks with the boys one night. They had a Hudson car and Simpson insisted we go up to the American PX (from which we were banned) to get some supplies.

"We can't get in to the PX. We're Canadians," I demurred.

"Sure, you can. You're friends of mine," he bellowed.

We got through the camp gates and went several hundred yards when a guard stopped me, stuck a gun under my snout and hollered: "Halt!"

"Those guys are my friends. You can't touch 'em," mumbled Simpson.

"You get out of the car, too," the guard ordered.

Joe wobbled out of the car and said: "Look, they're Canadians."

"Prove it," said the guard belligerently.

When I showed him my credentials as a UIC officer, he relented and gave me a green light to proceed. We proceeded to the PX where Joe bought us some much-needed scarce supplies for nearly nothing.

"You shouldn't be doing this, Joe," I remonstrated.

"Yah, you're my buddies."

I figured by morning Joe would forget who his buddies were. But two days later my little daughter was sitting outside our tent when who wobbles up but Joe Simpson. He was a real Brooklynite.

"Little goil, do you want some money?"

We had taught the kids never to accept gifts from strangers, so she refused it.

"Well, I'm a friend of your daddy."

He gave her a silver dollar which she had for years. I used to get Christmas cards from him and 40 others for years.

At the end of the 1943 construction season the PRA's involvement was pretty well at an end — except for some bridge construction. Its office was transferred along with some officer personnel from Fort St. John to the USED headquarters in Chicago to straighten up unfinished bookkeeping and to terminate management contractors' accounts.

13

Thousands Of Vehicles Convoyed From Edmonton

Although thousands of tons of construction machinery and supplies had arrived in Dawson Creek during 1942 via the frail Northern Alberta Railways, on Jan. 1, 1943, there was still a great backlog choking every rail siding between there and Minneapolis. There were several reasons for this logjam.

1. The NAR was so overloaded it couldn't begin to handle the movement.

2. The Americans in their zeal to pursue the war effort had ordered thousands of cars of military materiel out of engineering districts in the U.S. sent to the Northwest Service Command of the U.S. Army in Edmonton before they had come to grips with the problem of transporting it over hundreds of miles of semi-wilderness after it reached Edmonton.

There were 1,000 cars jammed in the several railway yards around Edmonton. Switch engines could hardly move.

True, a great deal of equipment had been shipped out via alternate routes through Waterways and the Mackenzie River system to Norman Wells; also via winter roads to Norman Wells. More had been routed over the White Pass and Yukon Railway to Whitehorse and even more on the Alaska Railway to Fairbanks. More of it could have been routed via Prince Rupert and the White Pass and Yukon but they had lost a bunch of barges on the north Pacific and had to resort to the rail movement.

During the winter American and Canadian construction companies which were going in over the preliminary army-built road had also amassed equipment for shipment to be ready for the 1943 construction season after the spring break-up.

All added up to the fact that Col. Theodore Wyman, Jr., of the Northwest Service Command was so desperate he was willing to offer a contract to any Canadian with enough savvy and upfront money who could unload those cars and arrange to convoy all vehicles that could travel under their own power to job sites on the twin projects.

The clearing of the bottleneck at Edmonton was further aggravated by Wyman. He had proved inadequate. His assignment was simply too big for him. Low morale resulted. He was demoted to Fairbanks and Gen. Ludson D. Worsham was sent in to get things moving.

A contract was awarded to Butler and Hawkins Ltd. The principals were Charles E. Butler, 49, a one-time contractor and service manager of a Calgary car dealership; Eric Hawkins, a salesman for Burrows Motors of Edmonton, who had a line into the Northwest Service Command, and James Boyce, a big game packer and small contractor in Banff. Their contract was to unload, service, repair and convoy the equipment out of Edmonton.

Butler and Hawkins received a bit of a shafting from smart and tough Americans with whom they negotiated the contract. The Canadian way of doing business was cost plus a percentage. The American way was signing up for their own estimate of cost plus a variable management fee. Well into the contract they found they were working for a pittance.

To accomplish this all-important job they organized an elite corps of Canadian civilians — one that received little recognition at the time, mostly because of wartime secrecy, which was very tight on the project.

Everyone on the job was required to have a security clearance. In my case, the permit was signed in Chicago by Herman P. Goebel, a major in the U.S. Cavalry. He was a first cousin of Josef P. Goebbels, Hitler's propaganda chief. Goebel's potential as a security risk came up in the U.S. House of Representatives. Consequently, he was never sent into a sensitive war zone. He was kept in Chicago. It was funny, however, that he got to sign my card as the Alaska Highway and Canol project were under the tightest security restrictions of any war zone in which the Americans operated anywhere in the world.

The contract called for hiring of 79 drivers within six weeks. At the peak of the operation the staff had risen to 750.

* * *

One of the convoy captains was R.G. (Rusty) Garrett of Banff, who had experience driving a semi for Imperial Oil Limited. He got his job because he beat out a U.S. Army test driver from Chicago — one of those who checked all the drivers Butler and Hawkins hired. He recalled:

Few Canadians had ever handled Diesel trucks previously. They were given three days' short course on them before the test. Those who didn't pass the Diesel test were given gas trucks to drive. Most had had experience driving buses or logging trucks.

One day Boyce and Butler got a bet going for $50 on gear-jamming with Clarence Yelldell of St. Joseph, Mo., a civilian expediter, and Bill Vinyard, a civilian engineer. I took out a big White Diesel with an army test driver. He undertook to show me the gear changes. When I took over, I said:

" There are a lot more gears in this rig than you showed me."

Then I started going up and down the gears. Butler won his bet and offered me a job as a convoy captain. Later I took over all the test driving.

* * *

Butler and Hawkins was in business the day after signing the contract and had incorporation papers from Ottawa five days afterwards. Butler recalled:

We easily spotted the reason for the general chaos. Between the Canadian National Railway and the Canadian Pacific Railway there were five unloading docks. But they were all too small for efficiency. Men had to be moved around to all these sidings to unload a car or two. For instance, at the CNR Cushing yards we could only spot seven cars on the sliding they assigned us. Men were sitting around with their hands in their pockets waiting for cars to be switched in for unloading. Cars were spotted on the siding as many as four times with orders to unload, then pulled back out again without being unloaded.

Through a friend I was able to get next to Walter Owens, western superintendent of the CNR, and told him the yards were so full it was practically impossible to carry on a switching operation and there was no co-ordination or co-operation with the Americans. Owens came to

Edmonton and had me tell my story to 30 army and railway brasshats.

We got what we wanted, although we had to build it ourselves: another spur line 700 feet long off our track in the Cushing yards. Then we set up a record of unloading 50 cars a day for 50 days. The best Bechtel, Price and Callahan ever did was 25 cars. Gen. Worsham came around frequently to watch us carry out our program. He stood there one night while we unloaded 10 cars of half-ton trucks loaded piggy-back — 30 vehicles — in 46 minutes.

This Worsham was a fine man, a good man to work with, the salt of the earth as far as I was concerned. He was willing to hear out a person with a good idea and treated civilians with courtesy and deference. He won a large circle of friends in Canada because he was a gentleman. He put me onto several other lucrative contracts besides the convoy work. However, he had no patience with the asinine in or out of the military.

He once received a letter from some stupid ass in Washington demanding to know the number of empty barrels on the highway. His answer was to walk over to a window and, seeing a jeep standing there with a number on it, noted down the number and told his secretary to write a letter of reply with that number on it.

The number was sent to Washington and everybody was happy, none the wiser that it was fictitious.

One Sunday Worsham came over and asked me to get in touch with his chief executive officer, Col. Kirkpatrick, to make plans for operating over the terrible roads during the spring break-up.

"Oh, no, general, please don't ask me to do that, " I replied. "He's your executive officer but if he was working for me as a civilian I'd fire that bastard in two minutes."

"I see you must have tangled with him," grinned Worsham. "I'll speak to him myself."

Kirkpatrick tried to be decent but he was one of those egotistical overbearing sons of bitches and he and I had tangled right off. He was a peacetime national guardsman and lacked practical experience. He treated me like a dog, barking orders into a telephone and generally making himself obnoxious.

When we got stuck we could call in army personnel. But some of us thought the U.S. had the biggest bunch of duds up there we ever saw. The Canadians did more work than them.

At peak times Jim Boyce worked 18 hours a day and had 18 foremen under him. We were driving every kind of vehicle imaginable: Turna-pulls, dump trucks, Caterpillar tractors, jeeps, scrapers, ambulances and graders. We even carried a Diesel switch engine to the NAR yards at Waterways.

Watson Lake was well supplied with jeeps. We convoyed 350 there — one for each five personnel on the base.

Much of the equipment was new but there was a lot of old stuff, some of it completely worn-out. Jim Boyce checked trucks that had 190,000 miles on the speedometers. Others were so decrepit they had bird nests in the cylinder heads. Others had flat tires.

Some were on lease from fleet owners in the U.S. They were rented by the army on a per diem basis and rent was paid even though they never turned a wheel; and they were too far gone to spend money on repairs.

We had a nine-acre holding yard. It was full most of the time. However, we couldn't accommodate the "deadline" vehicles and hauled them off to a yard on the east side. Eventually this grew into a whole hillside full of derelicts. Worsham ordered everything in this yard stripped and sent back to the U.S. as junk.

Some of the trucks came under guard with secret war materiel about which we were told not to ask questions.

Another unusual shipment comprised 470 11-ton White trucks with Cummins Diesel engines, worth $20,000 each. They had been assigned to the North African campaign against German Gen. Erwin Rommel. They had missed the convoy in New York so they were all shipped to the Alaska Highway job. They were equipped with smooth tires so they wouldn't boost sand in the desert. They were no good in Alberta gumbo even though they had tandem rear wheels (but not duals). We had a helluva job getting them up to Dawson Creek as they were in the ditch most of the time. But later on dry roads in summer they were marvellous.

When they arrived in Edmonton it was 40 below. Not a wheel would turn because they had been serviced with heavy transmission grease and 90 engine oil. We had to get a D-7 bulldozer and drag them off the New York Central cars and onto lowboys for hauling to the shops.

* * *

In despatching these and other trucks we were usually asked to carry supplies going up the highway. I carried everything from air compressors, hypodermic needles, ambulances, French safes, bulldozers and bulldozer tracks and shingle nails to electric motors. Ed Ibsen of Kamloops, B.C., was an assistant convoy driver under Charlie Pakalak, a former Edmonton policeman, whom all the boys called "Charlie Peckertrack." Ibsen recalled:

The last convoy Charlie's group took was eight blade-mounted snowplow trucks for clearing runways at Ladd Field, Fairbanks.

His most unusual convoy was 10 cabless open-air-style road graders for the Metcalfe-Hamilton Kansas City Bridge construction outfit at McCrae near Whitehorse. It took nearly two weeks to get them there in the fall of 1943. We did the truckers a favor by filling in all the ruts on that terrible stretch of road between Edmonton and Dawson Creek.

The Americans received a big splash of publicity when they drove the first convoy of 80 vehicles consigned to Metcalfe-Hamilton themselves. Only eight of them arrived. The rest were scattered along the road from Morinville north.

We sent our first convoy of 12 out five days later and we were in Whitehorse eight days before they landed in there. Our only casualty was a vehicle with a broken crankshaft — and we left it at a checkpoint.

They always wanted to do things big but they simply didn't know the North and the winter conditions they would experience. That's why Charlie Butler specified his convoys would be small — about 12 vehicles with 13 drivers so that if a man got sick or hurt there would be somebody to fall back on. A mechanic was usually taken along and he sometimes acted as spare driver.

* * *

The Americans were just like babes in the woods — and after this experience they let us do the driving. However, there were always greenhorns coming in who thought they could improve our methods. Maj. Sloan was one of them recalled by Charlie Butler:

He came from the deep south, hadn't been in a war before and had never seen Alberta mud. He came in to replace Ben Tibbitts as head of the equipment section. Tibbitts was a slob, unkempt, unshaven, sloppily dressed like a tramp, and a drunk. I saved him from getting court-martialled for being drunk a couple of times by spiriting him off to Waterways. But I wasn't around when Gen. Worsham encountered him drunk on duty at the American headquarters in the old Jesuit College. He was confined to barracks for 10 days and Maj. Sloan brought in to relieve him. He phoned me: "Mr. Butler, haven't you-all got any tow-bars in this heah part of the country?"

"They're awfully scarce, major. How many do you want?"

"I doan want any but ah see you-all sending 13 men out on 12-unit convoys. Why don't you-all get tow-bars and have each driver tow another unit?"

"Major, "I replied, "have you ever been over the Alaska Highway?"

"No."

"Have you ever flown over it yet?"

"No."

I sent a car over from the taxi pool and showed him a picture of what looked like a bunch of trucks travelling through a lake of mud.

"What's this hear supposed to be?"

"That's the Alaska Highway, " I said.

"There's no road there. It's disappeared."

"Major, are you telling me!" I then showed him a picture of a driver coming out the cab window of a truck. It was down so deep he couldn't get the door open. That was the general condition along the road during spring break-up.

We heard no more from Maj. Sloan about tow-bars.

* * *

Mud was the chief enemy in spring and summer. The worst mud was not on the Alaska Highway itself but on the ungravelled Highway No. 2 from Edmonton to Dawson Creek. Most of the time it would have been hard to dignify it as a road so deep was the mud. Rusty Garrett recalled:

I took convoy No. 121 out of Edmonton July 4 bound for Whitehorse. We found 140 trucks had been held up at the Athabaska River ferry because of road bans. But we had to get through — so we wired the U.S. Army at Edmonton to get us a permit. We received the permit by wire in a couple of hours. It took 10 days to reach Whitehorse when we got going again. The Alberta Department of Highways never turned down army requests for permits despite the fact the heavy vehicles made a terrible mess of the soft spots. We often drove wreckers in our convoys but most of the time we had army vehicles with winches and four-wheel drives and we were able to anchor in and winch the bogged-down vehicles through mud.

* * *

That stretch of road into Grande Prairie was terrible during the spring break-up. It was the worst mud I've ever seen: slimy black stuff. We just couldn't keep the vehicles on the road. Often it was the better part of valor to pull off the road for a day or two to let the sun get at the mud rather than churn it up some more, Ed Ibsen recalled:

The longest stretch I ever had without sleep was 37 hours. We took a detour through Spirit River to avoid a washed-out bridge. However, a cloudburst hit the area and turned the roads into gumbo. In addition, we also got lost.

I suspect the reason the Alberta government didn't upgrade this 350-mile highway was it figured the Yanks would do it. But they had no intention of taking on that road, too. It thus remained in terrible shape.

Under normal conditions it took two days for a convoy to reach Dawson Creek. In wet weather it could take a week.

After several trips of getting damned hungry during enforced delays miles from anywhere, we learned to take along some grub, build a fire and cook meals. We gained time by being patient.

The changeable weather was nothing to be trifled with, either, as the Toronto contracting consortium, R. Melville Smith Company, discovered when it shipped in several dozen General Motors trucks and, doubting our capability of unloading them correctly, did the job themselves.

They got them off the cars all right and parked them on 104th St. along the CNR tracks in 30-below weather. The radiators had been drained when they left the East. One of their men was ordered to refill the radiators. But the goddam fool didn't start the engines to mix water and anti-freeze. This left the anti-freeze at the bottom and the water at the top.

In the morning they found split radiators or cracked blocks on nearly every goddam machine. Then they came to us and asked for help. We refused and packed them off to a GM garage, as we didn't have the time or staff to play around with them. They had some of these vehicles tied up nearly two months; had to put new motors in some. Half water and half anti-freeze will protect radiators to 65-below.

* * *

Motorists who travel thousands of miles of all-weather roads in northern Alberta today in cruise control don't realize the difficulties of travel in 1942-3. There were only a few bridges on the main roads. Nobody could expect to get anywhere fast. An incident was recalled by Rusty Garrett concerning the 1943 spring break-up:

The Americans had a general somewhere in the U.S. with a shipment of medical supplies for the Soviets: operating equipment, drugs and everything. It was supposed to be delivered to them in Whitehorse and flown out of there via lend-lease aircraft. But he'd consigned it to Butler and Hawkins in Edmonton for us to deliver via convoy to Whitehorse.

We managed to make it to Dawson Creek despite many dangerous river crossings on the ice but the army had stopped traffic on the Alaska Highway. I had to phone Gen. Worsham in Edmonton for a special permit to go through.

"I'll issue you a permit but I don't think you'll make it. One of the worst stretches is in the Fort Nelson area. I can't understand why he didn't fly the stuff to Whitehorse but I guess he didn't realize how bad the roads can be here in the break-up," he said.

We got the stuff there but it took us nine days from Dawson Creek.

And thus was delivered one of the first loads of freight over that 1,250-mile route without a bit of fanfare or hoopla by a small group of Canadians who were doing their bit but not realizing at the time they had made history.

We used every trick in the book to get the vehicles over the road: even jumping flooded creeks — creeks that we could normally ford.

We'd build a chute or springboard as far over the banks as we could then get a run at it and try to jump the vehicle across the remaining distance — just like Evel Knievels. There would be a big clatter as the vehicle landed on the other side and kept on going. It was rough on the springs but they needed those vehicles up the line and we were determined they were going to get them . . . come high water!

We had the right-of-way over everything — even the authority to order out bulldozers to build shoo-flies around trucks which were bogged down and blocking our way. We often had to have troops corduroy bad mudholes with trees — sometimes as much as 100 yards.

Another priority which we had was on plane flights. The first few convoys went to Dawson Creek only and we drove back. But then Sloan started ordering convoys through to Whitehorse. This meant a long drive back so they gave us No. 1 priority by air. Some of the American brass used to get pretty sore when a dozen convoy drivers would show up at an airport and they'd get bumped. I've seen us come in and deliver a convoy and in half an hour we'd be flying back.

I thought one DC-3 flight out of Whitehorse was going to be my last. The pilot was making his first trip out of there and the co-pilot his second.

To gain altitude out of the mountains surrounding that airport, the pilots circled twice. But I noticed this pilot went around only 1 1/2 times. About an hour and a half out of Whitehorse he couldn't see any familiar landmarks and he got a bit excited. He was a good pilot from the U.S. but they had no navigational aids installed on this flight path yet. It was a terrifically bumpy ride and the wings began to ice badly. I went forward and said:

"Hey, what's going on."

"You see that lake down there? We're going to belly in," he said. It was likely Frances Lake.

"Not on your life," I said. "How about all my boys in the back. They're sick and would never be able to make it out."

"It's every man for himself," the pilot replied grimly.

"None of that for me. You get this craft upstairs right now."

"Well look what's up ahead," he said.

"Get this thing up to 11,000 feet and you can clear those mountains and we'll fly through this storm."

We were iced up pretty badly and it was hard to get the Gooney Bird up there but he did. He said:

"Which way would you go?"

"I think I would try the highway."

"You've flown this country quite a bit. Which way do you think it is?" the pilot asked.

"Well, head her straight up that valley," I advised.

He did — and came out over Watson Lake.

If I'm going to get killed I'd sooner take it from high above rather than belly into a lake.

He didn't have radio contact with Watson Lake. When the plane was overdue, Whitehorse reported it down in the bush. Word got out on the radio and my wife heard in Edmonton we were overdue. She was almost frantic because the Americans had lost quite a few aircraft in that area — and she figured this was another.

Butler was meticulous about keeping records and logs on all the vehicles his people handled. There was a staff of women checkers keeping track of every piece of equipment as it went up the road. Convoy captains were required to report their progress. Although the U.S. Army told him it wasn't necessary for this meticulous record-keeping as Edmonton had been classified as a U.S. war zone and accountability was not enforced, he did so anyway. When the Japanese were pressing the Americans in 1942 the motto was: Win The War: Expense Be Damned. Many contractors had helped themselves to vehicles in the Edmonton war zone and had forgotten to tell the army.

When the Japanese pressure abated in 1943, Edmonton was declassified, and accountability was enforced once again. Army engineering districts in Seattle, Chicago and St. Louis were shocked by the heavy requests for equipment by the Northwest Service Command and the subsequent "disappearance" of dozens of carloads after it had reached Edmonton. Investigation of the "losses" became a weekly fact of life and there were a lot of scared people running around until they found where it all was.

Our record-keeping system served us well several times and we were never cornered when it came to having to account for shipments. For instance, Bert Robbins, a convoy captain, was accused of "losing" a convoy of Studebaker six-by-sixes but because he had delivery receipts for them at Dawson Creek, the rightful blame went to the army. They eventually showed up.

We had to send Jim Boyce to Grande Prairie one time to locate a missing truck. It had broken down and a convoy had left it beside the road and pressed on.

Boyce found it in a farmer's barn — before he had a chance to use it to haul manure.

* * *

Rusty Garrett used to pick up a lot of stuff the other convoys had left around. He got quite a reputation as a clean-up man; also he got a reputation as having higher expense accounts than any other captain working for Butler and Hawkins. His travelling mechanic had brought a lot of missing vehicles back to life — and that took time, Butler recalled:

Our punctilious system enabled us to nail a project auditor named Baldman who tried to spear us with a bum rap. He had asked me to supply him and some buddies with a station wagon and enough rationed gas to go on a junket to Banff. I couldn't do this as Maj. Sloan was the only person with authority to order equipment out of the nine-acre yard. Sloan, of course, wouldn't give him an army vehicle for joyriding and he was furious. He alleged in a written complaint to Gen. Worsham I was holding equipment which was needed on the highway two to six weeks longer at Edmonton than need be. But this was crap as, once we had orders from Maj. Sloan to move it out, it was gone within 24 hours.

I was tipped off by Tiny Burdick, a big former football player in Worsham's office, what was about to happen: an inspection by Worsham, who was required to act on the complaint. Burdick tipped off the general and they laid a trap for Baldman.

I had Jim Boyce call out a crew to put the yard in top military shape. I had been in the army in the First World War and knew how the military thought. We used spit and polish and had all the truck radiators lined up so you could look down a straight line.

When Worsham showed up with 20 officers in a fleet of cars with flags flying I was ready for him. At that time I had a fellow named Graham. He was a bit of an outlaw; had been in jail several times. But he had a photographic memory.

Our company had records on every vehicle: serial number, who owned it, how much it cost, the car number of the railroad which shipped it, the date we received it, the date it went out on a convoy and who signed for it on the Alaska Highway.

Graham could reel off from memory every bit of information about every vehicle handled in the yard for as long as three weeks, including the serial number. I told him to stay at my elbow during Worsham's inspection.

Worsham would point to a vehicle and ask how long it had been there. I would look up the serial number and Graham could immediately string off its whole history. Worsham was very much impressed.

At the end of the inspection he arrived at the "echelon" or repair shop I had built for them. The flag was flying and below it was a sign which indicated we had gone 319 days without a man-hour lost due to injuries. The figures were compiled by Capt. Caldwell, his own safety and security officer.

"This is phenomenal," said Worsham; he walked over and shook my hand and took off. "You have the most orderly yard in the Northwest Service Command.

The next afternoon, I was called to the office of Col. R.W. Lockeridge, the district engineer, who said: "Mr. Butler, we have had several complaints from different sources about Baldman. You've never had anything to say."

"I haven't," I replied, "but on one occasion I told him to get to hell out of the yard when he was interfering with Boyce's work. Then I wouldn't give him this station wagon. It was getting so bad I was thinking of asking to be relieved of the contract if he remained on the job."

Baldman was given a posting to Prince Rupert. He was there 10 days when he was taken back to the U.S. under escort.

Rusty Garrett took convoy No. 121 through to Whitehorse from Edmonton July 4, 1943, starting at 7 a.m., with Boyce accompanying on an inspection trip. The other crew members were Reeder, Relling, Bretkreutz, Waugh, Morasse, Glover, Wagner, Williams, Weeks, Greening, Remnick, Dowhaniuk. Here is Garrett's log of the trip:

July 4 — Crew reached Clyde at 9:30 a.m. for breakfast. Arrived at Athabasca 12 noon. 12:30, finished gassing up and minor repairs. Dinner, 12:30 - 1 p.m. Vehicle GB-1507W, a car, had a blowout and it was necessary to mount a new tire. During this time the crew changed loads and tied down for half an hour. They found a new tire on the wheel of car No. 15-12019 for GB-1507W. Held up at ferry. Arrived at Faust 3:30 a.m. July 5. Tie rod on car No. 583 repaired at Smith. Put in for nine hours straight time and 6 1/2 overtime. Time carried over to July 5.

(Evidently they were working a nine-hour day but no more than 6 1/2 hours of overtime could be claimed in a day. However, any time put in after that could be carried over as overtime for the next day.)

July 5 — Crew started 8 a.m. Repairs made to tie rod ends and welding on car GB-1507W. Convoy went on way at 10 a.m. Wire sent to Edmonton on road conditions. Arrived High Prairie 1:45 p.m. Dinner High Prairie 1:45 - 2:45 p.m. Pick-up truck No. 14-11014 threw left front wheel. Car GB-1507 motor trouble. Tied up Falher 6 p.m. Nine hours straight time and three overtime.

July 6 — Left Falher 8 a.m. Dinner Sexsmith. Arrived Grande Prairie 3:30 p.m. Repairing flat tires. Supper 5 - 5:30 p.m. Two flats eight miles north of Hythe. Necessary to send truck back to Hythe for repairs. Arrived Dawson Creek 10 p.m. Nine hours straight time, four overtime. (At this time of year there is daylight until nearly midnight in this area.)

July 7 — Crew started 8 a.m. to make repairs and put cars through army shop for repairs, greasing and oil change. I advised No. 10 winter oil be drained and replaced by heavier summer oil. Crew tied up 6 p.m. Nine hours straight time, two hours overtime for Garrett and Boyce for making necessary arrangements to leave for Whitehorse.

July 8 — Left Dawson Creek 12:01 a.m., which was the only time allotted to cross by ferry at Peace River at Taylor. New suspension bridge not yet in service and temporary piling bridge knocked out first week in June. Crossed ferry 5 a.m. Breakfast at camp of R. Melville Smith Company of Toronto 6 a.m. Flat tires on 583, 15-12019, GB-1507W and 5565. Necessary to take carburetor off car 116 for repairs. Dinner at camp of Volck Construction Company of Rice Lake, Wisc., near Fort St. John. Arrived Fort Nelson 11 p.m. Supper at midnight. Very heavy truck and convoy traffic. Accommodation poor.

July 9 — Crew started 8:30 a.m. from Fort Nelson. Roads very tough and travel slow. Dinner at camp of Curran and Briggs Company of Toronto mile 35 from Fort Nelson. Rain and rough roads. Flat tire No. 5565. Supper at camp of Dufferin Paving Company of Toronto mile 98 6 p.m. Two more flats, 15-12019 and 5565. Very heavy rain and it's rumored road closed Summit Lake. Pulling vehicles through mud very heavy work. Rear spring removed from car No. 15-12019. Centre pin is broken but repaired. Two hours delay. Arrived at camp of McNamara Construction Company of Leaside, Ont., mile 120-N. Arrived Liard River crossing 1:30 a.m. Crew slept in cars as there was no room anywhere for drivers to sleep. Nine hours straight time, five hours overtime, 1 1/2 hours carried over.

July 10 — Breakfast mile 210 6 a.m. Flat tire No. 583. Dinner at camp of Emil Anderson Company of Fort William, Ont., mile 245-N. Impossible to make time owing to heavy roads. Car No. 565, key in left rear wheel stripped off. New key made at army camp. Flat tire car No. 583. Supper at camp of Morse Bros. of Rochester, Minn., Hyland River. Mechanic Waugh, driver Wagner No. 37, driver Reeder No. 212, driver Weeks No. 246, driver Remnick No. 227 and convoy captain Garrett making repairs to brakes, tires and greasing cars. Nine and half hours straight time, 4 1/2 hours overtime.

July 11 — Breakfast at Morse Bros. camp. Crew started 7 a.m. Car 15-12019 broken drive shaft bearing mile 323-N. Car No. 116 gooseneck on radiator shook loose on top. Ford sedan No. 116 put on deadline as valve stem broken; possible damage to No. 4 piston. Dinner at camp of McVaugh-Haynes of Dubuque, Iowa. Car No. 116 towed for five miles. Road heavy and bad holes. Cars giving trouble with water in gasoline and much delay caused. Supper at the camp of Bates and Rogers of Chicago. Half crew tied up at 11 p.m. at David Nassif Equipment Co. of Boston mile 59 north of Watson Lake. Nine hours straight time, six overtime. Rest had to sleep in trucks as no room account of heavy traffic.

July 12 — Breakfast at Nassif camp. Flate tire 1011. Repairs on two tires made at Brooks Brook army camp. Repairs brake line of No. 299811. Flat tires 5565, GB 1507W. Dinner at camp. No. 4E of Public Roads Administration. Flat tire No. 583. Rear main leaf of spring broke on No. 5565, and delay was encountered blocking and wiring up so as to be able to drive it. Arrived Whitehorse 8 p.m. Nine hours straight time and three hours overtime.

July 13 — Standing by for transportation at Whitehorse. Nine hours for crew.

July 14 — It was necessary I stay at airport till 11:30 a.m. standing by for plane. Nine hours straight time and five hours overtime for Garrett.

July 15 — Crew standing by at airport. One man left on plane. Six men left on another 6 p.m. Balance of crew stood by to board next plane. There were no accommodations as usual at Whitehorse.

14

Americans Built 2,850-Mile Phone System

In the last week of November, 1942, a 75-truck United States Army convoy pulled onto the main street of Pouce Coupe, a small fur-trading town and administrative centre for that area of northern British Columbia. The officers in charge believed they were in Dawson Creek, 12 miles farther north, the jumping-off point for the Alaska Highway.

* * *

The drivers grabbed all the parking available and the boisterous GIs spilled out of the vehicles and threw the villagers into consternation. One of those GIs was Sgt. Millard F. Tibbetts from the Rangeley Lakes area where he had worked for the Southern Maine Telephone Company. He came back to Pouce Coupe after the war and worked in the sheriff's office. He recalled:

The officers approached the Chinese restaurateur, a co-operative little man known as "Old Cook" and an institution in the small village. They asked him to undertake to feed the whole crew.

The hungry men soon cleaned out all the food. The field kitchen was backed up to the rear door of the restaurant to supply more meals. Then they had to scour the town to buy pies from any stores or housewives who would part with them.

Old Cook was given a chit for each meal he served. When it came to settle up he asked 75 cents a meal. Meals at that time were worth 40 to 50 cents apiece—and we knew it. But we added to Old Cook's windfall that day by giving him $1.50 apiece.

One of the few stores was a grocery and confectionery run by an aged lady. She became frightened by the huge men in their bulky uniforms and their funny-looking money. She refused to take it, shooed them out and locked the door. The GIs persuaded the officers to carry on negotiations with her to reopen the store. They went around to the back living quarters and persuaded her their money was worth a premium of 10%. She hesitantly opened up again and reaped a windfall of American greenbacks for chocolate bars, cigars, peanuts and drinks. Some didn't even bother to pick up their change.

The GIs comprised elements of the 843rd Signal Services Battalion of the U.S. Signal Corps assigned to operate and maintain the Alaska Highway telephone system, officially known as Cantel, under construction from Edmonton to Fairbanks.

It was started Aug. 15, 1942, at the Northern Alberta Railways Dunvegan Yards in Edmonton and, when completed two years later, the 2,850 miles of pole line linked all the air bases on the Northwest Staging Route and included a 600-mile circuit to Norman Wells at the east end of the Canol Road.

It was one of the longest open-wire toll circuits in the world at the time. By using Alberta Government Telephones circuits out of Edmonton to Great Falls, Mont., it was possible on completion of the line for an officer to contact Washington or Ottawa from Fairbanks.

Direct communication over this great distance was thus established before it was possible for a Peace River farmer to make a long-distance call to Edmonton. The only way he could communicate was via the overworked NAR telegraph line.

The importance of the line to northwestern Canada thus rivalled the importance of the Alaska Highway and the Canol pipeline. With the Japanese in the Aleutians and the U.S. Pacific fleet knocked out, communications over a vast uninhabited territory were essential.

The signal corps began the initial surveys in March and completed them by mid-summer. The route followed the NAR to High Prairie, thence across-country to Grande Prairie and Dawson Creek. From there it ran alongside the new highway to Fairbanks.

Actual construction was delayed until August as nobody really knew if a line of such length was possible. Tests had to be carried out on mock-up models in Bell Telephone Laboratories in New York. There it was established such a line was feasible.

Prior to the telephone line installation the signal corps provided essential communications for the armed forces by radio. However, this service was inefficient as it could be knocked out by atmospheric disturbances and there was danger of interception by the enemy.

Miller Construction Company of Indianapolis was awarded the prime contract for the line — and a schedule. The schedule called for completion of the first 442-mile stretch to Dawson Creek by Dec. 1.

Miller ran into an early winter and notified Maj.-Gen. Stoner, chief of the army communication service, the work could not be completed until Dec. 16. On Nov. 15 a blizzard had caught them at Grande Prairie with 90 miles of poles to be set and many miles of wire to be strung. Stoner decreed the deadline would be met and ordered in the 75-truck convoy from the 843rd to assist Miller. Wire crews from Canadian and American telephone companies were hastily requisitioned and thrown into the struggle, too. They received their baptism of Northern winter cold by working through snowdrifts six feet deep in 40-below weather in unsuitable clothing.

Despite the fact the ground froze solid post holes had to be dug. Various methods were used but the most successful was dynamite.

We secured several of those Alaskan boilers used for placer mining. They developed 100 pounds of steam pressure. A hole 1 1/2 inches in diameter was melted down and blown out to the necessary depth with steam pressure. Then a few sticks of dynamite were shoved down. They blew a hole out so that very little digging was necessary.

The holes were spaced 155 feet apart. A little arithmetic will show we had to set 95,000 poles.

Most of the poles were cut in the bush by local contractors. Although most were spruce, many thousands were tamarack. The tamaracks gave us trouble as, when dry, they develop a hard outer shell into which it is almost impossible to drive a lineman's spur. However, the tamaracks outlasted the spruce in the muskeg as the spruce rotted in it.

Many of the holes dug with dynamite were in frozen muskeg and in the spring thaw the weight of the poles caused hundreds to sink or fall over. Anchor guys let go, too.

Later when crews rebuilt the line across the muskegs they attached floating fixtures to each pole. Floating fixtures comprised a brace fastened horizontally at ground level. Braces which went into the ground were attached to the ends of the horizontal brace and carried in A-frame style to the pole and affixed to it. Farther up the pole, side guys were attached to big floating anchors. There were also variations of these. We had to invent and innovate as we went along.

On many of the rivers we had to cross it was obviously impossible to use the 155-foot setting. Catenary construction involving aerial spans was used here. The longest spans of this type used eight cross-arm fixtures suspended from six steel strands to cross a 1,250-foot-wide river. This span was held by 60-foot wooden towers on each bank.

Meantime, in the frantic scramble through darkness and cold in the fall of 1942 crews placed cross-arms on only alternate poles and attached the wire later. Temporary wire was also hung on NAR telegraph poles where the right-of-way ran parallel.

The cross-arms and poles were dropped at night ahead of construction and the wire was also strung. The poles were erected during the day.

The big push worked.

At 7:45 p.m. Dec. 1 Gen. Stoner picked up a telephone at the army headquarters in Washington and talked to Col. Heath Twitchell of the 95th Engineering Regiment in Dawson Creek.

There is more engineering to a telephone line than simply stringing wires to a pole. For instance, in every 256 poles there must be 128 transpositions to prevent disturbance of one circuit with another by induction. The voice does not go through the wire but around it. The farther it goes the wider it gets. The transpositions get it back again so a conversation is not being picked up by another circuit.

Those tests at Bell Laboratories showed more than the usual number of repeater stations would be needed for boosting the voice currents because the army specified the use of copper-weld wire to conserve scarce copper. Bell determined that wire with 30% copper welded around a steel core was the answer. It also gave the line greater tensile strength to resist the pounding to which it was subject. Catenary construction across the rivers was only possible because of this mechanical development. Otherwise poles would have been needed.

The steel in the wire had one big disadvantage. It caused loss of conductivity and this meant repeater or "booster" stations had to be erected every 70 to 100 miles rather than the 200 for lines built of pure copper.

The heart of the system was therefore the repeater stations and 28 of them were needed.

The equipment for them was manufactured by Western Electric, a subsidiary of Bell. Working together, the two produced in 26 days repeater apparatus that normally would have required 26 weeks to manufacture, assemble and ship.

Each repeater station was a small community in itself, with an amount of equipment equal to that of a large city toll office. Crews manned it 24 hours. Each required 50 tons of equipment to keep 20 telegraph circuits and 10 talking circuits moving 2,000 messages per day. Later radio hook-ups and wirephoto services were serviced by this line. The line fed into 1,600 army phones and teletypes.

Each repeater station had 2,100 vacuum tubes, 1,300 polar relays, 50 power units and a maze of highly intricate technical equipment.

Much of the equipment was flown in, even power units weighing over a ton.

There were hairy moments — as when six tons of equipment were involved in a train wreck at Dawson Creek; and a truck accident on the Alaska Highway. But it all arrived somehow.

Banks of storage batteries supplied the 500 kilowatts of current. The batteries were charged by six-cylinder gasoline engines but in case of engine failure the batteries were good for 36 hours.

A repeaterman needed the equivalent of eight years of experience: office manager, toll terminal workman, personnel supervisor and powerman. Besides the repeatermen, two linemen were assigned to each station for patrols. At strategic points 10 line crews of five men each were located.

As we proceeded to Dawson Creek, our convoy dropped off repeatermen. We were actually the first foreign troops with whom the people in the small towns along the way had rubbed shoulders. Other GIs had preceded us but they had gone in by rail.

I guess we overwhelmed a few. For instance, when we stopped at Smith the high-spirited GIs jumped down and took off pell-mell for the local restaurant for grub. It was across the street from the Royal Canadian Mounted Police barracks. A couple of red-coats bustled out to find out who had invaded the town.

They insisted in stiff upper-lip, brisk military fashion that the restaurant manoeuvre be carried out in "orderly fashion" and they would brook no rowdy hi-jinks. Their "outpost of empire" attitude amused us Yanks.

Of course, the Mounties had no warning of foreign troops — even friendly ones — and were not prepared to find a convoy at their front door that morning.

The 843rd overwhelmed the Town of Dawson Creek at Christmas, 1942. Christmas was always an important occasion for the boys in the services when they were far away from homes and families and likely to be feeling lonely and blue. Therefore, the officers and non-coms made it a point to see that extra efforts were made for a fine Christmas dinner and extra privileges were given the GIs.

In response to a suggestion box in camp, the signalmen decided to throw a big party and have as guests of honor the most needy family they could find in the district. This proved to be a farmer with a large family who lived six miles from town and was temporarily down on his luck. Each member of the family was given a new outfit of clothing, the kids were presented with loads of presents and the father was handed a purse stuffed with $1,000.

This made for a most memorable Christmas for those hard-up Canadian folk. It gave a deep sense of satisfaction and comfort to the young American soldiers thousands of miles from home and without hope of a furlough for 18 months. In fact, some of the boys were to be up there for nearly two years before they went out.

The commissioned officers and sergeants in the 843rd were trained telephone company personnel put in uniform and sent to boot camp for indoctrination. Lt.-Col. J.R. McKinley, our first officer commanding, came from Southern Bell Telephone and Telegraph Company. Maj. L.E. Van Nort, executive officer and chief engineer, was from the New York Telephone Company.

The green enlisted men were trained in the various trades at camps and later on the job by the company men. We figured an enlisted man had become a lineman when he could climb to a 20-foot mark on a pole.

Our outfit had more rank than any other on the Alaska Highway. It came about this way:

We had been sent to the Aleutian Islands to install radio beam equipment at Dutch Island in January, 1942. One of the installations was known as a diamond.

The essential part of the diamond was several 110-foot poles. We were all standing around the first pole we had erected waiting for somebody to make a move to go up to begin attaching hardware. It seemed a long way up to me because I hadn't been active in climbing for several years. Some of the new boys seemed to think it was a long way up, too. Sgt. Morse was the only experienced climber I had. I said to him:

"I'm going up there to tighten those guy wires."

"What do you want to go up there for? Are you crazy?" he demanded.

"Here, give me your climbing spurs. I'm going up there."

"You're crazy," he reiterated.

"All right, I'm crazy then. I feel I should set the pace. However, I'm not going to stand around yapping while I ask those young fellows to do something I wouldn't do myself."

So I put on the spurs and went up. When I finally made the top I took my pocket knife and stuck a $5 bill to the top of the pole. I came down. I looked over the crew and said:

"All right, the private who goes up there and gets that $5 bill will be a corporal when he comes down."

We made more corporals that way than we ever needed. But the challenge was the way we made climbers. We got the job done in no time.

The technical men were given a certain amount of relief from the regular army discipline. We were not often called out on parade for arms drill or calisthenics. But that irked some of the GIs, not to mention officers, in the other services to see our boys lying around not doing much, not realizing we got enough work climbing poles and building and repairing line.

A certain amount of hostility sprang up between us and those career army officers who attempted to interfere in our special field of knowledge.

Things came to a head in one instance when a cocky new lieutenant in the transport corps turned up at Summit Lake. He was a martinet who went by the book. Every day he had his men out on the parade square near the repeater station doing push-ups. It made him livid with frustration to hear ribald remarks coming from our boys lolling around the station.

The lieutenant undertook to write Lieut.-Col. McKinley in Edmonton and said he didn't see any reason our boys shouldn't go out for calisthenics just like everyone else. Although McKinley didn't realize we were too short of standby staff in the repeater station for such nonsense, he had no recourse but to go along with the lieutenant in the interest of keeping up morale. He therefore despatched Capt. William Ludwig, operations officer in charge of repeater stations, to look over the situation.

Now, Ludwig was a pretty good head. He had come from the New York Telephone Company. The orders had been cut and, while he thought they were stupid, he could do nothing but see they were obeyed. Next morning he showed up and bellowed:

"All right, every man out. Just pull the plugs on the switchboards."

He watched as the boys did 30 minutes of hard exercise. They were out the next morning and pulled all the plugs again.

But it didn't last for long.

There were loud squawks from Edmonton, Whitehorse and even Washington about the line going dead. Capt. Ludwig simply told them the crew was following orders. The nonsense ended in a hurry after that.

The cocky little lieutenant reminded Ludwig:

"You're in the army and you have to abide by army discipline." To which Ludwig responded scornfully:

"Well, if I'd known there was as much chicken in the army as I've seen here, I would never have joined. I just wonder sometimes if I am in the army, seeing some of the specimens it has produced."

That mountain at Summit Lake was plumb full of holes. When one of that lieutenant's drivers came in half an hour late from a trip or if he stopped at a civilian camp for a cup of coffee and left his vehicle, the punishment was: go dig a hole. There was no confinement to barracks there; the punishment was dig a hole.

Oh, he was a rough one. He wouldn't have lasted long in our unit. He'd have been hung and quartered.

A series of bush fires occurred south of Watson Lake in the summer of 1943. Eight miles of poles burned in the worst one. A career officer from another unit came along while we were making temporary repairs with field wire strung along the road.

"What are you fellows doing stringing that wire along the ground?" he demanded.

Of course, there was some snickering at his ignorance and some smart-alec remarks that wounded his pride. Hot under the collar, he put through a call to McKinley at Edmonton. Knowing there was likely to be trouble, I had phoned an advance report to McKinley to explain why we were laying the wire on the road. When the heated-up officer reached McKinley from Muncho Lake, McKinley said:

"Well, sir, where are you calling from?"

"I'm calling from Muncho Lake."

"Don't you realize there have been eight miles of poles burned out between you and me?"

"No."

"Well," said McKinley, "if it wasn't for those guys stringing that temporary wire along the road you wouldn't even be talking to me from there."

Put officer pips on an ordinary civilian and he can turn rotten, too. A skirmish occurred between Maj. Van Nort and me. Van Nort had borrowed my jeep to inspect some line near Smith River. The jeep had a flat.

But rather than change the tire himself, he walked four miles to a camp where some GIs were at work and ordered them to go out and change the tire. They were very hostile about this. They phoned me.

"Go up there and flatten another couple of tires," I told them.

With the Christmas, 1942, celebrations behind them, the next task that winter was to push on 900 miles to Whitehorse using the preliminary road built during that year. Men with a sub-contractor, Oman-Smith of Nashville, Tenn., found themselves working at temperatures of 40 to 50 below zero in winter and a sea of mud in the spring. But on May 1, 1943, they reached Whitehorse and by May 23 full service was initiated with all repeater stations manned.

Running the line 600 miles to Fairbanks was another story. The preliminary road had almost disappeared due to washouts and landslides. Even into July travel was impossible. A convoy sent out then bogged down. It was forced to return to Whitehorse, where it was put on a river steamer and taken down to Dawson City, Y.T., and thence to Circle, Alaska. Road conditions were better out of there but it wasn't until mid-October, 1943, the hook-up to Fairbanks was put into service.

Elements of the 838th Signals worked toward each other on the Canol Road with Bechtel, Price and Callahan crews from Johnson's Crossing to Norman Wells. This 600-mile pole line was not completed until February, 1944.

The toughest part of this job was laying three miles of submarine cable across the Mackenzie River in winter at 40 below zero. There were 6½ feet of ice on the river. Dynamite charges were set in holes drilled by steam. The charges were set off simultaneously and a steam shovel cleared away the scattered ice. Cable had to be spliced and laid rapidly before the river froze over again.

Some of the work had to be done over again when the ice went out of the Mackenzie in May, 1944.

The worst piece of line to maintain was the 110 miles along the White Pass and Yukon Railway from Whitehorse to Skagway. It was completed in the fall of 1942.

Winds of 60 miles an hour constantly wrapped lines together and snapped them off. Warm moisture-laden air from the Pacific put six inches of ice on the lines at the Skagway end and often snapped them. Patrolmen sent out to knock the ice off had to contend with snow drifts 25 feet deep. In some places the wires were buried and in others the linemen could reach them from snowbanks.

Despite our best efforts at clearing the right-of-way, many trees later fell across the line. On one September day in 1943, 150 trees were found across the line between Dawson Creek and Whitehorse.

* * *

Another duty of the 843rd was supplying lines to service teletypes to companies and army units needing them. Mrs. Florence English, Edmonton office manager for Bechtel, Price and Callahan, recalled:

Before the 843rd completed the telephone line to Fairbanks (and even after), BPC was despatching and receiving a total of 500 telegrams a day at Edmonton. This was more than most American cities at the time.

Messenger service would have bogged down under this load so we put in tie-lines with both main offices of Canadian National and Canadian Pacific Telegraphs. This made us, in fact, a branch wire office. This service was unique in Canada at the time, although it became standard service later, especially to newspaper offices. We had a working arrangement with the CNT to supply us with key or teletype operators.

For servicing the North, we used the telephone lines built by the 843rd, under Maj. O.F. Roberts, whose headquarters was in Edmonton.

When we made the move from our overcrowded office in the Mills Motors building to the Redwood Building, I wanted to install a tie-lie to connect the 843rd with us. However, Maj. Roberts said the only way he'd go for this was if I could get a teletype machine installed in his office. He didn't think I could do this because all had been commandeered by the forces.

However, I knew George McDonald, head of CNT in Winnipeg. I phoned him and asked him if he could dig up a teletype for me. He somehow got his hands on one in a remote station and sent it to me — much to Roberts' surprise. He told me afterwards I had pulled a fast one on him and had never expected I would be able to call him on that one. He had to fulfil his commitment as I had it from him in writing.

We designed continuous rolls for the machines, with the ability to make nine copies of each message. This became standard practice for many years. All messages were distributed through the routing desk system I organized.

* * *

During construction, a right-of-way 60 feet wide was cut with three bulldozers operating abreast. Sgt. Lewis was on one of these crews. He became so intent on his work he tipped over the edge of an 800-foot embankment. Fortunately for him there was a rollbar on his machine. This frame saved his life as the big machine turned turtle as it slid down the steep bank.

Lewis was jammed underneath unable to extricate himself and there was Diesel fuel pouring all over him when the boys reached the bottom. They managed to pull him out by brute force. Lewis later said:

"If you don't believe you see your whole life flash before your eyes in a situation which could be your last minutes on earth, you're crazy. I saw my whole life in review."

July proved to be trouble month for the crews. It is still trouble for everybody, including tourists, when the run-off from melting snow comes sluicing off the mountains.

The worst stretch was the 160 miles between Fort Nelson and Muncho Lake. At 3:32 p.m. July 10, 1943, a crew was sent out from the Muncho Lake repeater station to pull fallen trees off the wires. They had crossed a "wash" where water was spread 300 feet and a foot deep on the way out. Attempting to get home, they got hung up in water 12 feet deep and two miles wide.

As a temporary repair, wire was laid across Muncho Lake and supported by boats.

The Canadian section of the line was turned over to the RCAF in 1945. When peace came the Canada Department of Transport got it and placed Canadian National Telegraphs in charge. The land line was supplemented by a microwave system in the 1950s. In 1967, CNT phased out the pole line between Edmonton and Grande Prairie.

In only 25 years the most modern system the U.S. Army could build was rendered obsolete by more modern technology.

The pole line along the Canol Road remained in various states of repair until 1975 when the Canadian government had the poles cut off and the wire rolled into spools as a make-work project for Indians. Wilderness association activists, concerned for the safety of wildlife, advocated the clean-up as animals had become ensnared by the wire at times.

15

Women Braved Rigors Of Wartime Project

Although the Alaska Highway and Canol Project were initially staffed by men, women came onto the job in the later stages as the supply of non-draft-status males became scarce and uncertain.

In addition to women in the work force, some military and civilian wives were permitted on the projects. The easiest way for them to gain access was to get a work permit.

Walter Wright, an operating engineer for Dufferin Paving Company of Toronto, set out for Dawson Creek with his wife, Edith, and eight-month-old daughter, Elaine, in June, 1942. He became a permanent "emigrant" from Eastern Canada and stayed in Dawson Creek after the war to operate a cold-storage business.

* * *

Before taking off, they put their car in storage as they lacked gasoline ration coupons and a source of buying new tires. However, they shipped a new house trailer by rail. He recalled:

It was a 28-hour trip to Dawson Creek from Edmonton on the second section of a Northern Alberta Railways passenger train: day coaches only, no diner, no sleepers; these had been assigned to the first section filled with troops and other construction workers. I even had to go forward to get the fireman to heat the baby's bottle under the steam hose in the engine.

There were no rooms available in Dawson Creek. The NAR station agent told me the trailer had arrived but he wasn't too hopeful about getting the railcar spotted on the team track as the yards were jammed with cars of construction machinery.

"I'm in quite a predicament," I told him. "I have a wife and child in the waiting room and no place for them to sleep."

"I'll tell you what. Go and see the yardmaster—and he might be able to do something for you."

I finally contacted the yardmaster and told him my story. In the matter of an hour he had the car spotted for me on a team track. To get it unloaded was another matter.

In desperation, I stopped a trucker on the street. I learned what informal northern hospitality was all about as he did not hesitate to help me unload the trailer and park it in the railroad yard. In the meantime, I had met a friend from Niagara Falls, Ont., who lived in a rented shack.

Our introduction to Dawson Creek found my wife and baby staying at his shack and I slept in the trailer. The next morning the indoctrination of Edith (who had been a city girl all her life) continued. She sent me out to get milk. I ended up at the farm of Jack Kennedy, the drayman, and bought two quarts, fresh out of the cow; there was none in any of the stores. Edith refused to use it because it had become fashionable then in Toronto to feed kids pasteurized milk. So Elaine grew up on store-bought canned milk, which everybody in the North used.

I worked at the Dufferin Paving camp in Dawson Creek for a few weeks, then was assigned to a camp at Taylor Flats on the Peace River, five miles south of Fort St. John. I decided to take the trailer there a couple of days in advance, completing the move after supper so as not to miss a day's work. At that time of the year it was light until after midnight. Jim Pickard, the superintendent, was not to keen on me moving the family out to a line camp but I told him if they didn't go I didn't go. I guess I was even a bit dubious about such a move myself but I was determined that's the way it should be.

Nobody had seen a home on wheels around here before. It weighed 2 1/2 tons and took quite a lot of power to move it. The only car available with a trailer hitch was a 1936 Ford with an under-powered engine and no brakes owned by a clerk in the office of R. Melville Smith, the management contractor.

The worst part of the trip was negotiating the steep grades on both sides of the Peace. At that point the river was 350 feet below and the crossing was then by ferry.

I knew I was in trouble as soon as we took off. It was all the old Ford could do to pull the load up the first hill out of town. Later when we hit the steep grade going down to the Kiskatinaw River, the motor really wound up; I thought it was going to go through the hood. Starting up the other side, the old car powered out on the steep grade. I jackknifed it across the road to stop it from running back as Edith and Elaine cowered in fear. We sat there awaiting help.

It came in the form of an army six-by-six with a winch. The driver towed us up the steepest part of the hill out of the way. Then a man from Dawson Creek with a small Ford coupe came along and towed us 30 miles to the top of the ferry crossing, arriving about midnight,

"You won't need me anymore," he said. "It's all downhill from here."

"Is it very bad?" I asked.

"It's pretty bad," he replied. "I'd advise you to stay here overnight."

I couldn't do that. I simply had to get the trailer to Taylor and be back on the job in the morning as the big rush was on. I figured I'd give it a try. I put the car into low gear and there was no turning back from those hairpin switchbacks. It was terrifying and hair-raising. By the grace of God and sweaty palms we made it down.

The motor was just a-screaming as we came around those steep grades and into turns. Finally the bottom came and we pulled onto the ferry: and arrived at the gravel slip on the north side. The ramp there was built for bulldozers, other heavy equipment and big trucks. I was soon bogged down with the rear end of the trailer dragging in the gravel.

An army truck couldn't pull us out. However, the ferry man went back across the river, picked up a small crawler tractor and managed to get us on the road again.

By this time it was daylight and I could see a stiff climb up the north bank. I had just gotten around a sharp turn when the old Ford powered out again and back we came. I managed to jackknife it again to save us from plummeting straight down into the Peace. I waited until another truck came along. He towed me to Taylor.

Edith was reluctant to stay in the trailer parked in the company yard. She was very nervous in the wilds of British Columbia. I didn't get back for two days and that made it worse.

The next move was Sept. 20 when Dufferin Paving won a new contract 350 miles up the road — north of Fort Nelson. Once more it was rough travelling and getting located — especially going over Steamboat Mountain. It was pretty primitive living but by Christmas we had a good camp set up.

Then civilization came in the form of Greyhound buses. In March we went out on a holiday to Toronto. Edith and Elaine travelled by bus to Dawson Creek while I rode in the back of the company mail and ration truck. I don't know who got the better of the deal; Elaine was sick all the way as the bus negotiated the crooked rolling road.

When we arrived back from our holiday in April at the beginning of the 1943 construction season, the bears were just coming out of hibernation. One day I came home for lunch at noon and found Edith ready to walk out of camp.

She had been baking a cake and the aroma had drifted out to a black bear. Elaine was standing on the chesterfield looking out the window when all of a sudden she squealed:

"Mommy, look at the kitty! Look at the kitty!"

There was the bear standing up sniffing in the window. She made the right move by grabbing a couple of pans and banging them together — and the bear left. She also wanted to leave.

I mollified her by going to Caswell's camp and borrowing a rifle. A couple of days later at 3 a.m. I heard bears coming around and went out and shot two. But there were still plenty left. I moved the trailer alongside the warehouse where the bears didn't venture.

My last bout with the trailer came on the way out at the end of the 1943 construction season. It was being towed behind a R. Melville Smith truck loaded with six tons of crusher jaws and driven by a wild cowboy. He ignored the ice forming on the road till he started down a hill 79 miles north of Fort St. John and hit the ditch. The trailer broke loose and rolled over seven times down a steep bank, breaking the axle in the process. I know it rolled over seven times because I was in it with a chap from New York. Fortunately Edith and Elaine had gone ahead in the superintendent's car. Although I suffered a knee injury, I hitchhiked into Fort St. John, got a new axle machined at Okes Construction Company camp, went back and salvaged the trailer and hauled it to Dawson Creek. I sold it to a guy from Calgary — and never had anything to do with trailers since.

When I returned to the trailer after the upset, I found somebody had ransacked it but the only missing valuable was two boxes of photos I had taken on the job. I was upset as they were irreplaceable.

Two months later I was called into the R. Melville Smith despatch office and there was a package with my name on it. I opened it and there were my missing boxes of pictures. They had been brought in by a truck driver — but I could never trace down the thief who "borrowed" them.

* * *

Bears were an occupational hazard because the Yanks had also invaded bear country in their "invasion" of Canada. However, not all women reacted to them the same as Edith Wright. Sgt. M. F. Tibbetts of the 843rd Signals recalled:

Lum 'N' Abner's was one of the first two civilian roadhouses which followed construction of the highway. It was built at Mile 233 by E. A. Tucker, Montney, B.C., merchant, to supply meals, gasoline and beds for $1. The log construction was primitive but the place was welcomed by army and civilian truckers alike.

One day as I was passing, I heard shooting inside the door and stopped to investigate. Here was a bear on the floor and pies all over the place and this old woman cook standing there with a smoking shotgun yelling:

"Damn you, you won't steal no more of my pies."

She had set a row of freshly baked pies on a table in the living quarters in back, separated from the main cafe by a curtain.

The bear had smelled the pies through an open window and had come in on a pile of wood below the window. The cook heard him come in and grabbed the gun, running in and shooting as she went, madder than hell that her morning's work had been ruined.

I came through the front door with my sidearm at ready and this bear was lying on his back where he had fallen off the table. She was still blasting away and cursing and yelling.

Two days later she repeated the performance with her trusty shotgun on a big grizzly which came in and was tearing down the meat cache to get some sides of beef.

* * *

Generally speaking, women were more adept at handling bears than men. It was likewise established that Indians could handle their women better than white men. This apocryphal story by Herb Mowat, a foreman with Don

Construction Limited of Toronto, indicates this succinctly:

We had a band of Indians camped 400 feet below our camp on the river flats at the Kiskatinaw bridge site. They were fabricating creosoted pine culverts hooped with steel. The top Indian carpenter was Louis Ghostkeeper.

One night one of Louis's fellows scaled up the bank and knocked on the door of the bunkhouse in which there were 40 men asleep. The man nearest to the door opened it and said grumpily:

"Whatta ya want?"

"I want a bed," said the Indian.

"Whatta ya want a bed for? You live down in that valley."

"Yah. Want bed. Can't sleep in tent."

"Why can't you sleep in your tent? You slept there last night didn't you?"

"Can't sleep in tent," the Indian said. "Bear in tent."

Bears are mighty cranky just before hibernation and the natives avoid them; stay out of their way because they are so capricious they will tear the face off you just as quick as look at you if you cross their path.

Well, that was a damned good reason for not sleeping in the tent. The man in the bunkhouse said to him:

"Look here, you live in that bell tent with your wife, don't you?"

"Yeh," replied the Indian.

"Do you mean to say you come up here and ask for a bed for yourself because there's a bear in the tent — and you've left your wife down there with a bear in the tent?"

Indignantly the Indian said: "All right for her. She sleep. Bear wake me."

* * *

As husbands and boyfriends went overseas and casualty lists became longer, many thousands of Canadian women joined the work force or went back to work. Mrs. Margaret Murray of Hussar, Alta., a cowboy's wife, was one of the latter. She recalled:

I got a job in Dawson Creek office of the R. Melville Smith company during the 1943 construction season. The amusing thing was that when we wound up the accounts the only item that we could get to balance was the vinegar supplies.

At the end of the season I joined Helen (Topsy) Banke of Calgary and Winnie Guest of Yellow Grass, Sask., to go to Whitehorse. The National Selective Service (predecessor to the Unemployment Insurance Commission) was reluctant to allow women to go north but when the manager saw we were serious he offered us jobs in the NSS office there, but made it clear we wouldn't be allowed to work for the Americans.

When we arrived we found one poor old fellow in the office trying to cope with the paper work on hundreds of people still coming and going.

He was at the end of his tether and had almost given up in despair. Our job was to make some semblance of order.

A big white house had become available for NSS staff but the day we arrived the owner had backed out of the deal and sold it to Bechtel, Price and Callahan for more money. We had no other choice than to stay at the Whitehorse Inn.

The old man became terribly annoyed because he knew we couldn't afford the high room and food prices. Since NSS could not keep its part of the bargain, he gave us a permit to seek employment with the Americans. We were quickly snapped up by the United States Engineering District for its auditing office. This allowed us to live in the army women's dormitory much more cheaply. I worked there until April 1, 1946, when the highway was turned over to Canada.

As might be expected when males outnumbered females by about 200-to-1, pregnancies occurred and caused problems. There were no facilities to handle births. Where was Dr. Henry Morgenthaler when he was really needed?

A great many girls knew nothing about sex. I was naive myself about some of the common sexual aberrations that are discussed openly today. It was because of this I suffered an embarrassing incident.

A couple of men discovered a young man had homosexual tendencies. They had a lot of fun at his expense. One day I overheard one of them say to him:

"Look, fruit, go with Mrs. Murray and help her on the payrolls." I though "fruit" was his nickname. So I said:

"Yes, come along, fruit."

Everyone in the office just about died laughing. I didn't realize I had done anything wrong until he became furious.

"I don't mind them calling me that. But don't you dare call me that again," he said.

I found the code of morals in the North very much different than on the Outside. There was more tolerance than was found there.

Take the case of Eva. She was a clever youngster with a good education, one of the few Canadian girls in the camp kitchen. She was treated as a favorite. When she became pregnant she was not given a big dose of public disapproval as she would have encountered Outside.

The whole office staff was solicitous about her condition and more or less adopted her. They saw she was taken out of the kitchen and given an easier job in the office until after a son was born. I never saw anyone treated so well. They even took up a collection to help her financially. Quite a few of the American couples in Whitehorse offered to adopt the baby. However, she wanted the baby to stay in Canada — and a Whitehorse couple adopted him.

* * *

One of the camps to which a large number of women were assigned was Norman Wells. Eventually there were several hundred of them in that area living in quonset huts or dorms. Although there were strict rules of conduct, Miss Wilson, the camp matron, found rule enforcement difficult. Some of them came in and got turned around pretty fast because of venereal disease and pregnancy problems.

Mrs. Florence English, Edmonton office manager for Bechtel, Price and Callahan, recalled going into Norman Wells and being drawn aside by Miss Wilson and asked for suggestions on handling the problem:

My father, David McEachern, and my uncle had spent time in the North and I and previously worked in the North a couple of years.

"Well," I replied, "from my previous experience in the North, the first thing I would insist upon is that all the women wear skirts. Although this may be wilderness country, try to keep them feminine. You won't have much trouble with the girls if they are put on a pedestal. When they fall off they go pretty far down. When people are thrown together like this a girl should remain a girl."

I found out later that when my advice was put into the camp regulations, I was pretty universally disliked. However, they had to admit it worked.

I was at the Norman Wells airport one day when six women passengers were leaving on the flight with one-way tickets; there were always pregnant women on outbound flights. Wally Bellig, Canadian Pacific Airlines agent, stood there with his hands on his hips watching the parade. He turned to the pilot, Joe Irwin of Rochester, Alta., and made this profound observation:

"There they go. You know, it's an amazing thing about these latitudes: when the gals are hit with the love bug up here they sure get chawed bad."

I was one of the first Canadians to go to work for Bechtel, Price and Callahan of San Francisco when it was awarded the management contract for the Canol pipeline. The first BPC people arrived to open an office in Edmonton May 11, 1942. Among them were Paul Grafe, policy committee chairman; Van W. Rosendahl followed him in this job once it was organized; the chief engineer, Ed Lane; the personnel director, B.C. Deane; comptroller, R.D. Grammater, and Neil Durkee, administration manager.

The executives and their secretaries were the only ones on the scene when Ben Deane hired me 11 days later. I was just a little native Edmontonian with normal small-town experience and good knowledge of Northern lore.

The first task to which I was assigned was setting up a filing system. It was based on the duo-decimal system but I knew nothing about the system until later. My aptitude at such work was recognized and I was rapidly promoted to office manager.

As time progressed I gained the reputation for organizing office routines. I had won plaudits for putting the mail distribution system in order and for a filing system for keeping track of thousands of persons coming and going on the job.

Our first office was in the dark and drafty cold Mills Motors building. It was next spring — when they had crammed 364 people in there — that they moved us into the permanent headquarters, the notorious and fabulous Redwood Building.

In the move we were under strict orders not to interrupt the operation of any department. The engineers executed this move by transferring department by department at night.

I'm not sure how many survived one of Edmonton's coldest and harshest winters on the bare concrete floor of that old garage, whose only source of heat was overhead heaters.

The floor was so cold the women had to wear overshoes. One of the girls in the teletype room tried to organize a strike to get better heating. Durkee solved that problem — as problems were usually solved then — by firing her.

I also had a big fight with Lane over having the floor carpeted for warmth. He refused on the grounds the expense would be unnecessary in view of the fact we were soon to move to the Redwood Building. That was at a time when BPC was bringing in redwood from the U.S. for construction, hence the reason for the new building's name.

We had a great deal of sickness — colds, flu and even pneumonia. However, my records showed the people who lost the most time were local Edmontonians and those from colder climates like Minnesota. People from sunnier climates like California seldom booked off sick.

On Saturday, Nov. 7, 1942, a fierce blizzard dumped 20 inches of snow on the city in 20 hours and drifted as high as seven feet. It took me from 7 a.m. to 11 a.m. to go two miles to work.

Public transport was bogged down three days in the biggest snowfall the city ever recorded till then. The Americans came to the rescue of the city with a fantastic number of bulldozers, graders and snowplows they had on hand there. Had they not worked day and night for two days, it would have been a week before all the streets were opened.

Stories of this cold winter filtered back to the U.S. I'll never forget a girl from Texas who came to the steno pool one hot summer day in heavy ski slacks and fur-lined boots. She hadn't brought a summer dress with her. She had to send back home for light clothing — and 15 hats.

Edmonton was a city of surprises to the Yanks. I don't know whether this Texan was more surprised at finding a city of 90,000 or bathrooms in the rooms at the Corona Hotel or five men for every woman!

Having survived the surprises Edmonton had to offer, the Yanks had a few surprises for us. I encountered an American engineer walking down the street one 20-below-zero day with a raincoat over his arm.

"What on earth are you carrying that for?" I gasped.

"Well, you can never tell what it's going to do in this country," he replied. And he was right.

With a large floating population and isolation, the crime rate all over northwestern Canada increased during the American "occupation," especially crimes toward women. I was personally involved in one instance.

I had hired a young woman, Mrs. Margaret Days, as a receptionist. Her husband was in the army and on May 24 weekend he was on embarkation leave. I told her to take an extra day off Tuesday.

She hadn't shown up Wednesday and I received an urgent call from a neighbor who had gone to the house and found her unconscious on the floor. I took our staff nurse and rushed to her house and we got her to the hospital. She died on Saturday. The doctor who handled this case told me several years later it appeared to be a bludgeoning death.

The R. Melville Smith camp at Dawson Creek was the scene of two murders. Roy Matthew Seline, superintendent of the USED garage, was murdered in the trailer there by his wife, a waitress, but a jury acquitted her because of extenuating circumstances.

Dances were held at the Smith camp but GIs were excluded unless they were invited by a female staff member. A carload of five GIs lured a stenographer to their vehicle for a drink outside a dance one night and gang-raped her. She died in hospital next day.

Since there was no accommodation in the camps up the road, there were no organized camp followers. The women hired by construction companies were flown in and housed in dorms as there was no other way of getting them there safely.

Dawson Creek, of course, had no way of barring the entry of prostitutes. Once they arrived, however, it was a different matter. One guy imported a whorehouse full of Negro women and put them up on the hill. They were "persuaded" to leave by the military police, whose terms of reference were to prevent the spread of venereal disease.

Behind the dry-cleaning plant was a six-girl whorehouse run by Freddie the Window Washer of Edmonton. Each night after work, the girls would all troop over to the Shangri-la Cafe for noodles and little Freddie would tip the waitresses $5. It was a real big deal for everybody. The waitresses looked for him to come in every night — and when he didn't come they were really disappointed.

* * *

Construction men could take their wives to camps near Dawson Creek as long as going outside didn't involve a trip longer than a day. Oscar Albanati, an independent trucker from Sexsmith, Alta., recalled one of those who received a permit was a man known only as Wild Bill:

It got to be a standing joke at the Dawson Creek checkpoint that he changed "wives" frequently. A GI guard at the local checkpoint would stop him:

"Who is the lady?"

"That's my wife."

"OK. You may proceed."

The next time Wild Bill showed up he was faced with the same question:

"Who's that lady?"

"That's my wife."

"Oh, she's got much younger."

"Well, she got her hair dyed and got a new hair-do yesterday."

One time he came through with a panel truck—and didn't have any company.

"Where's your wife today?"

"She isn't feeling well. She's lying in the back of the truck."

"We're sorry to hear that. Maybe we better look in on her and see if we can help her."

The guard went around and opened the door and found not one but three women in there!

At the end of construction, a system of check points was established every 50 miles along the spanking new road manned by military police. All travellers were required to be connected with the war effort, were required to have travel permits and have all shipments checked out against manifests.

* * *

With the war ending in 1945, limited civilian travel was allowed for adventure and business. But travel by women was still prohibited because of lack of accommodation for them. The road was in charge of a joint U.S.-Canada team.

Mrs. Joyce Yardley of Carcross, Y.T., claims to be the first woman to travel over the road when travel by civilians was first allowed. Her husband, Gordon, recalled:

My father-in-law and I were stopped at the Fort St. John check point with an old car we wanted to drive to Carcross. He told the guard he was going to work for the Anglican Church in Whitehorse, which was plausible because he was a member of the church and was supposed to work for it for the glory of God. They gave him a pass without question.

I had a little more trouble. They didn't believe I was a farmer and fisherman. But this was true as I had a few beef cattle and horses and fished to supply British Yukon Navigation boats. They reluctantly gave me a pass.

Having secured the passes, I remembered I had forgotten a couple of bags in Fort St. John. The GI at the checkpoint told me to go back, get them and go back through the gate.

The "bags" turned out to be Joyce, our daughter, Norma, age 1, and Joyce's mother. I put them in the back seat under some blankets. This scared Norma and she broke out crying. I thought the jig was up but Joyce managed to hold her hand over Norma's mouth at the crucial point and we were waved on. We made the trip with no difficulty and without incident.

* * *

Some of the women came to work on the projects with the unabashed aim of making a fortune or "getting into circulation" to find a husband, it was recalled by Mrs. English:

It was surprising how many Edmonton girls married American servicemen during the "invasion." Possibly it was because they wore brighter, flashier uniforms and had more money to spend. It was no secret their money gave them enhanced social status everywhere they went and, in particular, in hotels.

In the latter stages of the war, beer was rationed and was only served once an hour to whomever was on the scene at the time — if, indeed, it would go around. Some Canadians had to wait three hours for a drink. An American could get service any time as he usually had the money and knew how to tip.

There were some awful scraps in the construction camps when army officers in their shiny uniforms walked into the dances and monopolized all the women. The best most of the construction stiffs could muster was a clean pair of overalls.

I know one woman who came from Beaumont, Texas, to work at Bechtel, Price and Callahan in Edmonton with the avowed purpose of making enough money to start a liquor store. She was my secretary.

She transferred to Whitehorse where there was a greater shortage of women and, a year later, came out with $10,000 — enough to start her liquor store. But her salary wasn't $10,000. Some years later she wrote a Christmas card and told me she owned five liquor stores.

* * *

As the war continued it became necessary to set aside some of the rules to keep civilians on the job from starving. A shortage of cooks developed. Dick Panter, superintendent for the R. Melville Smith Company, recalled:

One of the toughest situations I ever faced was not with angry men but a gang of angry women. They were eight women I brought in to try out as cooks up the line in the spring of 1943.

They were headed for Dawson Creek on a Northern Alberta Railways train and all would have been well had not a temporary bridge on the Peace River north of Dawson Creek given out. For some reason the ferry was out of service, too, and since we couldn't get them across the river to a new women's dorm at Fort St. John or Fort Nelson that meant we would have to hold them several days in Dawson Creek. On that train were several carloads of construction stiffs from the Harold Harvey Construction Company of Kingston, Ont., which I found out about at the last minute. They were to occupy all the quarters available in Dawson Creek. As we had no separate women's quarters there at the time I wired the cooks in care of the train conductor advising them to detrain at Grande Prairie and stay at a hotel there until arrangements could be made to get them across the river.

The message never reached them — and the two groups arrived in Dawson Creek together. I had to do some fast footwork and rustle up a crew to run up a temporary barracks for them. Despite the fact this crew outdid themselves and built it in six hours, there was no pacifying this female crew; cooks are temperamental by nature anyway. They squawked day and night till we were finally able to ship them up the line.

* * *

Camp life for women in the Public Roads Administration, R. Melville Smith, Okes Construction Company and the U.S. Army at Fort St. John, B.C., was a combination of long hours and making their own recreational opportunities. Mrs. Irma Small Gray of Saskatoon, Sask., spent the 1943 construction season in the PRA office she recalled:

I had graduated from business college in Calgary and was working as a restaurant cashier when the National Selective Service sent me and several other girls north. After a train trip to Dawson Creek we were loaded into an army truck headed for St. John just as the Peace River ice was ready to go out. The ice had already shifted the plank road atop it into a zig-zag pattern. However, we were told by the soldiers if the ice went out we'd be there two weeks before the ferry could start spring operation. None of us wanted this so we chanced a crossing.

Our driver went like hell across the dangerous makeshift bridge. We could feel the ice moving up and down. We made it all right but the next afternoon — April 6 — the ice went out.

I went to work for the accounts and auditing department headed by W. Abbott Gorham of Washington, an efficient accountant and snappy dresser. His secretary was Marguerite Ward of Calgary.

My job was checking contractors' payrolls. They were checked for adding and accuracy and to make sure the companies didn't pay men higher rates than their job classification allowed. Only a few companies tried to gyp Uncle Sam. Our work day was 8 a.m. to 6 p.m. and on days when the payrolls arrived we went back and worked from 7 to 11 p.m. We did all this for $200 a month, with $1.25 a day deduction for room and board.

Even with these hours there were more entertainment opportunities than the girls in the office and kitchen could handle. There were regular dances in the "rec" hall — and we never lacked invitations.

The dances were eagerly awaited because it was a chance to obtain what we missed most : ice cream.

The garden party was the social event of the season. The social committee was not so much concerned that it rained and the event was cancelled but that some unidentified person misdirected the ice cream shipment to Wing's Cafe.

The rec hall was the scene of music hours on Sunday nights at 9:00 and movies were shown regularly by Mort Devitt of Kitchener Ont., YMCA director attached to the RCAF.

The rec hall was also the scene of the year's biggest celebration on July 4, despite the fact 100 women in the offices were Canadians. Because the nearest liquor store was at Pouce Coupe, 60 miles away, there was a shortage. However, this lack was made up by a potion called Kickapoo Joy Juice. The recipe was as follows:

During the year all the left-over fruit juice from the tables was dumped into a large barrel behind the kitchen stove. By July 4 it had fermented into a potent drink that packed a terrific kick. Not a few persons who quaffed a couple of glasses of that elixir found themselves flat on their ass that day.

Each outfit had a softball team. The medics had a keen young pitcher by the name of Spahn (Warren Spahn, who later became a star in the National Baseball League).

Our simple pleasures were not the pleasures of the big city, however, and many couldn't stand the austere conditions of our isolated location, even though we planted vegetable gardens in the spring. James Quong expressed it this way:

"People are so hungry for entertainment around here they would pay a dime to see themselves in the mirror."

There's dead silence in the big dining room at the camp at McCrae, Y.T., as Maj. H. and his girlfriend, Tex, are confronted by his wife.

16

Gwen Holmes Meets The Great Quong

By the end of the 1943 construction season, the main work of the U.S. Public Roads Administration in supervising construction of the Alaska Highway had been completed. The work of the civilian contractors was about 90% done. The U.S. Army's Northwest Service Command had taken over the road but had to leave small skeleton staffs of engineers behind to supervise some uncompleted bridges at the north end. Only offices at Whitehorse and Edmonton were open.

The PRA had hired some Canadians and among them was a young Winnipeg woman, Gwen Dempsey (Holmes). She recalled:

Many of my girlfriends had joined the armed services or gone to Washington to work. So I decided to go too.

Through the U.S. Consulate I got the address of J.S. Bright, chief engineer of the PRA in Washington, and asked if he had a job for me. I hadn't expected an answer but, much to my surprise, he wrote back telling me he had a job in Edmonton.

In January, 1944, I reported to PRA headquarters in the old red brick Empire Theatre building. Later I was transferred to the PRA bridge department under Raymond Archibald, whose office was temporarily located in the Mills Motors building which Bechtel, Price and Callahan had vacated. In September they moved us out to the old Jesuit College which the army bought and renovated. Still later, we were shifted to a prefabricated building near the college.

Archibald was regarded as one of the best bridge engineers in the U.S. Besides him, I had worked for several other highly qualified engineers — including a cost production man, flight strip designer and a historian. The latter, was a white-haired elderly man who stayed only long enough to record a lot of statistics then took off.

For many days he dictated his report to me beginning at 8 a.m. I nearly went nuts trying to produce an accurate transcript as he had a southern accent and I had some difficulty grasping his words. One phrase stuck in my mind for years: ". . . the trader, the trapper, the entrepreneur . . ."

I was young and naive and didn't know exactly what that meant and it bothered me — so much that one night about 3 o'clock I jumped up and looked up "entrepreneur" in the dictionary. I kept wondering:

"What were entrepreneurs doing on the Alaska Highway?"

I never did fathom it!

I wondered if I would ever get a chance to see any entrepreneurs in the Yukon. The chance came more quickly than I expected.

One day Archibald came around before his return to the U.S. and said in an off-hand way:

"How'd you like to go on a little trip?"

"I'm not eligible to go on the road in my job classification."

"I've looked after that," he said, and threw down some papers indicating he had "promoted" me to a field clerk.

And thus on a rainy day in May, 1944, I found myself and a motley crew boarding a wobbly old Barkley Grow on floats to fly to Whitehorse. The pouring rain prevented take-off until 10 p.m., however.

We had to sign away our lives before we boarded the craft — and it seemed as if the release might come in handy for the plane's owner as we hit wild turbulence in the mountains at Watson Lake. I had reason to believe the pilot had never flown the route before — but he put it down on Watson Lake.

Among the passengers in this motley crew was James Y.C. Quong of Moose Jaw, Sask., an engineer who had been ribbing me about getting airsick on my first flight.

When we arrived at Watson Lake I looked out the porthole and saw we were in the middle of the lake.

"I think we've crashed," I cried to Quong in fright. I hadn't realized the plane was on floats.

Quong didn't answer. He was too terribly airsick. In fact, he was green: the first green Chinese I'd ever seen. He was so terrified he refused to open his eyes the rest of the trip.

We finally flew out of the night and into daylight. I didn't get any sleep because I was too fascinated by the manoeuvres of the pilot and everybody on the plane. I was even more fascinated at finding myself in such a helpless position, depending on someone else for my safe-keeping. But it was one more of the "normal" situations in which I later found myself in the North. Less than two years ago I had been leading a sheltered existence in my home at Winnipeg.

The leader of our party was Harris Soleman, a prissy but clever little Jewish engineer from Albany, N.Y., who had never been in the field before. Edmonton was the farthest north he had ever been or wanted to be. The idea of going north simply stunned and horrified him. When we boarded the plane his lip was trembling. I have never before or since seen a person in such an agitated state.

The other person in our group was Stewie, a frail little office boy — a nice kid of 17 who had just graduated from an Edmonton high school. His mother asked me to look after him — but he ended looking after me!

There were some others on the plane I didn't know. One was a great big fellow lying on some mail bags. He had come out of Whitehorse for a few days leave and was returning. He wore two wrist watches and checked the time frequently on both watches. He was the first person I ever met who was really bushed.

Nobody met us in Whitehorse. We struggled forlornly into the terminal, a seedy-looking lot, early in the morning. Nobody knew who we were, or cared.

Soleman would venture forth across the room and approach a big burly truck driver or somebody and try to tell him we wanted to go to the PRA field office downtown but he was brushed off time after time and we retreated to our seats once more.

Only one man was left at the downtown office of PRA and nobody knew much about us or what we were supposed to be doing. Finally someone took us downtown in the back of a truck. Then they took us to McCrae to the Metcalfe-Hamilton-Kansas City Bridge construction company camp. They didn't know what to do with us and didn't really want us. It was a huge camp, especially the mess hall. Everything was confusing and there were a lot of drunks staggering around.

It was the middle of the afternoon before they found me a room in a shaky plywood prefab building. I remember the room vividly because it had been unoccupied for quite a while previously and there were a number of holes and two squirrels kept entering and leaving through one of them all the time I was there. There were some bedbugs or something on the blankets. I killed these.

Drunks kept pounding on my door (which would jump and rock) to find out "who the new people were."

We were there a week before anyone knew what to do with us — a situation I found incredible but I had never come against the U.S. Army system nor the north before. By the end of that time word had somehow reached the lone PRA resident road engineer in downtown Whitehorse that we were at McCrae. All the rest of the engineers were out on the road at the time.

We were supposed to pay $35 a month for our board. However, we never did pay because we couldn't find out where to pay it and nobody sent us a bill. They issued us pink mess tickets but they evidently kept no records on us. I was a bit concerned and consulted Quong:

"Don't give it a thought," he said. "Do as I do. Just forget about it."

At the time I took these things as a matter of course but in retrospect I realize how wild and funny the whole fantastic performance was as there didn't appear to be any organization.

The resident engineer finally informed Stewie and I we could join his staff temporarily.

He was a clever man but seemed slightly confused. We later learned he was from Pennsylvania and was supposed to leave when we arrived. But after two years in the North he'd become bushed and so used to the lackadaisical way of doing things he couldn't make a decision. He kept asking me day after day what he should do.

The chief piece of furniture in his office was a lovely liquor cabinet. He couldn't find anything else for me to do but drink gin from the cabinet. I would occasionally swallow a drink or two to keep him happy but I had been used to working in more conventional office situations and didn't like knocking back drinks on the job. When I wouldn't drink with him he would force drinks on Stewie.

One afternoon I returned to the office and found poor little Stewie quite drunk. It was one of those days this shouldn't have happened. We had gotten word that Mr. Archibald, the big boss, was flying in. It was Stewie's job to go out and pick him up. He could hardly keep his feet and kept mumbling:

"I'll go out there and get him. I'll load him in the truck."

Despite the fact I had a couple smashes of gin, I had enough presence of mind to dash some cold water over his head to sober him up a bit. We finally navigated out to the airport: a manoeuvre greeted by Archibald with composure that one couldn't have expected at an outside airport.

Later in Whitehorse we discovered Soleman was one of those people who just couldn't stand to rough it. He was completely out of his element up there, despite such accoutrements as running water and showers in the married quarters. He came into the boss's office one day almost in tears, overwrought to the point of hysterics. He had a long list of complaints about the food, the accommodation, the people and the environment into which he had to bring his domineering wife. Spousal dissatisfaction with roughing it was one of the reasons wives were discouraged from coming onto projects like this. Somehow Soleman had managed to get his wife in.

The boss sat there and listened to him for a while. The boss was an outdoors type who could thrive in any situation: from monkeys crawling over his bed in the tropics to freezing his ass in a sleeping bag in the Arctic. He looked at Soleman in a kindly way and said in a pleasant voice:

"Well, Harris, what did you expect — the Waldorf-Astoria?"

I was sitting there waiting to take dictation and I thought I'd die laughing at Soleman's distress. A hurt look came into his eyes, just like a kicked sheep dog — and he turned and went sadly away. I suspect the complaints had been largely framed by his wife.

Soleman's wife was larger than he. She was the take-charge type, especially in arranging social outings in which we were expected to take part.

One memorable outing was a junket to Kluane Lake in a carry-all. Harris was tired as we left at some ungodly hour Sunday morning. He had his head in her lap and she was rocking him. She turned and said to Quong:

"Quong, isn't it wonderful that I love my husband so much after all these years?"

Quong didn't reply; he sat there and stared straight ahead, a bit embarrassed. He was more embarrassed when she wanted everyone to join in a sing-song.

In the middle of nowhere the carry-all caught fire. The flames were shooting out of the motor. We put it out with a fire extinguisher but instead of turning back we kept on going to the lake.

We didn't arrive back until 7 o'clock the next morning because every few miles the damn thing would catch fire and we had to stop.

At one point on that ill-fated trip we decided to stop at a roadhouse and have a meal. Now, Mrs. Soleman used to insist that because the PRA was a small outfit we should always travel together and identify ourselves. As if anyone in the Yukon cared who we were! She led the procession into the roadhouse, announcing to a woman sitting morosely behind the counter:

"I don't suppose you know who we are. But we are from the PRA and would like some food."

This grand entrance had no visible effect on the woman. She made no move to rise, just sat there and stared at her and said:

"Well, if you want anything to eat you'll have to find it and cook it yourselves. All the cooks went to Whitehorse and got drunk and are in jail."

I though it a great lark that we had to rustle up cans of food, cook our own meal, and wash the dishes just like in a real restaurant. But Mrs. Soleman could never understand the way these Yukoners acted. She was highly offended. I think she thought the woman was going to spring to her feet and lay on a great spread. But the woman couldn't have cared less. She didn't even say goodbye when we left. She wouldn't have lifted a finger had Gen. Eisenhower walked in.

James Quong was one of the most unusual Canadians I ever met. He had graduated as an engineer from the University of Saskatchewan. He came from a well-known family. His uncle ran a famous Prairie restaurant across from the Canadian Pacific Railway station in Moose Jaw. Mr. Archibald told me he was a talented photographer and cartoonist. He had served in the Dawson Creek and Fort St. John PRA offices and at the latter was head projectionist for movie showings.

He referred to himself in the third person as "the Great Quong" — and everyone called him that.

I never saw a Chinese with a more subtle sense of humor — so subtle one had to be extremely alert to catch the point of his sallies. He was terribly disappointed if you missed the point.

One of his large India ink cartoons was captioned "Priority Zero." It showed Santa Claus trying to thumb a ride on planes buzzing overhead. It was a lampoon of all the people pulling strings to get Christmas leave.

"Oh, yes, I'm going on leave. I can get a seat on a plane because I know Col. So-and-So," we all heard 1,000 times. Despite all the talk nobody was going anywhere — not even Santa Claus.

One day this cartoon, hanging behind Quong's drawing board, attracted the attention of a big dumb blustering American officer who had come in to tell a few corny stories and stand around letting out a few huge brays. After studying it for a minute, he turned and said:

"Quong, did you draw that picture?"

Quong admitted ownership.

"That's a pretty good picture. But what does it represent?"

The Great Quong was so disgusted he just shook his head and didn't even answer. When he came across a real stupid person his large brown oval eyes would develop a kind of sleepy expression and he would simply stare at the person.

This big braying Yankee came in a few days later with another of his corny jokes. Everybody laughed dutifully but Quong. He didn't even crack a smile, but cut him down with:

"Well, that's a good story. But what does it represent?"

His sense of humor was about the only way to handle the strange behavior that beset people in the Yukon and that poet Robert Service wrote about. It was demonstrated in the case of a young lieutenant in charge of kitchen supplies at our camp where about 300 people were being fed. He had fallen in love with a Canadian girl and gotten so carried away he wasn't ordering any supplies from the commissary. It got to the point where the cooks didn't even have enough butter or potatoes. They did their best but the meals were pretty horrible.

It took a hunger strike to settle the issue. I'll never forget as long as I live seeing all the army officers, road workers, married construction workers, us people from PRA and miscellaneous personnel sitting in the mess hall and not going back to work that afternoon.

That night there was a great change. We had olives, celery and steaks laid on. It was a real treat because we hadn't had much to eat for several weeks. It took the demonstration to shake up the young lieutenant.

His girlfriend was the daughter of a Canadian from Toronto who acted as liaison man between civilian workers and the army engineers. He was a weird little man and it was a rare day when he was sober.

One Saturday night about 11 o'clock I was heading for the shower. The door suddenly opened and in walked this Torontonian with a towel over his shoulder, drunk but dignified. He went into the women's shower. He didn't know where he was so I waited outside until he came out. I didn't say anything because this kind of thing was happening all the time and we didn't think it much out of the ordinary.

During the dark period before the strike, Quong's wife, Diamond, arrived in town from Vancouver and saved us all from starvation. She brought a hot plate — a very precious commodity. The meals had been so bad (mostly powdered eggs) he had lost 10 pounds. Powdered eggs were then in their development stage and we were used as guinea pigs for them in camps all along the highway. When cooked, a green mess came out. Many people were getting trench mouth. I recall Wong saying one day:

"You know, Gwen, this isn't the Great Quong you see walking by. This is his ghost. I haven't had a decent meal for three days."

"Neither have I," I replied.

However, after the hot plate arrived, the PRA staff would go down-town and buy some groceries and make such snacks as mushroom soup and toast. He'd come by my desk and look at me with his big round eyes and announce:

"The Fourth Adequate will be at nine o'clock."

We were all thankful to be able to gather at his place for some edible food.

Living in the North tended to develop in people a strange lethargy and the inability to make decisions. One developed the attitude there was no hurry to do anything; not even the most important tasks. It was hard to pull oneself back into reality. I also found this phenomenon when it was time for me to leave the project in late November, 1944.

Mr. Archibald had arranged a boat trip out for me as a treat. I was almost frantic that I wasn't going to be able to make the boat because of an engineer named Ricketts who became infected with this lethargy. He looked like Edward G. Robinson, the movie actor, only was taller and never smiled and he'd been in Whitehorse over a year.

He and Stewie and I were the only ones left in the office. Our job was to pack all the files and forward them by the White Pass and Yukon to catch the last boat out of Skagway. But I found out Ricketts didn't really want to leave and he didn't want me to leave, either.

"There's a month's work here," he insisted. But there was really nothing to do. He wouldn't requisition a reservation on the boat for me – and I got into an awful flap about that. He thought if he had a staff around him he could justify his existence there.

At any rate, the arrangements for my departure finally got made. Two days before I left the Great Quong got one of his spells of melancholia. He and Diamond were not going. He had agreed to stay on as manager of technical services for the Canada Department of Public Works when Canada took over the highway. They were in the Yukon for 25 years. Diamond came over and said: "Gwen, Quong is very sad." She was almost in tears herself. "He wants to see you."

I went over and he broke out a mickey of rye he had saved for sad occasions. We all had a drink.

"Now it's all over," he said. "But some day if you are walking down the main street of a big city and you see two people from the Yukon with noodles hanging out their ears (that's what they had been feeding us for weeks) you stop and say: 'My old friend, the Great Quong!'"

The Quongs knew I was going to stop off at the Georgia Hotel in Vancouver. About an hour after I arrived there was a knock on the door and I was greeted by five Chinese. They were members of the Chan family. For the next three days I was treated to real Chinese hospitality. They overwhelmed me so much I didn't even have a chance to visit my own aunt.

The Chans were members of Diamond's family and she had set this up. She and Quong were from old Chinese families. They were newly married and their marriage had been arranged in the old traditional Chinese fashion. She was a sweet girl who had never been out of Vancouver and suffered spells of homesickness.

At Whitehorse there wasn't much she could do (they lived in the married quarters and ate in the dining room) except help him in the darkroom. He had a deal with the PRA for taking progress pictures of many of the bridge. Before Diamond arrived I received an 8x10 print for a shirt I had washed and ironed for him. He was self-effacing about his work.

"Why don't you see if some of the people in the offices won't buy some of your pictures?" I asked him.

"My pictures won't become famous till after I'm gone," he said in a serio-comic voice. "I'll be like Michaelangelo. They'll say 'the Great Quong once sold his pictures in the Yukon for 10 cents apiece.'"

He ran up a bunch of his best photos and I went through one of the military offices and sold the lot in nothing flat.

"Quong, you're famous and you're not even dead," I said handing him the money.

I had a portrait taken in Edmonton and the prints arrived in Whitehorse when Quong happened to be around.

"You look like a solid Canadian citizen," he said after an appraisal —and broke into snickers. He took one of me that did me more justice.

"You don't look like a good solid Canadian citizen now. You look like a product of the Yukon," was his further appraisal.

When I left Quong gave me more Yukon photos. One night in a Winnipeg hotel somebody went through my effects and stole only photos of the bridges. I still speculate it could have been a spy.

Away from the "spell of the Yukon," back home I found myself thinking back over some of the fantastic and unbelievable events in that big floating population around Whitehorse. For instance, as the days become shorter late in the fall one tends to lose track of time.

One day I asked Quong what time it was. He told me it was five p.m.

I packed up and went home. On the way out I said "good night" to Mr. Archibald. He gave me a funny look. When I reached the dorm the phone rang and Archibald was on the line:

"What are you doing?"

"Oh, I'm getting ready to go out for supper."

"Come on over. I want to see you."

I went back and there was Quong looking at me over his rimless spectacles with a small grin. It was only 3:30 in the "afternoon."

Isolation also brought out the original and interesting in human nature. Take the case of Marion:

She was a secretary in her 30s, had a big deep voice, was very bossy, looked like Gracie Fields and had formerly worked for the Toronto Star.

Her boss had suggested she go outside for a holiday as she had been in Whitehorse a long time. But she had become bushed.

"You know, I don't want to leave. I think I'll stay right here — because I like the soft water."

"What did you say, Marion?" I asked her.

"I said I liked the soft water" — and she gave me the funniest look, as though it was me who was bushed.

A woman of 40 named Vinnie travelled around with Marion. They had been at Fort St. John before coming to Whitehorse. She appeared an extremely conventional type of woman.

But all of a sudden, after a two-week courtship, she married a Russian type and moved to Anchorage, Alaska. She simply vanished one day and that's the last we ever heard of her.

The camp at McCrae was semi-isolated from the main stream of the Whitehorse social whirl. I hadn't been any place for the first six weeks but then the office staff at Standard Oil Company of Alaska decided to hold a big July 4 U.S. Independence Day sports day and party at Carcross. Standard Oil crews ran a tank farm and pumping station on the Canol there.

"I guess I've arrived," I told Mr. Archibald. "They're going to charter a White Pass and Yukon train to take us to Carcross."

"Yes, they'll be able to play ball to midnight at this time of year up here," he said.

A carry-all was despatched to camp to pick up all us girls. When we boarded the train I knew it was going to be wild because they had smuggled in liquor from Skagway, Alaska, where there was no rationing, were drinking it straight before they left and most were so drunk they couldn't stand. Many of the girls were so smashed by the time they reached Carcross they couldn't make it off the train. The big baseball game was cancelled as the teams were so plastered they couldn't even see the ball.

The dance, held in a big quonset hut, was a terrible affair. If one man was found monopolizing a girl, several others would march up and grab him and drag him outside and knock him down on one of the sand dunes. There were fights all over the place and bodies lying all over the sand. Men would come flying out the door and land with a sickening thud.

I'd never seen anything like this before nor since — and neither had some of the others. There were far too many men and not enough women. Many of the girls I had started out with had simply vanished.

I really didn't know anyone there. At one point I found myself being pursued by a horrible drunken character. I took refuge with a couple of fellows in RCAF uniforms and asked them to pretend they knew me. One of them said:

"We have just come back from an overseas tour. But we've never seen anything like this before."

During the buffet at the intermission the fights began again with plates of salad thrown. It was a wild, fierce, indescribable scene.

Around midnight I attached myself to a man and his wife for protection and boarded the train for home with them. Things were even wilder; they had now begun to get ugly and fight with knives.

Before we had gone far all the windows in the coaches had been broken. I was horrified by the smashing of glass and crunching of feet over it in the aisles. But later it just got monotonous.

Back home, about 5 a.m. I was awakened by a pounding on the door. It was that horrible drunken character who had been pursuing me at Carcross. He said:

"You know where I've been all night?"

"No," I replied, "and I couldn't care less."

"I've been in jail. If you'd have stayed with me I wouldn't have gotten so drunk and in a fight. I was only at the party for an hour."

"I'm very sorry," I replied.

"Oh, that's all right. I've been in jail before."

That was the conversation — and he left.

Getting put in jail was an occupational hazard around Whitehorse. I know. I had been there. God, it was funny.

One evening two girls and I were standing down by the Yukon River watching one of those big sternwheelers moving out.

All of a sudden up marched two burly U.S. Army MPs and said:

"You're under arrest."

We looked at them in surprise. I thought it was a joke at first and that they were trying to be funny.

"What law are we breaking?" I asked.

"You're sightseeing in a restricted area," replied one gruffly.

I knew we were in real trouble when they loaded us into a truck and started towards the provost marshal's headquarters, where the jail was located. In summer it was just a stockade — a big tent with a high wire fence around it. Seeing the jail compound frightened one of the girls and she started to cry.

"Do you think they'll put us in there?" she bawled — and was going on something terrible.

They unloaded us and marched us on the double before the provost marshal. It struck me excruciatingly funny that people were being murdered up there and getting off and we three women were arrested for the heinous crime of sightseeing. I think I would have been tempted to laugh out loud had I been sure we were not in a bad spot.

The provost marshal was serious at first but then he adopted a slightly amused look and told us we could go when this girl started sobbing and heaving and making a terrible scene. They were serious about their job and told us if we ever repeated our offence we could be given 10 days in jail. This really scared my friend; she went home and cried all night. She was in terrible state over the disgrace of being arrested and brought before the military authorities.

The general boom-town atmosphere and isolation of Whitehorse made lawbreakers out of gentle people and sent others halfway around the bend (a condition generally known in the North as "getting bushed").

One of the waitresses downtown was a very proper white-haired widow in her late '50s, who answered an ad and found herself in Whitehorse. She came from Chilliwack, B.C. At first, she was shocked at seeing other waitresses rolling drunks.

She didn't want to stay there for the winter but she didn't have enough for boat passage back. She raised the cash by obtaining a liquor permit and selling several bottles at $50 a bottle.

"I just had to get out of there," she said. "That was the only way I could raise the money. My girl wrote and told me she never expected to end up a bootlegger's daughter!"

Violence and pressure seemed to plague the Americans. Murders were committed. Two or three officers disappeared while I was there. One was found hanging from a tree. There were rumors of murders, knifings and muggings.

An American GI working in the dispensary at Whitehorse married a Canadian girl. Later they moved back to the U.S. He went berserk one night and made her get into the car. He took her out and shot her. We always remembered him because he was such a nice chap.

One murder came close to home. I was visiting the officers' mess of the U.S. Army Air Force base one night with a friend from Minneapolis. A sergeant of about 24 and his girl came over and spoke to us. I saw my friend the next day and just as casually as if she was making a comment about the weather she said:

"You remember that young sergeant we were talking to last night?"

"Yes, vaguely."

"He was bumped off last night. They found him in a ditch."

"Why would anyone want to kill him?"

"Oh, I don't know. I heard someone was laying for him."

Nobody got excited over this — and they never did find out who killed him.

The Americans were nonchalant about things like this, but somehow they managed to avoid publicity. Accounts seldom appeared in the local papers. There would be a knifing at a dance or some other social event and it would be general knowledge, but when a reporter showed up American officialdom denied any knowledge of any misdemeanor. They protected their own.

I had a ringside seat to a hilarious marital triangle which raged up and down the highway from Edmonton to Whitehorse and had repercussions as far away as Texas.

At the camp I lived next door to a personal secretary from Texas, whom we all called "Tex." She was having a torrid affair with her boss, Maj. H. — an affair which started in Edmonton.

Little note would have been taken of this circumstance had it not been for a fight between Tex and her sister, who was also working in Edmonton. The sister wrote their mother in Texas and told her about Tex's affair with her boss.

The mother got on the phone and called the officer commanding the United States Engineering Division at Edmonton and told him to tell his major to leave her daughter alone. From then on the affair became the talk of the town.

Maj. H. was from Detroit, Mich., a real nice guy, efficient, smart, had excellent deportment and was very quiet. He was not the kind of man one would expect to be involved in such an affair; it was a queer affair I could never understand.

Not only did Tex follow the major to Whitehorse but his wife and 11-

year-old son arrived, too. The son and wife lived in a cabin near a small lake five miles from camp. However, they came to camp for their meals. Mrs. H. tried to break up this affair by attempting to publicly embarrass her husband at every opportunity.

How Mrs. H. got to Whitehorse I don't know. I do know he didn't bring her because he was too busy fooling around with Tex who, I might add, had a staff car at her disposal most of the time. I used to hear her on the phone in the dormitory hall screaming like a fishwife ordering the major to send the car around. This was truly an amazing performance for, when the car was brought around, she would appear so composed and demure with all her pancake make-up on.

When all the rest of us were getting on the shuttle bus to go to Whitehorse, Tex would order out the boss's car and, with all flags flying, would run into town for a sandwich or a package of needles. We all found this performance highly amusing.

I only ran into Mrs. H. once — and that was by a strange coincidence. I accompanied Mr. Archibald and a driver on a trip to Teslin bridge (one of the major structures on the highway) to pick up a report from the resident engineer and to watch a pour of concrete. Somehow, Mrs. H. and her son went with us.

I could see she was in a terrible state. I would say Tex was fortunate she didn't try to kill her because I think she had a good mind to. When we got to Teslin she began to quiz me about Tex, having found I lived next to her. But I didn't want to become involved. She ended the conversation by saying:

"Something's got to be done about that woman."

She made one last effort to insult her — but it had no effect. I was there.

Somebody had made a decision to provide the women with a separate dining area in the mess hall. The construction stiffs were notoriously inconsiderate at the table. Unless a girl had long arms she didn't get anything to eat. They cordoned off a small area seating about 25 for us.

The inevitable happened one day when Maj. H., Mrs. H. and Tex all blew into this dining area at the same time. This situation had been avoided before, but now the atmosphere became electric. Since everybody knew about the affair, an embarrassing silence ensued.

Mrs. H. turned and stared at Tex. This made Tex a bit flustered and glassy-eyed. Tex was a bit stupid anyway. In a voice dripping with sarcasm, she said to Tex:

"Are you going to have a staff car at your disposal today?" She looked her right in the eye. Tex kept mute. Mrs. H. pressed her advantage:

"I imagine you will — so you can drop me off at my residence on your way to Whitehorse and before you pick up Maj. H."

It was so weird. Everybody was trying to pretend they weren't there. And Mrs. H. had one final sally:

"I'm going to contact someone in Washington. I think so many of these girls are wasting their time. I think they all should be working for Maj. H."

The affair had a spectacular ending. Maj. H. and Tex got very drunk one day and had a huge running fight in which they broke things and shouted imprecations at each other all over camp.

The military couldn't stand for this any longer. They bundled up Maj. H. and put him on the next plane — which left in three hours.

To me, the most uproarious aspect of this marital battle was that while it raged in one part of the Eastern Theatre of Operations a most vicious war was raging in another. I have often wondered if there were such sexual liaisons going on in the Japanese army.

But what can I say: The Americans won the war!

Army guards protect the bank
but ignore bank clerks toting
$60,000 arriving from post office.
COMMERCE

17

Post Office And Bank Grossly Overburdened

On the day after Easter Monday, 1943, Ralph Daw and a woman clerk from the Canadian Imperial Bank of Commerce walked along the rickety board sidewalk in Fort St. John, B.C., trying to keep out of the mud as they carried several bundles wrapped in newspaper under their arms. They had just left the post office and were headed toward the bank where Daw was accountant.

They absent-mindedly said "hello" to a few local residents. Their attention was riveted to three U.S. Army jeeps parked in front of the wooden bank building. Two burly soldiers armed with machine guns and sidearms stood on guard at the front door casing bystanders for any signs of unusual activity.

"This is pay day for the army," muttered a passerby. "I hope it's a unit up the Alaska Highway and they won't be able to leave camp and come to town to raise hell Saturday night."

Daw and the clerk passed through the front door and saw a paymaster sergeant at a teller's wicket and two more GIs bristling with arms observing strict security measures and military discipline. At the back door they could see two more armed GIs patrolling back and forth.

As the sergeant was busily stuffing $6,000 into a bag, Daw and his companion walked behind a row of teller's cages and casually dumped their bundles onto a table. They then began sorting the $60,000 cash in the bundles.

* * *

"We used to laugh quietly to ourselves about the way the Americans set up armed guards to protect their petty cash while we lugged $20,000 to $60,000 around wrapped in newspapers to make the contents less conspicuous with no security or fuss. We just didn't have the time or the police protection for that," said Daw. He recalled further:

The demand for cash was so great we had a standing order with the Edmonton branch to ship in $20,000 in every mail. That was a lot of money in any day. Over a long weekend there could be several shipments to pick up on Tuesday morning.

At one time we were handling army and construction company payrolls worth $2 1/2 million a month. We were forced to handle money more casually than would ordinarily be countenanced; for instance, stacking cash around the tellers' cages in boxes.

New premises were built in the summer of 1942 but by the time I arrived in October they were inadequate. We had eight women on the counter and ledger work was done after hours. There was no room for any more tellers' cages to be set up, otherwise we could have put more to work.

Up to this time women had occupied only minor positions on bank staffs. But old-fashioned standards took a terrific beating when women decided this was their war as much as men's. There was no human rights commission around to recommend they go into combat duty in the armed forces so they were recruited into banks to replace staff shortages. Here they were given heavy responsibilities and worked long hours under pressure.

In the time I was in the Bank of Commerce at Fort St. John to March, 1944, the female staff made only one serious error. A construction worker from Minneapolis was short-changed several hundred dollars. It took the bank a year and a half to find him and make restitution.

Bank of Commerce branches at Edmonton, Pouce Coupe, Dawson Creek, Whitehorse and Prince Rupert won designation by the U.S. Treasury as depositories of public moneys with authority to accept and maintain deposits to the official credit of finance officers of the U.S. Army as the result of the alertness of our Edmonton branch manager. He was on hand for more business when Gen. W.M. Hoge and his party came through on an Alaska Highway route feasibility.

The head office in Toronto immediately offered through the bank's New York agents the services of these branches — and subsequently opened for various periods a sub-agency at Dawson Creek (which was in a quonset hut and was used largely by the U.S. Army from April, 1943, to April, 1944, to relieve pressure on the main branch); Fort St. John, opened as a sub-branch in May and as a branch in September; Muskwa (Fort Nelson) in March, 1943, to April, 1945, and a sub-agency at Johnson's Crossing from March to September, 1944.

The system under which we worked was this:

An authorized representative of the U.S. Treasury, known as a paying officer, opened an account at our branch of $1 million to $2 million. He kept the account replenished with cheques on the U.S. Treasury. From that account we would honor cheques of all contractors and the armed forces which had been approved by the paying officer. I understand some of the management contractors had some difficulty in getting approval for all the accounts submitted — but this is another story.

We attempted to have as many of the civilian and army personnel as possible on the job open accounts with us so they could deposit their cash or cheques and thus lessen the demand for the amount of cash that had to be brought in. However, at any given time we had at least $500,000 in the vault.

Linemen for the various contracting companies on the road would come down the road with perhaps 50 or 60 cheques for the number of men on their payrolls. Each cheque would have marked on it what each payee wanted to have done with the money — so much for his dependents on installment purchases (we would credit the payment to the seller), so much deposited to his account and some in cash.

Each lineman would leave all these cheques with us and we would go to work on them after 3 p.m. closing hour till midnight or 2 a.m. Next day the lineman would return, after a night in town, and take them back to camp 100 or 150 miles up the highway. Thus we didn't have to deal with the men individually — or they'd have needed 10 banks in town.

We dealt only in Canadian funds, converting all American payments. However, we issued money orders in American funds to those who wanted them. American funds were then at a premium of 10 per cent. Large amounts of U.S. currency had to be imported from our Seattle branch to meet the demand of purchasers.

Pay parades and mail calls for people working in lonely and hazardous jobs were tremendously important to morale, it was discovered by the armed forces and civilian contractors. Such people write more letters in wartime than peacetime. Mail is a great morale booster, and receipt of it was a "must." Much of the big labor turnover at the start of the project was directly attributable to lack of good mail service.

Although there was little chance for many of the troops and workers to spend their pay, it was important they receive the money. Many had obligations to wives and families back home. They counted on both money and letters. Many had bought cars or houses on time and these had to be paid off. Not a few wanted to save money to re-establish themselves in business after war.

Of all the bank branches on the American projects, Dawson Creek saw the greatest expansion. The staff had jumped to 24 in 1943 from 4 in 1941. Premises had to be expanded three times with added staff living quarters. However, Whitehorse saw more frenzied activity than either Dawson Creek or Fort St. John as more of the 20,000 military and civilian personnel stationed within a 20-mile radius could personally get to the bank. Staff had to be increased to 20 from 2.

The building which housed the bank was the same that a clerk named Robert W. Service had worked in and written "Songs of a Sourdough" during the Yukon gold rush. It was enlarged twice, and finally contained an apartment for the manager, A.E. Hardy, and separate living quarters for male and female staff. One thing was not changed, however. That was a big set of gold scales which sat in the window.

Volume of business increased 20 times in two years and Hardy estimated money transactions in the Yukon were over $ 1 million a day. At the height of the boom the branch was selling as many as 400 money orders a day as well as servicing hundreds of complicated new accounts.

The Edmonton branch was just as busy. In 1943 it was called upon to negotiate 5,000 salary cheques a month for American employees of contracting firms, drawn on the firms' bankers in U.S. Counter business in the U.S. exchange reached unprecedented levels. It was not an unusual occurrence to see several hundred workmen arrive at Edmonton by train leaving jobs in the north and surge into our office to cash wage cheques drawn on our branches in the North.

In view of the bank's great dependence on computers today, it might be pointed out that all this work was done by staff which was hurriedly trained and who had little background in mathematics and accounting. They didn't stand around wondering what to do or how to do it, they jumped right in and did it.

* * *

Maj. F.H. Johnston, manager of the Dawson Creek army tire plant, recalled:

The American Army put on quite a show for the locals in Dawson Creek, too, handling payrolls. To many of us it was just like a Western movie. The fellows with the bags of money came out ready to shoot down any thief who stuck his nose around the corner. I never saw such a splash of arrogance. The army always let us know they were in command.

I recall one incident when I stopped at the bank one day while driving a jeep the army had assigned me. The army took pity on me after seeing that my personal car was falling to pieces. However, when they issued this jeep nobody mentioned anything about needing a special permit to drive it on the highway.

The fact I was a civilian drew the attention of a couple of "the sticks," our derogatory term for military police, and when I came out of the bank I found my jeep in their possession. They placed me under arrest when I couldn't produce a permit; they wouldn't even allow me to drive it back to headquarters where I knew an explanation would be forthcoming.

I was marched in there as a prisoner and only released after it was established it was a misunderstanding. However, I didn't go driving army jeeps without proper certification from then on.

I have been told that people who wished to avoid the inevitable congestion tried mailing their deposits from across the street only to find the post office suffering in a similar manner as it took as long as four days to effect delivery.

* * *

It was quite true the post office was overloaded as were all the post offices in the small villages along the Alaska Highway. Their staffs were overworked trying to keep the millions of pounds of mail moving in and out during construction.

Marjorie A. Giles, later Mrs. Ralph Daw, postmistress at Dawson Creek during the hectic period, described the conditions under which she and her staff worked:

Before the American invasion got under way, we were in a small two-room building, the main room being 14x20 with a sorting room 20x20. This building became inadequate immediately after the first U.S. Army Quartermaster Corps detachments moved in and set up temporary headquarters in the 5¢-to-$1 Store. We handled all their mail for a while until they were able to receive it directly from the Railway Post Office (RPO) cars on the Northern Alberta Railways passenger train from Edmonton.

We had nicely gotten this problem cleared up when the construction companies and their hundreds of workers began to arrive. These firms rented boxes and the complete mail for each firm and its employees was handed to a mail courier, whose signature was good with us. The RPO clerks assisted with the handling of this by making up individual special packets for the firms so this mail didn't have to be sorted when it reached our office.

Because of the lack of space for installing lock boxes, we had to handle most of the mail through one general delivery wicket. This inevitably caused delays as there was a high transient population in the area. It was a matter of sorting through and through the mail in the general delivery slots. In time we became proficient at this and got to know many of the names. The "old-timers" around town weren't pleased with this situation at all as it meant line-ups of half a block long to pick up their mail.

On occasion, the person at the end of the line had to wait an hour.

It was fortunate, in a way, the building burned down in mid-summer because we were given new and enlarged quarters in a large quonset hut. We operated out of the Legion building a week while it was being built.

It was shortly after this another difficulty beset us when Alfred Sharp, the postmaster, was called into the RCAF. That left me, a small inconspicuous-looking woman, with a nucleus of five women in the rough-and-tumble environment of Dawson Creek charged with seeing the thousands of people in the area were given mail service. However, I was not without experience as I had been in the postal service all my life, dating back to post-high-school employment in England.

Many found it hard to believe a woman was postmaster.

One night a man came in and asked for the postmaster. A clerk came back and called me and I went up and asked him what I could do for him. He stood there and laughed his head off.

"You can't be the postmaster!" he said in amazement.

I proved the North wasn't entirely a man's country. This was one place not cluttered up with men.

We were always short of help. The five women on permanent staff couldn't handle the volume of mail, so we had to recruit whatever girls were available. Most were part-time help and girls coming into town looking for work to tide them over till they found a job elsewhere. Civil servant pay was low in those days and it was difficult for me to hire, much less keep, competent help. Any waitress — and that was a low-paid job even with tips — could make more than post office help. Most of them stayed with us till they were offered higher-paid jobs in the construction companies.

At the peak employment we had 12 extra helpers. Some of these "casual" helpers were pretty awful and we didn't keep them long, which added to our worries. Efficiency was low: Letters sorted into wrong boxes, C.O.D. parcels given out without collecting the money and general mix-ups.

Although the new quonset hut was a great deal longer than the original building, working conditions still weren't fit for human beings and I didn't blame many of the girls for quitting. The cold and dirt were real miseries in winter. There was no running water, just a hand bowl. We had no water barrel anyway and the men who delivered water at first rarely came near us. The army later piped in water, chlorinated water, too, and everyone at one time or another had diarrhoea. An outdoor privy at 30 or 40 below is no fun, I can tell you. In winter we adopted the old northern trick of wearing flannelette pajamas under slacks and sweaters plus an overcoat and a mitt on the left hand to keep warm in this uninsulated building. We had thermogene wool inside our shoes and never took off our overshoes. In summer time a heavy rain brought water up underneath the floor.

Things were too busy for us to stop to think about the abominable working conditions. We just carried on. There were a lot of laughs and there was always something to comment and laugh about going on in the town.

Ottawa didn't realize the problems we were up against in our small quarters but couldn't have cared less. Just so long as we did the work, didn't complain and carried on with the job, they left us to our own devices.

Nominally we should have been in the Vancouver postal district but since there was no direct connection from there we were attached to the Edmonton district office as we were directly connected to it by the RPO on the Northern Alberta Railways. We called Vancouver the "old men's office." We never thought they were too bright as, when any mix-ups in the mail occurred, they usually originated in Vancouver.

The Edmonton district office gave us all the help possible. For a period I sent in the daily accounts to Edmonton where they were written up and returned to us. This helped a lot. At the peak of the rush our office, Fort St. John and Fort Nelson were exempted from inter-office accounts. Edmonton did not complain (much) when my official mail got behind!

Despite the fact several hundred bags of mail were dumped on top of us daily, all the first-class mail was sorted after the arrival of the NAR passenger train each night before we went home. However, sometimes we were two weeks behind with the second (newspapers) and third-class mail (parcels).

The largest number of bags dumped in on us in one day was near Christmas of 1942. Christmas was pure hell. We had to walk sideways between the stacks of parcels. Christmas Eve we all worked till 2 a.m. then came back in the afternoon.

I had to be back at 5:15 every morning to put mail on the train which left at 6:15. I had a 10-minute walk to work and the police didn't like to see me making the trip afoot because it was a pretty rough town. They usually arranged to have a cruiser on hand to take me to the office. Two of the clerks lived two miles out of town and more often than not the U.S. Army would send around a truck to take them home.

After my early-morning chore I went home for breakfast about 8 and returned at 10 and was usually on the job until 8 p.m. to midnight. We would often drop mail at our friends' doors on the way home. These were the old days of the post office when we believed in giving good service. We did a good job and were proud of it. (Canada would have lost the war with today's postal service.)

Quite a lot of mail ended up in the dead letter office. We tried to send it down there promptly but just couldn't keep up with it. It would be a month sometimes before we could ship the undeliverable mail down there.

We also handled thousands of dollars in bank packets as matter of routine. We generally didn't know how much was in them but one day the RPO clerk told us there was $250,000 in them. Just for the thrill of being able to say we had a quarter of a million dollars underfoot we all went over and stood atop the pile.

May 22, 1943, was a trying day for us. In the middle of it all, in walked Edna Jaques, a well-known Canadian author of the time. She was doing a freelance story for Maclean's Magazine on Dawson Creek. She said Ottawa had sent her to inquire what help we needed. Being extremely busy at the time and in none too good humor, I was very short with her:

"Tell the idiots we don't need any more help. But we do need more room so we needn't walk sideways nor freeze to death while doing it."

My bad temper evidently had some effect as a couple of months later I had word that a new building would be erected. Sharp had been agitating for new quarters before he left but he was getting nowhere. He had a letter from Ottawa saying:

"There's no hope of getting a new building. You'll just have to carry on."

We were very happy to see our new building and when we deemed it far enough advanced to move in we did so on a Sunday. Later we had a visit from one of those silly-ass postal inspectors who was a stickler for regulations. He came around and informed me we shouldn't be here as we had no permission. I told the fool we were already here and what was he going to do about it and added a few more choice words that were definitely not lady-like.

The whole town was in an uproar over the story Edna Jaques wrote for Maclean's. It started off: "Of all the rip-snortin', hell-raisin' towns that ever mushroomed to fame overnight, Dawson Creek heads the list. It's 100 boom towns rolled into one, 100 army camps, a stampede, a madhouse were human emotions run amok and the devil lurks behind every hitching post."

This was all right but the people of Dawson Creek weren't ready to admit Miss Jaques found roustabouts, hangers-on, sharpers, gamblers, bootleggers and swindlers — the scum of the earth that follow every boom town — in their midst.

She also saw fights, drunks being dragged away and vice so bad "no woman dares to go out at night alone. . . . Army police stalk the streets day and night — strong young men with wooden clubs strapped to their wrists . . . the 'chocolate soldiers' constitute a real problem. It is forbidden by law to sell Negroes alcohol but rum-runners sell them hush-hush stuff and so many 'incidents' have happened the town is off-limits to them."

I'll never forget the old devil. What aroused my ire was not the fact she didn't write that the post office was expected to handle 100 times the amount of mail it was built to accommodate or that the girls were glassy-eyed with fatigue because they had to work 14 hours a day. She wrote that among the signs she saw around town was one which said:

"Post Office Closed Till We Get Squared Around."

This bloody well wasn't true. We, like most rural post offices, did close while we were sorting the mail but that was routine. There might have been a lot of mail around but there wasn't, as she said: "Half a ton of unsorted mail in great heaps on the floor. They seem to manage the letters all right but no one expects to get papers or magazines — the post office staff just can't get around to sorting them."

She had a great imagination and she turned it loose on Dawson Creek. Another result of her representations was that some of the people and the U.S. Army who had been complaining about the mail service used her article to put pressure on the post office to improve conditions. Grant McConachie, president of Canadian Pacific Airlines, flew in post office officials to take a look at the situation — and they were horrified. I don't think anybody outside quite realized how many people there were in the area.

Those flown in by McConachie were T.J. Reilly, acting district postal superintendent from Edmonton; J.B. Corley, who held the same job at Vancouver; George Herring, chief superintendent from Ottawa; W.E. Allison, officer in charge of postal service for the Northwest Service Command, and Capt. Yeiser, Northwest Service Command postal officer from Edmonton.

This delegation didn't come around to bother me — and I couldn't have cared less. I guess they were too scared to face us. They went straight through Fort St. John. Actually their trip was a waste of time.

Corley suggested the best way to break the logjam of third-class and second-class mail (this was more pertinent at Fort St. John) was to take it all back to Vancouver and sort it out and get it moving again as there was more personnel there to do the job.

On Saturday, Feb 13, 1943, Dawson Creek suffered a catastrophe during a garage fire when a gigantic dynamite explosion occurred. The blast damaged the post office only slightly — the back windows were blown in.

I became involved in the events of that terrible night when two of the women on the staff went out to see what had become of the young son of one of them during the fire. They found he was home and they returned to the post office. One of the women, Ann, said:

"That's quite a fire burning down there, Marj. They say there's explosives in it."

I went down to have a look at it and was standing in front of the glass windows of the 5-and-10-cent when it went off. Fortunately it blew all the glass inward and I received only a small scratch. But people were being flung down all around me and injured. I guess I must have been in shock momentarily for I said to myself:

"I should be back in that office or there'll be hell poppin' if they hear I'm away."

I took off like a rabbit.

Because of the fire threat after the explosion we decided to remove all the first-class mail, seven liquor sacks and the C.O.D. parcels. I went around to Bechtel, Price and Callahan, the prime contractors on the Canol pipeline which had an office in town, and arranged with them for the use of their mail station wagon and a driver. We had to guard those liquor sacks with our lives. Ottawa was awfully fussy about them. We had to institute more security precautions on them than the bank money shipments!

We tumbled all the mail out of the general delivery slots into bags and took them over to my house on the edge of town. We were able to move back to the post office over the weekend.

The staff members excelled themselves under difficulties that night. We never lost a registered letter then or any other time during those difficult days — and all the liquor got through.

The whole job was a terrible strain on me. After things simmered down in the fall of 1943 I went on part time and wasn't much good for a year after that.

Bechtel, Price and Callahan had developed its own mail service — a post-office-within-a-post-office. This set-up became necessary to serve the large number of people BPC brought onto the Canol project.

* * *

The person who organized the system was Mrs. Florence English of Edmonton, the office manager for that company. Mrs. English recalls:

Our mail problem was complicated by several factors.

First, we had hiring halls all over the United States and persons hired would nominally be sent to Whitehorse via Edmonton. However, by the time they reached the marshalling camp in Edmonton, their destination might change to Norman Wells, Whitehorse or elsewhere, according to the demands of the various job foremen. The camp was located at Calder on the outskirts of town near a CNR rail yard. There were bunkhouses, cookshack and post office, the latter being located in a quonset hut.

With the uncertainty as to where the workers would be despatched on the project, I instituted a system where change-of-address cards were given to the men as they were hired. They could send these cards back to the mail room in Edmonton whenever they moved.

Secondly, when the Americans first went north there were many locations like Norman Wells where there was only one mail delivery a month. We had a number of spots where there were foul-ups not only in getting the mail to the north out of Edmonton but in getting it to men stationed at isolated construction and maintenance sites. However, we organized a system in six months which made it possible to carry all our mail by plane and gave all the men daily service even in remote points. This was an immense break-through.

Thirdly, there were nine departments in the big Edmonton office and I had nine departments — each headed up by supervisors and assistants — to look after. This involved intensive organization seeing that the mail was properly distributed and despatched.

To prevent bottlenecks in mail handling, there was a big meeting between the Canadian and American military and civilian people with their opposite numbers in the post offices on both sides of the line. I represented the contractors. It was agreed that some of the stringent postal regulations would be waived in order to expedite the movement of mail.

I knew Tom Reilly, the acting district postal superintendent at Edmonton, and he arranged for me to inspect the postal set-up at Edmonton. Then I went back to BPC and designed an operation to fit in with theirs — somewhat like a sub-post office. At Edmonton our mail room was 40x60 with 16 mail clerks. Our bags were despatched without being sorted again right onto the railway post offices. We despatched mail to points throughout the project from our Edmonton set-up — by train wherever possible (such as to Waterways and Dawson Creek) and by plane to the points where land service was slow.

Our company mail operation in Edmonton was an operation bigger than most towns and cities in the west at the time.

I think we had one of the first postage meters in the country. We had a great deal of outgoing mail. Harvey Spivey, who had come in as secretary to Edward V. Lane, the first chief engineer and was later promoted to assistant office manager, had seen these in operation in the United States and suggested we order one to speed up this operation which, up to that time, was a hand-stamping deal. We did. It was a large machine, much bigger than the compact models they have today.

Our mail operation worked well for at the peak of operation there was a turnover of 20,000 employees on the job of whom 7,000 were female. There were 2,000 at Edmonton alone. However, these 20,000 were not all working. There were about one-third coming, a third working and a third going.

Even the post office was impressed by the job I did in organizing the mail service for BPC and expediting it. Our set-up at Whitehorse was inspected by Mr. Turner from the district postal office at Vancouver. He congratulated me on the despatch with which we moved mail through the system. In fact, he informed me I had, without prior knowledge, set up a system similar in that used by the army overseas.

To expedite things I travelled thousands of miles by plane into the field to inspect our mail set-up and delivery.

When it first moved in, the U.S. Army assumed the Canadian postal service would be able to service its engineering troops over the far-flung project. This wasn't possible and the Army Post Office moved its 996th Regt. in to try to service the forward units. They had found it often took letters from the U.S. three to six weeks to reach elements of the 341st Engineering Regt. in the bush north of Dawson Creek. Later, the day after pay day, APO mail clerks managed to reach the lead companies on horseback to sell money orders to GIs who wished to send home money. Nearly $25 million worth of money orders were written by the APO in two years.

With the set-up of activities and the establishment of the Northwest Service Command, the inability of the Canadian postal service to adequately handle the mail over far-flung projects in unsettled areas was responsible for the inauguration of an army truck service along the Alaska Highway. Canadian postal officials co-operated fully with Maj. Walters, who was in charge, and stretched rules to accommodate speedy handling. The result was all American and Canadian civilian and military personnel were served by APO. This service began Nov. 1, 1942, and ran as far as Watson Lake.

Service was speeded up on the south end but service on the north end continued slow for a year after that. It required 21 days for a letter to travel by water from Seattle to Whitehorse. Therefore, the truck run was extended the full length of the highway to Fairbanks, cutting 11 days off delivery time.

It was claimed the longest mail run of its kind in the world and was continued for many years after the war by the Canadian post office.

The Northwest Service Command moved about 42,000 pieces of mail a day. At the peak of the projects in 1943, there were 63,000 persons on the job.

* * *

A year before the Americans arrived, Western Construction and Lumber-

ing Company, headed by James Millar, worked on an all-weather landing strip at Fort Nelson. The location was some miles from the trading post at Musquwa and difficult to reach when infrequent mail deliveries came in. Millar applied for and was granted permission to set up a post office in his on-site construction company office and was named postmaster. Alex Johnston, superintendent, recalled the difficulties for him that move entailed:

All of a sudden I was legally barred from the office when Mr. Millar wasn't there (which was most of the time) due to government postal regulations. To abide by the regulations and eliminate the comical foul-ups he had to have me sworn in as assistant postmaster.

Then the American 35th Engineering Regt. and other forces moved in. One night at 11 o'clock I went out when a plane came in and there were 44 bags of mail waiting for me to sort. It had been held up at Fort St. John for some weeks, then they decided to dump it on top of us. Besides the mail for the troops, they sent along all the mail for other northern points.

I called Millar on the radio next day and told him if he wanted to retain the job of postmaster he would have to come up and run the office himself or get somebody else to do it.

Ultimately, a full-time man, Stanley Jacobs, was sent in to do the job. He also became police magistrate and held several other official jobs.

One day we sold $90 worth of air mail stamps to the Yanks. T.J. Reilly sent a signal from Edmonton saying:

"You can't do that."

"What are you going to do about it? I've already sold that amount," I replied.

It seemed that under postal regulations we weren't classed as a post office big enough to handle that amount of money.

The PRA installed one of Canada's first computers — but it had to be replaced by people.

18

No Tenders Called On This Project

Canadian contracting firms on the Alaska Highway and Canol projects found themselves in a highly unusual situation. Having undertaken contracts with a foreign government on Canadian soil, they discovered they were unable to sue that government because of any contractual dissatisfaction, it was recalled by George C. Andrew of Toronto:

They were under the manifest handicap of not being able to make representations through their members of Parliament or cabinet ministers. The official attitude could only be "let the contractor beware. If he is going to accept contracts under these conditions, it is up to him to make the best deal he can without reference to Ottawa. The only assistance we can give is through diplomatic channels and that is a long-drawn-out process." At that time the most direct channel was between the British and American Foreign Offices as Canada was then not a sovereign country being under the British flag.

Many did not know the predicament they were in until long after they'd signed the contracts.

When the U.S. Public Roads Administration received its assignment from the war department to build the highway in March, 1942, and moved its forces onto the job along with engineering troops, the Americans were desperate to get the job done fast at any cost. PRA unofficially advised the Canadian contractors it would be in order to set aside some of the contract provisions to expedite the work. Money seemed to be no object. "Do the job and let bookkeeping take care of itself," was the order of the day.

Many contractors working under the management contract of the R. Melville Smith Company Limited of Toronto were only too willing to abide by these unofficial directives — but it was a different story when the trend of battle turned against the Japanese and less generously inclined fiscal agencies in the U.S. government stepped in and tied them up in reams of red tape and paper work when it came time for the pay-out. At that time the PRA was nowhere in sight with either moral assistance or pens in hand to sign work orders which would have cleared up the difficulties.

A special form of contract had been chosen by the U.S. War Department — and approved by Congress — for use in wartime situations where time did not permit the preparation of detailed plans for rush projects. This was cost plus a fixed fee for management services and a fixed fee for construction services.

The joker was the fixed fee in both cases was based on the estimated cost of a plan of operations — but the PRA never furnished the plans. The reason was that the plan was changed several times by the Edmonton district engineering office of the Northwest Service Command of the war department, later known as the USED.

Once the preliminary road was holed through in 1942, uncertainty took hold of the project. Several changes in the plan of operations ordered by Gen. C. L. Sturdevant, assistant chief of the U.S. Army Corps of Engineers, put the army in conflict with the PRA.

Being caught in the middle of the "warfare" and being forced to spend too much time on the exacting requirements of the PRA interfered with the smooth running of the Smith organization and cost it a great deal of money. Before the end of the 1943 construction season expenditures of $18 million had been made on a contract estimated at $12 million. The PRA said the job was costing too much but couldn't tell or show the Canadians where.

It disturbed the Canadians the management fee didn't rise accordingly. In other words, the actual cost couldn't be taken as a reason for an upward adjustment of the fixed management fee.

This situation was further complicated by the U.S. auditor-general's office holding back payment of $1 million worth of work performed by various contractors under Smith management up to July, 1943. Smith was overdrawn by that amount at the Canadian Bank of Commerce at

Fort St. John. The aged manager, who was nearing retirement age, was worried to death about the huge overdraft. But the auditor-general was supreme and no final payments could be made until that office gave the OK — and that took a long time.

Conditions on the project did not allow for letting contracts to the lowest bidders. There was neither time nor means of transportation to permit contractors to send men in to inspect the work they were expected to do as a basis for bidding. (Had the latter step been taken, the formidable obstacles could have scared most contractors away!)

Even had these obstacles not existed there was another reason that reasonable bids could not have been obtained. The work was to be done in a wilderness region far from sources of supply. It would be necessary to establish complete facilities for housing, feeding and medical care of workers on the job site. Complete facilities for repair and servicing of equipment would have to be shipped in. Contractors were in no position to even estimate these costs in the northern wilderness under wartime conditions. Everything had to come in from the outside at enormous cost.

Utter confusion would have reigned had each of 40 or 50 small contractors undertaken independently to establish his own purchasing and transportation services. Back home, highway construction was done by contractors whose men lived in nearby population centres and report to work each day. The unskilled help was supplied by an employment agency. The contractor called the nearest machine shop or equipment dealer when breakdowns occurred. He could hire trucks on a contract basis. An oil company delivered fuel when needed.

None of these services were to be found in this isolated area. The PRA undertook to supply them all and to pay a rental on all machinery brought in by the contractors.

The work done by the contractors then was on cost plus a fixed fee based on an empirical estimate. Canadians had never experienced such a wide-open basis before and a great deal of laxity ensued.

I was brought into this situation in December, 1942, by Smith. I had been connected with a northern mining development corporation, Anglo-Huronia Ltd., and a small munitions plant in Parry Sound. He asked me to go to Fort St. John to assist in trying to obtain a financial accounting. He had received no statement from any of his contractors at the end of the 1942 construction season and didn't know where he stood. (Smith forces had been moved onto the job right behind the army in the summer of 1942 to upgrade the provincial road from Dawson Creek to Fort St. John.)

I arrived in Fort St. John Jan. 26 when it was 60 below zero. It took me two months to prepare a financial statement as the books all along the line were in bad shape. It was a case of them not having sent enough qualified accountants onto the project. They had excellent construction personnel but few knowledgeable bookkeepers.

As the result of knowledge I gained on this stint they asked me to go back to Fort St. John as office manager, a job which put me in charge of all finances until the contract was almost complete in November.

I discovered the inexperienced help was prone to foul up things. They unloaded freight cars for other than Canadian contractors at Dawson Creek, then had to load them out again. There was no organization in the way mixed truckloads going up the line were loaded so lading could be dropped off in progression at the camps.

I therefore revamped this warehouse, got some system about the operation and placed it on a better accounting basis. I found contractors coming in and asking for repair parts but the parts men would not make any attempt to ascertain if they had been placed on order. They'd give the company the part — and later find out it had been ordered for the account of some other contractor. For instance, a repair part would be ordered for Caswell. McNamara would pinch it. Curran and Briggs pinched parts from both of them.

It wasn't actual theft. There was a job to be done but this system made it impossible to tell the state of the Smith inventory at any given time.

The commissary system was in a mess and I had to make a special week-long trip up the road to the contractors' camps to straighten them out and improve procedures for handling goods and accounts. Much of the difficulty revolved around carelessness or neglect by employees.

For instance, at McNamara camp an inventory statement showed a loss of $2,500 which the accountant, Jack Combs, thought to be too great. He and I went to another camp and found nine boxes of cigarettes and tobacco which were property of McNamara. They reduced the loss to $500.

Accountants were added to Smith staff and sent out on the line to help contractors' bookkeepers keep their records current and in order. However, we had to continually return invoices to the different contractors for checking. Then we had requests — as in the case of Caswell — from as far back as 10 months asking us to check out gasoline invoices for as much as $2,000 and $3,000.

Although there were many invoice mix-ups, the Smith organization was at fault, too, in sending out conflicting orders and memos from offices at Fort St. John and Mile 8.

Another difficulty was Smith's chief accountant (before I came) allowed some laxity to be practised by the staff in controlling invoices coming in. In one instance, a list comprising 23 pages of invoices unpaid from the previous August was sent up from the Edmonton office in March, 1943. This gave us a poor corporate image as J.L. Zoller, our vice-president, had just finished having C.F. Capes, construction engineer of the PRA at Edmonton, approve for payment another long list of accounts. Capes had been told this list was all the outstanding accounts up to this time.

When I came back in May they moved me in over the head of this accountant. He did not take too kindly to having his authority reduced. By that time relations between the Canadians and the PRA had begun to deteriorate as the U.S. auditor-general had stepped in and had begun refusing accounts. For the auditor-general's part, there had been several investigators sent up from the U.S. to find out why expenditures had been running wild.

We, in turn, were having difficulty with our suppliers. There was Don McLaren of Snap-On Tools worried about his account and pressing for payment.

By June the U.S. government had held back approval of our telegraph account so long the telegraph companies had threatened to cut off our credit and put us on a cash basis.

It is apparent not all the fault lay with the Americans. They made the assumption we were taking Uncle Sap for a bit of a ride, I'm afraid. They saw he had done some sloppy work in the preparation and computation of payrolls for Canadian contractors. I discovered many payroll cheques were issued and later cancelled. Men were being paid in December for work done in September. Some were paid for the same period by both Smith and PRA; then it was necessary to cancel one of the cheques. There were internal duplications created by issuing cheques too soon after work periods ended and making improper deductions.

The biggest bugaboo was a clumsy IBM computer bookkeeping system the PRA installed at Fort St. John to handle the payroll.

This was probably the first computer operation in Canada. If it taught anything about computerization it taught that it was usually more trouble than it was worth even though electronics were later introduced. For the key punch operators, the job was more boring and deadly than working on a high-speed assembly line. Yet computers have mesmerized the whole world.

The system was first used in the U.S. on construction of the Pan-American Highway. The theory was that it could maintain construction records on every mile of the highway. However, on the Alaska Highway the theory was good but the practice unsatisfactory.

The IBM people came in and filled up hundreds of square feet of office space with huge boxes which handled the punched-out cards. Everybody was excited and vied for training as key punch operators.

A combination of circumstances fouled up the system, which was dependent upon keeping in close touch with the field. When punch cards were not made out correctly the computer would kick them back out and not issue a cheque. If there happened to be a weak pencil mark on a card, the machine wouldn't accept it and we'd have to send the card on a 1,000-mile round trip to have it done properly.

The temporary pile bridge across the Peace River caused trouble by washing out. For several weeks we had no way of getting the cards from our office at Dawson Creek to the PRA office at Fort St. John.

The results of all this difficulty put the project behind two months with the payroll at several points. Lack of competent operators also resulted in delays. Invariably the PRA would show up at our office on the 20th of the month to get our figures because their staff had punched the cards incorrectly or generally buggered up things. The operators soon found out how boring the job was, hence the reason for the mistakes. Many applied to be transferred to something else but, like any army, the "nothing" jobs had to be done by somebody — and key punch the operators were frozen.

We had employees coming to us beefing:

"The finance company is threatening to repossess our refrigerator unless I get my pay cheque."

I could see the computer application to this job was a failure and finally recommended we abandon it and put our payroll back on a manual system. This enabled us to get out our accounts by the 10th of the month following.

It's too bad business managers later on didn't have this perception and the guts to throw out systems that didn't work. Computers have cost and are costing companies millions today, yet the top brass is too embarrassed to admit their mistakes and keep on repeating them ad infinitum.

As the result of the U.S. auditor-general holding back approval of the $1 million worth of accounts, the Smith company called in its auditors, Clarkson, Gordon, Dilworth and Nash (Walter Gordon, who became Liberal government finance minister in the 1960s, was the most prominent member of the firm), to make a detailed audit of all the reimbursable items. However, the Americans remained obdurate and concerned only in continuing the red tape tactics.

Smith found it expedient to bring in Leopold Macaulay, a Toronto lawyer who later became deputy minister of highways for Ontario, to help frame our claims and work with lawyers for the companies. Smith and the contractors' representatives held many meetings through July and August to discuss the problem and map strategy.

At a meeting Aug. 11, 1943, Macaulay pointed out that while, during the early stages, the Smith organization had considered PRA men of honor who would carry out all undertakings, he had now come to the conclusion PRA was unreliable.

The whole matter would have been settled had the PRA issued work orders — and PRA personnel had assured George Morris of Dufferin Paving Company that a work order would be issued to cover work done in excess of estimated cost. However, this was not done and the PRA was starting to run out of money. There was an added threat the USED was going to take over the job. Contractors felt if PRA went off the job it would be difficult to reach a settlement.

Because of the activities of several companies, the PRA had developed the suspicion the Canadians were charging the PRA with machinery rentals to which they were not entitled. One of the Canadian companies was a flagrant example of this.

All companies which brought in machinery leased it to the PRA. The PRA, using wartime parts procurement priorities, was obligated to restore the machines to the condition in which they reached the job. But this company took the opportunity to completely overhaul all their machinery.

PRA turned a blind eye to this as all companies were doing it. And nothing would have been said in this case had the company not been caught stealing. Employees had cut open a sheepsfoot packer, filled each half with small and scarce parts, rewelded it and painted it over. Somebody blew the whistle. Uncle Sam sent in the FBI to investigate. They opened the packer with a cutting torch and the contraband was revealed. The PRA was so mad they pulled all the new motors and tires off company vehicles and gave it the boot.

Up to this point the PRA had used the contractors well on the rental deal. Now they began making it hard for everybody by disallowing full repair costs and/or ordering machines off the job earlier than the contractors expected.

Any contractor who was on the good side of the PRA came off all right. For instance, Curran and Briggs had a Diesel shovel whose motor went haywire. No repair parts were available; not even the Smith company could obtain them on their priorities. It was essential to get the shovel going for a gravel contract. The superintendent, Al Cuthbertson, was at wit's end until the PRA offered him an engine out of a White Diesel truck. It worked well until the end of the contract, when the PRA told Cuthbertson he could not only keep it but to take his own motor with him to repair when parts became available.

Macaulay had warned Canadian contractors to get it out of their heads a complete overhaul would be allowed on any machinery — only repairs on ordinary wear and tear. However, contractors on this job figured wear and tear amounted to 80% of the original cost as mud and cold played havoc. It ended up ultimately, however, after the shenanigans pulled by several companies, in the PRA establishing a policy of making a cash settlement in lieu of allowing actual physical work to the machinery.

* * *

Another inequity was recalled by Charles Butler, president of Butler and Hawkins convoy firm:

Government regulations required Canadian truckers to put in a 54-hour work week of six nine-hour days straight time before they could put in for time and a half overtime. The America drivers were paid on the basis of 40-hour week, time and a half to 54 and double time there after. Their basic hourly rate was twice as high as ours. Here's a case history of how wages were paid:

I sent Dan Letcher, one of our convoy drivers, with a load of personnel stuff to the army brass at Fairbanks. A driver for Metcalfe-Hamilton-Kansas City Bridge was involved and the U.S. Army sent a Negro soldier as a guard.

The American was driving when they arrived at a "suicide hill" on an icy road. The truck began swapping ends. The Negro went out one side; the driver out the other. Letcher moved over and grabbed the wheel and took the truck safely to the bottom. The American driver never touched the wheel again the rest of the trip.

They were gone 28 days. When they got back I signed wage vouchers of $1,000 for the American driver and $500 for Letcher. We knew they were padding overtime and expense — but nobody seemed to care.

Lloyd Wilder, a Canadian trucker, had a difficult time collecting some of the money. Two years after the war he received a cheque from the U.S. Army for work performed and signed for by army personnel at Fairbanks.

It was a surprise as he had written it off. However, the army got it passed for payment after it had been turned down a couple of times.

Several discrepancies in American auditing showed up. These further delayed final settlement.

When the smoke all cleared, Smith management and its contractors came out all right in the end despite some of the financial roadblocks.

* * *

Canadian civilian truckers found themselves on the wrong side of the U.S. military in the summer of 1943. Harold Havig, a Stettler, Alta., real estate dealer, was in the midst of the whole situation, and recalled:

The two big dogs in the trucking business at Dawson Creek were E.J. Spinney and Gordon Wilson.

Spinney got big because he had enough guts to step in and sign a management contract when the Americans first arrived and nobody else would tackle it. He had successfully completed the Fort Nelson airport hauling job in the winter of 1941-42 and this encouraged him to sign the huge hauling contract.

Wilson won a 17 million ton-mile contract.

Spinney and Wilson were paid 27 cents a ton-mile. They paid small sub-contracting truckers only 7 to 10 cents of this.

During July, 1942, a group of independent small truckers decided to cut out the middle men and formed an association called the Alaska Highway Truckers. W.E. Miller was elected president and W.B. Miller, secretary. I was appointed manager at $300 a month July 21.

Because we weren't a legal entity, the Americans wouldn't sign any contracts with our outfit until we secured a charter. We obtained a charter under the name of Dominion Truck Lines Ltd. Our terms of reference called for it acting as a clearing house for small truckers. The company was required to supply an office and parking space in Dawson Creek, to receive monies and to pay administration and office costs.

I paid the $400 legal fees out of my own pocket to have this charter drawn up and the understanding was I would recover these and other expenses out of the initiation fees of $25. Things were going along well,

I thought, when a new and confusing development entered the picture. One of the truckers, George M. Miller, had co-op religion. He agitated among the truckers for formation of a co-op to take over the Dominion Truck Line charter. Over my objections and those of company officers, he signed up pledges for $35 to form a trucking co-op. He was suppose to turn over $25 out of each pledge collected to me until I had recovered all my expenses.

At the end of the 1942-43 winter hauling season the 1,700 small Canadian truckers on the job were a bit desperate for more money, what with expensive break-downs and hard-to-get repair parts and tires. The co-op tried to win support for its cause by pointing out the prime contractors were making 17 to 20 cents a ton-mile and were fast becoming millionaires at the expense of the small truckers who were bearing all the expense and risk. Their pitch was that they could have the whole packet if they would band together. Of course, they overlooked the fact that had not Spinney and Wilson been hard-headed enough to undertake the initial risk none of them would even have been sub-contractors.

The co-op undertook a campaign to force the prime contractors to loosen their grip on the contracts. During June, 1943, all small trucks hauling for Wilson and Spinney developed mysterious break-downs: tire trouble, lost tailgates, engine failures.

Not a wheel turned for nine days. This was a rather ticklish situation. As this was a war zone no strikes were tolerated. However, the truckers were able to concoct logical reasons why they couldn't move.

The American military saw it had a situation on its hands it couldn't handle. It asked the Canadian government to send in someone to straighten out the matter. The man turned out to be none other than Gordon Wilson. He had by then been pressed into service as a $1-a-year man in Ottawa governing the trucking industry. When I found out Wilson was coming I deputized two other truckers to do the talking to him as I had quit his employ the year previously under difficult circumstances.

"I feel like a sheep in a den of wolves," Wilson said when he attended a meeting of our board. "But, fellows, we have business to do. We're not here to argue, or try to tell each other what to do. I have a job to do for the Canadian government and it has to be done right away."

He was nice about it and I had to admire him though he was on the opposite side of the fence. A mass meeting had been organized the day Wilson arrived. But during the afternoon Wilson and Spinney had gotten together and cooked up a deal.

When Wilson showed up that night he threw a bombshell into the meeting by announcing his company was willing to give us 16 cents and Spinney was willing to follow suit. The boys didn't know if they should go for this deal or not. If they could afford it now why had they chiseled all along? They didn't quite trust the big boys. The meeting dragged on until midnight as we tried to make up our minds.

At the stroke of midnight our minds were made up for us by a deal which was also cooked up that afternoon, I have no doubt. Col. Albert Lane, who was then in charge of the railhead at Dawson Creek for the U.S. Army, drove up in front of the hall in a command car and called me out:

"Are you fellows ready to roll?" he asked.

"I think we will be."

"What's the hold-up?"

"The boys are just getting their repairs finished and getting reorganized."

"I'll tell you something. I'll give every trucker on this job until 4 o'clock this morning to be completely mobile — or there will never again be a civilian trucker on the Alaska Highway."

Now I knew this was an empty threat. Maj. R.J. Haffner, executive assistant to the USED division engineer at Dawson Creek, had spread a rumor the army had mustered several trainloads of trucks and was ready to order them to Canada to put on the highway to replace civilian trucks.

The U.S. Army could have carried out this threat provided it had drivers available. However, under Canadian Unemployment Insurance Commission regulations the Americans weren't allowed to hire Canadians and I don't think they could have gotten enough drivers. I could have taken a tough stand and told Lane he was bluffing — but I kept this threat to myself. After all, there was a war to win. I went back in and told the meeting we had been given the great squeeze sideways.

Do you know that in less than 10 minutes there weren't enough guys left in that hall to help me carry the scrap paper off the floor? The colonel's threat had really defeated all opposition and whipped them into line. They simply flew out of there with their raise and went back to work.

They forgot all about Dominion Truck Lines, the co-op and every other thing except getting those trucks back on the road. They forgot all about their pledges, too. Although they had doubled their pay they forgot all about me, too.

I had received only $75 to pay off the organizational expenses and had to make up the rest out of my own pocket.

From then on when the army said "go," those truckers went. Of course, this all happened because our ranks had been split from the first — and the Americans knew it.

Femme fatale Trixie Stickles triumphantly got the trousers off the preacher, Rev. Don Amos.

19

Parka Padres Filled A Key Function

Besides the men in overalls and uniforms who struggled with muskeg, mosquitoes and motors during the construction of the Alaska Highway and Canol pipeline were the men of God — a small contingent to be sure but one whose members gladdened the hearts of all, from the youngest and loneliest to the oldest and toughest. One of these ministers was Donald C. Amos of Brampton. This is his story, with supplementary details by others involved in the ministry:

The parka padres were more than peripatetic preachers who packed into camps with portable organs, sleeping bags and knapsacks full of hymn sheets and New Testaments. They were cheerful understanding types who could engage in a bit of gossip or bunkhouse banter, maybe show a film, lead a sing-song or just participate in a good bull session.

With each unit the U.S. Army sent in a chaplain experienced in leading recreation activities. However, during the first year on the road many of the old-time civilian construction bosses were unaware of the importance of this matter. They figured if they provided a small room at the end of the bunkhouse where the men could sit around and swap lies their obligation was ended. Then they wondered why the labor turnover was so high in the 1942 construction season. When the reason finally dawned on them, they took steps to institute a chaplaincy service for the 1943 season.

I used to hear good friends of mine in the contracting companies say men would make their own fun. However, isolation lowered morale more than they knew — especially when hundreds were stuck in the middle of nowhere on a wilderness job.

Word got back to Protestant church heads they should look at the Alaska Highway set-up as a "wartime community." They agreed it could be classed as such — and an inter-church committee decided to send in a group of travelling chaplains.

I heard first of the need during a United Church of Canada General Council meeting in Belleville, Ont., in September, 1942. Rev. Charles Kitney, who had a widely acclaimed radio ministry in Grande Prairie, made it his business to travel up the highway to investigate. I went to Kitney and told him that, although I had had no experience in working with construction men, I knew a bit about the country as I had served as a student minister in 1934 at Kinuso near Lesser Slave Lake.

When someone from the home missions board at the United Church of Canada general office in Toronto phoned me at my study at Sydenham United Church in Brantford, Ont., and asked if I would be interested, I didn't hesitate and said yes. I was told to be on the job in Dawson Creek by Dec. 31, 1942. Leaving my bride of a few weeks, I set off to become a travelling chaplain among unknown men.

Arriving in Dawson Creek, I was taken in tow by Rev. Wes Hutton, the United Church minister there, and Rev. Selwyn Willis, rector of St. Martin's Anglican Church at Fort St. John, and given introductions to the top men in the construction companies I would be serving. They were both busy men, their small congregations having mushroomed during the American invasion and they didn't have time to visit the line camps.

Donning the parka and other winter clothing supplied me by the home mission board, I began my first tour by visiting five Canadian construction company camps between Dawson Creek and Fort St. John. The only part of my anatomy that gave me any problem in the intensely cold winter was my second chin which persistently stuck out over my parka cord.

There was a chill of another kind at some of the camps. I found it no piece of cake to break through the reserve of a camp full of grizzled old construction stiffs. I found the ice harder to break at Canadian camps than at American camps.

When I would show up at a camp manned by men brought in by companies under the management of Okes Construction Company of

St. Paul, Minn., I'd be welcomed with:

"Oh, padre, we've been looking forward to your visit. You're going to have a service for our men tonight, aren't you?"

In about three breaths I would find myself welcome. It was a great thrill to go into this type of camp to get acquainted with men who had not seen a minister or given the church or Master much thought for many weeks. They were willing to make an announcement of my presence at the dining room and provide me with all the facilities I needed.

It was quite a different reaction from many Canadian camps where the office manager would mumble: "Well, I guess it's all right." He'd turn back to his work and leave it to me to make my own arrangements.

This would require consultations with the mechanics and the blacksmith and guys in the bunk shack who could play musical instruments; and the boss. That meant elbowing my way to try and sit beside the camp boss when he came in for the evening meal to ask him if it was all right to hold a service in the camp dining room that night. Often his reply would be:

"You better check with the cook. I won't OK anything in the dining room without his say-so."

I'd have to leave my supper, go find the cook. He would generally accede upon learning I had an OK from the front office. Then I'd have to rush back and make the announcement — and do it before the first fellow had left the table.

This required fancy footwork as some of those hardened construction men had a record they didn't want to go back on. They could sit down and eat a meal from soup to dessert in seven minutes. If I didn't make my announcement before these fellows started to move I was licked. The usual reaction when I announced myself was to lift their heads out of their food long enough to say:

"Huh! What does that bird think he can do around here?"

I went onto the job with the expectation of having to break down this kind of case-hardened reserve and knew I had to meet them on their own terms. Showing any wimpishness would be fatal. So I early on learned to treat the rough and the gentle with equal aplomb. The only distinguishing insignia I ever carried to denote my work was a small gold cross on my tie.

However, there was no hostility; never once did I find hostility, just indifference. They left me to myself sometimes but the rest of the time they showed enough interest to come and hear what I had to say.

I preached in some odd places. At the A.E. Jupp Company we held church in the commissary by pushing aside the barber's chair and using the counter for a pulpit.

As time went on I learned to size up a camp situation quickly—and developed two kinds of services to meet the need.

Where there were no entertainment possibilities I'd arrange a quiet 25-minute service about 8 p.m. They'd sit at the dining hall tables with plates and cups turned over so the place wouldn't get messed up. I'd arrange for somebody to play the organ and we'd sing.

At other camps I'd dig up some talent for holding a recreation program then end up with a story and prayer.

They used to say I had a penchant for locating hidden talent. I suppose my reputation followed me after a concert I organized in March at Caswell Construction Company camp. I was lucky that night to find a violinist, banjo player and guitar player who enthralled the audience. The men even loosened up for a bit of community singing. The antics of the fiddler as he shuffled out a dance ditty brought down the house, as did Ed Potter who recited "Little Baptiste."

Even more impressive was the organ player on this occasion. I had brought along Rev. Willis for a tour of camps as far north as McNamara Construction Company on the Liard River. He came by his excellent musicianship well: his family were the Willis piano people in Montreal.

Later, when I had a car at my disposal and didn't have to depend on hitchhiking and was able to set up small rotational libraries in the camps, the apathetic or indifferent warmed up to the chaplaincy service. I had three boxes of books which circulated to help fight boredom of camp life.

I was able to bring in National Film Board reels from Vancouver and had a loose working arrangement with the Canadian and American air force and army units to borrow their equipment for civilian construction camps in exchange for double bills of my films. I was the most popular man in camp when I showed a double bill.

Later when we installed moving picture projection outfits in the line camps there was criticism about pampering and extravagance. However, a U.S. Senate investigating committee had some encouraging words for our efforts:

"When it is realized the workers were stationed in outposts more remote than many military posts on the fighting fronts and, once on the job, could not leave, this committee doesn't believe any criticism should accrue to those in charge of providing some form of recreation."

Some of the Canadian construction bosses looked upon provision of recreation facilities as a sign of weakness on their part, catering to the more frivolous nature of their employees. The whole attitude was exemplified in a statement by J.L. Zoller, vice-president of the R. Melville Smith Company:

"One thing I cannot understand with regard to help on the Alaska Highway. When they were here applying for work they were told of conditions: that there would be long hours and no holidays; in fact, there would be very little of anything they could look forward to in the way of enjoyment. After they arrived they found things were so much better than they expected it would appear they are now demanding certain privileges which, in the first instance, they did not expect."

There was no such a thing as gas rationing on the highway. In fact, as a chaplain I didn't even have to pay for my gas — and this led to an embarrassing circumstance at a Toronto service station later when I arrived back home. I was equipped with a pass which read:

"This is to certify Rev. Donald C. Amos is acting as a chaplain for the Canadian Protestant churches. He is to be given food, accommodation, gasoline and transportation such as he needs to fulfill his work."

I'd pull up to a gas pump at a check point, have them fill it up, have them check the oil and drive off.

I forgot myself at this service station and jumped in and drove off without paying. The attendant took a look and, despite the fact I was wearing a clerical collar, didn't feel I had the right to free gas. There was an embarrassing few minutes until I gave him an explanation.

Incidentally, I nearly lost the car in July, 1943. I came out on leave in late May, 1943, and stayed till late June. I found out that women could come up on the road if they had signed up for jobs. So to meet army regulations, I signed up my wife Margey as a cook and she came back in with me and stayed for five months.

Arriving in Dawson Creek by train, we took a Greyhound bus to camp north of Fort St. John where I had the car parked near a river.

Had we not driven the car away that day it would have been washed away in the fierce floods that closed the highway for several weeks.

For the first while we lived in an old infirmary in the Wallace Mackey camp at Muncho Lake. It had been left when the army engineers moved out. Later we lived in married quarters built for us.

Although I never made a pitch for collection I began to find the boys passing the hat and taking up collection in recognition of my extracurricular services. Later taking collection became an accepted thing during my visits.

My diary shows Dec. 21, 1943, I received an offering of $24.65 at the McNamara Construction Company camp at Mile 213 north of Fort

Nelson. However, a few days previously the boys at the USED camp at 117 miles north of Fort St. John were not so generous, and I didn't get much of a reception. They were a "stiff" crew — and the stiffest, by the way he talked, was the company clerk. He gave me $3 for what he called "the work you are doing."

Actually, once the boys in the camps began to see the value of the work by the chaplaincy service, they were very good to the preachers. In the latter days of the American "occupation," Chaplain Stephen Krizen of Bethlehem, Pa., served the Roman Catholics from Watson Lake to Fairbanks and William J. Brown of Wilkes-Barrie, Pa., the Protestants.

Chaplain Brown had a Dodge pick-up truck with a chapel fitted on the back. The chapel effort all began when Brown requested some form of permanent protection for his equipment during the winter. The boys at Haines Jct. camp built the small house with windows and doors at the rear.

The Anglican Church sent George M. Doolan, a divinity student from Wycliffe College, Toronto, to temporarily cover the road from Whitehorse to the Alaskan border and the Haines cut-off during summer holidays. Rev. Robert Ward of Carcross covered the section from Watson Lake to Whitehorse for them.

Doolan used to conduct song-fests in camp and he said these became popular. The men used to ask him to come back every week. A tough old superintendent grudgingly admitted to him after a while:

"I can see such activities are a good outlet for their energies — and it makes for better esprit de corps."

Often the men used to stick around after service to sing a few songs not on the sheets. It was surprising to him to discover these grown men requested again and again the children's hymn, "Jesus Loves Me, This I Know."

Doolan wasn't as lucky as I in regard to transportation. He had been promised a car but it didn't materialize. He had to resort to hitchhiking, no easy task with all the gear, including the field organ.

His classic story about "thumbing" concerns a ride with a driver hauling a load of 12x12 bridge timbers on a big International truck. They hadn't gone far when the radiator boiled over.

They stopped at a small creek to fill it up — then set out again. However, it boiled over again and continued to do so every couple of miles. They stopped to see if they could find out the trouble.

They took it off the radiator, drained it and found the trouble and proceeded to try to put it back on again. The nuts refused to turn on.

Finally the driver turned to Doolan and said:

"This is enough to make a preacher swear."

"If you think that nut will go on if you swear at it, go ahead," Doolan replied cautiously.

At which remark the driver looked at him for a moment with a curious air and without a word once again turned his attention to the task, chuckling to himself.

At "services" a wide cross-section showed up. For instance, at the R. Melville Smith camp at Fort Nelson I would expect to run into the jolly carpenter who acted as my town-crier and choir leader, a bewhiskered Mennonite, the Swede who was troubled that his friend's wife had never heard of Jesus and the colored man who was on hand at every service.

Fortunately, I never had to conduct any burial services but I had several memorial services. One was for two girls and a young fellow who went over a cliff into Muncho Lake. The girls, who were working in the kitchen at the W.H. Harvey Construction Company of Kingston, Ont., took off with three fellows. The girls rode in the cab with the driver and two fellows stood in the back of the pick-up truck.

Coming back from another camp, they ran off the narrow cliff along the lake and dropped into 150 feet of water. Only the two in the back escaped.

Many of the office personnel of the construction companies originated in Ontario and that gave us something in common. It opened a few doors for me. Then I met a few workers who had known of my work previously.

I was an unpaid messenger. A fellow would come to see me as I was leaving camp:

"I hear my daughter's gone to work at another camp, padre. What are chances of you taking a note to her?"

"I'll wait half and hour for you to write it and I'll take it along." He'd be relieved and happy.

"What have you heard from home?" I'd ask a truck driver. The look he gave me would make me say to myself: "I better have a talk to that guy later. I'd go hunt him up as he possibly realized the folks at home should have heard from him but he hadn't bothered to write. It was this kind of thing that prompted me to give individuals spiritual help.

Some of the most delightful times were the bull sessions after a service.

"Hey, padre, you don't believe all that stuff you told us?" somebody would bait me at the Wallace A. Mackey Ltd. bunkhouse. This would get a real good discussion going.

I had more weddings in a year than I would have performed in a lifetime. One day an embarrassed Texan came around and said:

"Parson, I aim to get married. Can you do the job?"

When I was filling out the papers for them afterward, I asked for the name of the mother of the Ukrainian girl he had married:

"Why, parson," he gasped, surprised at the question "I wouldn't know. I can hardly remember HER name!"

Besides Willis and Hutton, I rubbed shoulders and neighbored with many other padres. Most could tell about hardships they suffered as they walked, hitchhiked and travelled in every kind of weather to reach the men. At least one froze to death and two had nervous breakdowns.

Capt. James R. Cox, a chaplain with the U.S. Army Air Force base at Fort Nelson, made hair-raising flights and ferried across the Peace River when it was running 20 miles an hour and had washed away three temporary bridges. Maj. Ben Harrop, the Protestant chaplain of the 341st Engineering Regt., conducted outdoor services in rough GI fatigues. Rev. Lyman E. Jones, a pastor from the Lutheran Church's Missouri Synod, travelled from camp to camp. An Anglican laywoman, Miss Storrs, worked out of Fort St. John and underwent many hardships. Capt. Willis C. Gardner, chaplain with the 95th Engineering Regt., fell into the Clearwater River when a barge lurched. He could not swim. Sgt. Robert Hayes of Columbia, S.C., and Pvt. Hubert Massie of Waynesboro, Va., were awarded the Soldiers Medal for Heroism for saving him. On Dec. 13, 1943, I visited in hospital W.E. Walker, Jr., another Southern Baptist chaplain at Fort Nelson, who had suffered a slight heart attack on a rescue mission in which he should never have been involved. But he thought he should go because the airman down in the bush was another Southern Baptist, Lieut. Carpenter.

Lieut. Carpenter had gone down in a light pursuit plane in a valley north of the Smith River emergency flight strip. Walker was along with the search party. One of the search planes found Carpenter and a Norseman was despatched to pick him up. However, before this happened another search aircraft, a DC-3 with Maj. H.E. Wheeler, the Fort Nelson base commandant at the controls, had crash-landed four miles from the end of the Smith River strip when it developed fuel line problems.

Walker thought he should be part of the rescue party, although he was neither fit nor properly equipped for wading through the deep snow. He froze his feet and then suffered this heart attack. This meant the rescuers had to bring out two men. Fortunately, Maj. Wheeler wasn't badly hurt.

Wheeler, however, thought he owed Walker a debt of gratitude and later made an attempt to repay him. This was a time when religious discrimination was a hardship which had not yet been overcome by the spirit of ecumenism in this country.

An event which set off some denominational bitterness was the construction of a beautiful peeled-log church and attached community centre for Rev. Pierre Paulet of St. Peter's RC Church at Watson Lake.

Paulet was one of the priests like J.L. Coudert of Whitehorse, Father Yungblut of Fort St. John and Rev. Yvon Levaque of Fort Nelson who had been in the North many years at missions centred at trading posts. They were ready to assist when the road builders came on the scene.

Father Paulet ingratiated himself to the personnel of the U.S. Army Air Force stationed at Watson Lake with his dramatic rescue of two of their pilots who had crashed in the bush near Target Lake, a bombing range 24 miles to the north. While the Americans were frantically trying to figure a way of getting to them, Paulet calmly took off with his dog team in 30-below-zero weather and brought them out. For him it was just another routine trip with the dogs.

Although he was awarded a medal by the U.S. government for his feat, the men at the base felt he should have a more tangible reward. They undertook to build this church. Paulet thus had a chance to become close to many of the young airmen — many away from home for the first time, lonesome and homesick.

When the church was officially designed as St. Peter's RC Church rather than a community church, somebody set up a squawk based on "religious discrimination." There was an investigation during which carpet tramping was done and a few heads rolled. Paulet was temporarily dispossessed.

This denominational infighting spilled over to Fort Nelson when Chaplain Walker held dedication services for a new chapel. He and his assistant, Cpl. Robert Wheatley, had worked their hearts out to get it ready. It had been built out of four houses (and included craft, reading and study rooms) by GIs during their spare hours under general direction of the post engineers commanded by Maj. W.W. Finley as part of the Air Transport Command's plan to have chapels on every base. Cpl. Daniel H. Lewis and some of his post engineers buddies had worked late the night before putting on the finishing touches. Maj. Wheeler repaid his obligation by telling the personnel:

"Boys, we want everybody out for the opening of Chaplain Walker's chapel. This is going to be a great asset to this station."

Poor Walker was badly disappointed when only 26 showed up. The local RC chaplain had quietly spread word among his denomination to boycott the dedication.

I arrived May 7, 1944, accompanied by an RCAF chaplain on my last tour of the highway a few weeks before my job ended. I found Walker in despair, dead tired and sleepy. However, my friend and I cheered him up by promising assistance for the evening service. We talked to some of the RCAF personnel and construction workers.

About 100 showed up for the evening service and, of course, Walker felt much better. He led the "rousements" with Pte. Lyle Olsen at the organ. He defined "rousements" as good lively singing which brought the place to life. The chapel turned out to be a success.

In November, 1943, I was asked to make a survey of the Norman Wells side of the Canol project to determine whether the chaplaincy service was meeting the needs. I recommended a chaplain be sent to Norman Wells and Camp Canol to be with personnel forced to over-winter there.

The Presbyterians had also posted Rev. Dick Williams of Regina there. Williams had never before lived in the rowdy atmosphere of the construction camp away from civilization, where the men didn't have an outlet for their energies in their spare time. His first observation was that although he met many who were Christians, there was great need for a chaplain as there was plenty of gambling, drinking and swearing. He was upset one night when "a few of us got together for hymn-singing in a small room off the 'rec' hall. We were hardly able to make ourselves heard above the noise of bingo, poker and dice games."

However, due to the supportive efforts of the padres like Williams the camps were relatively free of drinking and big-time professional card sharps and gamblers. Camp bosses gave short shrift to them when discovered.

Williams and I made an unrecorded bit of Northern history a few months later. I was in Whitehorse in March, 1944, and asked somebody there how Williams was doing.

"Why don't you call him and ask him?" I was asked.

So I picked up an army phone and placed a call. When I got on the line I was amazed when the operator told me this was the first call to be placed to Norman Wells over the newly completed 625-mile phone line. I'm not sure if the man who told me to do this had intended it as a practical joke; anyway I heard Williams loud and clear.

The new link gave Norman Wells direct communications with any point in North America — and made these people in the northern wilderness realize that civilization for good or bad was on its way north. The line was abandoned when the Canol road was abandoned several years later.

On my trip north to do my survey I had some exciting entries to make in my diary as I did most of the travelling with bush pilots.

On a 5 a.m. flight out of Edmonton to Fort McMurray Nov. 21 on a Northwest Airlines plane, one of the passengers was a man named Boyce, who was superintendent of the United States Engineering District at Fort Smith. He was financial secretary for the Hennepin Ave. Methodist Church in Minneapolis, where Dr. Richard C. Rains was the minister. Rains was one of the pillars of Methodism in the world. Boyce told me about his great works.

For a man who liked to eat I was treated by Ralph Schidler, foreman for Bechtel, Price and Callahan at Fort McMurray, to a supper of fried chicken, ham, cherries and cake. This fare was only exceeded two days later by an American Thanksgiving Day dinner at the Hudson's Bay Company Mackenzie Hotel at Fort Smith. I was asked to bless a meal consisting of fruit cup, roast turkey, cranberry sauce, potatoes, asparagus, salad, hot rolls, assorted cakes, ice cream, hot mince pie and coffee.

How the Americans managed to come up with such a meal on food ration stamps nobody stopped to ask. However, every camp had a Blue Room, a special section for VIPs in which blue-colored plates were used. It was not a matter of pulling rank or of extravagance but one means of keeping top people on the job. It was also another indication of civilization encroachment on the North.

At Fort Smith I ran into Dr. John Melling, an Edmonton medical man and pilot and one of the North's remarkable people. He had been in Fort Smith for some time and was pulling out for good. He had flown into the Arctic with Oblate missionaries and had instructed them on administering elementary medicines.

We visited a small Roman Catholic hospital while he examined two patients with gonorrhea. The arrival of the American personnel all along the river saw several disease outbreaks where none had ever existed before. Medical offices had wide powers to deal with the situation to keep the spread under control.

I was told to be ready to fly early Monday morning with George Dalzeil, one of the North's most legendary, famous and notorious bush pilots. Despite the fact he was allegedly awaiting my arrival, we didn't take off until 2:35 p.m.. Also carried as a passenger was Lieut. Lawrence P. Spencer of Elmira, N.Y., a geologist who was officer in charge of pipeline construction between Norman Wells and Whitehorse.

That afternoon was the coldest I ever experienced in my life. I was lying atop some telephone hardware picked out of the snow that were urgently needed up the line. Despite the fact I was in my fartsack wrapped in my parkas, two pairs of mitts and other miscellaneous heavy clothing, I was chilled to the bone. Dalzeil and Spencer were up front chatting away, oblivious to the fact my teeth were chattering. We arrived at Fort Simpson in the dark. When I finally got warmed up I went down to the mess hall for a movie showing of "Hit The Ice." Wow! I had been doing that all afternoon!

A few days after nearly freezing me, Dalzeil nearly killed me. Once again he was flying telephone hardware for Bechtel, Price and Callahan — but this time he was overloaded when he took off from Norman Wells. Besides being overloaded there was another hazard: a large road grader which, for a reason I couldn't fathom, had been sitting at the end of the packed-snow runway at Norman Wells for weeks.

On take-off I didn't realize we were in danger until we were well past the control shack located half-way down the run-way. We should have been airborne by then but we weren't — and I could see that big road grader coming at us faster and faster.

What a man this Dal — which everyone called him — was! An able and cool pilot in any man's plane.

He used the full runway length and we were heading right for that machine. At the last moment he gave the engine one last goose and jerked back on the wheel and up went the nose of that Norseman, skimming over the top of the grader — and away he went.

I recounted the story to some of the boys and was told of another close call a few weeks previously by Harry Marsh, another bush pilot flying for the U.S. Air Transport Command. He had flown in there after dark, came in for a landing and, not seeing the grader, let the plane down on the runway.

When he went out the next morning he saw the grader and nearly had a heart attack. Out of curiosity he measured the distance between the grader and the start of his ski mark. He estimated he had missed it by only two feet. Had he been two feet lower at 100 miles an hour he wouldn't have had a chance.

Norman Wells, on the east side of the Mackenzie River, was a civilian operation run by Imperial Oil Limited for producing oil. The population was 450 when the action began but soon Imperial employed 500 and 150 more were engaged in oil exploration and development out of there, plus a U.S. Engineering Division set-up. The centre of activity was a two-storey building called "the hotel," in actuality a bunkhouse with civic services added on to it. It was for visitors and officers.

They put me up here in a room with Lieut. H.W. Reinke of the U.S. Army Air Force. I was taken in tow by Miss Wilson, the matron, and Mrs. Watson, the steward, of the dormitory accommodation outside the hotel, and they asked me to officiate at the opening of the new "rec" hall Dec. 4 and to conduct church service Sunday. There was trouble about putting me up but a wire from Col. R.W. Lockeridge, USED district engineer at Edmonton, ordered them to give me free quarters but charge 50 cents for meals. The people at camp found it odd I had to pay for the meals.

Walker Taylor, field supervisor for Imperial (who was on loan from the Royalite Oil Company at Turner Valley) and Miss Wilson had a good joke at my expense at the church service. Sitting in the front row was Trixie Stickles. I told them later I thought it was good of her to press my pants so I would look presentable at the service. They greeted this with gales of laughter. It was only then I found out she was giving them a bit of trouble in the dormitory. She could now say she got the pants off the preacher, too! And she had showed up at church to observe at first hand to results of her workmanship.

Camp Canol was on the west side of the river. It was strictly a U.S. Army camp of 2,000, with a 800-seat dining hall and large office building. My task was to visit construction camps to the end of the construction 150 miles along the road. In a week I was there I made several trips between Norman Wells and Canol by plane and by jeep four miles across the river ice. Lieut. Jack Davies took me across once. It was rough because of pressure ridges which we had to crawl over and it turned out to be a 40-minute trip.

The original location of the camp was Hoosier Ridge, 17 miles south, but it was moved to a mud-and-muskeg site four miles from the river after a location change for the road terminus. A third change was made in 1944 to escape that dreadful mud.

I killed time in camp as I had a bit of trouble getting permission from the army boss, Capt. R.E. Westling, to visit the camps. He finally radioed Edmonton for the necessary clearance for me.

During the wait for clearance I discovered two other clergymen who were doing excellent work there: Maj. J.B. Mackenzie and Father Pierre Beauregarde. Then there was Lieut. Wally Harrison who was attached to the USED. He broke down for an hour and a half one night relating how difficult things were in this wilderness camp. He seemed to think he was carrying the white man's burden for the area.

I immediately christened Mackenzie "Dear Doodles." He bustled around the North officially designated as a "special service officer" for the Northwest Service Command. He had been with the Salvation Army; also, as he had once toured with the famous Arthur Pryor Band in the U.S. as a trombone player, his specialty was band music. He had breezed into Camp Canol a few days before me and loaded with king-size cigarettes and good humor.

Within four hours he had organized a Negro band. Twelve hours after his arrival the band gave its first concert in the rec hall before a movie — despite the fact it possessed no instruments.

Dear Doodles had persuaded Bechtel, Price and Callahan to buy band instruments. They were supposed to have been sent out from Edmonton on the first available plane but had not arrived yet. Such a small matter as lack of instruments did not faze him. He opened his duffel bag and brought out some slide trombones and a valve trombone and a few trumpets. The matter of a drum posed a tricky problem. It was solved quickly by Mackenzie who commandeered a blacksmith's apron, tightened it with rawhide thongs over the end of Chef Victor Leval's biggest stainless steel mixing bowl and proceeded to bounce out a Gene Krupa form of rhythm that provided a solid background. The players filled in with washboards and kazoos.

Most couldn't read the sheet music Mackenzie provided but they were all natural musicians and performed well under Cpl. Oles Bredges of Oklahoma.

Father Beauregarde had a neat little set-up in a quonset hut. The Roman Catholics kept up their services and managed to look after their people better than the Protestants. His most famous words were:

"We both have the same troubles. It is the materialism, the materialism! Materialism is rampant!"

He was very open and evangelical in his anxiety for the men. We were both anxious about the camp.

Everyone regarded him as one of the most interesting sights at Camp Canol, this delicate slight friendly little Oblate priest who had been a watchmaker by trade and who came directly from a seminary in France to this rough army-civilian camp. He had won over every man and woman there.

He could speak only French when he had arrived the year previously but when I met him he could talk good English and Indian. He had run the gamut of Northern experience — froze his feet while mushing in a blizzard to a sick man's bed, was swamped in his funny little motor boat, the St. Pierre, and nearly died from having to eat camp food.

He was the most popular man I ever met in my travels. It was typical of him that he had white men from the Deep South attending a service at which a Negro accordion player provided the music for a mixed Negro and white choir. And they loved it.

He was a game little man. In 1946 he was helping to carry a casket downstairs in the Aklavik hospital — a job much too heavy for such a small man — when something went wrong and the casket came tumbling downstairs atop him and fractured his skull. He was flown out and recovered — and later ended up at Fort Smith.

I learned an elementary lesson of the North: never try to do anything or go anywhere in a hurry. One can spend more time trying to find people and waiting for rides from them there than it takes to get a liberal arts education. I'd be told to be on hand at a certain time and place and found this was just an estimate. I'd be waiting hours later for a driver who never showed at all.

I was called at 6:45 a.m. Tuesday — the day I was supposed to start a tour of the camps — but when I got to the USED transportation assembly office at 9:15 I found the scheduled ride with a driver named Jim Garrison had not materialized. In the late afternoon I couldn't disguise my annoyance and frustration at sitting around waiting for something to happen when some kind of soul put me in in touch with Garrison ("Oh, phantom man, whom I have seen but once.") He had been delayed but would be leaving at 8:30 Wednesday. I had then been hanging around there a week but he seemed airly unconcerned.

Garrison was to be my nemesis all during the tour of the pipeline camps.

Wednesday I was around early again but I didn't find him until 9:30 a.m., at which point he said he had to see a carpenter then would call for me at the bunkhouse. But I never saw him again. No, not once. I waited until 11:20 when Ed Sullivan, who was trucking supplies out to the camps, picked me up and we were on our way over a terrible road that made the Alaska Highway look like a superhighway. It had long steep grades through the mountains, was full of rocks and heartless river bottoms.

At 5 p.m. we reached the Mile 76 camp, where the boys were busily engaged in making catapaults, of all things, to shoot rabbits.

The following day I continued to Mile 150, the farthest camp from Canol at the time. I was supposed to catch a ride back with Garrison next morning but he took off that night. Driving at night, I subsequently learned, was a standard practice on the Canol Road. There were day-time whiteouts which made it impossible to see the road; but at night the headlights would pick out the turns. The road wasn't wide enough for two vehicles to pass and in daytime the drivers couldn't see an approaching truck. However, at night the headlights could be picked up. In passing, one driver pulled off the road but the other driver waited until he saw him safely back on the road again.

Once again Sullivan came to my rescue and took me back to Mile 122. There the wireless operator, Forrest Sandow, had a surprise for me. He told me about the religious services welder Rex Schulbert, Ernest McCurry, Bob Page, Barnes and Hoffman were holding every Sunday in Caboose No. 19. I sat and talked to them until 3 p.m., well past the time when they should have been back to work.

McCurrey, a Congregationalist from Avalon, Catalina Island, it turned out had sent home for his hymn book and the boys met and sang hymns and read Scripture — and sometimes an article out of a magazine. One particular article they showed me was "There Are No Atheists In The Sky."

I arrived back at camp Canol to find big excitement. During the week I was away on the line a big fire had broken out at the Bechtel establishment, causing more the $1 million worth of damage. Things were sure a mess. There was nothing left of the brand-new H-shaped building nor 10 trucks, a jeep, a Galion grader, eight bulldozers, the machine shop, battery shop, tire shop, tool shop, generators and all the mechanics' tools.

That night I shared a room with a man named Guthrie, a safety engineer flown in from Brooklyn to investigate the cause of the fire and help Mac Macdonald, the camp safety engineer, set up a camp-wide safety group. He told me somebody had carelessly used a compressor to pump some gasoline out of a barrel, unaware that on the other side of a partition a welder was at work.

I was one of the few outsiders who knew anything about this fire. Always wary of sabotage, the army had clamped a tight cloak of censorship over the incident.

(In fact, the account in this book may be the first mention of the fire ever published in Canada outside of the camp itself. There were mentions of it in the Canol Pipeline, a camp paper edited by Booth Eddy, and in the Norwell News, edited by Donald E. McRae, a man who later climbed up the Imperial Oil corporate ladder. Since there was no communication with the outside except the army radio, it was possible to maintain complete secrecy.)

Firefighters at Camp Canol were up against it because there was no water available from hydrants in winter. In fact, water was almost non-existent, except for drinking.

* * *

I left Norman Wells and flew to Fort Nelson. There I ran into Father Yvon Levaque in the visiting officers' quarters. He was a real northern pioneer priest who had left Montreal at age 18 to provide services for the Indians. Biographical notes by Levaque revealed:

Ofttimes I was gone six months without ever seeing another white man. In 1940 I was sent by the bishop into Fort Nelson from Fort Vermilion overland to try to re-establish an Indian mission there. When I arrived I found there was no proper church or living accommodation. The abandoned mission had been taken over by an independent trader. I finally found a place to live in the house of a man who was in Vancouver jail charged with murder. Then I cut logs to build a church.

I reported back to Fort Vermilion and in the summer of 1941 was told to fly back to Fort Nelson to continue my work. By that time Western Construction and Lumber was in there building the new airport.

In the spring of 1942 the slow pace of my life changed radically with the arrival of the 35th Engineering Regt. The 35th had been rushed over the 325-mile winter road from Dawson Creek and didn't have time to recruit some of the amenities of army life such as a chaplain. Since I was the only clergyman on the scene, the army asked for my services as a chaplain.

Since the two Indian parishes had only limited financial support, the bishop gave me permission to accept a retainer from the army as a civilian clergyman. But I had to take care of the Indians first.

This proved to be a transient parish. As the 35th worked both ways from Fort Nelson, my territory eventually extended from the Sickanni Chief River to the Liard River. This elongated parish covered 52 camps which I managed to visit once a month by holding services at two camps a day. I continued serving this parish for three years, although the camps and populations constantly shifted as the army construction units moved out and the civilian contractors moved in. The army assisted my work by building a chapel near the Public Roads Administration hospital at Mile 8 north of Fort Nelson. They also provided me with a 1939 Chev car.

I don't think the Indians were as awestruck and excited by the arrival of the GIs as the GIs were of them. Because of the construction around the airport, the Indians had become used to large construction machines. But when the GIs emerged at the end of the bush trail it was quite a revelation for them to find a settlement and a missionary priest. They were really amazed at this. One GI said to me:

"I suppose you like working with white people better?"

"My dear boy," I replied, "if you only know it there isn't much difference between a white Indian and a black Indian."

And he didn't like that lesson.

Because of my constant travel over dusty roads and around dirty camps, I was usually dirty. In 1944 I was asked to consider taking a commission in the RCAF at Fort Nelson. The officer commanding didn't like me. I overheard him telling the head chaplain from Winnipeg:

"I don't think Levaque will make a good chaplain for us. He's always filthy dirty. We want a white-collared chaplain."

I'm afraid the scene that ensued was un-Christian on my part as I told him where he could stuff his job.

* * *

When Don Amos finished his business in Fort Nelson, he once again became embroiled in the dreary old business of fighting construction bureaucrats at Dawson Creek. He recalled:

While I was away I found out many of the companies had pulled out their crews but had left skeleton maintenance crews in the camps for the winter. I had made several attempts previously to pick up juke boxes to send up the road for some of these boys. The R. Melville Smith Company had several of them in their rec hall. I had been promised them by Dick Panter, the superintendent.

Therefore, now that I was back I was annoyed to find the U.S. Army had stepped in and bought them out from under me. When camp broke up they decided to sell them to the first comers and since Panter wasn't on the scene at the time and the army was on the spot and I wasn't, the army got them. The old army game: lie as much as you can and steal as much as you can.

* * *

Bishop J.L. Coudert of Whitehorse had the most common understanding of any of the higher clergy, it was recalled by L.A. Pedee of Toledo, Ohio, a driver in the 18th Engineering Regt.:

He came to visit me at home years later. We sat each with bottle of beer and he with his big black cigar reliving Alaska Highway construction days.

His first contact with U.S. Army personnel was April 18, 1942, when many of the RC boys in Whitehorse came to visit his rectory. On the following Sunday we filled the old Sacred Heart Church which had been practically abandoned for several years. Shortly after he received a visit from the commanding officers of the 18th, 340th and 93rd asking the help of his Oblate missionaries in attending the spiritual needs till a regular RC chaplain was assigned. He assigned Rev. Charles Hamel to cover the territory between Lower Post and the Alaskan border. Hamel was relieved in July by Rev. Gilbert, an army chaplain.

In late September Hamel, Gilbert and Coudert visited all the camps as far as the Donjek River. They heard confessions seated on stumps at freezing temperatures. Coudert said the mass in the hospital tent at 6:30 a.m. while the military band played marches around the tent to add to the solemnity of the occasion.

On the way out in January, Col. J.V. Johnston, the officer commanding of the 18th, paid Coudert a short visit in Whitehorse. Although not a Catholic, he asked him to say a short mass for us all. He told the bishop then what none of us knew at the time: that we were on the way to the Aleutian Islands and our first actual contact with the Japs.

Many Americans thought they were seeing a mirage with the arrival of Greyhounds in Dawson Creek.
DAWSON CR
Bus to DAWSON CREEK

20

Greyhound Buses Followed The Army

On Nov. 23, 1943, scheduled Greyhound bus service was set up on the Alaska Highway between Dawson Creek and Fairbanks.

Operation of Greyhounds over a road through territory which had not even been explored two years previously impressed many Americans more than any other accomplishment on the Alaska Highway.

It all started during a drinking bout in 1942 when Ralph Bogan, vice-president of American Greyhound Corporation, boasted to Gen. J.A. O'Connor, boss of the Northwest Service Command of the U.S. War Department, that Greyhound could run buses anywhere O'Connor could build highways. From that encounter came a letter of intention by the command to give Greyhound a contract to supply transportation on the Alaska Highway project.

Because Canadian Greyhound had buses and drivers available, it was decided to move buses from the Canadian headquarters in Calgary to Dawson Creek.

To further conserve already tightly rationed gasoline supplies in Canada, the national transportation controller proposed in 1942 to prohibit bus lines from scheduling runs of more than 50 miles from any city. Canadian Greyhound vigorously protested the proposal on the grounds it would be financially disastrous. It was hard-pressed to maintain any kind of service with rationing then in effect; it already had buses sitting on the dead line for lack of gas rationing coupons; private cars were being forced off the road and it was nearly impossible for the public to obtain space on trains.

In the public interest the transportation controller's ruling was eventually adopted — but in the meantime the U.S. War Department had come to Canadian Greyhound's defence and rescue. The company signed a cost-plus fixed fee contract which called for drivers to work on a monthly salary plus expenses.

* * *

Drivers from Calgary, Edmonton, Saskatoon, Vancouver and Lethbridge volunteered to drive Alaska Highway buses — and became the only Canadian drivers ever to have the U.S. articles of war read to them. W.E. (Bud) Armstrong of Calgary, who later became Canadian president, went to Dawson Creek as dispatcher. He recalled:

We despatched two buses and a command car on a CPR flat car from Calgary early in November, 1942, to Dawson Creek. Then we sent a crew of four to Dawson Creek to receive them and to do what charter work was required by the U.S. Army for the first year.

The CPR "lost" the buses. They sat on a siding at Red Deer for three weeks. Our drivers going by on regular bus runs saw them sitting there.

In the meantime, other drivers sat on their asses in Dawson Creek and became the laughingstock of the entire system. This was only a portent of things to come in our dealings with the U.S. Army.

Finally word filtered through to the Calgary head office about the buses' location and we chased down the proper railroad officials to get them moving again. We decided not to ship any more by rail. We drove the other 10 called for in the contract to Dawson Creek. Six more were delivered that fall and four more for the following spring. I made the trip in the first of these driven to Dawson Creek by E.R. (Ted) Bavin and Charlie Elkins.

This Elkins was a first-class practical joker. I saw him deep in conversation with a construction worker at a line camp one day. He handed the man a couple of pills.

"What was that you gave him?"

"Oh, he wanted to go to the hospital in Fort Nelson. They didn't think he was sick enough and didn't issue him a transportation badge."

Tickets weren't issued — but anyone needing bus transportation was given a special lapel badge. No badge, no ride.

"So," said Elkins, "I asked him if he had a pain in his stomach and he said yes. Then I asked him if he felt nauseated and he said yes. So I told him to take these two pills — and he went away happy."

"What were the pills?"

"Oh, damned if I know. One of the medical officers at Watson Lake gave them to me. But I think they'll cure him."

Elkins was the same stamp of practical joker as Ted Field, a bush pilot for the Yukon Southern Air Transport, a predecessor of Canadian Pacific Airlines. He picked up a rheostat in Edmonton, which is an electrical attachment that makes lights in display cases flash on and off. He brought it to Whitehorse and attached it to the jukebox in the lobby of the Whitehorse Inn owned by T.C. Richards, also a famous northern character.

This was the only jukebox in town and it usually attracted a crowd sitting around the fireplace feeding nickels into it to play the latest hits.

When the machine began to stop and start as the result of Field's rheostat, all the mechanics in town were brought in to take a crack at trying to find the trouble. Nobody had any success. T.C. was just on the point of shipping it outside for repairs when somebody discovered Field's fiendish gadget.

Needless to say, Field was not popular with T.C. for some time thereafter.

When we arrived in Dawson Creek accommodation was very tight. The only thing we could get was one room on the second floor of the Dewdrop Inn. The new arrivals ended up on the floor or slept in beds in the daytime as the hotel couldn't supply more rooms. Office accommodation wasn't much better. It was a small building in an alley and we could tell by the smell its former occupants were chickens. For the first month and a half I was designated as dispatcher under Norman Lord, the superintendent.

The Americans brought up 16 more buses from shipyards and assigned them to commuter runs, moving personnel around the camps, plus a few longer runs to Fort St. John and Fort Nelson. Greyhound drivers drove them while on lay-overs.

As a publicity stunt and propaganda effort, the U.S. Army decided to move some Negro troops out of Whitehorse on furlough for Christmas, 1942, by bus over the new road.

* * *

This movement made history as it saw the first bus ever driven in to the

Yukon. It was the start of one of the longest and farthest-north runs in the world. W.H. Brown of Calgary was one of the drivers. He recalled:

The buses we were using were 37-passenger jobs, the same as those on regular runs. We were allowed to fill only 30 seats as the army contract called for keeping seven seats open at all times for emergency use. Also we couldn't carry overloads on those synthetic wartime tires. As it was, we left a trail of rubber between Dawson Creek and Fairbanks. Two drivers were assigned to each bus — for several reasons. The most important was to negotiate the hills until Lorne Frizzell, the superintendent at Calgary, went back there and shipped us low-speed rear ends. Our buses were underpowered and geared too high without them.

It was the job of the relief driver to stand on the step with a jack and, when we powered out on a grade, to drop off and shove it under the rear wheel to hold the bus until help arrived to haul us up the grade. It was customary to keep going day and night, with drivers spelling each other off after two hours. Later the 1,000 miles to Whitehorse was being made 44 hours.

On this historic run to Whitehorse to pick up the Negroes, we had a crew of telephone line builders on board. All kinds of trouble developed, the most serious of which was a shortage of gas — a shortage which had already put the road maintenance crews out of business. The army felt the road was in too poor a shape that winter to operate gas tanker trucks over it. They hadn't learned how to use graders to make snow base on it. In addition, it was slippery in the daytime.

To spin out gas supplies we visited army supply dumps and found that in many supposedly empty barrels there was a gallon or two which could be siphoned out by tipping them on their sides. One outfit gave us half a barrel of diesel fuel for our 210-horsepower Hall-Scott pancake gasoline engine. We mixed it half-and-half. The engine smoked like hell but we kept on running.

When we reached Watson Lake we found the only fuel available there was aviation gas which we couldn't use. The army decided our progress was too slow and moved the telephone workers to Whitehorse by plane.

The bus created a sensation when it stopped at the army camps. Soldiers who had been away from urban sights and delights for months could not believe their eyes when this symbol of paved roads showed up on what was then a dirt track. The Negro soldiers kept insisting they were seeing a mirage. To complete the contrast we passed an Indian woman with two kids and a dog sleigh near Teslin. We unwittingly brought one of the evils of white society to those kids for we stopped and filled their pockets with tooth-rotting candy.

We ourselves were taken by surprise to find an Indian with a car at Teslin Bay. He had brought it in on a sternwheeler river boat before the highway came and had run it up and down on a half mile road he had built. He had painted the vehicle white and, dressed in white, had used it to run down timber wolves on the ice-covered bay. The wolves couldn't see him against the snow.

When we arrived in Whitehorse the only sleeping accommodation we could find was in the post office.

Next morning we were ready to board the Negroes and start down the highway. However, without a supply of gas along the road to get us back to Dawson Creek, there was danger of the project falling flat on its face. This would be an embarrassing show for the U.S. Army as their public relations types had pumped up a ballyhoo, razzle-dazzle effort with newsreel cameras and radio interviews. Those GIs were really excited about getting out.

Walter Hyssop of Lethbridge and I went around to see Col. Herbert Soderston, the fuel controller, who was pacing the floor wondering how he was going to get the busload of Negroes over the road. He congratulated us on our ingenuity in obtaining enough gas to make the trip up. But he was mystified how we made it when trucks weren't running. I told him:

"This is our job and we did it. We carried axes, saws and cant hooks to remove trees which had fallen across the road. We had some help from the A.E. Jupp Company and a couple of civilian road contractors. When the roads became too slippery for daytime travel, we travelled at night. A guy would drive a half-ton truck through the sags and over the next hill. Walter and I could see his lights and have an idea of the road ahead. Then we'd swoop down one side and up the other at full speed — and always guessed right."

Soderston was impressed and excited.

"Well, by God, if you fellows got here with the clumsiest vehicle on the road I don't see why trucks can't use the road," he said. "You can certainly make it back despite the fact my people tell me it isn't open. I'm going to get some trucks out hauling gas and get things running again."

He got on the radio and ordered gas to be hauled to Whitehorse. Only a few of the first convoy of tankers made it.

After a couple of rough trips up the road the army didn't have any more charters for us until spring. We sat around most of the winter driving shuttle buses. We were offered $2 an hour to drive gasoline tankers up the road but didn't think it was right to be getting paid for two jobs and anyway we were on call to the army so we turned down the moonlighting jobs.

* * *

During February the army ordered Greyhound to send a crew to set up a schedule and meal stops between Dawson Creek and Whitehorse, Bud Armstrong recalled:

On Feb. 19, 1943, Hector Leonard, Guy Roberts, Walter Zeh, a mechanic, and I took off in a bus for Whitehorse to carry out the project. We duly arrived and reported to the U.S. Army. To our surprise and frustration they refused to put us up in their barracks because we were still operating on a letter of intent and this wasn't good enough credentials for them. In a way I couldn't blame them because I looked like a bum from the street, wearing an old railroader's cap, a beat-up old parka and pants held up by a piece of binder twine.

I went around to Signal Corps and asked them to notify Lord in Dawson Creek of our arrival so he could make arrangements with the army for our accommodation. The signal corps accepted our message and — I learned later — never sent it. There was something I didn't understand about a blackout on civilian messages because of the trouble the Japanese were giving them in the Aleutians. I'd appear daily and ask if a reply had been received:

"No, sir. Sorry."

"Will you send another signal to Dawson Creek?"

"Yes, sir," but it would never get sent. I had met Inspector H.H. Cronkhite of the RCMP whom I had known in my home town of Lethbridge, but even he couldn't do anything about clearing me with the army. We finally got a room at the Whitehorse Inn only because I met a friend, Bill Jewett, a pioneer pilot-prospector, who was leaving town and got us his room.

After we had been there for three weeks we began to run short of expense money. Only the fact that Homer Meer of the Canadian Bank of Commerce lent us some funds to tide us over saved our skins. Norm Lord finally found out what had happened to us through Col. Soderston — but we didn't receive any further orders — so we just sat there and waited and waited — and waited. We waited for six more weeks until communications were restored. The irritating part was nobody seemed to care about our plight. They were fighting a war.

When I finally returned from "exile" to Dawson Creek I set up a daily schedule of three buses each way to Whitehorse, with one continuing on to Fairbanks. This was a 365-day-a-year schedule.

I did not try to understand the unfathomable. It was six months before the army got around to putting my schedule into effect. When we did get the schedule running we were required to have 75 drivers and 75 mechanics on staff due to the army's official regulations. However, they were paying for this inefficiency so we could do nothing about it. Maybe that is the way to win wars. The Americans certainly did win.

Under ordinary circumstances bus drivers are paid by the mile so they are mile-hungry and would fight to get trips. However, working on a monthly salary, they put up all kinds of excuses when it came their turn to take highway schedules.

"It isn't my turn. I only had a 10-day layover," would come the reply when I called a driver to take a scheduled run up the highway. And, you know, some of the drivers actually were drawing 10-day layovers. But that was the way the army was running things.

Because of army regulations, a Greyhound bus steering wheel assembly ended up in the Soviet Union. Here is how:

The army had put governors on all its trucks and placed a 35-mile-an-hour speed limit on the highway. It was a disciplinary offence to be caught removing a governor seal. On hills many of the drivers put the trucks into "Russian overdrive," i.e., out of gear. Of course, many trucks got away from them because of this dangerous practice. When this happened the drivers jumped and let them go.

E.W. Evans and Doc Chalmers were hit by a truck in Russian overdrive on a Fairbanks schedule in the spring of 1944. It smashed the steering wheel assembly. A spare was ordered shipped to Fairbanks on a lend-lease plane bound for the Soviet Union. When it arrived they forgot to unload it and as far as I could learn it ended up in Stalingrad.

This was the only bus which was caught at the north end of the road by the spring break-up and was unable to move out of there for three months while the road was being rebuilt and repaired.

The boondoggling that went on was incredible. For instance, Metcalfe-Hamilton Kansas City Bridge had a contract for building the Whitehorse army headquarters, hospital and other buildings which were located two miles west of town. To accommodate the 700 men brought in to do the work, the company built a barracks and messing set-up four miles east of town. This meant we had to move 700 people three times a day.

Despite a few accidents and mishaps, we drove out the same 12 buses we took in on the contract. We had a few close calls: like the time Ron Jaques and I were rushing back from Fairbanks just before the 1945 spring break-up one night. I was sleeping and he was driving. He came to a slippery hill where a truck had jackknifed. He was able to swing around it but lost momentum in doing so. Two-thirds of the way up he spun out.

The minute the noise of the engine stopped I was wide awake and realized we were moving backwards to beat hell. There was a drop of 250 feet at that point and we were only saved from going over when we crashed into a stalled truck.

We managed to find some sand and got up the hill. Although we had smashed the radiator it was cold enough to run without it into Whitehorse.

We usually carried a mechanic with enough tools to make minor repairs on the road. It was a comfort to have a mechanic with a tool kit aboard when something went wrong 30 miles from nowhere. This was brought sharply to me when I started out one night with a bus full of GIs and a joker named Don Turney, a driver on layover in Whitehorse who wanted to see the bright lights of Fairbanks. Half-way there I turned to him and said:

"Did you bring along a toolbox? Mine was stolen in Dawson Creek."

"Hell, no," he replied, "why carry a toolbox when we aren't carrying any mechanics?"

This caused a general guffaw but it occurred to one or two of them that we were in the middle of the wilderness without a thing to make repairs if we broke down. Some sections of the road were very bad and occasionally it was necessary to have the passengers out and almost lift the bus through.

By September, 1943, Col. Joseph P. Glandon, Portland, Ore., officer in charge of transportation on the Alaska Highway, was able to report the buses hauled more than 6,000 passengers a month for 2.1 million passenger miles. This included troops, civilian workers on airports and many Canadian and American VIPs. The VIPs included Canada's governor-general, the Earl of Athlone; Mayor F.H. LaGuardia of New York, chairman of the Canada-U.S. Joint Defence Board; members of a U.S. Senate investigating committee and Gov. Ernest Gruening of Alaska and Col. O.M. Biggar, chairman of the Canadian section of the joint defence board.

William S. Howland, chief of Life magazine's Atlanta bureau, was completely awed by being able to travel 917 miles from Whitehorse to Dawson Creek early in October, 1943, "in a streamlined Greyhound bus exactly like those which travel between Birmingham and Atlanta." He further recalled:

When I got on the bus in Whitehorse the American landmark we passed was the airport, a field bigger than most American commercial airports. Among the 15 passengers were Congressman Homer Angell of Portland, Ore., making an official study of the road; Capt. Richard Neuberger, aide to Brig.-Gen. Patsy O'Connor, and Dave Rivkin, a civilian photographer with the army. The rest of the passengers were soldiers — 10 of them going on furlough — and two less fortunate GIs who had boarded at a checkpoint to ride back to the next camp to drive trucks.

We came to a long grade which men and machines were working after crossing the Teslin River. It had begun to rain and the grade was slick. Our drivers looked worried. The bus lunged at a hill in second gear, then low. We made a couple of hundred yards, then we stood there as the wheels ground the wet dirt to mush.

"Hell, we're stuck," said Charlie Elkins, the driver.

Stuck we were: not in the ditch or on the soft shoulder but right in the middle of the road.

"This is the third time this month we've been stuck here," said Craik, the relief driver. "We never make a trip without getting stuck three or four times and when it rains we don't try to drive between Watson Lake and Fort Nelson. We lay over there until it stops."

We weren't stuck long. Craik waved to a bearded "catskinner." He put the blade of his bulldozer against our back bumper and shoved the bus up the hill as though it were a toy. When our wheels took hold again he backed off.

But we were not through with that hill. A couple of hundred yards away there was a turn on which we gently slid sideways into the ditch. Our catskinner tried to push us but this time he got stuck. He had to yank us out with a cable.

* * *

Before their tour of duty ended, Canadian drivers had taken buses to Circle, Alaska, on the Yukon River, and to Valdez and Anchorage.

Following withdrawl of service by the U.S. Army, British Yukon Navigation started a freight and bus service between Dawson Creek and the Alaska border. Nick Koepke, assistant superintendent at Dawson Creek, went over to them to become superintendent of this operation. The first schedule required three days, with overnight stops at Watson Lake and Fort Nelson.

21

Tire Plant Largest Ever Assembled By Allies

Up until 1943 the Americans were not aware the Japanese drive into the Aleutians was a feinting action. They thought the enemy was serious about taking Alaska. In panic the war department ordered the American military to prepare a transport plan to roll 1,000 tons of freight daily over the 1,520 miles from Dawson Creek to Fairbanks as a precautionary measure should the sea route between San Francisco and Skagway be cut.

This meant that heavily loaded trucks would leave Dawson Creek every six minutes 24 hours a day. It also meant enough tires would have to be provided to operate 3.2 million tire-miles a month.

* * *

Gen. Theodore Wyman, Jr., called in J. Lance Rumble, Canadian manager of the General Motors truck division, as adviser in August, 1942, to help evolve the plan. Rumble recalled:

For Dawson Creek the most tangible result of this plan was the construction of a tire retreading and rebuilding plant, said to be the largest ever assembled by the Allies.

When the Japanese strategy was at last revealed and they began to pull back from the Aleutians, the need for the plant was diminished and the plan abridged. The main elements were there, however: engine and tire repair shops, trucks and trained men, a despatching system, telephone line, the camps, supply depots, restaurants and supplies of gas and oil.

Every 100 miles at the check points was a service station known as a No. 2 echelon. The word in French means "step-by-step maintenance." No. 2 echelons housed gas pumps, air hose, battery chargers, greasing equipment, hoists, service and wrecker trucks.

Between No. 2 echelons at 50-mile intervals were No. 1 echelon sheds for emergency repairs to be performed by drivers plus phone, stove, first aid kit, gas, oil, jacks and tool kit.

No. 3 echelons were located at Dawson Creek, Fort Nelson, Whitehorse and Fairbanks. Qualified mechanics were assigned to them for heavy repair work with stocks of repair parts, work benches, pressure hoses, welders and tools.

No. 4 echelons were machine shops capable of rebuilding carburetors, motors and rear ends, relining the brakes, replacing radiators, glass and electrical systems. Attached to these at Dawson Creek, Whitehorse and Fairbanks were tire retreading and rebuilding plants. The echelon at Dawson Creek was designed to run a truck in at night and in the morning it could emerge with a new motor and new tires, if need be.

In February, 1943, it was estimated there were about 12,000 trucks on the job all told. Keeping them running wasn't easy since we often failed to get engines and parts when and where they were wanted even with the unscrupulous use of the highest priorities by high U.S. Army officers. Coupled with that were operating conditions in cold weather we had never before been exposed to and drivers who treated trucks like shovels on the assumption if they wouldn't run the army would supply another.

The road was not only hard on tires but so were most of the civilian drivers. Overloads were common. The tire situation was the most critical of all. One road-building contractor, for instance, received only 250 of the 1,250 tires he ordered. He was forced to put many pieces of equipment on the dead line for lack of rubber. The army was forced to take action to augment the tire supply and get those echelons set up. It drew on some pretty big names to tackle this problem.

Leo Smith, maintenance superintendent of Smith Transport Ltd., Toronto, was sent to Dawson Creek in November, 1942, to set up No. 3 and 4 echelons. He organized a staff of 75 mechanics. He managed the work until June, 1943, when the shops were taken over by the U.S. Quartermaster Corps.

Throughout the winter night after night Smith would have 100 or more trucks standing outside the shop in below-zero weather covered with frost and ice and with the wheels so solidly frozen they would have to be hauled, pushed or skidded into the shop. The grease in the rear end was so stiff the mechanics would have to heat them to drain them and replace the grease with oil. The shop was nearly burned twice as the result of the considerable heat that had to be used. Gas and exhaust fumes were so concentrated it was not unusual for him to send 15 or 20 men home before the end of the shift to get fresh air.

My involvement in this plan came as the result of my friendship with Col. Fred Horner, an old General Motors man, being chief of transportation for Wyman. He asked me to get some men with experience in terrain like this.

I put the finger on Col. Herbert Soderston, formerly with Abitibi Pulp and Paper Co., whom I had known in early days in the lumber business. The other was R.G. Caley, superintendent of maintenance for British-American Oil Company of Toronto. Both went to Washington and signed up as lieutenant-colonels: Soderston for laying down gasoline supplies for the vehicles moving over the road and Caley to see the trucks were kept running to move the supplies.

Soderston and I had been to Fort St. John in August and had flown over the road. At first we figured the job was hopeless. We found a 10-ton truck loaded at Dawson Creek with gasoline, oil and food would be completely empty by the time it arrived at Fairbanks. We decided the only way to go was to use fleets of trucks to move stockpiles every hundred miles along the road, then assign trucks to these stockpiles to move them on. For a while we had some difficulty getting this system working but it finally went.

There were always hang-ups in the system. For instance, a load of essential telephone parts arrived in Whitehorse. The driver for the return trip hadn't realized they hadn't been unloaded and took off back down the road with them. The telephone people went crazy trying to locate them.

* * *

The manager of the Dawson Creek tire retreading and rebuilding depot at Dawson Creek was Maj. F.H. Johnston of Calgary, who recalled:

I had been in the Canadian Army and had been discharged for medical reasons and returned to my job as treasurer of Motor Car Supply Company in Calgary. Lt.-Col. L.A. Cavanaugh, the company president, sent me to manage the Dawson Creek operation. We had a Firestone tire dealership and won the contract for the largest of the three plants capable of handling 225 to 300 tires a day.

The other two were at Whitehorse and Fairbanks. At the former location, Canton Tire of Billings, Mont., a U.S. Rubber Company dealer, had two 20x100-foot former Civilian Conservation Corps buildings equipped with six recapping moulds, four vulcanizing moulds, five spreaders, buffer, steam plant and a light plant. Despite the fact new tires arrived there by the trainload, Canton was underequipped for the enormous job there was to do. Their equipment couldn't possibly meet the demand.

At Fairbanks, the army took over the plant of the Fairbanks Exploration Company, which was a Guggenheim subsidiary, and operated it as a workshop.

When I arrived at Dawson Creek there wasn't a solitary thing on the ground. However, it wasn't long until we had a building 150x450 feet erected for us. While it was being erected I was out scouring the country trying to find the equipment. It cost $1 1/4 million, but the U.S. War Department picked up the bill. We began operations Dec. 15, 1942. The war department made us change our name, adding "USED" to it, i.e., United States Engineering District.

Fraser Jamieson, a Firestone sales engineer, was sent in to help set up the plant as he was a tire man. We were still using all crude rubber for tires. Synthetic rubber hadn't yet been perfected.

Capt. Walter Venter was the liaison officer from the USED. There was one thing I liked about him: he knew nothing about our operations and processes and admitted it, so he left us alone to do our job.

Venter was always on the job in the daytime — but at night he used to go on some fierce benders — from which he earned the nickname, "Capt. Bender."

One night I hit the sack early but was wakened by an explosion. However, it was only Capt. Bender and a couple of his buddies with a jeep trying to knock down the hut. They were drunker than skunks and they bashed into the hut three or four times. But they didn't accomplish their mission.

I used to like the meals Capt. Venter put on in the officers' mess. Whereas the country was on rations, his meals were always tremendous and we were eating delicacies like asparagus tips.

Bert Onions, a tire expert from Moose Jaw, came up for two weeks to help with the installation of the machines. We later persuaded him to quit his job and become shop boss. He had a work force of 100.

For the official opening of the plant, Motor Car Supply laid on a big party at the hotel in Pouce Coupe. We had invited a large number of dignitaries. At the last moment, Col. J.E. Canary, who was then head of the Transportation Corps at Dawson Creek, forbade his officers to attend. He didn't think it was right to have his men drinking on duty. He was quite decent about it but we were greatly disappointed they didn't accept our hospitality.

It was just as well in the end, however, as it was our plan to have every one of the recapping moulds filled with tires and bring them all back to open them. We had 5,000 tires awaiting repairs. Just before the official guests were to arrive at the plant we made the horrifying discovery that only one tire was cured. The rest of the moulds were filled with water.

We managed to get the attention of the VIPs concentrated to the one mould—and they didn't know there wasn't a single recap in any of the others. We were sitting on tenterhooks for a while, I can tell you.

Much against my advice small steam generators had been installed —and these were at fault. They just couldn't deliver enough heat. Later we corrected the problem with the installation of a large steam boiler in a separate building.

I was involved in another unpleasant incident with Col. Canary.

I got a phone call from him one day:

"I'm sending a car for you. I want you to come to my headquarters."

I arrived and found myself before a board of inquiry. Canary said I was there to face serious charges: that the retreads on four tires we had done peeled off a Greyhound bus. I had been given a report on this by one of my people before I went down. I was sort of expecting something like this and was ready for him.

Col. Canary went on and on about the seriousness of the business for some time and other members of the tribunal added their condemnation. After that they all had their say, I stood up and said:

"Gentlemen, I don't think you know what you're talking about."

Just like that. It startled Col. Canary. He immediately figured I was insubordinate.

"What do you mean, Maj. Johnston?"

"Just what I say. You don't know what you're talking about. Those four tires that peeled were four new Goodyear tires."

The reason I knew about it was the distribution point for Goodyear tires was at a building at the rear of our plant — and we happened to hear about it by accident. Such a thing seldom happens to four at once — as once one goes it puts stress on the others and weakens them.

Before we put this plant into Dawson Creek, Don Leach, who ran Union Tire Shop, kept his place going 24 hours a day trying to keep up with the demand for vulcanizing. He wasn't equipped to do much retreading.

The army wanted him to do contract work but he couldn't get the necessary equipment. He just couldn't handle it.

As the army usually does when on a war footing, it is here today and gone tomorrow. The tire plant was closed without notice March 17, 1944, and the next day the Americans started moving some of the equipment to Italy to a plant where 1,000 persons were employed. Much of the equipment was badly damaged in the move — but no matter, there was a war on!

THE BOB HOPE SHOW
Bob Hope, Frances Langford and Jerry Colonna drop in unexpectedly on GIs at Watson Lake.

22

133 Bridges Built On Mass Production Basis

The bridge-building program for the Alaska Highway was almost as spectacular in concept as the highway itself. In fact, Public Roads Administration engineers devised for the first time in construction history the mass production of 133 major steel bridges.

Standard end designs were prefabricated so that steel mills could be put to work assembling 40, 50 and 60-foot Warren truss standard bridges that could be placed end-to-end across a river as the need be.

Although it was not one of the assembly-line structures, the 2,200-foot suspension bridge costing $3.5 million for the Peace River at Taylor Flats, a few miles south of Fort St. John, was PRA's crown jewel.

Unfortunately, the bridge was ill-starred from the outset and collapsed in ignominy Oct. 16, 1957, only 15 years after its completion.

Two of the main contracts for its construction were let to Dufferin Paving Company of Toronto. For nearly $2 million Dufferin built the approaches, abutments and piers. Bizarre as the fortunes of war are, the contracts were let to a company whose front man, James Franceschini, was in a Canadian internment camp for enemy aliens at the time. He was being held unjustly and was released only on compassionate grounds of poor health under pressure from opposition Conservative members of Parliament.

If there is such a thing as laughter from the grave, it could be heard from Franceschini when the 25,000-ton north concrete anchor slipped due to scouring and allowed the graceful centre span to fall into the swiftly flowing river.

The Peace, like most rivers in the Canadian North, has a high bank on the north and a low bank on the south. This necessitated building a high fill on the south and a deep cut on the north.

The bridge had to be built on a grade. For the sake of appearance, the entire structure was made to conform to a vertical curve with a middle ordinate such that at maximum live load and temperature the spans would not develop a sag in the grade.

* * *

During the summer of 1942 Dufferin Paving had a crew at Taylor Flats which included Walter Wright, a top mechanic, who recalled:

We had a young fellow, Max Sexsmith, who assured us he could operate a bulldozer and scraper. He was put on the night shift with my brother, Henry, working on the approach. One day about 4:30 a.m. a bulldozer was pushing Sexsmith's outfit from behind to help him load. This operation required him to go almost to the high bank of the river, make a sharp right and haul the material half a mile.

Max got all interested in operating the scraper. The dozer operator had quit pushing him because he could see Max was getting near the cliff. But Max kept right on going. He just forgot all about the cliff. The first thing he knew the bulldozer had dropped 200 feet over the cliff.

When Henry reached the scene Max was standing there shaking in his boots. Max had jumped clear before the machine went to the bottom and piled up.

At daylight they sent me down to salvage the outfit. I had to walk a dozer down the old road to the ferry then climb up the first ledge above the river, where Sexsmith's machine had lodged. Although it had jackknifed, miraculously it had remained upright. Damage was slight: only a bent running board, minor dents in the works and a couple of pads torn off the track. I hooked onto it and, after a little digging around it, it came free. We put it back to work that day.

Poor Sexsmith was fired, of course. He was gone by afternoon. He knew enough to pick up his things and go without being told. I overheard Jim Pickard, the superintendent, and Larry Kelley, the paymaster, talking it over:

"Jim, I'm making up Max's time. What will I pay it out to?" Kelley didn't know what time of the night it had happened.

"Make it out to an hour before he went over the bank," said Pickard. "That's when I should have fired him."

There were no unions to protect him, no sociologists to cluck about an unhappy childhood as the cause of his carelessness. He was simply paid off.

Maintaining control of vehicles on this job was difficult. Brakes bleeding off a big White Diesel truck sent it hurtling downhill into the middle of Dufferin's office at Taylor. It was quite a job to rebuild the office and get the files together again.

A dump man named Costello was killed by a truck backing over him. He was half-frozen and failed to move fast enough. Costello was one of several Italians who was retained, although demoted, in the company when Franceschini was put in the internment camp.

The bridge itself was given its first test of strength when a truck lost its brakes and ran over it at 70 miles an hour.

During July and August, Dufferin made good progress on the job of building the approaches and reconstructing the road between the Peace River and the Okes management camp north of Fort St. John this side of Charlie Lake.

When the PRA's Raymond Archibald, who was in charge of bridge design, determined that a suspension bridge was required for the Peace River, he notified William K. Greene and John W. Guppy, who had set up a design office in New York. They contacted John A. Roebling's Sons Co. of Trenton, N.J., builders of the Niagara Falls and Brooklyn bridges. They found Roebling was building a suspension bridge at Oakland, Calif., and, using wartime priority, commandeered it for the military project.

In the meantime, while the steel was being re-routed, Dufferin Paving was awarded a contract Oct. 1 to build two piers in the river spaced for a centre span of 950 feet and two side spans of 485 feet each. The river piers supported 195-foot steel towers. The cables strung across the towers on which the concrete deck was hung were tied to 25,000-ton anchorages at each end. There were 24 cables on each side 2 1/8 inches in diameter. The cables weighed 13 tons.

The stiffening steel work carried the load of the bridge and the cables carried the live load.

The contract called for locating the anchorages at the outer ends of the approach spans and serving also as the abutments supporting them.

The question of whether the anchors were properly positioned was raised at the time, it was recalled by Bruce Ballah, head of the Unemployment Insurance Commission in Dawson Creek:

Wallace Mackey, a contractor from Weston, Ont., whose specialty was bridges, walked into the bridge contractor's camp one day and in his profane, but positive, manner said:

"Now, look you bastards, you gotta go back another 100 feet with your anchor weights."

Naturally, he was told to mind his own business. After all, who was he to be giving advice to Walter Voght, general superintendent of Roebling of Brooklyn bridge fame?

"OK, but I'm betting that inside of five years you'll have trouble with her. That bridge will collapse. She won't take it."

He was right in one particular. She didn't take it. But it lasted longer than he predicted. He knew the type of materials in the bridge were not strong enough to stand the stress of heavier loads he foresaw coming.

* * *

The specifications for the piers were 38x80 feet at water level. They had to be sunk through 12 to 20 feet of water then through an estimated 27 feet of gravel to bed rock. The concrete was poured in winter by heating it and curing it with salamanders.

The Peace has always been a river feared and respected by engineers all along its length. Bridge piers were difficult to place because of unstable riverbed conditions and scouring action of the current.

To overcome these conditions, huge expensive bridges were required and for many years the population density didn't justify them. Crossings were made with ferries.

The piers for the Peace bridge were constructed in the worst possible weather conditions in temperatures that fell to 50 below. Although the ice was treacherous in November and December, it was three feet thick in January. At that time the steel was being erected from the ice with boom towers and a 68-foot crane.

Whether PRA engineers had time to properly make soil tests is a point that has been widely debated. It was a distinct possibility they had never reached bed rock but had only hit hardpan. It was later established there was gravel for 30 feet below the troublesome north pier.

By January, 1948, the Canada Department of Defence revealed that during the annual inspection by army engineers the previous summer, it was suspected scouring action of the water was undermining the north pier. Divers later found a hole 30 feet square by eight feet deep had been scoured out underneath the pier. A report by Dr. P.L. Pratley, a Canadian consulting engineer, resulted in a repair program. This was designed to base the whole pier on a firm foundation "instead of resting on gravel as it does now," said the department.

The work was done in January, 1948, to keep the pier from toppling in the spring floods. While the work was in progress the bridge was kept open for traffic.

In ordinary times, such a structure would have required two or three years to build. Bridging a comparable river would be a massive undertaking even in a well-populated area where men, supplies and tools were readily available. In this case the structure was built in less than a year. Forty-five per cent of the steel was erected in 15 days. Actually, it took longer to dismantle the bridge at Oakland than it did to re-erect it.

* * *

Harold W. Hills, resident engineer for Roebling, arrived from Trenton, N.J., in December, 1942, to arrange for the recruiting of labor, trucks, camp equipment from Dufferin, machinery, food, phones and dishes. He had his problems, it was recalled by Walter Wright:

Supplies were very tight and facilities were very primitive. When Voght arrived later with eight men to get the camp going, it was 30 below. They damn near froze to death in a camp built for summer use they had taken over from Don Construction of Toronto. No carpenters were available so they had to hire what labor they could find to insulate the buildings. I was told to buy some warm clothing and take out to them.

Although good progress was made on the piers, they were not ready to erect the first steel for the south tower until March 25. Then the weather turned unseasonably warm and water rose over the ice. The riveting gangs from New York City and Lake Charles, La., worked overtime and, in the 10 days between then and April 5, erected both towers. Records for fast erection were broken.

The ice broke up April 11. It took with it the temporary bridge the army had built in November. This was not the first temporary pile bridge that had been wiped out by the violent force of the river.

The vicious floods made it impossible to use falsework in the channel. This is why the PRA engineers selected a suspension-type bridge for the Peace.

The Peace was a terror for ferrymen, especially during high water. At Taylor Flats there was an old provincial government ferry with a turbine drive which used to have engine failure periodically and be swept downstream. It broke away four times that I remember.

I was on it one night when it took an eight-mile detour.

Traffic line-ups of four to five miles were common. To alleviate this situation before the bridge was opened, the army brought in a tugboat from the Canol project at Waterways for added power. An engine failure on this tugboat resulted in a two-mile detour and required cables attached to two bulldozers on each side of the river to retrieve it.

The bridge was ready for use Aug. 3, 1943. A big official opening was planned for Aug. 31. The ribbon was scheduled to be cut by the Earl of Athlone, Canada's governor-general. However, at the last minute he was called back to Quebec City for a conference between Prime Minister Winston Churchill of Great Britain and Prime Minister Mackenzie King of Canada. The earl didn't get to see the bridge until he came back to Dawson Creek on a tour of the highway two weeks later.

* * *

There was a bit of pique surrounding the bridge opening, it was recalled by W.W. Bradley, an expediter for Bechtel, Price and Callahan:

First of all, the bridge was closed for a couple of days in advance of the opening ceremonies and hosed down to have it clean for the VIPs. Traffic was rerouted via the ferries.

Second, with several hundred dignitaries arriving from Dawson Creek by car, convoys were ordered halted so there would be no dust to plague them on the road. The American GIs and civilians didn't go for this royalty stuff like their Canadian cousins. There was a lot of swearing, cursing and imprecations about "this long-geared old English lord" disrupting traffic. This sort of pomp and circumstance was foreign to them during this time of urgent haste. Had the same kind of "subversive" talk been heard among Canadians, discipline would have been meted out. But nothing was done to the Yanks. There was more grousing in the PRA camp at Fort St. John when everyone was evicted from Barracks G to accommodate the visitors.

In place of the Earl of Athlone the dedicatory address was given by James D. Scrugham of Nevada, chairman of a U.S. Senate sub-committee on post roads and post offices, which was carrying out an investigation of highway projects. This choice drew snide comments from the PRA about the bridge being opened by "self-appointed openers."

The Fort St. John PRA staff published a camp paper, financed by jukebox profits, called The Northern Light. It was dedicated to a "light-hearted look at the PRA." It came out with a singular item, written deadpan, considering the bridge was one of the major suspension structures in Canada. It ran:

The Peace River bridge was opened Aug. 3rd.

1. Everybody in camp went to the bridge.
2. Senators, generals and others spoke.
3. The wind blew.
4. Ribbons were cut.
5. Trucks drove across the bridge and back.
6. We came home.
7. Nobody fell off.

A stiff wind had sprung up several hours before the hour-long ceremonies. Since the deck was 145 feet above the river, quite a noticeable sway had developed. This made many in the party air sick and they lost their breakfasts over the rail. Several were saved from falling off when they were dragged back.

Some of the PRA staff made an appearance in a flotilla of canoes. They had travelled to Hudson Hope and launched them from there.

The bridge was responsible for helping to bring the petroleum industry to the Peace River country after the war. That industry was blamed for the collapse of the bridge. Refinery loads as high as 95 tons were trucked over it in the construction of Pacific Petroleums refinery and scrubbing plant at Taylor. It was never built to carry that weight. When the B.C. Department of Highways refused truckers permits for overloads, they went to Ottawa and received permission from the Canadian Army which had taken over the road in 1946. The army figured its repair work on the north pier in 1948 had been effective and everything was in order.

Pacific Petroleums had built a large pumphouse at the river capable of supplying the refinery with 80,000 gallons of water per minute. Three high-pressure water lines ran between the north pier and the abutment. One of these lines had been broken for a period of several days before it was detected and the high-pressure water had scoured a large quantity of gravel from underneath the abutment.

By the time it was discovered, the abutment had started to slip and the anchorage pulled away. Walter Wright, who had remained in Dawson Creek after the war, recalled:

Shortly after 9 a.m. Oct. 16, 1957, I heard the news on a radio broadcast. I packed my cameras and went over the Burbidge Studios and got young Hanson to go with me. I met Henry on the way back. He'd been on his way to Fort St. John and police stopped him at this end of the bridge, telling him it was unsafe to cross so he had to return.

We got a boat and went across to the north side and could plainly see where the abutment was pulling away from the bank. Just before the collapse I was discussing with an engineer from the refinery how soon it would go down:

"I don't imagine it will give away for another six or eight hours," he said.

In less than 30 seconds from the time he said that it was down.

There was no resting until the B.C. government replaced the jinxed bridge with another type of structure. Despite the fact it had a black mark against it from construction days, the bridge had become an important factor in the economy of the newly developing area.

I was one of the few who worked on construction and was there at its death. It was hard to believe this could ever happen.

* * *

The instability of the Lower Liard River was the reason the PRA ordered another suspension bridge — a bridge still in place 210 miles north of Fort Nelson. This one was of new steel, not salvage material.

During the road location the 35th Engineering Regt. was in doubt which bank of the river the road should be taken along. Using their aerial mapping technique, R.N. Johnston and Ken Siddall, two Ontario highway engineers from Toronto, were asked to make an assessment. They recommended the 35th erect a bridge over the river which was 700 feet wide at that point, often ran 10 miles an hour, was subject to flooding and carried considerable floating timber.

"We finally came to the conclusion the expense of bridging the river would produce more benefits than the better north-bank location," said Johnston.

It was realized the temporary bridge the 35th built would never hold out against the ice in the spring so a company of the 341st Engineering Regt. was sent in there March 10 to set up a sawmill and produce timber for a substantial bridge. Some 250,000 board feet of timber were sawed. It was built six feet higher than the 35th's. Piles were used that required dynamiting holes in ice four feet thick.

Eight days after completion April 22 the ice broke up and a five-acre block seven feet thick took out the centre bents. Other blocks followed and in a short time 63 of the 80 bents were carried downstream as if they were match sticks.

Another bridge was built and by June 17 water had risen 13 feet. A 24-hour vigil was kept for seven weeks, during which time 80 cases of dynamite were used to keep the spans clear of debris.

Seeing the difficulties, the PRA stepped in and ordered construction of a 1,143-foot suspension bridge worth $2.8 million. McNamara Construction Company of Toronto had the contract to build the approaches and footings for the 94-foot-tall towers. The American Bridge Company had the steel contract and used Caughnawaga Indians from Montreal in construction. The main span was 543 feet and the side spans 233 feet.

Delivery schedules of steel were so casual they made contractors' hair stand on end as trucks broke down and essential components were left standing beside the road. In fact, one truckload of steel never made it; it just disappeared from the face of the earth and was never found.

Floods continued to wash out temporary bridges so often that in November, 1943, this suspension bridge was opened prematurely. Planks were laid on the girders before the deck and railings were installed and trucks inched their way across the precarious temporary roadway.

When the PRA engineers came onto the job in March, 1942, they were faced with the best means of crossing numerous rivers ranging up to the size of the Missouri or the upper Mississippi. Would the bridges be temporary or permanent?

Although the U.S. War Department in its original directive of Feb. 14 specified permanent structures, in the initial penetration of the country only temporary low-level bridges were to be installed. It later became policy that the temporary wooden bridges should be left intact if they stood up.

Because the rivers in this mountainous country did not behave like ordinary rivers (they were wild, tricky and highly uncertain) the decision to build permanent bridges was made — even though it was estimated the U.S. armed forces would only require use of the road for four or five years and there was then no commitment from the Canadian government to keep the road open after they were through with it.

The usual placid appearance of the broad, gently flowing Peace, Tanana and Liard Rivers belied their ability to rise with startling rapidity to full flood or to carry block-busting ice floes that smashed everything in their path.

Engineers who happened to see for the first time glacial streams like the Duke, Donjek, Robertson, White and Johnson as only trickling currents meandering through mile-wide debris-strewn valleys could scarcely believe these rivers could gush into bank-full torrents within a few hours, rise and fall with the sun as glaciers melted and congealed in varying temperatures of the high mountain ranges, or could pile valley-wide layers of ice up to 30 feet deep.

Other streams of mountain origin like the Muskwa, Sickanni Chief, Racing River, Toad, McDonald, Trout, Hyland, Coal, Takhini, Yerick, Tok and others are innocent enough at times but could lash out with flood-swollen tongues with devastating suddenness.

All these rivers were as untamed as the country itself. They treated man-made structures with contempt. It took something more than temporary bridges to stand against their fury.

There was no question the major bridges would be permanent ones. The only other question was economy and speed. The engineers looked around for materials immediately available.

A survey by the Army Corps of Engineers determined structural timber was in short supply due to wartime priorities and unprecedented rains having bogged down lumbering operations. Steel was more readily available. Upon contacting five leading bridge fabricators, it was found substantial investories of steel were on hand and there was shop space for fabrication. Further studies showed there was little difference in cost between wood and steel. It would be easier to transport steel to the sites.

The deciding factor was the bridges had to be high enough and strong enough to allow flash floods and ice to pass underneath.

Having settled the question of type and materials, the next one was speed. This was accomplished by having standard designs prefabricated and having them made up while at the same time having the approaches built all along the highway to accommodate the number of prefabricated spans necessary.

With the standardization of designs, the letting of contracts, manufacture and rolling of steel and fabrication could proceed as soon as the designs were finalized. By the time it was necessary for details to be filled in for individual bridges, fabrication was well on the way and the field information sent in from Fort. St. John and Edmonton to complete the package. Thus there was a great saving of time when time was an important factor.

To further speed up the mass-production technique, the American Bridge Company was awarded a contract for preparation of material lists and shop details for all standard spans for distribution to eight U.S. and Canadian fabricators. These were prepared in consultation with design engineers in the field.

* * *

Whereas the majority of bridges resembled peas in a pod, one stood out as an oddity; and is a historic sight today. This is the bridge over the Kiskatinaw, 20 miles north of Dawson Creek. Herb Mowat, a foreman for Don Construction Ltd. of Toronto and later chairman of the administration committee of the United Nations Association of Canada, recalled this unusual structure:

It was creosoted fir timber construction 100 feet above the water, but the unusual feature was it was built on a nine-degree curve with a deck super-elevated two feet in its 24-foot width. The necessity for its unusual construction was dictated by a horseshoe curve in the river where the river crossing was effected. Moose Creek also joined the Kiskatinaw inside the horseshoe.

Complicating the crossing was a "pimple" of land between the prongs of the horseshoe, one side of which formed the inner bank of the river. It rose 200 feet above the river. Further complicating the crossing was the fact the river had a steep outer bank which was 400 feet high.

To overcome this forbidding terrain, it was necessary to bring the route of the road into the crossing on a hairpin turn. The bridge was part of the hairpin turn; it was on a nine-degree curve at the apex.

You'd see a carload of American engineers drive down the road and they'd hit the bridge at 40 miles an hour. They'd stop, climb out of the vehicle and stand in awe of the curved super-elevated structure they'd just passed over.

"My God," one would say, "that curve was a bridge."

They'd never seen anything like it before and, of course, they had to give it a thorough inspection to see how it could stand the stresses. Curved bridges on both roads and railroads are not unusual in British Columbia.

The structure, comprising a main span of 190 feet flanked by two 114-foot spans and three short approach spans at each end, was built under severe weather conditions. It was not until mid-October, 1942, excavation for the north-tower pier was completed and concrete pouring started. Work on the timber tower and falsework was carried out during weather that dropped to 40 below.

By the end of January all was ready for the arrival of the timber from the coast. However, the first of 500,000 board feet was delayed and didn't show up until early April.

In April a flood washed out 500,000 feet of falsework. Crews had to be sent into the bush to cut timber for new falsework.

The temporary bridge downstream was also washed out and this had to be replaced with another temporary structure. This structure was washed out in June but by the that time the permanent bridge was ready.

A few days after it was opened there was an unofficial test of safe allowable stress on this bridge. A four-wheel-drive truck moved slowly over the structure hauling a float carrying a 40-ton power shovel; ahead was a 20-ton bulldozer being planked across; this procession was overtaken by two White Diesel trucks with gross weight of 20 tons each; it was met by three gravel trucks carrying 20 tons each: for a total of 120 tons.

Maintenance of temporary bridges until structures of a more permanent nature could be erected in the second construction season provided many headaches for the engineering regiments held on the road during the winter and spring of 1942-3. In the spring of 1943 it was discouraging for the companies of the 341st Engineering Regt. to see the ice systematically knock out wooden bridges built with hand tools before it was possible to get piledrivers and portable sawmills onto the scene.

* * *

Plenty of trials and tribulations and many innovations were required to get the work done, it was recalled by Herman Engel, Jr., Houston, Texas, a lieutenant in the 340th Engineering Regt.:

I guess that's why the Americans won the war. We always had some compensations for rough going to make us forget our difficulties. The touring troupes of Hollywood stars were one of them.

At the end of November, 1942, Bob Hope, Frances Langford, Jerry Colonna and guitarist Tony Romano stopped overnight at Watson Lake on their return from entertaining troops in Alaska. They were very tired, having gone all out doing as many as half a dozen shows a day at isolated camps in the Aleutians.

It was Miss Langford's first tour for the troops — and it could have been her last. At Anchorage the plane encountered fog, couldn't land and circled for hours. The pilot said he didn't think he was going to make it and told them to put on their parachutes. This elicited from Hope one of his famous one-liners:

"All I could see flashing through my mind were all the bad shows I'd done."

On the pilot's last run he was aided by a searchlight crew on a nearby mountain — and he made it.

As an indication of the kind of guy Hope was, he ordered a special trip and put on a special show for the lonely grateful searchlight crew.

Although they were shook up from that experience, someone mentioned there were 100 of us GIs building a bridge on the Upper Liard who hadn't seen an American female for eight months. Hope said:

"Bring 'em along, bring 'em along. We'll give 'em a show!"

We thoroughly enjoyed the impromptu show the troupe put on for us on a couple of tables in the air force mess hall at Watson Lake.

I was right in the front row.

* * *

The Hyland River bridge 213 miles north of Fort Nelson was one of the most difficult, requiring over a year to build, it is recalled by Bobbie Hill of Missoula, Mont.:

I spent some time with Morse Bros. and Associates of Rochester, Minn., after July, 1943, working on the approaches. We encountered a peculiar shale formation which was hard to handle with machinery. George Allen, the foreman, figured his 250-man force would never hack their way through it.

We did and we survived. We were lucky. My buddies told Allen we could handle dynamite — but never had. We threw it around with mad abandon and when we had some left over we simply hid it in the woods nearby.

Prospectors like old Bob Bloom had a free supply for several years. All they had to do was find the cache.

For this bridge a deck structure 600 feet long was needed. Such a structure had been designed for the Goascotan River between El

Salvador and Spanish Honduras on the Inter-American ...
it was decided to duplicate that structure for the Hyland River and

* * *

The longest steel truss bridge to be completed in 1943 was the one across the Muskwa River at Fort Nelson. It is 970 feet over-all. It was designed by Raymond Archibald and his associates to utilize second-hand steel from bridges abandoned by the Southern Pacific Railway in the Shasta Dam reservoir area. Prime contractor was Bay Cities Engineering Co. of San Francisco.

Archibald quoted from notes on difficulties encountered:

". . . In the latter part of May and during June the Muskwa flooded three different times, taking part of the work trestle which had to be replaced before operations could proceed again. The main channel spans, erected during the high-water period, were only completed a few days before the heavy rains of July 9 and 10, 1943, which caused a 33-foot rise in 22 hours that washed out the entire work trestle and all buildings at the bridge site."

* * *

William Tunny of Mayerthorpe, Alta., recalled:

We lost 37 temporary bridges 200 miles on either side of Fort Nelson.

Although I worked mostly as a carpenter, I had some experience as a steam engineer and was working on the Muskwa on a pile driver.

Our camp was located on a river bench about 10 feet above the normal flood line. July 9 we were sitting down to eat when some boys from the army came in:

"You fellows had better move up to the army camp at Fort Nelson. There's a big flood coming."

"Should we finish supper?"

"No," they said, "you better go now. Have your supper at the camp."

We threw our belongings into a couple of trucks and took off to the camp a couple of miles down the road.

About 9 p.m. I decided to drive back and look over things. When I got back to camp it had disappeared. There were about 20 feet of water over the campsite. The Muskwa was a wide and angry river that night and it's lucky we got out of there.

A 55-ton crane was sitting on a bend of the temporary mud-sill

...ith the cab under water and it was being battered by logs and brid...wood. When the water receded the crane was still there but the bridge was washed away on either side of it.

The water rose to within a foot of the top of the new bridge. The Indians said it was the highest flood crest they could ever remember. Many trucks were washed downstream and some other heavy machinery was smashed beyond repair.

A bridge over the Tetsa River 68 miles north of Fort Nelson gave us an unusual problem.

The army had stockpiled 150,000 board feet of lumber and squared timber for a permanent bridge. The flood scattered this timber for miles. That wasn't so bad as they had plenty to replace it.

The real problem came up when the flood caused the Tetsa to change course and left the temporary bridge high and dry. They had to divert the river back into its old channel again after we had erected a 300-foot permanent steel bridge.

* * *

While most of the bridges were completed by the end of 1943, a few still had work to be done in 1944. PRA engineers like S.A. Engdahl of Providence, R.I., quickly learned a few tricks to assist them to fight northern elements. One was the use of ice on the rivers as a base from which to drive piles and build falsework used in the erection of steel; and to run truckloads of steel across rivers and lake ice.

The Teslin River was unusual as it had been designated by the Canadian government as a navigable stream as river streamers used it to service Teslin Lake traders from Whitehorse via the river system. In fact, that's how the engineers got some of their equipment into the middle of the Yukon wilderness to start building the highway south.

Engineers were faced with building either a high-level bridge with clearance for shipping or one with a swing section. They chose the former as less maintenance would be required. The clearance was 62 feet. Water was 40 feet deep in the 550-foot-wide channel. The bridge was built on a two per cent grade and was 1,300 feet long.

The engineers had many problems with the pier foundations because of the shifting river bed. At the 240-foot mark the drills were still in mud. The concrete piers were built on piles 50 to 75 feet long. There were 170 piles under each of the eight piers and two abutments. The caissons were sunk 25 feet below the river level.

The Nisutlin Bay bridge on Teslin Lake gave problems. The freeze-up of 1942 halted the ferry being used by the army for the Fairbanks Freight. Something had to be done in a hurry to restore the road. The engineers of the 340th used another trick. When the ice was thick enough to hold a man, men were sent out to lay slabs from a portable sawmill. Water was sprayed atop them. When this layer froze, they placed more slabs atop that layer and continued until they had an ice bridge three feet thick. It was 2,200 feet long and was strong enough to support heavy equipment.

Later they drove piles from the ice and built a temporary one-lane bridge with 200-foot turn-out lanes for passing.

This temporary rickety wooden roller-coaster bridge remained "temporary" until 1956 when the Canadian Army built a permanent structure.

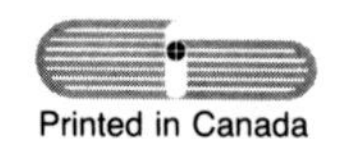

Printed in Canada